Cilicia, its former history And present state

with an account of the idolatrous worship prevailing there previous to the introduction of Christianity

WM. Burckhardt Barker

(Editor: WM. Francis Ainsworth)

Alpha Editions

This edition published in 2019

ISBN : 9789353704735

Design and Setting By
Alpha Editions
email - alphaedis@gmail.com

This book is a reproduction of an important historical work. Alpha Editions uses the best technology to reproduce historical work in the same manner it was first published to preserve its original nature. Any marks or number seen are left intentionally to preserve its true form.

THE BIRTHLAND OF ST. PAUL.

CILICIA:

ITS FORMER HISTORY AND PRESENT STATE,

WITH AN ACCOUNT OF

THE IDOLATROUS WORSHIP PREVAILING THERE PREVIOUS TO
THE INTRODUCTION OF CHRISTIANITY.

BY

WM. BURCKHARDT BARKER, M.R.A.S.,

MANY YEARS RESIDENT AT TARSUS IN AN OFFICIAL CAPACITY.

EDITED BY

WM. FRANCIS AINSWORTH, F.R.G.S., F.G.S.,

Corresponding Member of the Geographical Society of Paris.

Illustrated by numerous Engravings from existing Remains.

"I am a man which am a Jew of Tarsus, a city in Cilicia, a citizen of no mean city."
ST. PAUL, ACTS xxi. 39.

LONDON AND GLASGOW:
RICHARD GRIFFIN AND COMPANY,
PUBLISHERS TO THE UNIVERSITY OF GLASGOW.

CONTENTS.

INTRODUCTORY PREFACE 1

CILICIA AND ITS GOVERNORS.

CHAPTER I.

Early period of Cilician history. Scriptural mention of Tarsus. Ancient religion. Notice of the Cilicians by Herodotus. Cilicia under the Assyrians. Burial-place of Sardanapalus. Dominion of the Medes. Cilicia overrun by Scythian hordes. The Prophet Daniel's tomb. Crœsus, king of Lydia. Persian satraps. Invasion of Greece by the Persians. Syennesis, king of Cilicia. Treaty of Antalcidas. Alexander the Great in Cilicia. Battle of Issus. 11

CHAPTER II.

Plistarchus. Battle of Ipsus. Ptolemy Evergetes. Antiochus the Great. Zeno and Chrysippus. Cilicia under the Seleucidæ. Invaded by Tigranes. Reduced to a Roman province by Pompey. Cicero's campaign in Cilicia. Marc Antony and Cleopatra at Tarsus. Cilicia invaded by the Parthians under Labienus. Athenodorus. Vonones slain in Cilicia. St. Paul. Insurrection of the Cliteans. Cossuatianus Papito governor. Polemon, king of Cilicia, marries Berenice. Cilicia declared a Roman province in Vespasian's time. Fate of the Roman empire decided on the plain of Issus. . 23

CHAPTER III.

Legend of the Seven Sleepers. Sapor invades Cilicia. Zenobia's conquests. Cilicia overrun by the Alani. Maximianus dies at Tarsus. Death of Constantius at Mopsuestia in Cilicia. St. George, patron saint of England, born at Epiphanea. The Emperor Julian buried at Tarsus. Invasions of the Huns. Belisarius in Cilicia. Campaigns of Heraclius and of Chosroes (Kusru Anushiriwan). . . 36

CHAPTER IV.

Rise of the Saracens. Cilicia overrun by Harun al Rashid. Al Mamun dies in Cilicia. Exchange of prisoners at Il-Lamas. Sack of Mopsuestia by the Khalif Mutassim. Mopsuestia retaken by Nicephorus Phocas and John Zimisces. Rise of the Turkmans. Alp Arslan and Romanus Diogenes. Turkman dynasty at Nicæa. Persecution of the Christians. First Crusade. Tancred and Baldwin in Cilicia. Alexius annexes Cilicia to the Greek empire. . . 45

CHAPTER V.

The Emperor John Comnenus killed in a wild boar hunt in Cilicia. Description of Anazarba. The second Crusade. Third Crusade. Death of Frederick I. (Barbarossa) in Cilicia. Fourth Crusade. Cilicia under John Ducas Vataces. Devastations of Yanghiz or Genghiz Khan. 54

CHAPTER VI.

Rise of the Osmanlis or Usmanlis. Victories of Bayazid. Invasions of the Moguls. Capture of Constantinople by Muhammad II. Bayazid II. Annexes Cilicia to the Ottoman empire. Campaigns of Sulaiman the Magnificent. Amurad IV. invades Cilicia. His house at Adana. Reforms of Mahmud II. Abd'ul Masjid. . . . 65

CHAPTER VII.

Modern history of Cilicia. Rise of Kutchuk Ali Uglu. His means of revenue. Acts of cruelty. Bayas. Mode of life and characteristics. Seizes the master of an English vessel. Captures a French merchantman. Bribes the Turks who are sent against him. Puts his friend the Dutch Consul of Aleppo into prison. Forces a caravan of merchants to ransom him. A characteristic anecdote. . 73

CHAPTER VIII.

Dada Bey, son of Kutchuk Ali Uglu. His piratical expeditions. Repels the attacks of the Turks. Is taken by stratagem. Is beheaded and burnt. History of Mustafa Pasha. Kil-Aga killed by Haji Ali Bey. Dervish Hamid. Story related of Haji Ali Bey. Conquests of Ibrahim Pasha. Mustuk Bey placed in power. Comparison between the Egyptian and Turkish governments. . . 84

CHAPTER IX.

Muhammad Izzet Pasha. A pretender to the Turkish throne. His strange history and rare accomplishments. Disappears at Kuniyah. Ahmed Izzet Pasha. Grants permission to Mustuk Bey to murder his nephew. Sulaiman Pasha. Durwish Ahmed's expedition against Mustuk Bey. His chief officers taken and stripped. Bayas captured and sacked. 92

CHAPTER X.

Anecdotes of Sulaiman Pasha. Gin-Jusif, rebel of Kara-Tash. Arif Pasha. Murder of a pasha. Hasan Pasha. Anecdotes of the council. Christian members of council. Employés of the Porte. Toll at Kulak Bughaz. Hati Sheriff. Courts of justice. . . 101

CHAPTER XI.

Geography of Cilicia. Tarsus and Adana. Missis (Mopsuestia). Sis (Pindenissus). Bayas and the coast. Pylæ Ciliciæ. Population of Cilicia. Europeans and their influence destroyed. Consuls and their authority. English consuls allowed to trade. Climate. Stagnant lake (Rhegma). Marsh of Alexandretta. Country-houses. Nimrud. Sea-ports. Kaisanli. Mursina and its road-stead. 110

CHAPTER XII.

Advantages and disadvantages of Tarsus in a commercial point of view. Tables of navigation. Tabular view of the trade of the interior of Asia Minor. Table of exports. Table of imports. State of agriculture in Cilicia. Produce of the country. Cotton. Wheat. Barley. Linseed. Wax. Fruit-trees. Silk. Olive-trees. Pay of a day-labourer. Pasture of land. Tenure of land. Timber and woods. Geology and mineralogy. Extracts from Mr. Ainsworth's work. Plain of Tarsus. Falls of the Cydnus. First, second, third, and fourth range of hills. Mines of iron and lead. Argentiferous Galena. Revenue of the Pashalik. 117

CHAPTER XIII.

Il Lamas (Lamum). Kurkass (Corycus). Aski Shahir. Soli, afterwards Pompeiopolis. Great Mausoleum at Tarsus. Strabo's description of the coast of Cilicia. His account of Tarsus and neighbouring towns. 128

LARES AND PENATES.

CHAPTER I.

Introductory 145

CHAPTER II.

Discovery of the terra-cottas. Lares and Penates of Cilicia. Evidences of promiscuous worship. Apollo of Tarsus. Perseus, Bellerophon, and Pegasus. Radiated Apollo. Identity of physiognomy. Ugly faces. Deification of children. Deification of princes. Deification of ladies. Character of Cilician art. Progress of Christianity. Destruction of the Lares and Penates. Atys. Apollo, the Syrian Baal. Cybele, Ceres, and Isis. Eleusinian mysteries. Cybele and Atys, Isis and Osiris, Venus and Adonis. The cat, dog, and horse. Harpocrates and Florus. Isis and the Nelumbium. Sacred bulls. Egyptian art. Morpheus 152

CHAPTER III.

Apollo. Apollo Belvedere. Caricatures of Midas. Apollo of Tarsus. Senator in the clavus latus. Lion attacking a bull. Telephus or Mercury (?). Ceres. Victory. Date of destruction of the Lares. Metamorphosis of Actæon into a stag. Remarks of Mr. Birch. . 184

CHAPTER IV.

ON CERTAIN PORTRAITS OF HUNS, AND THEIR IDENTITY WITH THE EXTINCT RACES OF AMERICA.

Monstrous head in a conical cap. Portrait of a Hun (?). Identity with American sculptures. Emigrations of Asiatic nations to America. Testimonies from Stephens, Schomburgk, Humboldt. Analogies of language. Evidences from Klaproth and d'Herbelot. 203

CHAPTER V.

ETHNOLOGICAL SUBJECT OF THE HUNS CONTINUED.

"The ugly heads" of the collection. Standard of beauty. Monuments of Central America. Parallel case in Hayti. The Hittites of Scripture. Reference to Egyptian sculpture. Effects of the Egyptian invasion of Cilicia. 208

CHAPTER VI.

ADDITIONAL WORKS OF ART. GODS, DEMIGODS, AND HEROES.

Apollo. Mercury. Hercules. Bacchus. Silenus. Fauns and Satyrs. Pan. Minerva. Venus. Cupid. Europa. Marsyas. Leander. Laocoon. Æsculapius. Fortune. Caius Caligula (?). Priapus. Harpy. Marsyas. Abrerig or Nergal (?). Summary . . . 213

CHAPTER VII.

SIBYLS AND DOLPHINS AND THEIR RIDERS.

Sibyls. An African sibyl. Head-dress of the virgin-prophetesses. A matron sibyl (?). Dolphins and their riders. Apotheosis of deceased children. Story of Arion. Radiated heads. The Bulla. . 228

CHAPTER VIII.

Magi and Monks. 232

CHAPTER IX.

Monsters and Idiots. 237

CHAPTER X.

HUMAN FIGURES.

Bards. Priests. Miscellaneous. Female figures. Deified children. Undetermined. 243

CHAPTER XI.

ANIMALS.

Dogs. Oxen. Bulls. Buffalo. Horses. Lions. Panther. Wolf. Boar. Ape. Hippopotamus (?). Cat. Goats. Rams and Sheep. Crocodile. Snake. Eagle. Swan. Ostrich. Cocks. . . . 249

CHAPTER XII.

DOMESTIC AND RELIGIOUS ART.

Chariots. Vases. Bowls and dishes. Wine-jars and drinking-vessels. Lamps. Handles. Table and chair. Ring and glass. Round disc of pottery. Net. Butter-print (?) 253

CHAPTER XIII.

MUSICAL INSTRUMENTS.

Lyres. Syrinx. 259

CHAPTER XIV.

COMPARATIVE GEOGRAPHY.

Arsus (Rhosus). Myriandrus. Iskandrun or Alexandretta (Alexandria ad Issou). Godfrey de Bouillon's fort. Baylan (Pictanus, Erana?). Primitive Christian church. Castles of Ibn Daub and of Baylan Bustandah. Altars of Alexander. Castle of Markatz. River Kersus. Gates of Cilicia and Syria. Bayas (Baiæ). Issus. Nicopolis. Kara Kaya (Castabala). Epiphanea. Matakh. Tamir Kapu (Iron Gates, Ammanian Gates). Ayas (Ageæ). Ammodes. Kara Tash (Mallus and Megarsus). Aleian plain. Pyramus. Mopsuestia. Castles on the plain. Sari Capita. Rhegma of the Cydnus. Yanifa Kishla. Mazarlik. Castle of Kalak Bughaz. Kara Sis. Anabad and Dunkalah. 262

CHAPTER XV.

ANTIOCH AND SELEUCIA.

The Bay of Antioch. Village of Suwaidiyah. Grotto of Nymphæus. Island of Melibœa. Ruins of Seleucia Pieria. Projected re-opening of the port of Seleucia. Mount St. Simon. Mount Casius. Temple of Ham. 267

CHAPTER XVI.

NATURAL HISTORY—ZOOLOGY.

The ounce. The lynx. Bears. Hyenas, wolves, and jackals. The Fox. Hares. Fallow-deer. White gazelle (ghazal). Greyhounds. Gh'aik, or ibex. 276

CHAPTER XVII.

GAME BIRDS.

Game birds. Manner of taking quails. Manner of taking francolin and partridges. Capture of wild doves. 281

CHAPTER XVIII.

Falconry. 284

CHAPTER XIX.

Medicinal Plants 299

APPENDIX.

	PAGE
Narrative of Nadir Bey, written from his own dictation (in French)	301
Translation	310
Petition of Nadir Bey (in Italian)	320
Translation	325

HISTORICAL DOCUMENTS: Copy of a Buyurdi from Muhammed Izzet Pasha. Insurrection of Lattakiyah in 1804. State of North Syria in 1805 and in 1814. Petition from the Chief of the Trades to Mr. John Barker, 1841. Notice of Badir Khan Bey, the extirminator of the Nestorian Christians. Story of Fahel, chief of the Arabs of the Zor, or forest district on the Euphrates. . . . 328

Burckhardt's Account of Cilicia 355

COMMERCIAL TABLES: I. Commerce of Kaisariyah with the chief towns of Asia Minor. II. Summary of the Commerce of Kaisariyah one year with another. III. Exports of the Pashalik of Adana and Tarsus. IV. Imports of the same Pashalik. V. Prospectus of the Navigation of Mursina, roadstead of Tarsus, 1844. VI. Table of Duties paid at Constantinople. 372

INDEX 387

LIST OF ILLUSTRATIONS.

	PAGE
VIEW OF SIS . . . . *Frontispiece.*	
MAUSOLEUM AT ELEUSA	10
MAP OF CILICIA	11
SARCOPHAGUS AT SELEUCIA PIERIA	35
RUIN AT ANAZARBA	64
SACCAL TUTAN	91
PLAIN OF ANTIOCH—OVERFLOW OF THE ORONTES—MOUNT AMANUS IN THE DISTANCE	109
MISSIS	110
VIEW OF ALEXANDRETTA	113
ALEXANDRETTA AND CAPE KHANZIR	116
SARCOPHAGUS AT SELEUCIA PIERIA	131
GROUND-PLAN OF MAUSOLEUM AT TARSUS	133
TOMB AT ELEUSA 242, 258
RUINS OF AN AQUEDUCT AT ANAZARBA	275
VALLEY OF THE ORONTES	275
SCULPTURED ROCKS AT ANAZARBA	283
GOS-HAWK AND FALCON	295
GESRIL HADEED, IN THE PLAINS OF ANTIOCH	298
BETIAS: SUMMER RESIDENCE OF MR. BARKER	300
MR. BARKER'S VILLA IN THE VALLEY OF SUEDIA	360

LIST OF ILLUSTRATIONS TO LARES AND PENATES.

	PAGE		PAGE
Actæon	189	Bacchante	200
Adonis as Apollo	178	Bacchus	195, 216
Apollo . 157, 161, 162, 164, 178, 195		Bard playing	243
Apis	182	Boy and Dolphin	230
Ariadne	216	Caius Caligula	223
Atys, young 174, 227		Captive, kneeling	211

LIST OF ILLUSTRATIONS.

	PAGE		PAGE
Ceres	176	Macrocephalus, a	238
Chronos	193	Magus	232
Commodus	167	Man riding a Bear	226
Cupid and Swan	219, 220	Mask, comic	177, 178
Cybele	192	Mercury	158
Davus	198	Messalina	158
Diana	156, 284	Midas	185
Eros	166, 194	Monster, head of a	236
Gladiator	244	Musical Instruments	260
Harpocrates	181	Osiris	14, 161
Head, tutulated	192	Pallas	169
Heads, monstrous	203, 204	Pan	155
Hercules	169	Perseus	197
Hero	193	Phree (the Egyptian Sun)	252
Horse, leg of	175	Phrygian Head	197
,, head of	180	Priest with attributes of Apollo	164
Idiot head	268	Priestess	199
Incense-burner	155	Saturn	193
Iris	177	Senator	186
Isis	191	Serapis	14
Juno	157, 167, 177	Sibyl, African	228
Jupiter	157	Silenus	218
Lady, head of	168, 188	Somnus	183
Lamp	156	Tartarus	248
Leander swimming the Hellespont	222	Venus	170, 193
Lion attacking a Bull	187	Victoria Aleta	189

INTRODUCTORY PREFACE

BY THE EDITOR.

The author of this little volume, and the first to bring to light the Lares and Penates of the ancient and interesting city of Tarsus—Mr. William Burckhardt Barker—is the son of John Barker, Esq., who died at Suedia, or Suwaidiyah, near Antioch, on the fifth of October, 1850, in his seventy-ninth year. He is also the godson of the eminent traveller and Oriental scholar Louis Burckhardt, whose footsteps he has most worthily followed, having prosecuted the study of the Oriental languages from his early boyhood, and being now as familiar with Arabic, Turkish, and Persian, and the many dialects which emanate from these languages, as he is with the chief languages of Europe. He lately made an extended tour in Persia, whither he went to perfect himself in the language of that country before his final return to England.

Mr. W. Burckhardt Barker is further already known in this country by an account of the sources of the river Orontes, of which no previous description had been published, and which appeared in the 7th volume of the Journal of the Royal Geographical Society.

The father of our author for a long period occupied posts of honourable trust under the British government. He was appointed Consul and Agent to the East India Company at Aleppo in 1799, where he exercised his functions and practised a generous hospitality to his countrymen and to strangers till 1826, when he was promoted to the post

INTRODUCTORY PREFACE.

of his Majesty's Consul-General in Egypt. Here he remained till 1834, when he became entitled to his retirement from public service. He then fixed his residence in the beautiful valley of Suedia, ancient Seleucia Pieria, on the banks of the Orontes, and about fifteen miles from Antioch. Here he built a commodious house, and planted his grounds with the choicest flowers, shrubs, and fruit-trees of Europe and Asia. At a subsequent period he added to this general residence a summer-house at the village of Betias, on a commanding eminence of Mount Rhosus, where there was an abundant supply of water, the air was always refreshing and cool, and the prospect magnificent; and here his mortal remains were consigned to the tomb.

The presence of an Englishman of a liberal and benevolent mind had a great influence upon the native population, who looked up to him and his family with sentiments of love and respect. This feeling was shared as well by the Muhammadan inhabitants as by the Christian. His services to Eastern travellers have in numberless instances been called into action, and have been gratefully recorded in many published works of those who partook of his hospitality.

Mr. Barker's family came from Bakewell, in Derbyshire, where they have long been established. He married Miss Hays at Aleppo in 1800, who survives him. This lady's mother was a daughter of Mr. Thomas Vernon, a Levant merchant of Aleppo, when that city was the grand emporium of the commerce of India. He was of the family of the Vernons of Hilton, in Cheshire, and a near kinsman of Admiral Sir Edward Vernon, of Porto Bello celebrity. By this lady, who was a remarkable linguist, for it is stated she spoke five languages fluently when only six years old, Mr. Barker had three sons and two daughters, all of whom possessed a great facility for acquiring languages, and became proficient Orientalists.

Mr. Barker's latter years were much occupied in procuring from all parts of Asia the best kinds of fruits, which he cultivated in his gardens at Suedia with a view to prove their merits, and afterwards of transferring them to his native country, so as to improve upon the varieties grown there. His attention was especially directed to the peach, nectarine, and apricot; and from specimens that have already been produced from his stock, there is but little doubt that in a few years a very superior order of what we denominate wall-fruits will be in common cultivation in England. Some hundreds of Mr. Barker's trees are now under culture in the garden of an eminent nurseryman in Devonshire, and are destined to be spread over the country. They all possess the peculiar property of having sweet kernels, in contradistinction to those common in Europe, which have bitter kernels: this imparts a greatly improved flavour to the fruit. The famous Stanwick nectarine, declared by Dr. Lindley to be incomparably superior to any thing we have, was introduced by Mr. Barker into this country through the assistance of his Grace the present Duke of Northumberland. In this gentle and humanising pursuit Mr. Barker spared neither exertions nor expense. He was in the habit for many years past of sending agents into distant countries of the East, including Bokhara, Samarkand, Kandahar, and Shiraz, to procure for him scions of all such trees as bore the best fruits.

He was, indeed, enthusiastic in the pursuit of whatever he thought would benefit mankind. Thus in 1848, when the cholera committed great devastation in the north of Syria, a remedy is stated to have been discovered by which many persons were cured even in the advanced stages of the disease. Mr. Barker verified the efficiency of the proposed remedy by personal observation; and once he was satisfied, he spared no pains or expense to spread the knowledge of what he deemed an important discovery to all parts of the world.

During a residence of fifty years in Syria and Egypt, Mr. Barker never lost an opportunity of obliging in his private capacity all persons who came within his reach; and such was the reputation he had acquired by his general hospitality, that often a letter of introduction from him to any of the chiefs around was of more real value than the best passport from the government authorities. During the campaign of the French in Syria he also rendered good service to our old ally the Porte, from whom, under Sultan Selim, he received a gold medal and a snuff-box set with diamonds, which were sent to him through his friend Sir Sydney Smith.

Mr. Barker had a final opportunity of being useful to his country by forwarding the objects of the Euphrates expedition, which landed at the mouth of the Orontes in 1835, and of extending his characteristic hospitality to Colonel Chesney and the officers and men of the expedition.

This true-hearted Englishman, indeed, spent all his income in keeping up to the last the honour and respectability of the British name.

As a farther proof of what has been here stated, I have been induced, with the kind permission of the publishers, to introduce into the work a brief notice of Mr. Barker, with some account of his residence at Suwaidiyah and of the immediate neighbourhood, from Mr. Neale's work, recently published by Messrs. Colburn and Co., *Eight Years in Syria and Palestine, &c.*

The interest of the present work will be found upon perusal to be much greater than might be expected from its more or less local character. Cilicia, properly so called, is not less remarkable for its physical configuration, than it is as the scene of varied historical events, many of which have by their importance influenced the destiny of the world.

Physically speaking, the alluvial deposit of the Cydnus and the Sarus, the Pyramus and the Pinarus, all rivers of ancient renown, the great Aleian plain, the lower and wooded ranges of the Taurus and of the Amanus, the snow-clad summits of which gird this province like a wall of rock, and the narrow slip of land forming the shores of the Issic Gulf, constitute the whole of the country of Cilicia Proper.*

But politically and historically Cilicia derived its importance from being the highway between the nations of the East and the West. When the Persians, under their powerful monarch Xerxes, advanced against the first seat of European civilisation, or when the Greeks in their turn marched in the train of a Persian satrap to the plains of Babylonia, Cilicia was alike put under contributions by both parties. When the already aged civilisation of the East and the young civilisation of the West had in Alexander the Great's time become more balanced, the fate of the two was decided half-way on the plains of Cilicia. Petty chieftains, like the successors of Alexander, made of it a continuous field of strife; and so warlike had the experience of the past made its

* Strabo divided Cilicia into Cilicia Aspera and Cilicia Campestris; the latter is called by Ptolemy, Cilicia Proper.

inhabitants, that it required a Pompey, a Cicero, and a Mark Antony in the palmy days of Rome to bring the same rock and sea-girt province into subjection.

Even the short-lived powers of Zenobia affected Cilicia; and in the long struggle for domination that took place between the Emperor of Byzantium and the Sassanian Kings, Cilicia still continued to be the field of oft-repeated and sanguinary conflicts. This was still more the case upon the rise of Muhammadanism; and in the times of the early khalifs, when the population of the country appears to have attained its maximum, its soil was more than ever stained by the blood of victims to men's lust for power and dominion.

The Saracens were succeeded by Turkman races, which have ever since held most tenaciously by a country which they have found peculiarly adapted to their habits and mode of life. Three times the Christians of the West, as they were rising into power upon the past civilisation of Greece and Rome, advanced to battle for the empire of the Cross through Cilicia; and fatal experience ultimately taught them to take other routes. For a time, as under the wily Alexius or the less fortunate John Comnenus, Cilicia was once more a Greek province: but the dread power of the Osmanlis was already on the ascendant; and with the exception of the temporary sway of the Mamluks, and of the devasting inroads of a Janghiz Khan or a Timur-lang, which were as evanescent as they were sweeping, and of a brief Egyptian domination in the time of Ibrahim Pasha, Cilicia has ever since remained under the control of the Osmanlis, or of their more or less dependent vassals, the Turkman chieftains of the country.

The peculiar position of this sea-and-mountain-girt province has always influenced the character of the inhabitants. The father of history tells us that the Cilicians were among the few nations in Lesser Asia whom Crœsus could not bring into subjection. Mr. Barker notices the bad character for piracy and unfaithfulness that Artemisia, queen of Halicarnassus, gave of the Cilicians; so familiar indeed were these features in the character of these isolated people of antiquity, that *Cilix haud facile verum dicit* became a proverbial saying.

From the same mountains where Cicero found the " wicked and audacious Tibarani," and where dwelt the rebel Clitæans, Armenians (not always very warlike in *other* countries) descended to ravage the plains or harass the Crusaders; and what is more curious, as shewing the persistency of character among tribes similarly situated, the Aushir and Kusan Uglu tribes of Turkmans, scarcely subjected by Ibrahim Pasha, are in the present day merely *nominal* vassals of the Sultan.

A curious feature also belongs to Cilicia, which is its fatality to crowned heads. It is doubtful if Sardanapalus, notwithstanding certain not very authentic statements to the contrary, did not die in this province; the river Cydnus, which had nearly proved fatal to Alexander, was certainly so, nearly a thousand years afterwards, to the Emperor Frederic, surnamed Barbarossa; Seleucus VI. was burned to death in a palace at Mopsuestia; Labienus and Vonones were slain in the same province; Pescennius Niger was killed on the ever-memorable battle-field of Issus; Trajan died at Selinus; Florianus was killed by his troops at Tarsus; Maximianus died in agonies at the same city; Constantius perished at Mopsuestia, and Julian the Apostate was buried at Tarsus; the best and wisest of the khalifs, Almaamun, died in Cilicia; and the pride of the Comneni, Kalo Joannes, lost his life in a boar-hunt at Anazarba.

Three times the fate of the world was decided on the plain of Issus. First, when the Greeks and Persians met there; secondly, when Severus and Pescennius Niger engaged there in a life-struggle for dominion; and thirdly, when Heraclius and Chosroes contested there for the superiority of the West over the East. There also, in the time of Bayazid II., the Osmanlis contested with the Mamluk dynasty of Syria the empire of the East. Yet in the present day it is difficult to determine, in a truly positive manner, the exact site of this famous battle-field, to which so melancholy and so sad an interest attaches itself.

The modern history of this remarkable country, as detailed by Mr. Barker, possesses all the interest of a romance. It could scarcely be imagined that, within almost our own times, the high-road between the East and the West was held almost independent during the whole lifetime of one bandit-chief, Kuchuk Ali Uglu, and during a portion of that of his son, both of whom levied tribute on all wayfarers, imprisoned or murdered inoffensive travellers, and committed all kinds of excesses, even to capturing English and French merchantmen and imprisoning a Dutch

Consul, without any effective interference having taken place on the part of Europe or the Turkish government! Happily those days are gone by, —it is to be hoped for ever.

The history of the five pashas who succeeded to the Egyptians is replete with curious matter, highly instructive to those who wish to be truly informed as to the mode of administration in Turkish provinces. The commercial details, more complete and satisfactory than any hitherto presented to the public, will also prove interesting to a large community.

In regard to that part of Mr. Barker's work which illustrates the political and administrative affairs of Cilicia, it must, however, be understood that the condition of that province is very exceptional, and in one peculiarity anomalous. The population is mixed, the majority being Turkmans; next in number, but at a far-off distance, come the Fallahs, or agricultural peasants, mostly Ansayrii and deists; after these the Christians, chiefly Armenians; next come the Kurds, dwelling at Kars and other places in the mountains; and lastly, the Turks or Osmanlis, chiefly *employés* of the Porte, police, &c. The Turkman tribes of Taurus are as independent as the Miriditi, Sagori, and other mountain tribes of Turkey in Europe; and the Ayans, or Turkman nobles of the tribes inhabiting both plains and mountains, constitute the council, and thus hold the provincial, more especially the financial, administration of the district so entirely under their control, as to put insuperable impediments in the way of reforms projected at Constantinople being as yet brought into operation in a district so remote, so peculiarly circumstanced physically, and having a population of its own—not precisely ill-affected towards the Sultan of the Osmanlis, but having no feeling or tie of nationality.

The antiquities of Cilicia are the monuments of its past glory; the more interesting and suggestive from comparison with the actual fallen condition of this once prosperous, populous, and powerful country. Towns that could boast of their 200,000 inhabitants, like Mopsuestia, now scarcely contain 200 ! Anazarba, the home of Dioscorides and Oppianus, is now level with the ground; and Epiphanea, which gave birth to St. George of Cappadocia and of England, is an untenanted, desolate, black ruin. The city dignified by the birth of the great

Apostle to the Gentiles remains, but alas how fallen! The dominion of the Greeks and Romans has, however, left its traces in a few noble monuments of olden time. The public edifices of Soli or Pompeiopolis, the ruins of Anazarba, the tombs at Sebaste or Eleusa (for an illustration of which I have been indebted to the distinguished traveller Dr. Layard), the Amanian gates, and the presumed altars of Alexander, still attest the taste and magnificence of bygone times; above all, a new interest has been imparted to Cilician archæology by Mr. Barker's important discovery of terra-cotta illustrations of the Lares and Penates of the Cilicians of old. Epiphania is still a great ruin; Sis and Arsus are remarkable sites of early Christianity; and hills and mountains are still dotted with the castles of Saracens, Venetians, Genoese, and Crusaders. Almost all that has been done by the Muhammadans still exists; and Bayas, on the site of the Baiæ of the Romans, is for its size the most complete epitome of an Oriental town that I ever met with.

Much has been done in recent times to illustrate the comparative geography of Cilicia. It was impossible that, in the absence of current topographical information, former commentators on the old geographers could throw more light upon the subject than existed in the days of Pliny, Strabo, or Ptolemy. Take, for example, the commentaries of the distinguished classical editors Gronovius and Vossius upon Pomponius Mela: Issus is identified with Laissa, Ammodes with Amanoides, Tarsus with Tarso, &c. Cellarius, in his admirable Compendium of Ancient Geography, wisely refrains from identification with actual sites.

The beginning of a new era in respect to a more intimate acquaintance with the geography of Cilicia dates from the publication of Captain (now Admiral) Sir Francis Beaufort's *Karamania*, and Colonel Leake's *Journal of a Tour*, &c. The surveys of the Euphrates Expedition completed what Admiral Sir Francis Beaufort had left undone, and enabled the editor to publish a first detailed notice of the comparative geography of the Cilician and Syrian gates in the fourth volume of the Journal of the Royal Geographical Society, and which has been amplified and corrected in subsequent publications.

Much, however, still remains to be done by future travellers. The site of Myriandrus has never been positively determined; Cicero's campaign in Amanus is by no means thoroughly understood.

The route given in the Antonine Itinerary as leading from Nicopolis to Zeugma on the Euphrates appears to be the same as the pass through Amanus by which Darius advanced in the rear of the Macedonians; but the details of this road are wanted. The sites of Aliaria and Gerbidissus are unknown; and the total distance of seventy-two Roman miles from the Euphrates to the shores of Cilicia is unsatisfactory. No traces have been met with of the Serropolis of Ptolemy, supposed to be the same as the Cassipolis of Pliny. Cadra and Davara, the strongholds of rebels at the period of Tarsus's greatest glory, are also unknown sites.

Mr. Barker has not omitted the consideration of the produce and agriculture of this rich and fertile country. His notice also of the natural history of Cilicia, if not scientific, is still replete with curious and original information. Gazelles and other small deer, as also their natural enemies the feline tribe, abound in Cilicia. The Amanus is spoken of in the Song of Solomon as the mountain of leopards. The naturalist Ælian, and the poet of the Argonauts, Valerius Flaccus, speak of the tigers and of the deer of the same district. The editor has seen six panthers while hunting in one small valley; and Mr. Barker describes Abdallah il Rushdi as leaving Adana, after a short residence there, with forty-two panther-skins in his possession.

The plains of Cilicia abound in game. It is scarcely possible to ride across these fertile grassy expanses, dotted here and there on the western side with the evergreen carob-tree — the locust-tree of Scripture — without seeing herds of gazelles browsing in the distance. The large bustard stalks along the same plains, and the smaller bustard is seen at certain seasons soaring in flocks of myriads. Wherever there is cover, the beautiful *francolin*—the prototype of our pheasant—abounds. The marshes teem with wild fowl. The sea swarms with fish, which may often be seen parading its depths from over the ship's side. Turtles are so abundant, that Mr. Barker tells us that hundreds may be taken in a day. This is truly a country as favoured by nature as it is neglected by man.

But by these very peculiarities it gains in human interest. Its remarkable configuration and physical features, its mountains, forests, and wild animals, its natural resources and produce, its history and vicissitudes, its associations and existing monuments, its prostrate and oppressed population, and above all its commercial capabilities, and its claims upon the sympathy of a wide-embracing humanity, entitle it as a country to a moment's attention, and as a population of various origin and creeds to a thought of kindness from English readers.

MAUSOLEUM AT ELEUSA. FROM A SKETCH OF DR. LAYARD.

MAP OF
CILICIA
and the north of
Syria.

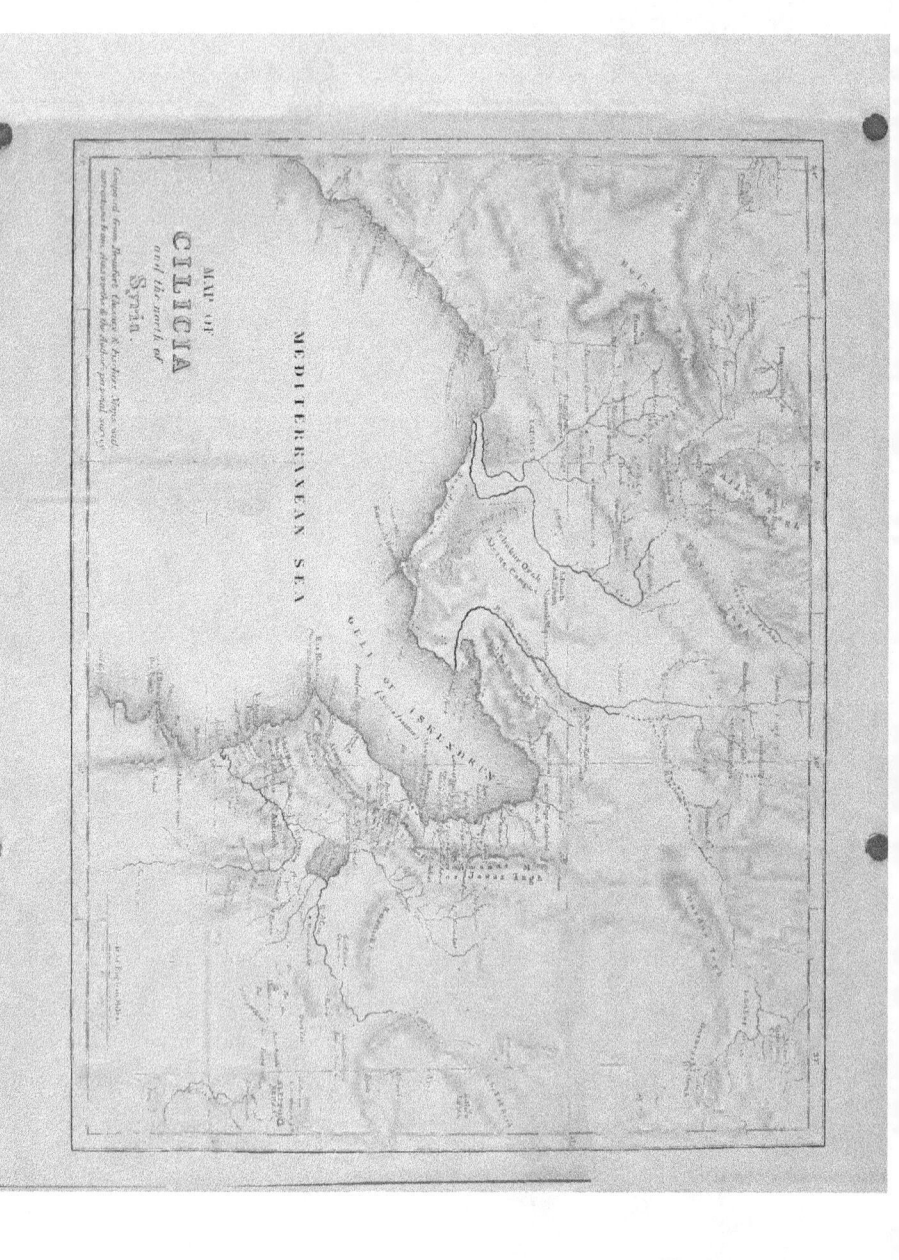

CILICIA AND ITS GOVERNORS;

BEING AN

INTRODUCTION TO THE HISTORY

OF

THE LARES AND PENATES.

CHAPTER I.

EARLY PERIOD OF CILICIAN HISTORY — SCRIPTURAL MENTION OF TARSUS — ANCIENT RELIGION — NOTICE OF THE CILICIANS BY HERODOTUS — CILICIA UNDER THE ASSYRIANS — BURIAL-PLACE OF SARDANAPALUS — DOMINION OF THE MEDES — CILICIA OVERRUN BY SCYTHIAN HORDES — THE PROPHET DANIEL'S TOMB — CRŒSUS, KING OF LYDIA — PERSIAN SATRAPS — INVASION OF GREECE BY THE PERSIANS — SYENNESIS, KING OF CILICIA — TREATY OF ANTALCIDAS — ALEXANDER THE GREAT IN CILICIA — BATTLE OF ISSUS.

THE early history of Cilicia, a country replete with interesting associations, as having been the theatre of many great events, is unfortunately, like that of most ancient nations, involved in obscurity; and it is extremely difficult to construct, out of the scanty materials which have reached our times, a chain of narrative so complete and satisfactory as to connect, without the absence of some essential links, the history of its past grandeur with its actual condition. It has been my main endeavour, the more effectually to dispel the cloud which hangs over the ancient portion of its history, to select from such writers as have given this country a place in their pages what may be considered most worthy of insertion, in order to form a connected and complete history. But the gleams of light which, from time to time, break through the mist are partial, leading only to conjecture; and they do not sufficiently fill up the gaps which the ignorance of some and the unwillingness of others have left us to regret in this inquiry.

There is, however, the best reason to believe that those passes or natural defiles which break the barriers that Nature has placed between the elevated plains of Asia Minor and those large tracts situated east of the Mediterranean, were considered by the nations of antiquity of so much importance that they were made an object of the particular attention of monarchs; and hence Cilicia became, from its position, the scene of strife between contending empires. Connecting, as it were, the eastern and western world, it was also, at a very early date, the first to benefit by the continual influx of strangers; and civilisation, consequent on the intercourse of man with man, was an early feature of its character; while wealth, flowing rapidly on its precursors, civilisation and trade, laid a foundation for that opulence which, in after times, attracted the cupidity of the Romans, and reduced it finally to a Roman province. Hence we find Cilicia mentioned by several historians as the first commercial power which made any figure in this part of the world.

But it is not only the fables of Pagan theology that bear witness to the high antiquity and power of this country, by informing us that Tarsus was built by Perseus, son of Jupiter by Danaë; but Scripture historians also affirm that the sons of *Tarshish*, the great-grandson of Noah, who were settled on this coast, had made themselves famous for their navigation and commerce; so that "the ships of Tarshish" had become a common appellation for all vessels of trade, and "to go to Tarshish" a proverbial expression for setting out to sea in such vessels. In Isaiah xxiii. 10, Tyre is called "the daughter of Tarshish," which would lead us to infer that the nautical celebrity to which the Tyrians subsequently attained had its rise in Cilicia, and that a colony from this country settled on the Syrian coast and laid the foundation for Phœnician grandeur and fame.*

* There are few questions in sacred geography that are involved in greater difficulties than the position and extent of Tarshish, or of the several Tarshishes mentioned in the Scriptures. Some have argued that the word itself applied to the *sea* generally. One of the latest authorities, the Rev. J. R. Beard, D.D., has attempted in a similar manner to cut the gordian knot, by arguing that all the scriptural passages in which the name occurs agree in fixing Tarshish somewhere in or near Spain. (*Cyclopædia of Biblical Literature*, edited by J. Kitto, D.D., art. "Tarshish.") Heeren (*Ideen*, &c. ii. 64) goes so far as to translate (Ezek. xxvii. 25) the ships of Tarshish, &c. by "Spanish ships." And Bochart, in his *Geographia Sacra* (*Phaleg*, iii. 7), is undecided as to the superior claims of Carteia or Cadiz, or the Tartessus of Aristotle, Strabo, Pausanias, Arrian, and Avienus, which was between the two mouths of the Bætis or Guadalquiver, and which is the most likely site of the Spanish Tarshish, being of Phœnician origin.

But there was another Tarshish in Ophir or Arabia; for in 2 Chron. xx. 36 it is recorded that Jehoshaphat king of Judah joined himself with Ahaziah king of Israel to make ships to go to Tarshish; and they made the ships in Ezion-geber—that is, on the Elanitic Gulf, on the eastern arm of the Red Sea. And in the parallel passage, found in 1 Kings xxii. 49, these vessels are described as "ships of Tarshish," which were intended to go to Ophir.

So also there appears much probability that there was a Tarshish nearer to Judæa. An important testimony to this effect occurs in Ezek. xxxviii. 13: "Sheba and Dedan, and the merchants of Tarshish, with all the young lions thereof." Now, here Tarshish is mentioned in conjunction with two eastern sites; and we shall have occasion to shew

Strabo says of the nations of Tarsus, that they did not, like other nations, stay at home, but, in order to complete their education, went abroad; and many of them, when this was accomplished, became attached to their residences in foreign countries, and never returned. To this roving disposition we must attribute the circumstance of their having factories at Dedan and Sheba on the Euphrates, with which places they trafficked in silver, gold, &c., as we are told by Ezekiel (xxxviii. 10);* and it confirms the assertion of Tacitus, that Thamiras the Cilician was the first who introduced the science of divination into Cyprus during the reign of Cinyras, as far back as 2000 years B.C., and that the priesthood continued to be hereditary in his family for many generations, until, for want of male heirs, the sacerdotal functions merged into the descendants of the king. Here we find an enlightened Cilician quitting his native country, and bearing with him the riches of superior knowledge, which he imparts to a less civilised nation, establishing for himself and for his posterity an imperishable monument of fame.

What that knowledge was, or to what particular worship it related,

that the Amanus was in ancient times as renowned for its lions as Cilicia is to the present day distinguished by the number of its panthers, while it does not appear that there were lions in Andalusia.

Again, when Jonah (i. 3; iv. 2) wished to avoid the duty imposed upon him to go and prophesy against Nineveh, he took ship at Joppa and fled to Tarshish. It is not likely that he fled as far as Spain; but it is not unlikely that he fled from Judæa, and took refuge in Tarsus.

The transit of the Phœnicians from Cyprus to Cilicia was easy. Apollodorus relates, that Celendris, now Chalindrah, was founded by Sandocus, i. e. Sadoc, father of Cinyra. It was afterwards a colony of Samians. The name of the country itself is said to have been derived from Cilix, the brother of Cadmus. According to Bochart, Corycus, on the same coast, derived its name from the celebrity of its crocuses or saffron,—*carcom* in the Hebrew, and *corcum* in the Syriac (Solomon's Song iv. 14). It is not certain if the Amanus is meant in the 8th verse of the same canticle, "look from the top of Amana," because the mountain so called is mentioned in connexion with the Lebanon. The allusion to "the lions' dens"—"the mountains of the leopards"—makes it, however, extremely improbable that it is the Cilician Amanus that is referred to. Bochart, in his *Phœnices in Cilicia* (*Phaleg*, i. 4), entertains no doubt of the commercial relations of Tarsus and Tyre: "*Nec desunt*," he adds, "*quibus Tarsus Ciliciæ metropolis, Pauli Apostoli ortu nobilis, videtur esse Tarshish et Cetis*" (Cethim).—W. F. A.

* Very little is known as to the locality peopled by the descendants of the Cushite Dedan. It is supposed that they settled in southern Arabia, near the Persian Gulf; but the existence in that quarter of a place called Dadan or Dadena is the chief ground for this conclusion. The Rev. Charles Forster has, however, shewn in his *Historical Geography of Arabia*, that correlative testimony is given of this opinion by the juxtaposition of kindred names (vol. i. pp. 38, 63). With regard to the descendants of the Cushite Sheba, there seems no reason to doubt that their ultimate settlement was in Ethiopia; while the descendants of Sheba, son of Joktan, peopled Yemen in Arabia. Hence the distinction between the African Sabæans and Arabian Sabæans; but there were also Badwin or "wandering" Shebans (Job i. 15) and Chaldean Sabæans, or, more properly, *Tsabians*, particularly described by Mr. Rich and the Rev. Mr. Wolff.— W. F. A.

the learned historian does not proceed to say; but in another passage we learn from him that the Egyptians, in the reign of Ptolemy Philadelphus, B.C. 284, obtained the statue of the god *Serapis* from Sinope in Pontus; and although the epoch when this image was introduced and placed in the quarter of the city of Alexandria called Rhacotis is comparatively of modern date, the circumstance may go far to establish that this god was worshipped in Asia Minor; and if we are to believe Herodotus, who says the Egyptian priests attributed the origin of their nation to the *Phrygians*, close neighbours of the Cilicians, we may conclude that a great similarity existed in the worship and religious ceremonies of the two countries. This subject is more particularly illustrated in that part of the work which refers to the newly-discovered terra-cottas, among which have been found heads of Horus and other deities of the Egyptian pantheon, as also the god Osiris, represented under the form of an ox, and of which we give an illustration here. The two accompanying woodcuts of Serapis and Osiris are taken from some terra-cotta antiques found at Tarsus, and of which the reader will find a more circumstantial account further on.

SERAPIS.

We are told by Herodotus that the original inhabitants of Cilicia were called *Hypacheans*, and that it was not until the arrival of *Cilex*, the son of *Agenor* king of Phœnicia, that they obtained the appellation of Cilicians. Cilex, it is related, set out in search of his sister Europa, who had been carried away by pirates; and after seeking her in many countries by sea and land, disgusted and worn out by his want of success, and attracted by the fertility of the soil, he settled down on the coast of Asia Minor, and gave his name to the country which forms the subject of this history, about 1552 B.C.*

OSIRIS.

Tarsus in Cilicia is said to have been founded, according to heathen mythology, B.C. 1326, by Perseus son of Jupiter and Danaë, while on his expedition against the Gorgons; but other historians attribute its origin to a colony of Argives.

* According to others (Apollodorus, iii. c. 14), Cilex was son of Cinyras, and brother of Cadmus, which Cinyras first colonised these countries from Phœnicia, and built the town of Celendræ or Celendris, afterwards a colony of Samians. Bochart (*Chanaan*, i. 5) argues that the country derived its name from the abundance of chalk and limestone,—*challek* or *challak* of the Hebrews, and χάλιξ of the Greeks.—W. F. A.

CILICIA UNDER THE ASSYRIANS.

However that may be, this city became famous for its maritime commerce as early as the days of King David, B.C. 1055 (Ps. xlviii. 7), and from that circumstance gave its name to that part of the Mediterranean contiguous to Cilicia, which was thence called the Sea of Tarshish. Pamphylia was also colonised from the same district.

But under what government Cilicia existed, or whether it rose to fame in a state of independence, is a matter of great uncertainty. It would appear probable that this country paid tribute to the Assyrian monarchs, because the *Cilicians* are not mentioned by Homer in his catalogue as having sent subsidies to Priam at the siege of Troy, B.C. 1184, with the rest of their neighbours, the different states on the coast of Asia Minor. Certain it is that the kings of Assyria subdued the principal petty nations of Asia; and as the Taurus formed the natural boundary of Mesopotamia, Cilicia must have been the first to fall under the yoke of the successors of Nimrod.

But we are precluded from learning at what precise date this country was overrun by the Assyrians, because from the death of Ninias, the son of Ninus and Semiramis, B.C. 1600, down to the revolt of the Medes against Sardanapalus, during a period of eight hundred years, there is a chasm in the history of Babylon to be filled up. The fables of Berosus in reference to this subject are not worthy of credit, as the work which passes under his name is evidently a fabrication. But that it was subdued and formed a part of that kingdom previous to the time of its dissolution is an historical fact, as we find Sardanapalus made it his favourite residence; and we are informed by some historians that the ports of this country were considered of great importance by that dynasty, as being their chief maritime station in the Mediterranean.

Grecian historians have attributed to Sardanapalus, the last king of the Assyrian monarchy, the foundation of the city of Tarsus, B.C. 820; but as it is also reported that he was buried at Anchiale* by his par-

---

* Anchiale may have begun even in the time of Sardanapalus to be a necessary port to the commerce of Tarsus, in consequence of the increasing alluvium brought down by the river Cydnus, and which is always filling up the lake, that formerly served as a harbour (called by Strabo Rhegma, and which he says preserved some remains of its naval arsenal). This Rhegma resembled a lake by its extensive and shallow bed, and could no longer admit of large vessels, because earth, stones, and rubbish were continually brought down into it from the heights of Mount Taurus by the winds and torrents. It is now a stagnant marsh, with four or five feet water, and no longer communicates either with the sea or the river Cydnus, although not more distant in some places than a thousand yards from either. The original beds of the canals, which served as a means of communication with the sea, are filled up by earth and sand; but the traces of them exist, and could with no great difficulty be cleared, and made to serve as an exit for the water. The whole of the surrounding country, with

ticular desire, we may infer that he was more probably the founder of this latter place, and the embellisher only of Tarsus. On the site of Anchiale is a ruin to be seen which may have been the foundation of the tomb; but no vestige remains of the celebrated statue mentioned by Arrian of this ill-fated monarch, or of the inscription in the Assyrian language commemorating the intemperance and dissipation that distinguished his life, which so provoked the satire of Aristotle. The fact that Sardanapalus was really buried on this spot would seem to contradict the accounts of other writers of celebrity, who assert that he burned himself in his palace in the city of *Nineveh*, with all his household and treasure; or, at all events, the two statements can only be reconciled by supposing that his body was carried by some faithful surviving attendants, by whom, we hear, he was *deified*, to repose in the city of his predilection, which owed its origin to his choice.* Different accounts of the same event occur frequently in ancient authors, and cause us to regret how much this question is involved in obscurity.†

On the dismemberment of the Assyrian empire, Cilicia fell into the

the bed of the lake itself, having risen considerably by alluvial deposits—a circumstance universal wherever rivers flow into large plains, and particularly in the vicinity of such a high range of mountains as the Taurus—Anchiale was for centuries the depôt of Tarsus, and received such vessels as could not by their size enter the lake; and it continued to serve as the port of Tarsus in after ages until modern times, when Kaisanli was chosen for its proximity; and lately Marsinah has been preferred to either for the safety of its roadstead, and is rising into the notice of the commercial world.

* The partiality that Sardanapalus seems to have evinced to Anchiale was natural enough; it was to him, with its wide expanse of sea, what the Indian Ocean would have been to Alexander,—the furthest point of his conquest: for in the Bay of Issus the land may be seen on the other side; while at Anchiale the Eastern monarch might have considered himself as having reached the farthest bounds of his Western World. From this place, which he prided himself on having built in one day, he could look on the broad blue sea, and ordain that his tomb should there be formed, where it might remain as a monument of his grandeur, washed by the waves that alone impeded his conquest. There is a ruin at Karadoghar which may be supposed to form a part of this monument; and the whole coast is lined with buildings that are now broken down and covered with sand by the sea, which has retired full a hundred yards: these must have served for quays, and greatly facilitated the landing of goods, which now have to wait the calming of the wind and sea. When we see the gigantic works of the ancients, wherein they spared no trouble for the smallest good, we cannot but wonder at the vastness of population which enabled them to carry out such undertakings. We might well take a lesson of perseverance from their example.

† Professor Grotefend states, that after Shalmaneser king of Assyria had reigned twenty-five years, he extended his conquests over Asia Minor, and took up his abode in the city of Tanakan, a strong place in Etlak, by which perhaps Tarsus in Cilicia is meant, of the building of which by Sennacherib a fabulous account is given by Alexander Polyhistor and Abydenus in the Armenian version of Eusebius. After he had introduced into that place the worship of Assarde (Astarte) or Nisroch, and received gold and silver, corn, sheep, and oxen as a tribute, he reduced the neighbouring pro-

hands of the *Medes*, and so continued until the reign of Cyaxares, B.C. 624, when the barbarous hordes of Scythians overran all Central Asia, and overturned the government. After remaining twenty-eight years in possession, the Scythians were in their turn driven out, their chiefs being murdered by Cyaxares at a feast. The Medes then recovered that power which the invaders had lost by their licentiousness and ignorance of civil administration.

As Daniel the Prophet flourished about this time (550 B.C.), I take the opportunity here of stating a remarkable circumstance connected with an Armenian tradition in the country. The Turks hold in great veneration a tomb which they believe contains the bones of this prophet, situated in an ancient Christian church, converted into a mosque, in the centre of the modern town of Tarsus. The sarcophagus is said to be about *forty feet below* the surface of the present soil, in consequence of the accumulation of earth and stones; and over which a stream flows from the Cydnus river, of comparatively modern date. Over this stream, at the particular spot where the sarcophagus was (before the canal was cut and the waters went over it), stands the ancient church above mentioned; and to mark the exact spot of the tomb below, a wooden monument has been erected in the Turkish style.* The waters of this rivulet are turned off every year in the summer, in order to clear the bed of the canal; and if ever this country falls into the hands of a civilised nation, it will not be difficult to verify the authenticity of this tradition, which the fanaticism of the Turks now prevents us from doing. However extraordinary this may appear, and difficult as it may be to establish the identity of this sarcophagus as containing the relics of the *prophet*, without the assistance of history or inscription, little doubt can be entertained of the existence of a tomb of *some holy* personage, or of one whose memory was held sacred, from the well-known permanence of oral tradition in the East; and it is a remarkable instance of the tenacity by which events are rescued from oblivion, and the power of tradition to record the exact locality, at so great a depth under the accumulated ruins of so many years.†

---

vinces to subjection, and appointed Akharrizadon or Assarhaddon as king over them. This is one of the triumphs supposed to be alluded to in the celebrated obelisk of Nimrud or Athur.—W. F. A.

* This monument is covered with an embroidered cloth, and stands in a special apartment built for it, from the iron-grated windows of which it may occasionally be seen when the Armenians take occasion to make their secret devotions; but generally a curtain is dropped to hide it from vulgar view, and add by exclusion to the sanctity of the place.

† The burial-place of the prophet Daniel is not historically known. Epiphanius says

It is a curious coincidence that the supposed tomb of Daniel the Prophet at Susa is said to be, like the one above described, under a running stream. This would prove the great increase of alluvial deposits in the East. (Vide *Journal of the Royal Geographical Society*, vol. ix.; article by Colonel Rawlinson.)

During the anarchy attendant on the wars of the *Medes* with their neighbours the Babylonians and Persians, Cilicia became independent; for we are informed by Herodotus that (B.C. 548) Crœsus king of Lydia subjected almost all the nations which are situated on this side the river Halys. The *Cilicians* and *Lycians* alone were not brought under his yoke; and we find them again (B.C. 504) governed by their own kings and increasing in maritime power, but subject to pay tribute to Darius Hystaspes, third king of the Persian monarchy, who divided his dominions into *satrapies*, of which Cilicia was the fourth. The Cilicians were obliged to furnish 360 white horses and 500 talents of silver annually: of these, 140 were appointed for the payment of the cavalry who formed the guard of the country; the remaining 360 talents were received by Darius. On the resolution taken by Darius (B.C. 490) to invade Greece, Datis and Artaphernes his nephews were ordered to man a fleet and collect an army for the purpose. Accordingly they proceeded to Aleium in Cilicia, a plain at the mouth of the river Pyramus* and near the port of Mallos (Kara-Tash), where they collected a large body of infantry; here they were soon joined by a numerous reinforcement of marines, agreeably to the orders which had been given; and soon after, the vessels which the preceding year Darius had commanded his tributaries to supply having arrived, the cavalry and troops embarked and proceeded to Ionia, in a fleet of six hundred triremes, or three-oared galleys.

that he died at Babylon; and he is followed in this by the generality of historians. Monumentally and traditionally, however, the tomb designated as that of Daniyali Akbar, "the greater Daniel," at Sus, ancient Susa, in Susiana, records the burial-place of "God is my judge." The great Saracenic building which adorns the site at the present day in Sus or Shush, is represented in the Baron de Bode's *Travels in Luristan and Arabistan* (vol. ii. p. 188). It is also described by Major Rawlinson in the *Journal of the Royal Geographical Society* (vol. ix. p. 83). The Major spoke of sacred fish being also preserved at the spot. Layard (ibid. vol. xvi. p. 61) says that the small stream which washes the tomb certainly contains fish, but he does not believe that they are generally esteemed sacred. A black stone or aerolite, such as played so conspicuous a part in the early religions of the Semitic nations, is preserved there. Great suspicion as to the intentions of Europeans towards this sacred stone is unfortunately entertained by the guardians of the monument.—W. F. A.

* The Aleian Plain has always stood prominent in the history of Cilicia. Pliny calls it Campus Aleius. Strabo relates that Philotas led the cavalry attached to the Macedonian army under Alexander the Great, 'Αλήιον πεδίον, "over the Aleian Plain."

INVASION OF GREECE BY THE PERSIANS.

Xerxes, son of Darius, on undertaking (B.C. 484) his great expedition against Greece, exacted one hundred ships from the Cilicians, at which epoch Herodotus says they wore helmets peculiar to their country, and small bucklers made of the untanned hides of oxen; they had also tunics of wool, and each man had two spears and a sword, not unlike those of Egypt. At a council called by Xerxes before the battle of Salamis, Artemisia, queen of Halicarnassus, spoke very disparagingly of the Cilicians, as a people addicted to piracy and not to be trusted, and on whom no reliance could be placed. Whatever may have been the character of many of the Greek colonies of the coast, it is certain that the inhabitants of Tarsus maintained a fair reputation in their commercial transactions, and which was absolutely necessary to them in their intercourse with foreigners.

At the death of Xerxes (B.C. 410), Cilicia remained under the government of its own kings, but tributary to his successors Artaxerxes, Darius Nothus, and Artaxerxes, against whom Cyrus the younger revolted. Having been appointed governor of Lydia by his brother Artaxerxes, he assembled an army (a part of which was composed of the ten thousand Greeks whose courage and endurance have been immortalised by Xenophon), and entering Cilicia, arrived at Tarsus. The inhabitants of this city, with their king Syennesis, fled to a fastness in the mountains, now called *Nimrud;* but those of Soli and Issus, who were near the sea, did not follow their example.

Cyrus sent for Syennesis; but the latter replied, that he had never put himself in the power of a superior, and would not do so now. His wife Epyaxa, who had previously visited Cyrus in Phrygia, whither she had been sent on a diplomatic mission to meet the conqueror, dismayed by the reports regarding his formidable army, prevailed on her husband to change his resolution, and the two princes met on friendly terms. Syennesis gave Cyrus large sums of money to carry on the war, and received in return suitable presents, with the restitution of

---

Arrian describes Philotas as leading the cavalry across the Plain to the river Pyramus. This is important in a geographical point of view. Dionysius of Corinth alludes to this Plain in the 872d verse of his poetical geography:

Κεῖθι δὲ τὸ πεδίον τὸ 'Αλήιον'

which Avienus has rendered

"*Hic cespes late producit Aleius arva.*"

It was also on this beautiful and expansive Plain that Bellerophon wandered after his fall from Pegasus at Tarsus:

"Forsook by heaven, forsaking human kind,
Wide o'er th' Aleian field he chose to stray,
A long, forlorn, uncomfortable way."

W. F. A.

the prisoners taken by Cyrus. He was confirmed in his authority at Tarsus.

We may presume that the Cilician kings during the next twenty years sided with the Grecian colonies in the war carried on by the Spartans against Artaxerxes, and lost their independence; for we find, by the "treaty of Antalcidas," that Tarsus was included among the other cities and possessions in Asia Minor that were ceded to the Persian monarchs.

When Alexander had carried his victorious arms into Asia (B.C. 333), in his march against Darius after the battle of the Granicus, he advanced to the Pylæ Ciliciæ (Kulak Bughaz); and fearing an ambuscade, he ordered the light-armed Thracians to advance and reconnoitre that narrow pass, where only a few men abreast can be admitted at a time. He was astonished, and rejoiced at his good fortune, in finding that the Persians had not availed themselves of the advantages afforded them by the natural features of the pass to make an effectual stand at this important post, which a handful of men could defend, and hurl destruction on the invaders by throwing stones and other missiles from the heights above. This neglect on their part surprised him, but it was nothing more than what was to be expected; for the few Persian soldiers left there as a guard by Arsanes on his retreat, after laying waste the country, had fled in consternation at the approach of the formidable invader; and the Cilicians were so ready to throw off the Persian yoke, and to hail the Greeks their fellow-countrymen, that they never thought of offering any opposition. From this place the Macedonian hero marched his whole army to Tarsus, and arrived just in time to save it from destruction, as the Persians had set fire to the city, to prevent his becoming master of the treasures it contained.

It was here that Alexander nearly lost his life by bathing in the cold waters of the Cydnus, a river which passes by this town, and which in summer is nearly all of melted snow, flowing from the neighbouring heights of Mount Taurus; and here it was he gave an instance of that magnanimity of spirit which formed so distinguishing a feature in his character, by shewing perfect confidence in his physician Philip, and drinking off the medicine he administered, in utter disregard of the insinuations made to influence him against a faithful servant, and which accused the physician of having been bribed by Darius to poison him.

From this place, having sent his cavalry under Philotas across the Aleian plain to the banks of the Pyramus, where he ordered a bridge to be prepared, he proceeded to Soli, where he laid the inhabitants under a contribution of 200 talents, and evinced in what contempt he held the barbarians, by entertaining his followers with games in honour of Æsculapius and Minerva; he then proceeded along the coast to Megarsus, and from thence to Mallos.

This latter place, situated on a height according to Strabo, " was founded by Amphilocus and Mopsus, who having slain one another in single combat, were buried so that the tomb of the one should not be visible from that of the other." He next proceeded to Issus, the scene of the memorable battle which decided the fate of the Persian empire; for soon after, by the battle of Arbela (B.C. 330), Darius was dethroned, and with him terminated the line of Assyrian and Persian kings, which had lasted two hundred and nine years from Cyrus.*

* According to Plutarch, Darius was encouraged by Alexander's long stay in Cilicia,—which he regarded as the effect of his fears, instead of tracing it to its true cause, sickness,—to march across the mountains into Cilicia in quest of his adversary. "But happening to miss each other in the night, they both turned back; Alexander rejoicing in his good fortune, and hastening to meet Darius in the straits, while Darius was endeavouring to disengage himself and recover his former camp." This description of the two armies passing one another in the night indicates that Darius had effected the passage before Alexander had reached the Syrian Gates, and that the armies passed one another in the region of Urzin, and where are now the supposed ruins of Epiphanea; the Macedonians keeping the coast, the Persians occupying the interior. Calisthenes says, in the fragments of Polybius (lib. xii. cap. 8), that Alexander had reached the straits which are called the Cilician Gates, when Darius arrived with his army at the Amanian Gates. The philosopher of Olynthus evidently meant the Cilician and Syrian Gates of Xenophon (Markaz Kalasi), and not the Cilician Gates (Kulak Bughaz). Quintus Curtius (lib. iii. cap. 8) says, " The same night that Alexander arrived at the straits by which Syria is approached, Darius arrived at that place which is called the Amanian Gates." Arrian (lib. ii. p. 94) also says, " Darius having crossed the mountain *where are* the Amanian Gates, advanced towards Issus; Alexander having imprudently left him in his rear." Most scholars have read τὸ κατὰ τὰς Πύλας 'Αμανικῶν as " near to the Amanian Gates;" but others have argued that κατὰ with the accusative establishes identity, as in κατὰ τὴν χώραν ἐκείνην (Luc. xv. 14), " in that region," as well as " near to."

Thus, according to one version, the pass of Darius over the Amanus is identified with the road given in the *Antonine Itinerary* as leading from Nicopolis to Zeugma on the Euphrates, and is called the Amanian Gates: according to the other, the road remains the same, but Darius is made to descend near to the " Amanian Gates," now called Tamir Kapu, or Iron Gates. Arrian relates that Darius having advanced to Issus, he took that city and slew whatever Macedonians had remained behind, and the next day he advanced to the river Pinarus. Having heard that Alexander was about to retrace his steps and give the Persians battle, he sent fifty thousand horsemen across the river to keep the Macedonians at bay till the remainder of the army could take up its position. According to Plutarch, Alexander, whose army was small in comparison with that of Darius, took care to draw it up so as to prevent its being surrounded, by stretching out his right wing beyond the enemy's left. In that wing he acted in person, and fighting in the foremost ranks, put the barbarians to flight. Cicero (lib. v. ad Attic. epist. 20) speaks of a castle that Alexander occupied in the same neighbourhood. " We held for some days," he says, " a castle, the very same that Alexander held against Darius near to Issus."

Three streams descend from the Amanus in the regions here alluded to. The most northerly is called the Dali Chaï, mad or swift river; the central, Kui Chaï, river of the village; and the southerly, Yuslah Chaï, from a village of that name: all unite to form the ancient Pinarus before reaching the sea. The village of Yuslah has been identified by some with Issus, from a remote analogy of name; but it is certain from the description of the movements of Darius as above given from Arrian, that Issus was north of the Pinarus. Strabo also says, "After Ægæ comes Issus, and then the Pinarus." In the villages north of the Pinarus there are to the present day plenty of remains of antiquity,—hewn stones, fragments of columns and pilasters, friezes, &c., especially in the Muhammadan cemeteries,—to indicate the site of a city which was populous and opulent in the times of Xenophon, and once gave its name to the gulf of Alexandretta, but which was succeeded in the time of the Romans by Epiphanea, Baiæ, and other towns and stations, and in modern times by Iskandrun—Alexander's favourite little site. The distances given by Xenophon are satisfactory so far as regards the positioning of Issus. The army of Cyrus marched in two days fifteen parasangs, or thirty-five geographical miles, from the Pyramus to Issus; and from Issus, in one march, five parasangs, or fifteen geographical miles, to the gates of Cilicia and Syria. These distances would place Issus a little northward of the Dali Chaï. The course of this river has, however, been explored by the annotator from Yuslah to where it issues from the mountains, without any trace being discovered of the altars said by Quintus Curtius to have been erected by Alexander on the banks of the Pinarus. It is more likely that these were erected at the spot which Alexander had reached before he turned back to engage with the enemy; and that they are represented by the massive marble ruin called Sakal Tutan by the Turks, Jonas's Pillars by English sailors, and Bomitæ or altars by Pliny. Mr. W. B. Barker has in the present work identified Issus with Bayas, the Baiæ of the Romans (Bais, *Antonine Itinerary*), sixteen Roman miles from Alexandria. The details above given will explain the various reasons for which we differ from him on this point. It must not be omitted here that Mr. Edward B. B. Barker, her Britannic Majesty's Vice-Consul at Suwaidiyah, informs me that he has traversed the Amanus in the direction which Darius took to arrive in the rear of the Macedonians; that it is a hilly, rough, and exceedingly stony country, the road being rendered especially difficult by rounded stones, but that it is not all mountainous. This accords with the impressions received by contemplating the Amanus from the acclivities of the Taurus above Adana. The mountainous character of the range ceases abruptly beyond the parallel of the most north-easterly extent of the Gulf of Alexandretta.

The position of the various "gates" or mountain passes will be best understood by reference to the map; but to facilitate the reader's comprehension, they are as follow, proceeding from Asia Minor:

The Cilician Gates. Pass of Taurus, Kulak Bughaz.

The Amanian Gates. Tamir Kapu, or Iron Gate of the Turks: a Cyclopean arch, where the hills come down to the sea-side at the head of the gulf.

The Cappadocian Gates. The pass described by Strabo and explored by the Euphrates Expedition, leading through Taurus to Marash, ancient Germanicia.

Darius's Pass. Across the Amanus, north of Issus and near to (sard) the Amanian Gates; probably the same road which is given in the *Antonine Itinerary* as leading from Castabala to the Euphrates by Nicopolis, Aliaria, and Gerbidissen.

Gates of Cilicia and Syria of Xenophon. Ruins near Markaz Kalasi, and at Sakal Tutan (Jonas's Pillars of some writers, Bomitæ or altars of Pliny).

Gates of Syria. Pass of Bailan, Pictanus of the *Jerusalem Itinerary*, Erana of Cicero.—W. F. A.

CHAPTER II.

PLISTARCHUS — BATTLE OF IPSUS — PTOLEMY EVERGETES — ANTIOCHUS THE GREAT — ZENO AND CHRYSIPPUS — CILICIA UNDER THE SELEUCIDÆ — INVADED BY TIGRANES — REDUCED TO A ROMAN PROVINCE BY POMPEY — CICERO'S CAMPAIGN IN CILICIA — MARC ANTONY AND CLEOPATRA AT TARSUS — CILICIA INVADED BY THE PARTHIANS UNDER LABIENUS — ATHENODORUS — VONONES SLAIN IN CILICIA — ST. PAUL — INSURRECTION OF THE CLITEANS — COSSUATIANUS PAPITO GOVERNOR — POLEMON, KING OF CILICIA, MARRIES BERENICE — CILICIA DECLARED A ROMAN PROVINCE IN VESPASIAN'S TIME — FATE OF THE ROMAN EMPIRE DECIDED ON THE PLAIN OF ISSUS.

AFTER the death of Alexander, in the struggles for power carried on by his successors, Cilicia, like the other countries of Asia Minor, was overrun by the armies which they levied to oppose one another, and was the scene of war and bloodshed for several years, till it fell into the hands of Plistarchus brother of Cassander, and Demetrius son of Antigonus, and who ruled there until Antigonus, who had made himself master of all Syria, was killed by the forces under Ptolemy, Lysimachus, Cassander, and Seleucus Nicator, at the battle of Ipsus, in Phrygia. Cilicia then fell to the share of this last-mentioned general, and formed part of the empire founded by him, and known in history as that of the Seleucidæ.

Ptolemy Evergetes, the third of that name king of Egypt, invaded Syria and Cilicia (B.C. 245), and wrested the government from Antiochus Theos, grandson of Seleucus, in revenge for the ill-treatment of Berenice his sister, whom he had married; and this country remained tributary to the Egyptian dynasty during the reigns of the two succeeding kings of Syria, Seleucus Callinicus and Seleucus Ceracenos.

Antiochus, surnamed the great, their successor (in the year B.C. 233), not only re-established the power of the Seleucidæ in Syria and Cilicia, but also colonised the whole coast of Asia Minor (of doubtful fidelity) with Jews from Babylon and Palestine, from whom were descended the multitudes of Israelites scattered through those regions at the first preaching of the gospel, and among whom none more illustrious than the Apostle of the Gentiles; and thus Antiochus was an instrumen tin the hand of divine Providence in laying the foundation of the Seven Churches which take so prominent a part in the history of early Christianity.

About this date (B.C. 207) flourished Zeno, a philosopher of Tarsus, and Chrysippus, a native of Soli, an adjoining town,* who was a disciple of "Zeno the Stoic," and Cleanthus his successor; but being of a sophistical turn, he departed from some of the principles of these philosophers. He was nevertheless considered the most conspicuous ornament and the most zealous and able defender of the Stoics, so much so that

"Nisi Chrysippus fuisset, Porticus non esset,"

passed into a proverb. Some accuse him of incongruity, and say that he contradicted himself, as he did not act according to the evil maxims he inculcated. He wrote upwards of 300 books, on such various subjects that he appears, like Voltaire, to have aspired to be considered a universal genius. He admitted the possibility of a resurrection of the body, and maintained the mutability of the gods: even Jupiter was not to be exempted at the destruction of the universe. He died in the 81st year of his age, laughing at an ass eating figs out of a silver plate.

During the reign of Antiochus Epiphanes, son of Antiochus the Great (B.C. 175), the Cilicians revolted, and the king went in person to quell the insurrection; which when he had accomplished, he returned to Antioch, then become the seat of empire.

In the civil wars which disgraced the reigns of the succeeding kings, and the bloody contests they maintained from time to time with the Ptolemies of Egypt, we find little of note occurring in Cilicia until the

* Soli was, according to Strabo, a city next in renown to Issus, founded by the Acheans and Lindians of Rhodes. Polybius also speaks of the ambassadors from Rhodes and from the city of Soli in Cilicia coming together to the senate, as their interests were the same. When Pompey subjected the pirates of the coast, he appointed this city as their chief dwelling-place, and changed its name to Pompeiopolis. Ptolemy says (lib. v. cap. 8) Πομπηιοιπολις ἡ και Σολοι, Pompeiopolis, formerly Soli. The Latins often preserved the Greek diphthong: thus Pomponius Mela says nunc Pompeiopolis, tunc Solæ; Pliny also, Solæ Ciliciæ, nunc Pompeiopolis. Tacitus (Annal. ii. cap. 58) speaks of Vonones taking up his quarters there; and Dion Cassius (lib. xxxvi. p. 18) relates that the same city was devastated by Tigranes. Strabo makes Soli the first city (from the westward) of Cilicia Campestris; but Ptolemy seems more correct in naming Corycus. Livy and Pliny speak of Soli as a colony of Argives as well as Rhodians. The word "solecism," σολοικισμος, solæcismus, adopted in our language from the Greek or Roman, took its origin, according to Strabo, from the barbarian dialect of this city.

The site of Soli, now called Mazatlu, is distinguished at the present day by many interesting remains of antiquity. Among these especially is the beautiful harbour or basin, with parallel sides and circular ends, entirely artificial, and minutely described by Admiral Sir Francis Beaufort in his work on Karamania. There are also remains of a most noble portico opening to a double row of two hundred columns, once united by arches, forty-four of which are now standing; an elevated theatre, city-walls strengthened by numerous towers, an aqueduct, and other detached ruins, tombs, and sarcophagi.—W. F. A.

reign of Seleucus the sixth. This monarch fled from Antiochus Pius, and took refuge at Mopsuestia in Cilicia; where endeavouring to levy money from the people, he was burnt together with his followers in his palace by the revolted populace, who were excited to so severe an act of vengeance by his tyranny. Mopsuestia is now a small village called Missis on the banks of the Saihun (Pyramus), and on the high road from Constantinople to Antioch.*

Tigranes, king of Armenia (B.C. 69), son-in-law of Mithridates, during the latter part of these civil wars had laid waste Cilicia, and carried away the inhabitants of Soli, with many others, to colonise and people Tigranocerta, a city he had founded in Armenia and made his capital, and which Lucullus, the Roman general, took with great difficulty, and found there 8000 talents in ready money.†

B.C. 68. The vast body of pirates who had infested the whole of the Mediterranean during the war with Carthage had become formidable to the Romans, by intercepting the vessels laden with wheat and other provisions into Rome, and committing many great excesses. They possessed a thousand galleys and 400 cities in different parts of the Mediterranean, and hired themselves as subsidiaries to Mithridates, king of Pontus, with whom the Romans were then at war. Pompey was sent with the fullest powers that were ever given to a Roman citizen against them, and set out in a fleet of 500 ships and with 120,000 men. He divided his forces into thirteen squadrons, which he sent to different parts of the Mediterranean, and followed them up into Cilicia, which they had made their chief place of resort, and where they had fortified many places which they considered impregnable. After various engagements

* Mopsuestia, more correctly written by Strabo Mopsi Hestia, the house or abode of Mopsus the poet and soothsayer, was a holy city and an asylum, and became free under the Romans, by whom it was enlarged and embellished in the time of Hadrian. It was also, as we learn from Procopius, remarkable for its magnitude and splendour in the middle ages; and Abu-al-fada relates that 200,000 Moslems were devoted to death or slavery in this city by Nicephoras Phocas and John Ximisces. A great many misrepresentations, regarding both the situation of this city and its name, exist in the Byzantine writers, and are also propagated by Gibbon. It is now a mere village of about a hundred houses, known as Missisah, *vulgo* Missis, situate on the right bank of the river, connected with a mass of ruined dwelling-houses and a caravansarai on the other, by a bridge constructed in part of old materials, and from among which I copied a Greek inscription now in Colonel Chesney's possession, and possibly the same as that given by Gruter (p. 255, num. 4). There is also a large ancient mound or tumulus that might be worth excavating.—W. F. A.

† A careful consideration of all the circumstances connected with the details of the campaign of Lucullus against Tigranes have led me to identify Tigranocerta with the Amida of the Byzantines, now Dyar-Bakir. (*Travels and Researches in Asia Minor,* &c., vol. ii. p. 362.) St. Martin says that all the Armenian writers consider Tigranocerta the same as Amida, also called Dorbeta by Ptolemy.—W. F. A.

carried on for three months, Pompey overthrew the pirates in a pitched battle, by sea and land, at Coracesium, now Kurkass,* and took ninety men-of-war and 20,000 prisoners. This multitude of men he compelled to relinquish their roving and desperate life, and caused them to settle and people the cities which had been laid waste by Tigranes in Cilicia, particularly Soli, which was rebuilt by him and to which he gave his name, and which was afterwards called "Pompeiopolis" on that account.†

B.C. 65. The kingdom of Syria had been restored by Lucullus to Antiochus Asiaticus on the expulsion of Tigranes, king of Armenia; but four years after, Pompey, who was called upon to settle the intestine broils and factions of the royal family, dethroned Antiochus, on pretence that he, who had concealed himself while an usurper sat upon his throne, was not worthy of being a king. Syria and Cilicia, with their dependencies, were then constituted Roman provinces; and with this last scion of royalty terminated the dynasty of the Seleucidæ, which had lasted 257 years. Occasionally the governors named by the senate were, however, allowed to retain the title of kings, as we shall see later.

Cicero was named proconsul of the province of Cilicia B.C. 50, and set sail from Rome with 12,000 foot and 2600 horse; and by prudence and good government he effected the reduction of Cappadocia to the authority of Artobazanes. Cicero's administration was remarkable for the moderation and integrity he displayed; for, although "he drove out the thieves which infested mount Amanus," we do not find any brilliant action recorded; and on his return he refused the triumph which the senate wished to decree him, saying he preferred to see differences settled and parties reconciled to each other.‡

---

* Coracesium was, according to Strabo, the first town of Cilicia Aspera; and the barren ridges of Mount Taurus, which come down to the shore, sufficiently indicate the beginning of that rugged coast. Admiral Sir Francis Beaufort identifies Coracesium with the town and promontory of Alaya, where he found the remains of a Cyclopean wall, a few broken columns (the remains of Christian churches), and other fragments of antiquity. Sir Francis Beaufort says, in allusion to this last stand made at Coracesium by the pirates against the Romans, that certainly no place in the whole coast was so well calculated to arrest the march of a conqueror, or to bid defiance to a fleet, as this commanding and almost insulated rock.—W. F. A.

† Appian (Mithridates, p. 394) also mentions Mallus, Adana, and Epiphanea, as cities which the pirates were made to colonise.—W. F. A.

‡ The movements of Cicero in Cilicia require much careful study. The greater number of sites mentioned by the then proconsul are even now unknown. In his 20th Epistle (lib. v. ad Attic.) he describes himself as proceeding from Tarsus to that portion of Amanus which divides the waters between Cilicia and Syria. This would apparently coincide with the actual Gawur Tagh. This is further demonstrated by his occupying there a castle (which was formerly held by Alexander) near Issus, and

MARC ANTHONY AND CLEOPATRA AT TARSUS.

B.C. 41. We must not omit, in thus hastily recapitulating the principal events which took place in Cilicia, to notice the visit of Cleopatra to Tarsus, whither she went to meet Marc Anthony, and which meeting has been commemorated by the immortal bard of Avon. The Egyptian queen arrived and sailed up the Cydnus in a galley, the prow of which was inlaid with gold, the sails of purple silk, and the oars of silver, and the latter were made to beat time to the music of flutes and oboes. Under a canopy of cloth-of-gold curiously embroidered, Cleopatra was seen reposing, dressed as Venus is generally represented, with beautiful little boys like cupids around her, who fanned her, while her maids habited as sea-nymphs were employed, some steering the rudder, some working the ship, at the same time that perfumes exhaled from the vessel, and wafted by the breezes diffused themselves along the shore. Fancy can alone portray to the imagination the glowing descriptions given of this pageant, which attracted such crowds of all classes that Anthony was left on his throne alone,

> "Whistling to the air, which but for vacancy
> Had gone to gaze on Cleopatra too,
> And made a gap in nature."

Her entertainments, rendered particularly remarkable by an ingenious display of brilliant lights, so far exceeded any thing of the kind even in that luxurious age, that Anthony was astonished, and avowed himself outdone. He was subsequently induced by her artifices to make her a grant of the fine pasture-lands in Upper Cilicia, " the noble cedar-woods

against the Persians. From thence the proconsul ascended into Amanus and devastated the country. In the 4th Epistle to Cato, book xv., he says, that having pacified Amanus, he simulated leaving the mountain, and removed the distance of a day's march to a castle near Epiphanea. This would therefore appear to correspond to the castellated ruin which is seen about two miles south of the ruins of Epiphanea. Erana corresponds to Baylan. The sites called Sepyra, Commorin, and Porntino, all in Amanus, are unknown. The subjection of this portion of the Amanus having been effected by the destruction and burning of these strongholds, Cicero proceeded to Pindenissus, which he says was in Eleutherocilicum, and inhabited by the Eleutherocilicians, a people who were never subject to kings (15 ad Fam. Epis. iv. and v. ad Att. 20). Pindenissus has been identified by Mr. Barker with Sis; and as it is described as situated on so lofty and well-fortified a site, this is very probably a correct identification. Colonel Chesney and the annotator visited the ruins of two ancient castles north of Sis in the interior of the mountains, one of which was called Kara Sis, or the Black Sis, and the other Andal Kalah, and one of which probably represents the Flaviada placed in the Itinerary from Cæsarea in Cappadocia to Anazarba, eighteen Roman miles north of the latter. This is an interesting and unexplored route, on which the sites of Prætorium, Badinum, Laranda, and Cocuso remain to be discovered. The Flaviada of the Itinerary is called Flaviopolis by Ptolemy, Flavias by Hierocles and by Callistus, who says (lib. xiv. cap. xxxix. p. 529), Φλάβιας ἐστίν ὑπὸ τὴν Ἀναζάρβης μητρόπολιν, as if it was below or south of the metropolis of Anazarba.—W. F. A.

above Syedra,"* the iron-mines of Amaxia, and adjacent harbour for a fleet, in short all the mountainous part of Cilicia except Seleucia (Selefkeh), famed for its admirable police.

On the departure of Anthony for Egypt (B.C. 39), Labienus, a Roman officer who had enlisted in the Parthian service, and was chosen commander of the Parthian forces under Pacorus, the youthful son of their king Orodes, took advantage of the dissolute manner of life Anthony was leading at Alexandria, and the disorder and discontent in the provinces, to march with a large army into Cilicia, and from thence to Caria, reducing all the Asiatic towns one after another, and making himself master of all Asia Minor, except Stratonicia, a Macedonian colony defended by its impregnable situation. Ventidius, Anthony's lieutenant-general, was sent against this formidable force, and he surprised Labienus in Cilicia, where a battle was fought, though not a decisive one; but Labienus was killed by a skirmishing party in the mountains, whither he had fled. The Parthians, under Barzaphernes, the next in command, rallied and seized a narrow pass between the meeting ridges of Mount Amanus and the Taurus (now on the road to Mar'ash from Adana), where the passage is so narrow that a wall was built across, and gates put up to impede the further progress of Ventidius, but unsuccessfully, that general having overcome this obstacle and obtained a brilliant victory. Barzaphernes was killed, his whole army cut to pieces, and the victor passed on to meet Pacorus, who had assembled a large army and crossed the Euphrates: a complete rout of the Parthian forces and the death of Pacorus were the result. The Romans recovered the possession of Syria and Cicilia, and carried the terror of their arms, under Sosius and Canidius, two of Anthony's generals, over the whole country, and even to Mount Caucasus.

At the battle of Actium (B.C. 31), among the other tributary kings who supported Anthony against Augustus was Tarchondemus, king of Cilicia, who contributed to his assistance principally by a fleet of ships; and this leads me to notice the few remaining kings who, under the

* Συδρή, or Sydra, of Strabo, and Σύεδρα, or Syedra, of Ptolemy; next town on the shore east of Coracesium, and identified by Sir Francis Beaufort with ruins of a somewhat imposing appearance seen on the summit of a steep hill, whose rugged ascent from the sea-shore deterred the navigator from visiting it. Amaxia or Hamaxia comes next in order in Strabo to Syedra, but in Ptolemy it is Iotape. Sir Francis Beaufort found plenty of ruined sites in this neighbourhood, but no inscriptions to identify them. It would be well worth some modern traveller's time to give us better descriptions, with drawings, of this part of the coast, so replete with antiquarian interest, and which abounds in relics of past times.— W. F. A.

From this place a great deal of timber is now yearly exported to Egypt.

Roman protectorate, were permitted to rule the country, paying tribute to the military governor of Syria. Subsequently we find that Augustus deposed Philopater, son of Tarchondemus, and placed his younger brother, who bore the same name as his father, in authority (B.C. 4).

Augustus, victorious over all his enemies, shut the gates of the temple of Janus; mankind enjoyed a respite from anarchy and strife; and the eventful period arrived to which so many prophecies referred; —the long-looked-for and now anxiously expected Messiah was ushered into the world. Throughout the whole globe the sound of war ceased to be heard, and the emperor swayed the sceptre of that vast empire, to which so many nations were tributary, with moderation and justice.

I must here notice Athenodorus (Sandon), preceptor of Augustus, native of Tarsus, and one of the wisest philosophers and best men of the age, to whom virtue gave that dignity and weight which allowed of his taking liberties with his illustrious pupil. Athenodorus had often warned him, not only of the infamy, but also of the danger attendant on his dissolute life. Finding his expostulations useless, he resolved on carrying his reproofs home, and speaking directly to his senses. With this view he put himself into a litter and caused himself to be carried into the emperor's apartment, at the hour appointed for the reception of one of his fair visitors. Augustus lifted up the curtain, when, of a sudden, the philosopher sprang out with a drawn sword in his hand, which he pointed at his pupil's throat. The emperor fell back in consternation, when Athenodorus exclaimed, "Now, Cæsar, are you not afraid that this stratagem, of which I make an innocent use, may be used by some other person to take away your life?" The remedy was a bold one, but adapted to the evil, and had its effect, at the same time that it increased the esteem and confidence of the pupil in his master.* On retiring in his old age from the court, Athenodorus left Augustus, at his request, as the best legacy, the admirable advice, "When you find anger rising within you, repeat the twenty-four letters of the alphabet before you speak or act." There was another Athenodorus of Cilicia, an older man, of the Stoic school, and preceptor to M. Cato, son of Cato the censor.

* Dion Cassius, Zonaras, and Zozimus attribute to Athenodorus (surnamed Cananites, from Cana in Cilicia, a site I am unacquainted with, the birthplace of his father, whose name was Sandon, but himself a native of Tarsus) these freedoms with Octavianus, as also the expulsion from Tarsus of Boethus, a favourite of Antonius. The memory of Athenodorus was, according to Strabo and Lucian, honoured by an annual festival and sacrifice. There was also an Athenodorus surnamed Cordylio, a Stoic philosopher, born at Tarsus, but who dwelt at Pergamus and Rome; and an Athenodorus of Soli, a disciple of Zenon.—W. F. A.

About this time also flourished Athenæus, a peripatetic philosopher of Cilicia.

Vonones, son of Phraotes, king of the Parthians, fled (A.D. 19) to Creticus Silanus, governor of Syria, driven out by an insurrection of his subjects, in hopes of the support of the Roman republic, which had been promised him when placed on the throne by Caius Cæsar a short time before. Silanus at first favoured his claims, but afterwards thought proper to secure his person, and left him, under a strong guard, to enjoy the title of king and the parade of royalty. He was sent, by order of Germanicus, to Soli or Pompeiopolis, whence he attempted to escape into Scythia, with the hopes of obtaining assistance from the reigning king, his near relation. With this intent he went on a hunting party, and having watched his opportunity he betook himself to flight, and turning off from the sea-coast he struck into the woods,* and rode at full speed towards the river Pyramus. The inhabitants on the first alarm demolished the bridges. The river was not fordable; and Vonones, found wandering along the banks, was, by order of Vibius Fronto, the commander of the cavalry, loaded with fetters. He did not long survive; for Remnius, a veteran who had been entrusted with the custody of his person, in a sudden transport of pretended passion, drew his sword and ran the unhappy prince through the body. It would seem that this man had been bribed to favour the king's escape, and rather than be detected as an accomplice preferred to be an assassin.

In the next year (A.D. 20), Cneius Piso, after having poisoned Germanicus by means of his agents, afraid to face his accusers at Rome, whither he had been summoned by Cneius Sentius, fled to Cilicia, and by circular letters demanded succour from the petty kings of the neighbouring provinces. With a body of deserters and these auxiliaries he seized the castle of Celendris, a stronghold on the coast of Cilicia (now

---

* Tacitus here speaks of trees in Cilicia. In the country traversed by Vonones there are now but a few trees here and there, which serve to screen from the noonday sun the labourers who collect the abundant harvest of the plain, which might, however, be cultivated to an infinitely greater extent. In this plain of Adana and Tarsus I have observed the remains of ancient roads, so constructed as to be *much higher* than the *level* of the land, which bear witness to the high degree of civilisation to which this country was brought. It is a stupendous work to raise roads in this way; and they are very numerous, crossing each other in every direction. Although they have been allowed to go to ruin, they are still of the greatest importance, as without them there would be no possibility of crossing the plains in the spring, when the heavy rains that have fallen during the winter on the alluvial deposits, render the surface of the country so muddy that no animal can pass, and gazelles are often caught by the hand of man when surprised by sudden rains into a little island surrounded by a marshy swamp of a ploughed field.

Kilindriyah),* where he was besieged by Sentius at the head of the Roman legions. An engagement followed, but the victory was not long in suspense, for after the Romans had forced the ascent of the hill, the Cilicians were routed and driven back to the fortifications; the walls were then scaled after a vigorous resistance, and Piso desired to capitulate. He offered to lay down his arms on condition that he should remain in the castle till the Emperor Tiberius's pleasure should be finally declared. The proposition was rejected; but Sentius allowed him a safe-conduct to Italy, where he met the reward due to his crimes.

About this epoch (A.D. 30) flourished Antipater of Tarsus, who lived in the reign of Tiberius, and was preceptor to the philosopher Blossius, to whom he dedicated his philosophical lectures.†

Tarsus had now become the rival of Athens and Alexandria; numerous schools were established there, and numbers flocked from all quarters to profit by the lessons of the philosophers, and to study the liberal arts and sciences. But in the numbers of the learned who have, by the lustre of their reputation, reflected a glory over Tarsus as having been the place of their nativity, St. Paul is the most illustrious. Born of a good family of the sect of the Pharisees, he was early led to study eloquence and rhetoric, and thus laid a foundation for the taste and elegance which distinguish his writings. Initiated into the arts of Grecian disputation, he was well able to perform the difficult task of refuting the sophistry of the numerous sects, and to aid in the extension of the true doctrines he was chosen to preach; while being enrolled a free citizen of Rome, he became thereby a fit instrument in the hands of Providence, from the respectability attached to that title. St. Paul chose Cilicia as the first scene of his labours, being anxious that his townsmen and kinsfolk should be the first to hear the glad tidings he had to announce; and for several years we find him making this province of Asia Minor the field he loved most to toil in.

* Κελένδερις of Strabo and Ptolemy. Apollodorus says (lib. iii. cap. xiv. num. 3) that Celenderis was built by Sandocus, son of Astynous. Pomponius Mela and Tacitus write Celendris. Pliny speaks of the district of Celendritis with a town. It is generally spoken of as a colony of Samians, with a harbour strongly fortified and well provided. Admiral Sir Francis Beaufort speaks of Chelindreh, or Kilindriyah, the modern Celenderis, as a snug but very small port, from whence the couriers from Constantinople to Cyprus embark. Among the ruins of a fortress is a hexagonal tower, that has been rent down the middle as if by an earthquake. There are also arched vaults, sepulchral houses, and sarcophagi, and near the sea-shore a cenotaph, with a single arch on each side, supporting a pyramidal roof of large stones.—W. F. A.

† Antipater of Tarsus was the disciple and successor of Diogenes, and the teacher of Panætius, B.C. 144 nearly. Plutarch speaks of him, with Zeno, Cleanthes, and Chrysippus, as one of the principal Stoic philosophers; and Cicero mentions him as remarkable for acuteness (*De Stoic. Repugnant.* p. 144; *Cicero de Divin.* i. 3; *de Off.* iii. 12).—W. F. A.

About this time (A.D. 36), the Cliteans, a bold tribe of mountaineers in Cilicia, impatient of being taxed according to the system newly practised in the Roman provinces, retreated to the heights of Mount Taurus; and being possessed of inaccessible fastnesses, they were enabled to defend themselves against their sovereign and his unwarlike troops. To quell the insurgents, Vitellius, who was then governor of Syria, despatched Marcus Trebellius at the head of 4000 legionary soldiers, and a select detachment of auxiliaries. The barbarians had taken their post on two hills; the lesser was called Cadra, and the other Davara. Trebellius enclosed both with lines of circumvallation, and all who dared to sally out were put to the sword, and the rest were reduced by thirst and famine.*

Sixteen years had scarcely elapsed, when, in A.D. 52, the same predatory hordes, accustomed to plunder and trained to civil commotions, assembled under Trosobor, a warlike chief, and pitched their camp on the summit of a mountain, steep, craggy, and almost inaccessible. From this fastness they rushed upon the plain, and stretching along the coast, attacked the neighbouring cities. They plundered the people and the merchants, and utterly ruined the navigation and commerce of the environs. They laid siege to the city of Anemurium, and dispersed a body of horse, sent from Syria under Curtius Severus to the relief of the place. These freebooters were even bold enough to hazard a battle with the Romans; and the ground being rugged and disadvantageous to cavalry and convenient only to foot-soldiers, the Romans were totally routed. At length, Antiochus, the reigning king of the country, gained the good-will of the Cliteans, and proceeded by stratagem against their leader, the confederates having been excited to disunion among themselves. Trosobor, with his principal adherents, was put to death,

* In reference to this little episode in the history of Cilicia, it is worth while noticing, for the benefit of future explorers, that the mountain strongholds of Cadra and Davara have not been made out, at least to my knowledge. Admiral Sir Francis Beaufort says of the Ἀνεμούριον ἄκρα, or promontory of Anemurium of Strabo, that it was difficult, from the inflexions of the coast, to select a point for identification; but he identifies the city of Anemurium with the ruins at Aski Anamur. There is, however—excepting Strabo's statement of the distance of the confines of Pamphylia to Anemurium 820 stadia, and from Anemurium to Soli 500 stadia, and which Sir Francis himself thinks ought to be transposed—no authority for such a distance existing between the city and cape. Scylax speaks of Anemurium as a town and promontory; Pomponius Mela (lib. i. cap. 13) and Livy (lib. xxxiii. cap. 20) as a promontory; Ptolemy and Pliny as a city. There is therefore every reason to believe that Cape Anamur, the most southerly extremity of Asia Minor, is the same as the Anemurian promontory, the more especially as the city is close by, as the name is preserved, and as Sir Francis Beaufort could find no trace of a promontory at the point given by Strabo's figures.—W. F. A.

and by conciliatory measures the rest were brought to a sense of their duty, and returned to their several homes.

In the year A.D. 56, Cossuatianus Papito was governor of the province of Cilicia. He was a man of abandoned character, who at Rome had set the laws at defiance, and who thought that he might commit the same excesses and extortions in the government of his province. The Cilicians sent deputies to complain of his conduct to the senate; and the prosecution was carried on with such unremitting vigour, that Cossuatianus was obliged to abandon his defence. Being convicted of exaction, he was condemned to make restitution.

Polemon, king of Cilicia, A.D. 60, who had been previously confirmed on his father's throne by Claudius, was persuaded by Berenice, widow of Herod king of Chalcis* (and sister of the Agrippa before whom Paul had pleaded), to marry her, in the hope by the marriage to suppress the report of the criminality with which Paul had charged her brother Agrippa. Polemon was at the same time prevailed upon to adopt the Jewish religion; but Berenice abandoned him soon after, and he returned to his Pagan worship.

Vespasian proceeding to carry on the Jewish war, A.D. 74, saw the inexpediency of permitting the existence in his rear of a number of petty princes, who, although tributary to Rome, ever excited revolts and commotions. He therefore reduced them entirely to subjection; and Cilicia, and several other kingdoms, were finally declared provinces of the Roman empire. In the fourth year of his reign, A.D. 78, Cecenius Petus, president of Syria, bearing an enmity to Antiochus king of Comagena, a country north-east of Cilicia, wrote to Vespasian that Antiochus had leagued with the Parthians in rebellion against the Romans. Petus received from the emperor full powers to proceed against Antiochus; he fell at once upon Comagena, before the king could have any notice of his intention. Antiochus did not choose to make any opposition, and in order to evince his unwillingness to withstand the Romans, retired to a plain, and pitched his camp not far from the city of Samosata, his capital;† but his sons Epiphanes and Callinicus collected their forces, and made a firm stand against the Roman legions. They were, however, defeated, and obliged to disperse in different directions; some taking refuge in Parthia, and some in Cilicia. Antiochus, with his wife and daughters, repaired to Tarsus, where Petus seized his person, and forwarded him as a prisoner of war to Rome.

* See Josephus.
† Now Someïsat, on the Euphrates. (*Journal of Royal Geographical Society*, vol. vii. p. 422; and vol. x. p. 321 and 333.)

When Vespasian was informed of the arrival of Antiochus as a prisoner in chains, he remembered the friendship that had formerly existed between them. He ordered the fetters of Antiochus to be struck off, and appointed Lacedæmon for his residence. In the meantime, Epiphanes his son having reached Rome, he also made interest for his father; and during Vespasian's reign they remained at Rome, and were in favour with the emperor.

From the reign of Vespasian to that of Trajan, A.D. 117, nothing of any note occurred in Cilicia. This last-mentioned emperor, it is well known, marched a large army to the shores of the Persian Gulf, regretting "that he had not the youth and strength of Alexander, that he might add unexplored kingdoms to the Roman empire." On his return, he was taken ill in Cilicia, at Selinus (afterwards called Trajanopolis), where he died; but his ashes were conveyed to Rome, and deposited under the famous column which still exists, to perpetuate his name and celebrate his exploits.*

Hadrian, his successor, passed through Cilicia A.D. 129, with a large army, on his way to Syria and Egypt; but no monument remains in this province to record his magnificence, or even the fact of his having passed through it.†

After Severus had made himself master of the Roman empire by the death of Didius Julianus, A.D. 194, he marched his veteran legions

---

* Admiral Sir Francis Beaufort describes many remnants of antiquity as still existing at Selinty, or Salinti, the ancient Selinus, afterwards Trajanopolis. Among the most remarkable of these is a low massive edifice of seventy feet by fifty, composed of large well-cut blocks of stone, and containing a single vault. A flight of narrow steps, parallel to the wall, leads to the flat top, on which nothing now remains, though there is every reason to suppose that this building was formerly the basement-story of some splendid superstructure; but the columns, which either surmounted or surrounded it, have all disappeared, except a few fragments of some large fluted pilasters of fine workmanship. This edifice stands in the centre of a quadrangle, along each side of which there was a single row of thirty small columns; but they have been all broken off close to the ground and carried away: the quadrangle is about 240 feet in diameter. A similar sepulchral building, but of later date, has been joined to this greater mausoleum. "I cannot find," says Sir Francis Beaufort, "what honours were paid to his (the Emperor Trajan's) memory by the Cilicians; but it seems highly probable that a mausoleum should have been erected in the city where the decease of so accomplished and so popular an emperor took place; and if so, it is equally probable that this building was designed for that purpose."—W. F. A.

† The reign of Hadrian was more particularly distinguished by labours of pacification. With the exception of the revolt of the Jews under Barchochab (132-135), the East enjoyed profound peace during the reign of this wise prince. Towards the end of his reign the emperor visited almost all the Roman provinces with the view to the establishment of order. Cilicia profited by these judicious travels. Coins are extant which commemorate Tarsus as ΑΔΡΙΑΝΗΣ ΤΑΡΣΟΥ ΜΗΤΡΟΠΟΛΕΩΣ.

Mopsuestia was especially favoured and embellished by the emperor, and even

to oppose Pescennius Niger, who had put himself at the head of the Eastern army, and had usurped the name and ensigns of Augustus. After some skirmishing on both sides in Lesser Asia, a decisive battle was fought on the plains of Issus, the same plains which more than five centuries previously had been covered with the blood of the Persian soldiers of Darius, and which had also been the scene of Alexander's victory. Pescennius Niger was totally routed, with the loss of 20,000 men and of his own life. His head was sent to Rome as a trophy; and the troops of Europe again asserted their usual ascendency over the effeminate natives of Asia.

assumed his name. The citizens are called on coins of Antoninus Pius ΑΔΡΙΝΑΩΝ ΜΟΨΕΤΩΝ, Hadrianorum Mopseatarum. Gruter also records an inscription found at Missis, which he translates, *"Evergetæ ac servatori Hadrianæ Mopsuestiæ Ciliciæ sacræ, liberæ et asyli, suis legibus viventis, et fæderatæ ac sociæ Romanorum.—* W. F. A.

SARCOPHAGUS AT SELEUCIA PIERIA, OPENED BY MR. BARKER.

CHAPTER III.

LEGEND OF THE SEVEN SLEEPERS—SAPOR INVADES CILICIA—ZENOBIA'S CONQUESTS—CILICIA OVERRUN BY THE ALANI—MAXIMIANUS DIES AT TARSUS—DEATH OF CONSTANTIUS AT MOPSUESTIA IN CILICIA—ST. GEORGE, PATRON SAINT OF ENGLAND, BORN AT EPIPHANEA—THE EMPEROR JULIAN BURIED AT TARSUS—INVASIONS OF THE HUNS—BELISARIUS IN CILICIA—CAMPAIGNS OF HERACLIUS AND OF CHOSROES (KUSRU ANUSHIRIWAN).

During a long period, while the Roman Empire was subject to the rule of many iniquitous emperors, and while the capital was the scene of murder and dissension, Cilicia enjoyed comparative tranquillity. We may except the persecution which the Christians underwent in all parts of the empire, and which was particularly severe in the East, where the Jews have ever laboured under a public prejudice to their disfavour. The legend of the Seven Sleepers, who are said by Christian tradition to have fallen asleep in the reign of the Emperor Decius during the seventh persecution of the followers of Christ, and to have slept for 187 years in a cave near Ephesus, has been adopted and embellished by Mohammed.* The Arabian prophet casts a veil of mystery over this tale;† but some

---

* Mohammed or Mahomet. The first orthography is adopted, as being that which is now most generally accepted, after the manner in which the name of the Arabian prophet is generally pronounced. The correct orthography is, however, Muhammad.—W. F. A.

† Mohammed has invented and added to this fable the dog (Al Rakim) of the Seven Sleepers; the respect shown by the sun, which, in order not to shine into the cave, daily altered its course, and the care God himself took of the sleepers to preserve their bodies from putrefaction by making them turn to the right and left. He says in the Koran:

"And thou mightest have seen the sun, when it had risen, decline from their cave towards the right hand; and when it went down, leave them on the left hand. And they were in the spacious part of the cave. This was one of the signs of God. Whomsoever God shall direct, he shall be rightly directed; and whomsoever He shall cause to err, thou shalt not find any to defend or to direct. And thou wouldst have judged them to have been awake while they were sleeping; and He caused them to turn themselves to the right hand and to the left. And their dog stretched forth his fore-legs in the mouth of the cave. If thou hadst come suddenly upon them, verily thou wouldst have turned thy back and fled from them, and thou wouldst have been filled with fear at the sight of them. And so He awakened them out of their sleep, that they might ask questions of one another. One of them spake and said, How long have ye tarried

of his commentators have imagined that the site where this miraculous event occurred was not Ephesus, but a cave about ten miles north-west of *Tarsus*. Every Muhammadan who arrives at this place conceives himself bound to visit the spot, and thinks a pilgrimage thither obligatory from the countenance given to this fable by the prophet. Numbers flock there in parties of ten and more, on which occasions a sheep is killed and roasted, part of which is eaten, and the rest given to the poor.*

The kingdom of Parthia had been overturned by Artaxerxes Babegan, first of the Persian dynasty of the Sassanidæ, in A.D. 226; and the Persian carried his arms to the frontiers of Syria, declaring war on the grounds that Cyrus had conquered, and that his successors had for a long time possessed, the whole of Asia as far as the Propontis and the Ægean Sea, and that all Egypt had also acknowledged the Persian sovereignty. Artaxerxes, at his death, bequeathed his new empire and his ambitious designs to his son Sapor, who took the town of Antioch [A.D. 259], then capital of Syria, and marched into Cilicia, ravaging the whole country, and treating his prisoners with wanton and unrelenting cruelty. He devastated the city of Tarsus and many other towns of Cilicia, and proceeded to lay siege to Cæsarea (Kaisariyah), capital of Cappadocia, after having crossed the Taurus at the Pylæ Ciliciæ. At this point no opposition was made to his progress by the Roman garrison, although he might have been held in check by a handful of men. Sapor

here? They answered, We have tarried a day, or part of a day. The other said, Your Lord best knoweth the time ye have tarried."

After further reference to the other parts of the legend, he again leaves the principal fact in uncertainty, concluding:

"Some say the sleepers were three, and their dog was the fourth; and others say they were five, and their dog was the sixth, guessing at a secret matter; and others say they were seven, and their dog was the eighth. Say my Lord best knoweth their number; none shall know them except a few. Wherefore dispute not concerning them unless with a clear disputation, according to what has been revealed unto thee; and ask not any of the Christians concerning them. Say not of any matter, I will surely do this to-morrow, unless thou add, If God please (Inshallah)."

* The story of the Seven Sleepers is attached traditionally to many other places in the East, besides Ephesus and the cave near Tarsus. (See D'Herbelot in Ashab-i-Kahaf, and Assemanni, i. 336.) Shah-Abad or Jundi Shapur, in Khusistan, is, according to the Taskarati-Shusteriyah, believed to represent the city of the Seven Sleepers. Colonel Rawlinson says that wherever the tradition prevails in the East, it may be received as an evidence of antiquity. The tradition probably existed anterior to Christianity or to Muhammadanism. Mohammed's dog is a kind of antithesis to Ovid's cavernous abode of sleep, near which no cock or dog, or any animal accustomed to rouse men from their slumbers, was permitted to approach. (*Met.* xi. 592. See also Gibbon, 525; and Gregory de Tours, *De gloriâ Martyrum in Max. Bibliothecâ Patrum*, tom. xi. p. 856.)—W. F. A.

seems, however, to have despaired of making any permanent establishment in the country, and sought only to leave behind him a wasted desert, whilst he transported into Persia the people and the treasures of the provinces.

Odenathus, prince of Palmyra, attacked Sapor, pursued him into the very heart of his kingdom, and delivered all the provinces of Asia Minor from his tyranny, leaving to his wife Zenobia the splendid but doubtful title of " Queen of the East." But the power of Zenobia was not of long duration. Aurelian marched a large army into Asia A.D. 273, reducing the provinces, and annexing them again to the Roman empire. He took Zenobia prisoner on the banks of the Euphrates, about sixty miles from Palmyra;* and thus terminated the glorious but short career of this Eastern power. Aurelian, preparing for his Persian expedition, had induced the Alani, a Scythian people who pitched their tents in the neighbourhood of the sea of Azof, to assist him as auxiliaries with a large body of light cavalry. These barbarians arriving on the Roman frontier at the moment of the death of the emperor, and finding the war suspended, overran the provinces of Pontus, Cappadocia, Cilicia, and Galatia (A.D. 275). Tacitus, the successor of Aurelian, and grandson of the historian, marched to oppose them with the veteran legions. Great numbers of the Alani, appeased by the punctual discharge of the engagements entered into by Aurelian and confirmed by his successor, relinquished their booty and captives, and quietly retreated to their own deserts beyond the Phasis. Against the remainder, who refused to listen to his remonstrances, the Roman emperor waged in person a successful war, and delivered the provinces of Asia from the terror of the Scythian invasion.

The fatigues of a campaign at his advanced age were fatal to the health of Tacitus, and he expired soon after at Tyana in Cappadocia, A.D. 276. His brother Florianus instantly usurped the purple, without waiting for the approbation of the senate. Probus, the general who commanded in Syria, declared himself the avenger of the offended senate; and fortune was propitious to him, in spite of his having to contend against the European legions assembled at Tarsus, with the effeminate troops of Egypt and Syria. The hardy veterans of the north sickened and died in the sultry heats of Cilicia. Their numbers were also dimi-

* I have elsewhere explained the events of the decisive battle of Imma, as occurring on the marshy plain of the lake of Antioch, now called Al Umk; and there is every reason to believe that Aurelian's light horse overtook the unfortunate Queen of Palmyra, after the battle of Emesa, at her own favourite summer residence, the marble city at the pass of the Euphrates, the ruins of which still exist, and are called to the present day Zilibah, or Zenobia.—W. F. A.

nished by desertion, through the undefended passes of the Taurus. Tarsus opened its gates to receive Probus; while Florianus fell a sacrifice to the rage and contempt of a soldiery disgusted with him, and unwilling to protract the civil war.

During the reign of the prudent but artful Dioclesian, Cilicia enjoyed a respite of twenty-one years from war and bloodshed, although during that time two armies passed through the province on their way to carry on the Persian war. On the resignation of this emperor, Maximin, the nephew of Galerius, who had been created general of the Eastern army, and emperor in conjunction with Severus Constantine and Licinius, committed the greatest excesses in persecuting the Christians; and unhappy Cilicia became again the scene of pillage and confusion. Maximin, ambitious of supreme authority, collected all his forces and marched to attack Licinius his colleague, who met him with 30,000 men under the walls of Heraclea Perinthus, soon after he had crossed the Hellespont and possessed himself of Byzantium, A.D. 313. The result of the engagement was a decisive victory in favour of Licinius. Maximin fled so precipitately, that he reached in twenty-four hours Nicomedia in Asia Minor, one hundred and sixty miles distant from the scene of his defeat. His victorious enemy pursued him, and he retreated again beyond the Taurus to Tarsus, where he died in the greatest agonies of a dreadful disease, which ecclesiastical writers describe as a visitation of Heaven for his barbarities in the persecution of the Christians, and the horrid blasphemies which he had uttered.

By the death of Maximin, A.D. 331, Christianity was relieved from her last enemy. Constantine the Great, after his accession, ordered all the heathen temples to be destroyed; and by founding the new kingdom at Byzantium, he brought the seat of empire nearer to Cilicia. The rich plains of Cappadocia, and the plains as far as the banks of the Sarus, near Adana, were remarkable for a fine breed of horses,* which tempted the monarch to appropriate these choice pastures to his own use. With this view he founded private estates independent of the public revenue, regularly administered by a count or treasurer, and officers of inferior rank. These were stationed in all parts of the province, and had special bands of soldiers under them for this particular service, and were not subordinate to the authority of the provincial magistrate.

Constantius, the son of Constantine, was at Antioch A.D. 360, when

* The Aushar horse is to this day much prized by the Osmanli. He has not the superior excellence of the Arab in resisting fatigue, but he is a much more showy animal. He is almost as broad as he is long, and larger than the Arab horse, and his walk is unequalled by any breed in the world.

his nephew Julian was declared Emperor of the West, and he marched against him at the head of his Eastern army. A slight fever which he caught in Cilicia on his way to oppose Julian, and which was increased by the fatigues of the journey and the agitation of his spirits, obliged him to halt at the little town of *Mopsucrene*,* " twelve miles" from Tarsus, where he expired after a short illness, in the forty-fifth year of his age and the twenty-fourth of his reign.

It is not very generally known that Cilicia is the native country of the renowned St. George, the patron saint of England, who was born at *Epiphanea*,† a small town near the Amanian gates, in a fuller's shop. From this obscure origin he raised himself to the archbishopric of Alexandria, where, in the year A.D. 361, he was massacred by the fury of the populace. Although his remains were thrown into the sea in order that his party might not have an opportunity of revering them as the relics of a martyr, the manner of his death helped to obliterate the atrocities of his life, and he was canonised about a century afterwards, A.D. 494.

In the next reign, that of Julian, A.D. 363, Cilicia saw the return of another army on its way to attack the Persians. The apostate emperor

* Mopsucrene or Mopsi fons, the fountain of Mopsus, appears to have been in Taurus, near Tarsus.—W. F. A.

† There is considerable difficulty in determining the position of Epiphanea. The numbers given in Ptolemy would approximate to the site of Nicopolis; while the tables of Agathodæmon—the designer of the maps which accompany Ptolemy—place the two at some distance from one another. Yet nothing can be more certain than that it was not situate far from Issus; for Cicero expressly relates (lib. xv. epist. 4), that to deceive the hostile mountaineers of Amanus, he pretended to depart from the mountain and to go to other parts of Cilicia, and that he repaired in one day's march to the castle that is near Epiphanea. On returning from that part of Amanus which Cicero reached in one day from Epiphanea, as he afterwards relates, he repaired to a castle at the roots of Amanus, near the altars of Alexander. Quintus Curtius says these altars were on the banks of the Pinarus; but we sought for traces of them there in vain, and have been consequently inclined to identify them with the Bomitæ, or altars, of Pliny, Sakal Tutan of the Turks, and near which there is still a castle called Markaz Kalahsi; and this identification would be strengthened by Cicero's expression, " at the roots of Amanus."

Epiphanea might then be near Issus; and there are, besides the ruins on the Pinarus, other and more extensive ruins near Urzin, at the head of the Gulf of Issus.

Besides the walls of the city, which are still standing in part, and the ruins of numerous dwelling-houses, there are also ruins of a temple and of an acropolis situated on a mound in a central and commanding situation. Outside of the town there are also ruins of an aqueduct with a double row of arches, running E.S.E. and W.S.W. All these buildings being constructed of basalt, and the ruins and environs being totally uninhabited, give to the place a very sombre and gloomy aspect. They are situated on a plain at the foot of some low basaltic hills, only a few miles from the N.E. extremity of the Gulf of Alexandretta. Epiphanea is recorded as an episcopacy in the *Ecclesiastical Notices of the Lower Empire*.

Stephanus and Arrian, it may be observed, identify Nicopolis with Issus.—W. F. A.

was obliged to winter the troops at Antioch preparatory to his expedition; but he was so vexed and annoyed at the conduct of the Christian party there, who lampooned him, that he declared he would pass the next winter in Tarsus: but it was decreed otherwise, for he died a few months after of a wound he received from a javelin whilst animating his troops to battle on the other side of the Tigris. His body was embalmed and brought back by the army to Tarsus, where he was buried. A stately tomb was erected over his remains on the banks of the " cold Cydnus," in the city he had a few months before appointed to be his residence, and which was now destined to contain only his ashes,— another instance of the vanity of human projects.

Julian was succeeded by Jovian, A.D. 384. The latter was succeeded by Valens, during whose reign the king of Persia made many inroads into the Roman provinces, and particularly turned his victorious arms against Armenia—a country under the protection of the empire. Para, the king, fled to the Roman camp; but the general Trajan, acting under the direction of the Emperor Valens, meditated his destruction, and, under the semblance of friendship and the specious pretence of consulting with the emperor, enticed him into his power. The king of Armenia was received with due honours by the governors of the provinces through which he passed; but when he arrived at Tarsus, his progress was arrested, his motions watched, and he gradually found himself a prisoner in the hands of the Romans. He, however, managed to effect his escape with three hundred faithful followers, and succeeded in crossing the Euphrates and eluding the vigilance of the troops sent in pursuit. He thus reached his native country, but was soon after induced to come to a banquet prepared by the Roman general, where he was inhumanly murdered, in defiance of the sacred rites of hospitality.

During the succeeding reigns of Theodosius Arcadius and Theodosius the younger, bands of adventurous Huns, who had overrun the north of Europe and Asia, ravaged the provinces of the East, from whence they brought away rich spoils and innumerable captives. They advanced along the shores of the Caspian Sea, traversed the snowy mountains of Armenia, passed the Tigris, the Euphrates, and the Halys, recruited their cavalry with the fine breed of horses, and occupied the hilly country of Cilicia. Here they came in contact and clashed with the Isaurians, a savage horde who had possessed for several centuries the fastnesses of Mount Taurus, and who from time to time made predatory inroads on the sea-coast.

These bold mountaineers had maintained for 230 years a life of plunder and independence, and seriously disturbed at several epochs the tranquillity of Asia Minor, although sometimes soothed with gifts, and sometimes restrained by terror. When their countryman Zeno ascended the throne at Constantinople (succeeding Theodosius Marcianus, Leo I. and Leo II.), he invited a large and formidable band of Isaurians to surround him as a body-guard, and rewarded them by an annual payment of five thousand pounds of gold. After the death of Zeno, his successor Anastasius abolished their pension and banished them from the empire. In revenge for this treatment, they placed a brother of the late emperor at their head and marched towards the capital, it is said to the number of 150,000 men (including auxiliaries), whose standard was for the first time sanctified by the presence of a fighting Christian bishop. The valour and discipline of the Goths, who were sent against these Isaurian rebels, sufficed to drive them back to their fortresses, which were after six years' warfare successively besieged. All their bravest leaders were killed, numbers of those made prisoners were transported to Thrace, and the remnant submitted to Anastasius. Some generations, however, passed before they were completely reduced to the same level of slavery as the rest of the subjects of the empire, for we find from time to time that the *Counts of Isauria*, the Prætors of Lycaonia and Pisidia, were invested with full military power to restrain their licentious practices of rapine and assassination.*

No event of any moment occurred during the nine years' reign of Justin I. (A.D. 537); but his successor Justinian, in a long reign of thirty-eight years, saw his supremacy established in every part of the Roman empire in the East, by his victorious general Belisarius, and gained battles as brilliant as those which had rendered the ancient Romans so distinguished in the time of their republic. On preparing for the African campaign, the mountains of Cilicia contributed their quota of infantry, and the sea-ports furnished their complement of transports and sailors, to make up the number of five hundred vessels and twenty thousand mariners with which Belisarius set out from Constantinople (A.D. 541). Four years afterwards Justinian undertook the defence of the East, which had been invaded by Nushirwan, king of Persia. Nushirwan had destroyed Antioch, and carried away the inhabitants captives to colonise the new city he had founded at Ctesiphon; but Belisarius

* The general system of policy, rendered necessary by the weakness of the succeeding governments, and which we shall see particularly exemplified as we proceed in our modern history of these countries.—W. B. B.

Mr. William J. Hamilton was the first to bring to light in modern times the city of Isaura, the stronghold of the Isaurians; and he has given a peculiarly interesting description of the existing ruins in his *Researches in Asia Minor, Pontus, &c.* vol. ii. p. 331.—W. F. A.

compelled him to retreat with precipitation; and in a subsequent campaign (A.D. 543) repossessed himself of all the cities taken by the Persian king in Cilicia. He, at the same time, so strengthened the defences of the country, that no further inroads were made on that part of the kingdom for many years.

After the death of Justinian (A.D. 590), and during the reigns of his successors Justin II., Tiberius II., and Maurice, the Persian wars continued without any decided advantage on either side, the Persians never having been able to retain any conquest beyond the Euphrates. But in the lifetime of the latter prince, Chosroes, the grandson of Nushirwan, on the revolt of his subjects and the deposition and death of his father Hormuz, fled to the Roman emperor for support. He was ultimately reinstated on the throne of his ancestors, after two battles against the usurper had been fought, in which the Roman troops were the victors. Chosroes was grateful for this signal service; and until the death of Maurice peace between the two empires was faithfully maintained.

But the disorders introduced by the tyrant Phocas, who succeeded Maurice (A.D. 611-616), afforded a pretext to Chosroes to invade Syria and Asia Minor. The pretence was to revenge the death of his friend and benefactor; and the first intelligence from the East which Heraclius, the successor of Phocas, received, was the taking of Antioch. In five years the armies of Chosroes had overrun all Asia Minor, Syria, Palestine, Egypt, and Lybia as far as Tripoli, and the Bosphorus; and a Persian camp maintained its position for some time in sight of Constantinople.

The emperor Heraclius (A.D. 622), roused at length by such extraordinary successes, prepared to attack the Persians. He embarked his forces on board a fleet of transports, and landed near the Syrian gates (Markaz Kalahsi) in the Gulf of Alexandretta, within the confines of Cilicia. The natural fortifications of that country protected and concealed the camp of Heraclius, which was pitched near Issus, on the same ground where Alexander had defeated Darius. Cilicia was soon encompassed by the Persian army, who were astonished to find the enemy had taken up a position in their rear. Their cavalry hesitated for some time to enter the defiles of Mount Taurus; but by superior manœuvering, Heraclius drew them into general action on the plain; and having defeated and routed them, the emperor was enabled to cross the mountains, and winter his army in the province of Cappadocia on the banks of the river Halys.

In the next year (A.D. 623) Heraclius sailed by the Black Sea to Trebizond, passed the mountains of Armenia, and penetrated into Persia as far as Tabriz, which, with several other cities, he took and sacked, destroying all the temples and images, and retaliating on the Persians the horrors committed on the Christians at the destruction of Jerusalem nine years previously by Chosroes.

Heraclius next penetrated into the heart of Persia (A.D. 624), and by a well-concerted succession of marches, retreats, and successful actions, drove the enemy from the field into the fortified cities of Media and Assyria. In the spring of the next year, after crossing the Tigris and Euphrates, he returned laden with spoils to the banks of the Sarus, in Cilicia, to maintain that important position. He found the banks of the river lined with barbarian archers; and after a bloody conflict, which continued till the evening, on the bridge of Adana, he dislodged and dispersed the enemy, a Persian of gigantic size being slain and thrown into the river by the emperor himself.

In his fourth campaign (A.D. 627-628) Heraclius marched into Persia, obtained a complete victory on the plains of Nineveh over Chosroes (who fell and was put to death by his son Siroes), recovered three hundred Roman standards, delivered numerous captive Christians, and returned to Constantinople in triumph, after concluding an advantageous peace with the Persians. But these signal successes were not attended with any lasting benefit to the empire, for a very few years afterwards the followers of Mohammed possessed themselves of the same provinces which Heraclius had recovered with so much labour and bloodshed from the Persians; and even the kingdom of Persia itself, in less than thirty years from this date, was brought under the yoke, civil and religious, of the Arabian khalifs.

CHAPTER IV.

RISE OF THE SARACENS—CILICIA OVERRUN BY HARUN AL RASHID—AL MAMUN DIES IN CILICIA—EXCHANGE OF PRISONERS AT IL-LAMAS—SACK OF MOPSUESTIA BY THE KHALIF MUTASSIM—MOPSUESTIA RETAKEN BY NICEPHORUS PHOCAS AND JOHN ZIMISCES—RISE OF THE TURKMANS—ALP ARSLAN AND ROMANUS DIOGENES—TURKMAN DYNASTY AT NICÆA—PERSECUTION OF THE CHRISTIANS—FIRST CRUSADE—TANCRED AND BALDWIN IN CILICIA—ALEXIUS ANNEXES CILICIA TO THE GREEK EMPIRE.

The Saracens, who (A.D. 639) had just sprung up in a corner of Arabia, impelled by religious fanaticism, were carrying, under Khaled their chief, surnamed the *Sword of God*, all before them in Persia, Syria, and Palestine. Pursuing their progress to the north, they reduced Cilicia, with its capital Tarsus, to obedience. Passing on, they crossed Mount Taurus, and spread the flames of war as far as the environs of Trebizond. These conquests were soon followed by the siege of Constantinople (A.D. 677), by Sufiyan, general of the khalif Muawiyah, when 30,000 Moslems perished, and the Arabs were obliged to retreat and conclude a peace of thirty years with the Emperor Constantine IV. They also agreed to pay a tribute of three thousand pieces of gold, fifty horses, and fifty slaves; and the feeble hand of the declining empire was once more extended over unfortunate Cilicia.

A second attempt was made by the Saracens (A.D. 717), when they, to the number of 120,000, marched again through the provinces of Asia Minor, under Muslimah. Crossing the Hellespont at Abydos, they laid siege to Constantinople on the European side; but after some months of fruitless warfare, their fleet was burnt by the renowned Greek fire, and they were glad to retreat through Asia Minor, dreadfully dispirited and diminished in numbers. Five galleys only of their fleet of 1800 ships returning to Alexandria.

In the reign of Irene the Great (A.D. 781), Harun al Rashid invaded the Greek provinces at the head of 95,000 men, and the Christians subscribed to an ignominious treaty and an annual tribute of 70,000 dinars of gold, which bought the khalif's clemency. The payment of this tribute was delayed after he returned; but at eight different times the

Greeks were taught to feel that a month of devastation was more costly than a year of submission.

On the accession of Nicephorus (A.D. 800), open war was declared, and Harun al Rashid crossed the Amanus and Taurus in the depth of winter, ravaged Cilicia and Asia Minor, and sacked Heraclea, on the Black Sea. The famous statue of Hercules, with the attributes of the club, the bow, and the quiver, and the lion's hide of massive gold, was demolished by him. Nicephorus was compelled to recognise the right of lordship which Harun assumed; and the coin of the tribute, in servile obedience to the conqueror, was stamped with the image and superscription of the khalif and his three sons.

Al Mamun, the son of Harun al Rashid, undertook (A.D. 829) an expedition into Asia Minor, when he advanced as far as Tarsus, and took fifteen towns of Cilicia. On his way back he encamped on the banks of a little stream in Cilicia, which the Arabs call Bazizun, not far from Tarsus. Here he stayed to enjoy the shade of the trees and coolness of the stream, and expressed a wish to have some dates from *Azad*, which he said were alone wanting to make his felicity perfect. By an extraordinary coincidence, a caravan of mules happened to be just passing, and two baskets of dates, fresh from Bagdad, were set before him. Of these he eat so heartily, drinking at the same time so copiously of the cold waters in the adjacent rivulet, that he was seized with fever, of which he died. His body was transported to Tarsus, and there interred, but no trace now exists of his tomb.

Al Mamun[*] was a great encourager of science and literature. During his reign mathematics, astronomy, and chemistry were introduced among the Arabs; and the first library was established at Bagdad, to which all nations and sects were invited to contribute copies of their works.

The Emperor Theophilus, the son of Michael the Stammerer, marched in person (A.D. 838) five times through Asia Minor in his wars with the

---

[*] An extraordinary tale is told by an Arabian writer of the birth of Al Mamun. His father, Harun al Rashid, having won at chess from the celebrated and admired Sit Zibaidah (Zobaide of the *Arabian Nights*), his wife and cousin, the privilege of dictating to her any caprice which struck his fancy, compelled her to walk barefoot across the centre of the bath, over the hot stones, measuring the whole distance by putting one foot in succession before the other. This she was obliged to do; but she resolved to take signal vengeance for this unfeeling frolic on the first opportunity which presented itself after her recovery. She challenged him to renew the game for the same stakes; and being this time the victor, she chose the ugliest female black slave in the harim, and obliged him to take her to wife. Al Mamun was the fruit of this union, born about the same time as Amin the son of Sit Zibaidah, and he grew up as clever as his brother was stupid.

Saracens; and in his last campaign he destroyed the small town of Zabatra in Syria, in spite of the solicitations and remonstrances of the Khalif Mutassim,* third son of Harun al Rashid, whose casual birthplace it happened to be.

Mutassim levied a large army to resent the affront. The troops of Persia, Syria, and Egypt were collected together in the plains of Cilicia at Tarsus, and moved on over Mount Taurus to Amorium in Phrygia, the birthplace of the father of Theophilus. The emperor hastened the defence of what appears to have been at that time a most flourishing city, but to no purpose; for although 70,000 Moslems had perished in this war, Mutassim persisted in the siege, and totally ruined the town, slaughtering 30,000 Christians, and carrying off an equal number of captives to Tarsus, Syria, and Persia. These were treated with great cruelty; for although an exchange or ransom of prisoners was sometimes allowed‡ in the national and religious conflicts of these two parties, quarter was seldom given in the field, and those who escaped the edge of the sword were condemned to hopeless servitude or the most cruel torture.

The Emperor Constantine Porphyrogenitus relates with visible satisfaction the execution of the Saracens of Candia, who were flayed alive or plunged into caldrons of burning oil. Gibbon, in speaking of the taking of Amorium, makes the following observation: " To a point of honour Mutassim had sacrificed a flourishing city, two hundred thousand lives, and the property of millions. The same khalif descended from his horse and dirtied his robe to relieve the distress of a decrepit old man, who with his laden ass had tumbled into a ditch. On which of these two actions did he reflect with most pleasure when he was summoned by the angel of death?"

* Mutassim was the first khalif, according to an Arabian writer (Ibn Shuhny or Shuh-na), who added the name of the Almighty to his own—a practice continued by his successors, as if maintaining their right by divine authority. Thus we have epithets of *Billah, Biamr-illah, Lidin-allah;* as we should say, *By the grace of God,* &c. &c., *Prophet of the Faith,* &c.

† There is reason to believe that Zabatra corresponds with the place now called Rum-Kalah, or "Castle of the Romans," on the Euphrates; but there is great difficulty in determining this point satisfactorily, as the site is only mentioned by the mediæval writers.—W. F. A.

‡ Abu-l-faraj relates one of these singular and characteristic exchanges as having taken place on the bridge of the Lamas (now Il-Lamas), in Cilicia, the boundary of the two empires, and one day's journey westward of Tarsus, where, 4460 Moslems, 800 women and children, with 100 allies, were exchanged for an equal number of Greeks. They passed each other in the middle of the bridge; and when they reached their respective friends, they shouted *"Allah Akbar!"* and *"Kyrie Eleison!"* No doubt many o) these were prisoners of Amorium; but the most illustrious of them (*the forty martyrs* had been the same year beheaded by order of the khalif.

Arabian writers also mention a victory gained by Mutassim over the Greeks at Mopsuestia, called by them Mamuriyah, and state that 30,000 of the enemy were left on the field of battle. This engagement must have preceded the taking of Amorium, for from this date Cilicia came under the dominion of the khalifs; and Tarsus became a capital city of great importance, from its vicinity to the frontiers of the Muhammadan dominions.

During the whole of the next century the khalifs of Bagdad, the successors of Mutassim, retained possession of Cilicia; and the hostilities carried on between this Arabian dynasty and the Greeks were confined to some trifling inroads by sea and land, the fruits of their close vicinity and indelible hatred. But towards the middle of the tenth century the intestine broils and revolutions which convulsed the throne of the Abbassides, and reduced the khalifs to the position of royal prisoners, encouraged the Greek emperors Nicephorus Phocas and John Zimisces to make a last effort (A.D. 963) to obtain possession of the fine provinces which their predecessors had lost. The twelve years of their military command form the most splendid period of the Byzantine annals. An immense army laid siege to Adana (erroneously called Mopsuestia by Gibbon*), which double city, divided into two by the *Sarus*, was surrounded and taken by assault, and two hundred thousand Moslems were led to death and slavery.†

---

* See Colonel Leake's learned work on the *Ancient and Modern Geography of Asia Minor*. 1824.

It would appear, however, that Gibbon was in the right as far as regards the city in question being Mopsuestia. The mistake of saying that Mopsuestia was cut in two by the river Sarus originated with Zonaras and Cedrenus: it should be by the Pyramus. Adana does not appear to have been ever divided into two towns by the river Sarus, but Mopsuestia always was by the Pyramus; hence Colonel Leake appears to increase the confusion by changing the town to meet the error in the name of the river. Mopsuestia was also an important city in the middle ages; Adana did not rise into notice till after the time of the Khalifs; nor is it likely that two such excessive populations as those of Adana and Tarsus could have existed so close to one another.

It may be remarked also, that Abu-l-fada describes this butchery of Moslems—so much exaggerated as far as numbers are concerned—to have taken place at Mopsuestia, not Adana.

Sir Francis Beaufort, in his *Karamania*, remarks that Anna Comnena has made the same mistake, when she describes (Alexiad. lib. xii.) part of Tancred's army as proceeding up the Sarus to invest Mopsuestia.—W. F. A.

† "A surprising degree of population," says Gibbon, "which must at least include the inhabitants of the dependent districts." And yet there is more probability of this number being less exaggerated than that ascribed to Seleucia, near Antioch, computed to have had upwards of 300,000; as the environs of Adana are very extensive and fertile, and well calculated to afford sustenance for an infinitely large number, whereas the position of Seleucia is circumscribed within very narrow limits by the sea on one side, and the rocky Mount Rhossus on the other, which could never have furnished sufficient food for such multitudes; particularly in the vicinity of so vast a metropolis

The city of Tarsus was reduced by the slow progress of famine. The Saracens capitulated on honourable terms, and were dismissed with a safe-conduct to the confines of Syria. "A part of the old Christians had quietly lived under their dominion, and the vacant habitations were replenished by a new colony; but the mosque was converted into a stable, the pulpit was delivered to the flames, and many rich crosses of gold and gems, the spoils of Asiatic churches, were made a grateful offering to the piety and avarice of the emperor; and the gates of Adana and Tarsus were transported to Constantinople, and fixed in the wall there, a lasting monument of victory." Antioch was recovered, and subsequently all Syria (except Acre), and many cities on the other side of the Euphrates were overrun and despoiled. The Emperor Zimisces returned to Constantinople laden with Oriental spoils, and displayed in his triumph the silk, the aromatics of the East, and three hundred myriads of gold and silver. But this transient hurricane, the last efforts of a declining storm, blew over, and left few traces of its effects; for shortly afterwards, being unable to maintain their conquests, the Greeks evacuated the Asiatic towns, and the Saracens again purified their mosques, and overturned the idols of the saints and martyrs, the Nestorian and Jacobite Christians preferring their Saracen rulers to their heretical brethren. Antioch, with the cities of Cilicia and the island of Cyprus, were the only possessions retained by the Greek Emperor, and the sole advantages of this bloody struggle.

The Turkmans, wandering hordes of Scythians who had come from the north and overrun all China and Central Asia, had been invited some years previously (A.D. 1000) by the khalifs into Persia, to prop up by their military energy a feeble and tottering power, opposed by rebellious and refractory vassals. Converted to Muhammadanism by their new connexion with the Saracen Arabs, they seized upon the *monarchy*, but suffered the *monarch* to exist; they declared themselves the *lieutenants* of the Khalifs, and distributed their numerous clans over the whole of the countries between Bagdad and India, which they divided among themselves: hence the different dynasties of *Sammanides, Gaznarides, Suljukians, Karizmians*, &c., and at length *Ottomans* or *Osmanlis*, which last became the most celebrated from the duration and extent of their power, and which they have had the good fortune to retain to the present day. The Turkmans of the court and city have been refined by the business and intercourse of social life, and softened by luxury and effeminacy; but the greater number of their brethren still

as Antioch, which was said to contain 600,000 souls. Commerce alone might have been equal to the support of such numbers.

continue to dwell in the tents of their ancestors, and lead the same wandering life which they led eight centuries ago.

During the life of Tugrul Bay (A.D. 1050), one of the Suljukian family, many parties of Turkman horse invaded the provinces of the Greek Empire, and overran a frontier of 600 miles, shedding the blood of 130,000 Christians. But these incursions did not make a lasting impression on the Greek Empire, which still extended to Antioch and the boundaries of Armenia. The torrent rolled away in the open country, obscure hostilities were continued or suspended with various vicissitudes of good and bad fortune, and the bravery of the Macedonian legions renewed the fame of the successors of Alexander. The Turkmans, however, had the advantages of a new and poor people over an ancient and corrupt government, and were besides continually recruited by fresh hordes of their companions, impelled by the thirst of rapine, and the necessity of forming new settlements.

A.D. 1068. Tugrul Bay left to his nephew and successor, Alp Arslan (become, by the overthrow of the Gaznavide dynasty, the most powerful head of the numerous clans, and who had assumed the title of Suldan), the care of prosecuting the war against the Christians, and he invaded Asia Minor with a large army headed by his Amirs or generals. Laden with spoils, which they seized indiscriminately, and careless of discipline, these troops were, in the security of conquest, scattered in numerous detachments all over the provinces. The Greek emperor, Romanus Diogenes, who had been invested by the Empress Eudocia with the purple for the purpose of defending the state against these barbarians, surprised and defeated them separately, and drove them beyond the Euphrates in three laborious campaigns.

On the report of these losses, Alp Arslan flew to the scene of action (A.D. 1072) at the head of 40,000 horse, and overcame and captured Romanus Diogenes. He accepted, however, a ransom of a million of gold pieces, and sent him back on promise of paying a tribute of 360,000 pieces. But in the treaty of peace it does not appear that he extorted any province or city from the captive emperor, and his revenge was satisfied with the trophies of his victories and the spoils of Anatolia, from Antioch to the Black Sea.

Sulaiman, the son of Kutulmish, a relative of Arslan, and of the family of the Suljukians, invaded Asia Minor two years after (A.D. 1074), and declared himself in favour of Nicephorus Botoniates, in opposition to his rival Bryennius, and materially contributed to the success of the former, whom he settled on the throne of Constantinople. 2000 Turks were at this time transported into Europe, the first of that nation who crossed the Hellespont,—a fatal precedent, for the Turks took the opportunity of fortifying themselves in the country; and the elevation of a tyrant, who was soon deposed and put to death, was purchased by the sacrifice of many of the finest provinces of the empire; and from this date the Turks could no longer be expelled from Asia Minor, the whole of which they soon subdued, except Trebizond, which held out to the Greeks.

Sulaiman following up his successes, completed (A.D. 1084) the conquest of Anatolia, and established the new kingdom of the Suljukians of Roum. At Nicæa, the metropolis of Bithynia, 100 miles distant from Constantinople, "on the very spot where the first general council or synod of the Christians was held, the divinity of Christ was denied and derided; and the Kuran was preached in the same temple which had witnessed the assemblage of the heads of the Christian Church, now converted into a mosque. The Cadis judged according to the laws of the Kuran, the Turkish manners and language prevailed over the cities, and Turkman camps were scattered over the plains and mountains of Asia Minor. On the hard conditions of tribute and servitude, the Greek Christians were permitted to enjoy the exercise of their religion; but their holy churches were profaned, their priests and bishops insulted; they were compelled to suffer the triumphs of the Pagans and the apostacy of their brethren, and many thousand captives were devoted to the service or pleasures of their masters." Here I pause to observe how well adapted to the present state of the country is this picture drawn by Gibbon, from contemporary writers, of the degraded state of the Christians in those times, and which has continued to the present day with little or no alteration or diminution. In consequence of this tyranny, they have, in self-defence, been induced to resort to that cunning and deceit which are now their leading characteristics, and which *alone* are the features that distinguish them from their oppressors, for they have in every other respect adopted the manners and prejudices of the Muhammadans. None of their churches have been restored to them that were converted into mosques; but they are permitted, on payment of large sums, to build new churches, on heaps of ruins where it is impossible to say what edifice had stood, whether theatre, bath, or Pagan temple. Under the late Sultan some of the restrictions on Christian worship have been diminished, and firmans are to be obtained with less difficulty and comparatively moderate fees; and this they owe to the progress of civilisation, consequent on the march of intellect which produced in Sultan Mahmud an enlightened monarch and a man of genius.

On the establishment of a Turkman dynasty at Nicæa (A.D. 1095), which lasted 220 years, the provinces of Asia Minor came under its subjection, and were the scene of slaughter and rapine; while the pilgrims from every part of Europe, who began to flock to Jerusalem, encountered innumerable perils ere they were permitted to salute the Holy Sepulchre. A spirit of zeal, engendered by the exclusiveness of Muhammadanism, prompted these hordes to insult the clergy of every other sect. The Patriarch of Jerusalem, we are informed, was dragged by the hair along the pavement and cast into a dungeon, to extort a ransom from his flock; and the divine worship in the Church of the Resurrection was often disturbed by the rudeness of its masters. Peter the Hermit roused the martial nations of Europe to avenge their wrongs; and the Crusades were undertaken by our ancestors in a spirit of enthusiasm to peril their lives in the defence and rescue of their co-religionists—a feeling which seems to have been entirely extinguished in the hearts of their descendants.

Kilitch Arslan, the son of Sulaiman, was king of Nicæa (A.D. 1097) when the army of the first Crusaders besieged that city on its way to the Holy Land, and took it after a siege of seven months. The Turkman sultan, no way dismayed by the loss of his capital, retreated to Dorylæum in Phrygia, and assembling there all the forces he had in the province, resolutely attacked the Latins, and eventually engaged them in a pitched battle. But victory declared for the Crusaders; and Kilitch Arslan was compelled to retreat, and implore the aid, by kindling the resentment, of his eastern brethren, which he did, laying waste the countries he traversed. The Crusaders proceeded to Koniyah, Arakli, and Marash, and thence over Mount Taurus to Kucusus, now Kursun, a town remarkable as having formerly been the place of exile of St. Chrysostom. Two of the chiefs, Tancred and Baldwin, the brother of Godfrey of Bouillon, were here detached from the main army, with their respective squadrons of 500 and 700 knights. They overran in rapid career the hills and sea-coast of Cilicia, from the mountainous country to the Syrian gates, and planted the Norman standard on the walls of Tarsus and Malmistra (Mopsuestia). The former of these cities Baldwin, excited by jealousy and ambition, obliged Tancred to deliver into his hands; and he had the barbarity to refuse admission to 300 of the soldiers of Tancred, who were consequently obliged to pass the night outside the walls, where they were cut to pieces by a strong party of Saracen Turks. But Tancred by his moderation had gained the affection of the soldiers, and Baldwin was soon obliged to return to the camp, to endure the reproaches of the Latin chiefs. Tancred fortified and garrisoned the towns he had taken, and these were the most lasting possessions of all that the Crusades acquired.

A.D. 1118. While the brave Tancred and his warlike associates were winning laurels before the walls of Jerusalem and Antioch, the wily Alexius, Emperor of Constantinople, improved the opportunity afforded by the victories of the Crusaders, and recovered the provinces previously taken from the Greeks by the Suljukian Turkmans, by following in their steps, and taking possession of and fortifying all the towns on the coast, including the islands of Cyprus and Rhodes. The seat of power of the Turkmans was thus confined to the districts of Koniyah, where the dynasty of Alp Arslan fixed their debilitated throne. Their power eventually became nominal; for in spite of the high titles they assumed, the last of their race were happy to be considered as generals of the Great Mogul, and owe their sway to his bounty, until they were finally destroyed by Gazan in 1298, the year 706 of the Hegira. In the meanwhile the ambitious but prudent Alexius had resolved to annex Cilicia to his empire, and that the Syrian gates should be the boundary of his possessions: for this purpose he made war on Tancred and Bohemond, now tranquil masters of their conquests. Bohemond, unable to cope with this new enemy, left Tancred to govern at Antioch, and returning to Europe, levied an army of 5000 horse and 40,000 foot, with which he returned to punish the faithless Greek. But the sudden death of Bohemond happened about this time; added to which, the venal arts of Alexius, by which he won over his confederates, compelled Tancred to sign a treaty of peace, whereby all Cilicia was restored to the Byzantine empire. Thus the towns of Tarsus and Malmistra (or Mopsuestia), so bravely won by Tancred, fell under the government of the Greeks.

CHAPTER V.

THE EMPEROR JOHN COMNENUS KILLED IN A WILD-BOAR HUNT IN CILICIA—DESCRIPTION OF ANAZARBA—THE SECOND CRUSADE—THIRD CRUSADE—DEATH OF FREDERICK I. (BARBAROSSA) IN CILICIA—FOURTH CRUSADE—CILICIA UNDER JOHN DUCAS VATACES—DEVASTATIONS OF YANGHIZ OR GENGHIZ KHAN.

The crafty Alexius was succeeded (A.D. 1143) in the throne of Constantinople by his son John Comnenus, surnamed Kalo Joannes or John the Handsome, a prince whose reign of twenty-five years was marked by virtues rarely met with in such degenerate and guilty times. He introduced a gradual reformation in the manners of his capital, without assuming the tyrannic office of a censor. The only check on the public felicity was love of military glory,—the ruling passion of the emperor. But the frequent expeditions he undertook may be justified in some measure by the necessity of repelling the Turks and repressing their inroads. The Sultan of Karamania was confined to his capital, the barbarians were driven to their mountains, and the maritime provinces of Asia enjoyed a tranquillity which was highly appreciated.

John Comnenus repeatedly marched at the head of his victorious armies from Constantinople to Antioch and Aleppo; the whole coast of Anatolia to the north and south was subjected to his power, and in the sieges and battles of the Holy War his Latin allies were astonished at the superior spirit and prowess of a Greek. But while the Greek king began to indulge the hope of restoring the ancient limits of the empire, the decrees of Providence were about to frustrate his plans; and the thread of his life and of the public happiness was broken by an unfortunate and rather singular accident. While hunting a wild boar in Cilicia, near the town of Anazarba, he had fixed his javelin in the body of the furious animal, and in the struggle to recover himself a poisoned arrow dropped from his quiver, and a slight wound in his hand produced mortification and proved fatal to him.*

* La Cilicie dépendait des rois Seleucides; mais Tigranes roi d'Arménie ayant détrôné ce prince, la Cilicie, du moins la partie qu'on appellait Campestris, obéit au roi d'Arménie jusqu'à l'an 688 de Rome, dans laquelle Tigranes fut vaincu par Pompée. Cette partie resta soumise aux Romains. Jules-César confirma le titre de Métropole à la ville de Tarsus. L'Empereur Auguste lui conféra de nouvelles graces, et elle jouit

SECOND CRUSADE.

The second Crusade, under Conrad III. Emperor of Germany and Louis VII. (A.D.1147), experienced the same disasters that befel the first expedition. Misled by the guides in the pay of the perfidious Greek Emperor Manuel, who succeeded Kalo Joannes, and who was secretly leagued with the Saracens, the unfortunate Conrad and Louis were betrayed; and unable to penetrate farther than the Taurus and the confines

du titre et des prééminences de métropole jusqu'au cinquième siècle de Jésus-Christ. Les villes d'Anazarba d'Egès (Ayash) et Mallus (Kara Tash), et autres, lui étaient soumises. La ville d'Anazarba, décorée du titre de Césarée, était illustre; elle éprouva les plus grands malheurs; elle fut renversée par un tremblement de terre, et l'Empereur Nerva la fit bientôt rétablir. Cette ville resta dans un état florissant pendant plusieurs siècles; un autre tremblement de terre la ruina sous le règne de Justin ou Justinian. Elle se releva encore du milieu de ses ruines par la munificence des princes, et l'avantage de la situation et la fertilité de son territoire furent cause qu'elle fut bientôt rétablie. Anazarba riche, peuplée, et dans une position avantageuse, par une rivalité alors commun entre les grandes villes d'une même province, ambitionna le titre de métropole, et elle le prit suivant Vaillant sous le règne d'Elagabule ; mais elle l'avait obtenu auparavant : sur un médaille frappée en l'honneur de Caracalla l'an BAZ 232 de l'ère de la ville, 966 de Rome, 214 de Jésus-Christ, quatrième du règne de ce prince, elle prend le titre de ΜΗΤΡΟΠΟΛΕΩΣ, métropole, qu'elle conserva sous les empereurs suivant; mais ce titre était simplement honorifique, sans donner aucune juridiction dans la province; il donnoit la préséance après Tarsus, dans les assemblées générales Pareils honneurs furent accordés aux villes de Nicée en Bythinie, de Laodicée en Syrie, et de Sidon en Phénicie.

La ville d'Anazarba ne se contenta pas du titre de métropole; elle y ajouta l'épithète d'illustre, ΕΝΔΟΞΟΥΜΗΤΡΟΠΟΛΕΟΣ, qu'elle fit graver sur plusieurs de ses monnaies. Elle conservait encore ce titre sous le règne de Dioclétian. On lit dans les Actes des Martyrs publiées par Don Ruinart, que Taraque, Andronique, et Probus furent mis à mort pour la religion Chrétienne l'an 304 de Jésus-Christ ἐν 'Αναζαρβῳ τῃ ενδοξῳ μητροπόλει, à Anazarba illustre Métropole.—Dissertation sur l'Ere d'Anazarba par l'Abbé Belley, in the Mémoires de l'Académie, vol. 50, p. 350. Vide Journal, Jan. 18, 1848.

Tarsus under the reign of L. Verus had inscribed on its medals Π Μ Κ, which has puzzled antiquaries; the Abbé says it means προτης μητροπόλεως Κιλικιας. Anazarba had the same engraved on its medals, out of opposition.

Under the reign of Arcadius, Cilicia was divided into first and second provinces, of which Tarsus and Anazarba became the chief metropolitan towns.

Anazarba, under the Emperor Commodus, obtained the privilege of being αὐτόνομος, by which it had the right of choosing its own magistrates, and of being governed by its own laws.—W. B. B.

Anazarba, which appears to have been erroneously called Ain-zarbeh,—the name being merely corrupted by the natives to Anawarzah,—figured for a short period as one of the most flourishing cities of Cilicia. Ptolemy calls it Cæsarea ad Anazarbum; Pliny, Anazarbeni qui nunc Cæsarea; Hierocles calls it Metropolis; and it is enumerated among the Christian episcopacies in the Ecclesiastical Notices of the Low Empire. It was the country of Dioscorides, who is called by Suidas the physician of Anazarba, and of Oppian, the poet of the Cynegeticus. Carolus Stephanus, in his historical dictionary, says that this writer of elegant verses died of plague at his birthplace, which he calls Zerbus. This splendid town was destroyed by a fearful earthquake in the reign of Justinian. This is narrated by Procopius and by Cedrenus.

Little was known of the actual condition of this place till it was visited by a party from the Euphrates expedition. The walls still remain, but in a ruinous condition.

of Cilicia, they were obliged to embark with a few retainers only in Greek vessels for the coast of Syria, the one from the Hellespont, and the other from Satalia. The greatest part of their miserable and misguided followers, to the number of several thousands, were abandoned to their fate and exposed to the cruelty of the Saracens at the foot of the Pamphylian hills, and in the forests of Mount Taurus.

Andronicus, grandson of Alexius and cousin of Manuel, was twice sent during the lifetime of this emperor to govern the important province of Cilicia. His romantic adventures and hair-breadth escapes would fill a volume; I can but refer to the most striking passages in his life. In his first campaign he pressed the siege of Mopsuestia, which had been seized by the Armenians. By day his boldness was equal to his success; but the nights were devoted to the song and dance, and a band of Greek comedians formed the choicest of his retinue. One evening he was surprised by a sally of the vigilant foe; but while his troops fled in disorder, his invincible lance transpierced the thickest ranks of the Armenians. In his second command of the Cilician frontier, some years afterwards, the Armenians again exercised his courage and exposed his negligence, while he wasted his time at Antioch in balls and tournaments. Among three princesses whom he seduced was the Queen of Jerusalem, whose shame was more public and scandalous than that of either of her predecessors. He remained twelve years in prison, took the Cross as a Crusader, wandered as an outlaw to Bagdad and Persia, settled among the Turks in Asia Minor, became a robber of Christians and the terror of the kingdom of Trebizond, usurped the throne of Constantinople, and after a bloody reign of three years was put to death in a cruel and ignominious manner by the enraged populace.

The third Crusade, under the conduct of Frederic I. Emperor of Germany, surnamed Barbarossa (A.D. 1183), did not eventually meet with much more success than the last. After passing the Hellespont, his army was harassed by innumerable hordes of Turkmans during twenty days that he was traversing the dense forests of Bithynia; but he overcame all obstacles to his progress, and attacked and stormed the capital of the Turkmans, and compelled the Sultan of Koniyah to sue for peace. But the veteran warrior reaped no harvest from his exertions; he was not fated

Few public buildings exist, however, within the walls, beyond an extensive castle of various ages, built upon the top of a rocky hill, and many of the rooms of which are in perfect keeping,—but these appear to belong to the Muhammadan era. A great number of beautifully sculptured and highly ornamented tombs and sarcophagi still attest, however, to the opulence and civilisation of this former metropolis of Cilicia. Nor must we omit to mention the ruins of an aqueduct, which brought water direct from the mountains, a distance of many miles.—W. F. A.

to tread the soil of the Holy Land, nor to terminate the triumphs which he had begun. He was drowned while crossing a river in Cilicia, which had been swollen by the tropical rains,—*the Cydnus* according to some writers, and who have taken this occasion to draw a comparison between him and Alexander, to whom this river had nearly proved fatal above a thousand years previously. But I am unwilling to give credit to this story, as it seems unaccountable that a general at the head of his army should be lost in fording a river which is nowhere more than six feet deep; and I think it more probable that he was attacked by the malignant fever of the country. However this may be, his troops were decimated by sickness and famine, and his son, who had contrived to reach the Holy Land with a few remaining followers, expired at the siege of Acre. These losses led succeeding Crusaders, grown wiser by the fate of their predecessors, to abandon the overland route, and Cilicia was no longer trampled under foot by the zealous but little disciplined hosts.

The fourth Crusade, undertaken by the Venetians and French (A.D. 1204), was diverted from the coast of Syria, to which it was originally directed, by the enticing shores of the Bosphorus; where, on pretence of revenging the death of Alexius, who with his father Isaac had been murdered by Murzufli, the Latins made themselves masters of Constantinople, sacked and burnt the best part of the capital, and elected Baldwin Count of Flanders Emperor of the East. The successors of this monarch maintained themselves in the capital during a period of fifty-seven years. But Theodore Lascaris, the son-in-law and relation of Alexius, having fled, he set up the standard of the Greeks at Nicæa, and with the alliance of the Turkish sultan he saved a remnant of the falling empire. During a reign of eighteen years, this emperor extended, by his military talents, the small principality of Nicæa to the magnitude of a kingdom, in which Cilicia was included.

Theodore Lascaris was succeeded at his death (A.D. 1222) by John Ducas Vataces, his son-in-law, who fixed the throne on a more solid basis, and in a long reign of thirty-three years displayed both the virtues of peace and the energy of war. In the long administration of this prince, the provinces of Asia Minor, and among them Cilicia, enjoyed the blessings of a good government. The lands were sown with corn or planted with olives and vines; the pastures were filled with cattle and horses; the education of youth and the revival of learning were also serious objects of his care, and both by his precepts and practice, simplicity of manners and domestic industry were encouraged.

It was somewhere about this period that the Venetians and Genoese founded commercial emporia on the coasts of Asia Minor, in Cilicia, and in Syria, somewhat after the principle adopted by the early Hellenic colonists, fortifying themselves in their positions by adequate defences, and often by castles to command the passes of the interior, or to keep the surrounding populations in awe. Few records of the era of the foundation of these emporia exist, and equally few are to be met which record their history, their prosperity, or their adverses, and their final extinction.

Upon this subject the able historian Sismundi says, " The chronicles of the maritime cities of Italy throw very little light upon the colonies which their citizens founded in the towns of the East, or even at Constantinople. These colonies governed themselves, they named their own authorities, and did not receive them from the metropolis; and whatever their population or their wealth, they could not be considered as belonging to the state. Hence it is that the national historians have attached but little importance to the debates of a number of Venetian and Pisan individuals at the other extremity of Europe, although the results brought about by them still astonish us in the present day ; while, on the other hand, the continual wars of the Pisans and the Genoese, which appear to us in the light of freaks of pirates, captivated their whole attention."

There are, however, a few fragments referring to these conquests which it may be interesting to record here.

The earliest fleet of the Venetian republic that accompanied the first Crusade, A.D. 1099, was composed of 200 ships, and commanded by the son of the new doge, Vital Michieli. They fought off Rhodes a bloody battle against the fleet of the republic of Pisa, each forgetting that they were Christians and crusaders. The Venetian fleet took Smyrna at a later period, and assisted the land troops of the crusaders in taking Jaffa.*

The Genoese republic sent, in August 1100, twenty-eight galleys and six larger vessels into the East. The historian Caffaro was of the expedition. Another fleet was despatched about this time by the republic of Pisa under the Archbishop Daimbert, who became afterwards Patriarch of Jerusalem. The combined fleets passed the winter at Lattakiya ; and when the death of Godfroy de Bouillon had endangered his new kingdom, they kept the maritime provinces, including Cilicia, in subjection to the Latins.

The troops of the two republics undertook the siege of Cæsarea, A.D. 1101. Caput Malio, the Genoese consul, was the first to climb the ramparts, on simple maritime scaling-ladders, and the town was taken from the Musulmans and consigned to pillage. One-fifteenth of the booty was given to the sailors that remained on board the fleet.

* Andrea Danduli Chron. l. ix. c. 10, p. 256.

Constantinople was retaken by the Greeks under Stratigopulas from the Venetians, A.D. 1261; and Michael Paleologus, whose troops had been assisted by the Genoese, granted privileges to the latter which he had promised them beforehand, but established them at Galata, out of the city. The Venetians and Pisans formed each a separate quarter, and the three were governed by a separate magistrate, which their respective towns sent to them; and here were formed three small republics, which maintained their liberty and independence, in a city the emperor of which was still at war with the Latins. The latter ceded the island of Scio to the Genoese, which was the largest held by them (till 1556), the jealousy of the Greeks having induced them to look with favour upon the occupation of the island by the Musulmans.

The *final* conquest, by Melek Seraf, of St. Jean d'Acre, when 30,000 Christians were massacred, occurred A.D. 1291; and the taking of Tripoli of Barbary by the Genoese admiral Philip Doria, in A.D. 1355.

The Genoese of Pera attempted in the year 1376 to take the island of Tenedos, ceded to them by Andronicus, who had been half blinded by his father, John Paleologos. They were prevented by the governor of the island, who remained faithful to the deposed emperor, and called the Venetians to his assistance, thus defeating the objects of the Genoese.

Nicotia was taken June 16th, 1373, by Catani (Genoese admiral of some galleys sent by the Genoese to revenge the massacre), and seventy captive virgins dedicated to Venus were restored to their parents.

Famagosta was taken October 3d by Petre di Campo Fregoso, brother of the Doge of Genoa, at the head of thirty-six galleys and 14,000 men. Petro Lusignan, the young king, and son of the deceased king of the same name, was taken prisoner on that occasion, and the island subjugated to the Genoese. The young king, however, attacked the Genoese in Famagosta in 1378, assisted by the Venetian galleys; but he was repulsed, and forced to quit not only the island, but the seas of Cyprus.

Sinope (Samsun), Trebizonde, and Cerasus were taken by Mohammed II. A.D. 1462.

Pope Pius II. died in 1464, and thus the hopes of assistance entertained by the Christians of the Levant were destroyed.

Pope Paul II. endeavoured in vain to revive an interest in the Christians of the Levant, and the fleet that had assembled at Ancona (A.D. 1465) to proceed to the assistance of the Christians, was sent by the Venetian senate to attack and plunder the island of Rhodes, under the Great Master of the order of St. John of Jerusalem.

Petro Mocenigo, after ravaging, with eighty-eight galleys, the north of Asia Minor, attacked, A.D. 1472, Attalia, or Satali, a rich town of Pamphilia, which furnished Egypt and Syria with provisions, devastated the environs, and then returned to Rhodes. He also ravaged Ionia, opposite Scio, and Smyrna, without making any distinction between the Christian churches and the Muhammadan mosques.

Mocenigo received from Venice, A.D. 1473, the order to put himself in communication with Ozun Hassan, to whom the republic sent Josaphat Barbaro (a person advanced in age, speaking the Persian fluently, and of great talent and perspicuity), three galleys laden with presents and a great quantity of artillery, together with 100 artizans whom the republic offered to the service of the sovereign of Persia. It was through Cilicia that they had decided on passing into Persia to accompany the Persian ambassador. The latter was on his return to his master after having been received at Venice, to negotiate that mutual assistance should be given by the Latins and Persians against their common enemy Mohammed II. The princes of Karamania, two brothers, who had been despoiled by the Muhammadans of great part of their possessions, but who still defended themselves bravely in the remainder,* were awaiting them. One of these was besieging *Seleucia* (Sulufsky), which it seems was a place still of some importance even at so late a period.

Mocenigo, with forty-five galleys, two from the Knights of Rhodes and four from the king of Cyprus, proceeded to their assistance. Landing first at Cyprus, he had a meeting with Hassan Bay, the younger brother (the eldest, Pyramet,† being in the Persian camp), near Sulufsky, where his envoy, Victor Seranzo, was informed by the young bay that the Muhammadans kept the people of Karamania, who were devoted to the Christian prince, under subjection by means of three fortresses, Sichesii, Seleucia, and Coryco (Sikin, Sulufsky, and Kurkus), which they could not take for want of artillery. Mocenigo forced the Muhammadan troops occupying these three places to capitulate, and made them over to Hassan Bay.‡

These were the first attempts made to open a communication with the Persians; and they are of an interesting character, not only as regarding the country we are now engaged upon, but also as pointing out

* M. Antonio Sabellico, deca. iii. l. ix. f. 215 verso. Coriol. Copio, l. ii. p. 361.

† Many of the names used by Mr. Barker in this portion of his narrative are derived, as will be seen from the foot-notes, from Italian writers of the middle ages, and they are exceedingly corrupted. Pyramet, for example, could not be a Turkish name. —W. F. A. It is a corruption of Pyr and Ahmed, which conjointly mean *old Ahmed*, or the *chief* Ahmed.—W. B. B.

‡ M. Ant. Sabellico, deca. iii. l. ix. f. 216 vo. Callimachus Experiens de Venetis contra Turcos, f. 409. Coriolan Copio, l. ii. p. 352.

the progress of the human mind. They opened unknown regions to the observations of western nations; they brought together people that had been long separated; they threw the first dawn of light on geography, till then so confused; and they inaugurated the period in which we are now living, a period the most remarkable character of which consists in the *communication* established between all the nations of the globe.

After the taking of Sulufsky by Mocenigo, finding it impossible to penetrate into Persia with his suite, Josaphat Barbaro left in Crete the presents with which he was charged, and proceeded with the Persian ambassador to cross these barbarous lands, accompanied only by a few servants. He started from Tarsus through " Little Armenia," no doubt following the usual route that leads by Anazarba and Sis through a passage made in the mountains by the river Pyramus; thence he crossed Kurdistan, a country that has remained to this day as wild as its inhabitants are intractable. Here he was attacked by robbers; his companion, the Persian ambassador, was killed, as were also his secretary and two of their followers. Barbaro himself was severely wounded and despoiled of every thing; he did not, however, lose courage, but proceeded to join Ozun Hassan at Tabriz, with whom he remained five years, and received from that sovereign great marks of kindness and favour. In 1488 he returned to Venice by way of Aleppo.

Mocenigo in the mean time proceeded to attack different places on the coast of Asia Minor. He took Myra, having defeated and killed Arasa Bay, the governor of the province, who had come to the rescue. He then disembarked near Phygas in Caria, where he received a message from Catherino Zeno, who was accredited by the republic of Venice at the Persian camp, to come to Cilicia, in order to be able to afford any assistance in his power to the Persians, who were then advancing westward. On his arrival at Kurkus he received another messenger from Zeno announcing the defeat of the Persians, after their partial success, and their retreat into Armenia.

About this time we find that the Genoese still possessed some strong places in Cyprus;—among others, Famagosta. It would be beyond our limits to enter into the details of the wars between Charlotte, daughter of Janus III., the fourteenth king of Cyprus, and her natural brother Jacques, the Venetians siding with Janus, and the Genoese with the legitimate princess; suffice it to say, that in 1444 Famagosta opened its gates to Jacques de Lusignan, after three years' siege.

Mocenigo continued up to the year 1473 to make descents on the coast of Lycia, Caria, and Cilicia; but his attention seems to have been principally taken up with subduing the island of Cyprus to the adopted daughter of St. Mark, the niece of Marc Cornaro, a Venetian gentleman established in Cyprus, and who had been an exile from his country. This is the lady whom Jacques de Lusignan married, in order to contract an alliance which should qualify him as " son-in-law of the republic."*

The Genoese, up to the year 1475, possessed a colony in Caffa in the Crimea, anciently called Theodosia ; it had been more than two centuries in the hands of these people, and had acquired riches and a population almost equal to its mother city. It was the centre of communication between Europe and the East, by means of the Genoese, who received the spices of India, and the stuffs of silk and cotton manufactured in Persia, by way of Astrakan.†

Caffa was taken by Hamid, a commander of Mohammed II. (A.D. 1475). He conducted the Frank inhabitants to Pera, selecting therefrom 1500 youths to be brought up among the Janissaries at Constantinople; and thus was destroyed the dominion of the Genoese in the Black Sea.

An army of 80,000 men was sent by Bayazid II. (A.D. 1488) to attack Kayit Bay, the sovereign of Egypt, in whose hands, at this time, was Syria and Cilicia. This army, after having taken Adana and Tarsus, was defeated by the Mamluks at Issus, at the foot of Mount Amanus. The Ottoman fleet was dispersed and partly destroyed by a tempest, and the Turks renounced the invasion of Egypt.‡

Jam or Zezim, son of Mohammed II., and brother of Bayazid II., aspired (A.D. 1489) to the throne of his father, under the plea that he was " Porphyrogenetus," that is, born when Mohammed II. had become sultan, whereas his elder brother was born during the earlier period of their father's life, before he had reached to the height of empire. He was vanquished, however, in his endeavours to bring about a revolution in his favour in Asia Minor, and he took refuge in Cilicia, which which was then under the dominion (as we have just seen) of the Sultan of Egypt. From this he embarked for Rhodes, to solicit the assistance of the Knights of St. John.§

It would seem that the latter did not dare to keep him on the

---

* Marin Sanuto Vite du Duchi, f. 1185, vol. x. p. 330. Andrea Navaziero Stor. Veneziana, f. 1127-1131. Annal. Ecclesiast. 147, § 47, f. 229.

† Ubertus follata Genuens Hist. l. xi. p. 626.

‡ And. Navaziero Stor. Venez. p. 1197, and Raynaldi An. Ecc. 1488, § 9, p. 989. Sismondi, vol. ii. p. 321.

§ Raynaldi Annal. Eccles. 1482, § 35, f. 312. Turco Græcia Hist. Politica, l. i. p. 30. Demetrius Centimir, l. iii. chap. ii. § 7 and 8, p. 123.

frontiers of a state that had become so powerful; they therefore sent him to France, from whence he passed into the hands of Pope Innocent VIII. (A.D. 1489), who detained him in honourable confinement by the bribery of Bayazid, who paid the pope 40,000 ducats yearly for the "pension" of his brother!

In the year 1566 the Genoese lost the island of Scio, which was taken from the family of the Giustinianis by Sultan Sulaiman. They were on the point also of losing Corsica, which had been invaded by the French in 1553, had revolted in 1564, and continued to repel the oppressive yoke of this republic until 1568, when it was again brought into subjection.

The Venetians signed a treaty (20th October, 1540) by which they ceded to Sulaiman all the islands of the Archipelago already conquered by the Turks.

In 1570 the Turks attacked Cyprus, which was defended until 1573 by an immense sacrifice of men and money, till the inhabitants were forced to sign a treaty of peace, and abandon the island to its new masters.

To resume, however, the thread of our history, in and about A.D. 1255.

The three years of the reign of Theodore, son of John Ducas, were marked by cruelty and evil passions; and although he thrice led an army against the Bulgarians in Europe, he obtained no signal advantage. He left at his death the crown to his son John Lascaris, a boy eight years of age, who was soon set aside and blinded by Michael Palæologus (A.D. 1259), one of his relations, who seated himself firmly on the throne of Constantinople two years afterwards, by which event the Latin dynasty was superseded, and the Greek emperors triumphantly entered the metropolis, after a banishment of fifty-seven years (A.D. 1261).

But the removal of the seat of empire from Nicæa to Constantinople was fatal to the Greeks, as the countries on the Asiatic side of the Hellespont were left exposed to the Turkish invaders, and the barrier which had been effectual for so many years against their inroads was removed farther north. The attention of Michael Palæologus was also almost totally absorbed in propitiating the Roman pontiff, in order, by artful and hypocritical means, to avert the western storm which was hanging over his head, so that the eastern part of the empire was neglected and left to its fate. While the Greeks and Latins were engaged in disputes on trifling points of religion, a colossal and irresistible power had overturned all the Asiatic kingdoms; and even those of Europe were shaken to their foundation. The whole of Central Asia, China, Persia, part of India and Russia, were overrun by the Moguls and Tartars, who about the year A.D. 1206, under Yanghiz or Genghiz Khan and his followers, rendered themselves masters, during sixty-eight years of unparalleled success, of the greater part of Asia. The sultans of the Suljukian dynasty at Koniyah in vain attempted to stop the torrent in its course; they were swept away by the victorious arms of the Moguls, and Azzaddin fled to Europe, taking refuge in Thrace. The whole of Asia Minor felt the iron sway of the conquerors; and Hulagu Khan, grandson of Yanghiz Khan, laid the whole country waste with fire and sword.

But as these shepherd-kings soon returned to their own country with their spoils and captives, the destructive inundation ceased to flow after a while, and Cilicia once more formed a part of the Greek empire.

Michael Palæologus was succeeded by his son Andronicus, (A.D. 1282,) whose long reign of nearly fifty years was disgraced by superstition and weakened by the disputes of the Greek Church, and this at the very time that a new power, destined to subvert his own, was rising on the ruins of the Suljukian dynasty.

RUIN AT ANAZARBA.—(From a Sketch by Edward B. B. Barker, Esq.)

CHAPTER VI.

RISE OF THE OSMANLIS OR USMANLIS—VICTORIES OF BAYAZID—INVASIONS OF THE MOGULS—CAPTURE OF CONSTANTINOPLE BY MUHAMMAD II.—BAYAZID II. ANNEXES CILICIA TO THE OTTOMAN EMPIRE—CAMPAIGNS OF SULAIMAN THE MAGNIFICENT—AMURAD IV. INVADES CILICIA—HIS HOUSE AT ADANA—REFORMS OF MAHMUD II.—ABD'UL MASJID.

OTHMAN, son of Orthogrul,[*] a Turkman chief of a tribe of four hundred families who had settled in Lesser Armenia on the banks of the Euphrates, after his father's death enlisted in the service of Ala-addin, one of the last sultans of Karamania. Becoming emir or lieutenant of the feeble monarch, he founded a kingdom, the seat of which was first established at Brusa, then at Adrianople, and lastly at Constantinople.

The founder of the Osmanli dynasty first invaded the territory of Nicomedia, A.D. 1299, and during twenty-seven years he made repeated incursions on the Greek empire. At last, when oppressed by age and infirmities, he received the news in his camp of the taking of Brusa by his son Orchan, which then became the capital of the new dynasty.

Orchan afterwards subjected all the countries of Asia Minor, almost without resistance; but it appears that he allowed his brother-generals to divide the spoil, for we see that the emirs of Gharmain and Karamania (in the latter of which Cilicia was included) are said to have been in a condition to bring each an army of 40,000 men into the field. From these proceeded the vast tribes of Turkmans established all over Cilicia and Karamania, who maintain their original way of living to this day, and who are a separate race from the wandering tribes to the north,—of those, for example, in the districts of Kaisariyah. The latter are mostly of Kurd origin, and speak a perfectly different language.

Orchan, profiting by the civil wars of the elder Andronicus and his grandson, caused his emirs to build a fleet and pillage the adjacent islands, and even the sea-coasts of Europe.

---

[*] It is proper in names so long accepted as Osman or Othman, Orthogrul, and Osmanlis or Ottomans, to retain the accepted orthographies; otherwise, as there is no *o* in the original, a more correct orthography would be 'Usman, 'Usmanli, 'Urthugrul, &c.

F

John Cantacuzene, who, in conjunction with John Palæologus, son of the younger Andronicus, had become emperor, basely invited to his aid (A.D. 1346) the public enemies of his religion and country; and Orchan was induced to come to his assistance by the stipulated condition that the daughter of Cantacuzene should be given him in marriage. Parental tenderness was in this case silenced by the dictates of ambition, and the Greek princess was delivered over to her Asiatic lord without the rites of the Church. The Turks were thus introduced into Europe; and in the very first step they made they trod down with contempt one of the first and most sacred rites of the Christians, by taking the daughter of their emperor as a concubine in their harims! Sulaiman, the son of Orchan, marched at the head of ten thousand warriors into Europe to support the wavering power of his ally. In the civil wars of Romania he performed a small degree of service and a greater degree of mischief. By degrees the Chersonesus was insensibly filled with a Turkish colony, while the Byzantine court solicited in vain the restitution of the fortresses of Thrace. The walls of Galipoli, the key of the Hellespont, had been thrown down by an earthquake; they were rebuilt and fortified by the policy of Sulaiman, and Constantinople would have next fallen a prey to the ambition of the Turks, had the Turkish chief not died by a fall from his horse, and the death of his father soon after fortunately intervened to stay for a little while the shock of the impending storm.

A.D. 1360. Amurad I., second son of Orchan, succeeded to the throne, which he removed from Brusa to Adrianople. During a reign of nearly thirty years he subdued without resistance the provinces of Romania and Thrace, from Mount Hæmus to the suburbs of Constantinople; and John Palæologus, almost a prisoner in his palace, was obliged, with his four sons, to follow the court and camp of the Ottoman prince. The Bulgarians, Servians, Bosnians, and Albanians were all made tributary, and brought by a famous institution to be, by their bravery, the supporters of Ottoman greatness. The redoubtable corps of the "Janissaries" (Yani-chari), chosen from among the stoutest and most beautiful Christian youths, became the terror of nations, and in later times of the sultans themselves.

It was reserved to Amurad's son Bayazid, who succeeded him, A.D. 1389, to extend the conquest begun by his grandfather to the boundaries of the Greek empire in the East. All the countries from the Hellespont to the Euphrates acknowledged his sway; while on the other side, whatever yet adhered to the Greek empire in Thrace, Macedonia, and Thessaly, submitted to Turkish masters. Bayazid stationed a fleet of galleys at Galipoli to command the Hellespont. At Nicopolis he defeated a confederate army of 100,000 Franks under John Count of Nevers, whom he made prisoner.

At length (A.D. 1395) his attention was directed to the conquest of Constantinople; and the dreaded catastrophe was only averted by the consent of Manuel, successor of John Palæologus, to pay an annual tribute of 30,000 crowns of gold.

But this respite was of short duration; the truce was soon violated by the restless sultan, and an army of Ottomans again threatened the devoted capital. Manuel in his distress implored the assistance of his Latin " brethren," and a reinforcement of troops from this quarter (a forlorn-hope) protracted the siege until Timur-lang, known in Europe by the name of Tamerlane, the Mogul conqueror, diverted the attention of Bayazid by invading his Eastern possessions. Thus the fall of Constantinople was deferred for some fifty years longer.

A.D. 1402. Timur-lang, surnamed the *lame*, although a descendant of Yanghiz Khan in the female line, rose from the state of a shepherd-lad to the possession of an empire more extensive than that of Alexander. His first conquest was Sogdiana; from thence he advanced to the conquest of Persia, took Bagdad, penetrated to the farthest part of India, and on his return from thence he fell upon Syria and Asia Minor. His aid was solicited by the Muhammadan princes whom Bayazid had deposed, as also by the brother of the absent Greek emperor.

Timur summoned the Turkish sultan to raise the siege, and the two formidable enemies met on the plains of Ancyra (Angora) in Galatia. After one of the most furious battles ever recorded in history, Bayazid was defeated and taken prisoner, and put into an iron cage, according to the vulgar tale.* Thus the Moguls became masters of all Asia; and, if they had been possessed of ships they might have overrun Europe. But the invasion of these hordes led to no permanent conquests; Timur had no troops to leave behind him to maintain his power, and the populations were abandoned to anarchy.†

---

* Local tradition records the exact locality of this great engagement to have been the plain of Chibuk-Abad, north of Angora, now Anguri.—W. F. A.

† The Turks tell a characteristic story regarding the spirit of discord prevalent in Cilicia, which is not equalled in any part of the world. Each inhabitant would, if he could, drink the blood of his neighbour.

They say that Timur-lang used to carry with him forty cases containing his treasure, and that he had eighty slaves, to whom he confided the guard of his person and these cases, half of whom by turns watched while the other half reposed. Arrived before Adana on his way back, he overheard his guards concerting among each other to kill him, and divide the spoil between them; and he understood them to say that they would wait till their companions awoke, to be all agreed. Upon this Timur-lang,

Of the five sons of Bayazid who after his death contended for the sovereignty, Muhammad I. was the most conspicuous, and obtained the ascendency. He employed the eight years of his reign in eradicating the vices produced by civil discord, and in establishing the Ottoman power over Cilicia and the other provinces of Asia Minor on a firmer basis.

His son Amurad II. besieged Constantinople, A.D. 1422, with an army of 200,000 Turks and Asiatic volunteers; but after a siege of two months he was called away to Brusa to quell a domestic revolt excited by his brother. The effete empire was allowed a respite of thirty years, during which Manuel sank into the grave, and his son John Palæologus II. was permitted to reign in consideration of a tribute which he paid to the Turks of 300,000 aspres, and the renunciation and abandonment of all the territory without the walls of Constantinople. Amurad was much taken up with the Hungarian war, and twice abdicated the throne, preferring the prayers and religious practices of the society of the dervishes to the cares of royalty.

John Palæologus was succeeded by his brother Constantine (A.D. 1443), a youth of fair promise, and who defended his country bravely for a time. But it was ordained that the last of the Greek emperors should bear the same name as the first and founder of Constantinople. On the 29th of May, A.D. 1438, the ill-fated city fell into the hands of Muhammad II., the son of Amurad, who took it after a siege of fifty-three days. Thus was sealed the fate of the Christian government in the East, at the same time that the Turkish government was finally established in Europe.

Muhammad II. marched a large army into Asia Minor against Uzzum Hassan, a powerful Turkman chief, and obtained a complete victory over him on the plain of Gialdaran in Upper Armenia.

Bayazid II. succeeded his father A.D. 1481, and inherited his martial character, but did not meet with all his success in military affairs. During the long wars which his father had carried on in Europe the eastern provinces had been neglected, and the sultan of Egypt, taking advantage of this supineness, had made himself master of all Syria, Cilicia, and part of Anatolia. Bayazid undertook a great expedition into Asia Minor to recover these provinces, and two battles were fought by the rival sultans in Cilicia, and the cities of Adana and Tarsus were taken

pretending to awake, ordered the whole army in motion, saying that there must be something treacherous in the very ground whereon they were encamped, which could make the select of his followers so faithless. And that is the reason, say the Turks, why he did not take Adana.

and retaken by both parties with alternate success. At length Bayazid, although vanquished, had the tact to conclude an advantageous peace, by which all Cilicia was ceded to him as far as the Syrian gates (A.D. 1492). He then returned to prosecute the wars against the Venetians in the Morea; in which expeditions he caused all the dust from his shoes to be collected, in order that the same being put into his coffin, might witness in his favour at the day of judgment, of his having carried on the war against the infidels with unremitting vigilance.

Bayazid was succeeded, A.D. 1512, by his son Sulaiman I., who began his reign by poisoning his father and putting his two brothers to death. His next step was to make war on Shah Ismail Sufi of Persia, whom he defeated in the plain of Gialdaran in Upper Armenia (which had before been the scene of Muhammad II.'s victory), and obliged him to retreat to the southern part of his dominions. The city of Tabriz fell into Sulaiman's hands, and he at first resolved on wintering there, but was dissuaded by his officers on account of the intense cold; and he returned to Amasiyah, and soon after to Constantinople, to prepare for a greater expedition. A very formidable army was again levied, at the head of which he marched into Syria and Egypt, carrying every thing before him, and completely subduing both countries, the military sovereigns of which were both slain, and he led in triumph to Constantinople the last khalif of the second dynasty of the Abbassides.

Sulaiman II., surnamed the *Magnificent*, A.D. 1520, succeeded his father Selim. He is looked upon as the greatest of the Turkish emperors, for, independent of his great victories, he was the friend of literature and art, as well as a just prince. He took Belgrade, and also the island of Rhodes, after a gallant resistance, and won the famous battle of Mohatz (A.D. 1526). In the following year Buda fell into his hands. In his war with Austria he was not so fortunate; for after having made twenty assaults on Vienna, he was obliged to raise the siege and return to Constantinople. Unable to remain inactive, he set out on an expedition against Shah Tamasp of Persia, besieged and took Bagdad, and through the zeal of his lieutenants carried his arms into Africa. Many cities on the coast of Barbary were added to the empire during his long and victorious reign of forty-six years.

The short reign of Selim II., who ascended the throne in A.D. 1566, was distinguished by no remarkable event except the taking of the island of Cyprus and the loss of the battle of Lepanto in the Morea, in which it is said that 32,000 Turks perished.

Amurad III., son of Selim, began his reign (A.D. 1574) by strangling five of his brothers. The Shah of Persia having invaded his eastern provinces, he marched to attack him, and retook the city of Tabriz, which the Persians had seized during the last reign.

Muhammad III., one of the greatest monsters that ever disgraced the annals of history, succeeded the weak Amurad A.D. 1594. He began his reign by strangling nineteen of his brothers, and causing ten of his father's wives to be thrown into the Bosphorus, in the fear that they might prove pregnant. His reign of nine years was marked throughout by cruelty and treachery, and just before his death he executed his own son and his son's mother on suspicion of treason.

Ahmed I., second son of Muhammad III., succeeded to the throne A.D. 1604, at the age of fifteen; and after a reign of twelve years he was succeeded by his brother,

Mustafa I. (A.D. 1617), who made himself so odious by his savage disposition, that he was deposed by the Janissaries after a reign of three months, and his nephew

Osman II. was placed on the throne; and after a brief reign of four years and four months he also was deposed, and Mustafa I. was once more elevated to the throne by the intrigues of the Janissaries. These were at this time a real Prætorian body, and very soon after put the sovereign of their choice to death.

Amurad IV., son of Ahmed I., succeeded (A.D. 1622), and proved as sanguinary a tyrant as his grandfather Muhammad III. had been; for he perpetrated all sorts of excesses, some of which seem to be scarcely credible,— such, for example, as amusing himself by shooting his subjects from a balcony. The Pasha of Erzerum having thrown off his allegiance, and united with the Shah of Persia to devastate some of the Turkish provinces in Asia, Amurad marched at the head of 200,000 men to stop their progress. With this immense force he entered Cilicia, and laid waste the Taurus and other countries. Having reduced Trebizond and Erzerum, he marched into Syria, with the intention of proceeding on a pilgrimage to Mecca ; but it appears that he did not go beyond Damascus, and returned to Constantinople in 1635. Three years afterwards he undertook the conquest of Persia; but after taking Bagdad he was persuaded to sign a treaty of peace, and he again returned to Constantinople, to execute a project he had long been revolving in his mind, which was no less than the utter destruction of the Ottoman race. Death, however, put an end to his design. The house which this sultan inhabited at Adana is still to be seen, but in a dilapidated condition. The door leading to the upper story is walled up, as, according to traditionary report, it is unlawful for any one to occupy the seat of the monarch, to prevent which this precau-

SULTANS FROM 1640 TO 1807.

tion was taken; or perhaps, we might also conclude, in superstitious horror of his character and crimes.

Ibrahim I., the brother of Amurad, succeeded him A.D. 1640. This prince fitted out an expedition against Candia. The siege is remarkable in history for the horrible murders and atrocities perpetrated during its progress; but this island, the pride of the Archipelago, was not annexed to the Ottoman dominions till the reign of his successor.

Ibrahim I. was strangled by the Janissaries A.D. 1648, and his son Muhammad IV., a boy seven years old, was placed on the throne. In the early part of the reign of this prince the siege of Candia was pushed with vigour, and terminated favourably for the Turks. In the latter part of Ibrahim's life the reverses he had met with in Hungary so enraged him, that he swore he would feed his horse on the altar of St. Peter at Rome. For this purpose he prepared a large army, with which he besieged Vienna in 1683, but was completely foiled and compelled to raise the siege by the bravery of the celebrated Sobieski. After a long reign of nearly forty years he was succeeded, A.D. 1687, by

Sulaiman III. his brother, who only reigned three years.

Ahmed II., brother of Sulaiman, succeeded in A.D. 1690, and reigned four years.

Mustafa II., a nephew of the two former sultans, was elected by the Janissaries A.D. 1695, and, after a reign of eight years, was deposed in favour of his brother,

Ahmed III., who, after an inglorious reign of twenty-seven years, was obliged to abdicate in favour of his nephew

Muhammad V., who, raised to the throne A.D. 1730, reigned twenty-four years, and was then succeeded, in A.D. 1754, by his brother,

Osman III., who reigned only two years, and was then succeeded by his nephew (A.D. 1757),

Mustafa III., son of Muhammad V., during whose reign the wars with Russia began. Mustafa III. was succeeded (A.D. 1776) by his brother,

Abd'ul Hamid I., who was not more fortunate in repelling the encroachments of the Russians on his territory than his brother had been; at his death the throne was filled (A.D. 1789) by

Selim III., the only son of Mustafa III. This ill-fated prince sustained repeated losses in his wars with Russia, in spite of the reforms in the army and navy which he introduced, and the adoption of European customs and improvements, and which proved so displeasing to the Janissaries that they deposed him, and soon after put him to death.

Mustafa V., cousin of Selim III., was proclaimed sultan A.D. 1807;

but he reigned only one year, when he was also murdered. Of the pretended son of this prince, Nadir Bey, I shall have occasion to speak further on.

Mahmud II., the brother of Mustafa V., and the only surviving male of the Ottoman line, was raised to the throne A.D. 1808 by the Janissaries, and he proved himself superior to any of his predecessors in political courage and sagacity. He temporised and cajoled the Janissaries, until he could seize a fitting opportunity, which occurred on the 14th June, A.D. 1826, when he caused them all to be put to death, and restored tranquillity to the empire. His name will ever be memorable by the reforms he began, and which have since been slowly but steadily carried out by his son, Abd'ul Masjid, the present sultan, who ascended the throne on the 11th July, 1839, and a few months after gave to the world the before unheard-of spectacle of a despotic monarch granting voluntarily a constitution to his people, by the well-known Hatti Sherif of Gulhanah.*

* As this document is quite unique in Eastern history, we give a few extracts:

"These new institutions should have three objects in view:—first, to guarantee to our subjects perfect security of life, honour, and property; secondly, the regular levying and assessing of taxes; and thirdly, a regular system for the raising of troops, and fixing the time of their service.

"For, in truth, are not life and honour the most precious of all blessings? What man, however averse his disposition to violent means, can withhold having recourse to them, and thereby injure both the government and his country, when both his life and honour are in jeopardy? If, on the contrary, he enjoys in this respect full security, he will not stray from the paths of loyalty, and all his actions will tend to increase the prosperity of the government and his countrymen. If there be absence of security of property, every one remains callous to the voice of his prince and country. No one cares about the progress of the public good, absorbed as one remains with the insecurity of his own position. If, on the other hand, the citizen looks upon his property as secure, of whatever nature it be, then, full of ardour for his interests, of which for his own contentment he endeavours to enlarge the sphere, thereby to extend that of his enjoyments, he feels every day in his heart the attachment for his prince and for his country grow stronger, as well as his devotedness to their cause. These sentiments in him become the source of the most praiseworthy actions."

CHAPTER VII.

MODERN HISTORY OF CILICIA—RISE OF KUTCHUK ALI UGLU—HIS MEANS OF RE-
VENUE—ACTS OF CRUELTY—BAYAS—MODE OF LIFE AND CHARACTERISTICS
—SEIZES THE MASTER OF AN ENGLISH VESSEL—CAPTURES A FRENCH MER-
CHANTMAN—BRIBES THE TURKS WHO ARE SENT AGAINST HIM—PUTS HIS
FRIEND THE DUTCH CONSUL OF ALEPPO INTO PRISON—FORCES A CARAVAN
OF MERCHANTS TO RANSOM HIM—A CHARACTERISTIC ANECDOTE.

THE history[*] of the Ottoman Empire during the last two centuries, till we come to the epochs of Mahmud II. and of his son Abd'ul Masjid, furnishes little or no pleasing retrospect; but is on the whole a dark picture of tyranny, cruelty, and barbarism. The sultans, no longer permitted to be at the head of their armies, were buried in the effeminacy of the seraglio and the mazes of an intriguing court. They gave up the administration of affairs to their officers, who sold the government of the provinces to the highest bidder, while the purchasers were permitted to indemnify themselves by the plunder of the towns and villages. The population, oppressed by repeated acts of injustice, were glad to screen themselves behind a lesser evil, and submit to the usurped rule of factious chiefs who became rebels to the authority of the Porte, and erected *de facto* petty independent kingdoms, which they left at their deaths either to their children or to the most intriguing, brave, or impudent of their followers. The weakness of a government enfeebled by venality, and no longer maintained or held together by those principles which called it into existence, prevented the adoption of vigorous measures to punish rebellion, and subdue those chiefs who had availed themselves of the general discontent

[*] If a blank occurs in the history of Cilicia for the last two hundred years, the reason is, that no archives are kept in the provinces as at Constantinople, as each succeeding governor carries away with him in a bag the small bundle of official documents; and that for two reasons: first, because he is afraid to leave behind him any traces of his misrule, which might be employed subsequently by his enemies against him; and secondly, from the summary way in which business is transacted,—mostly by word of mouth,—very few papers are necessary, and the small stock can be transported with great facility, the whole object and aim of these governors being to make money as quickly as they can before the order for their recall is obtained by their enemies.

to flatter their followers with the hope of impunity, and who were thus enabled to depose or set aside the pashas sent to execute the orders of the Porte; and the ministers at Constantinople, unable to carry on the business of the government (or even to maintain themselves in their posts,) from the exhausted state of the treasury, drained by increasing luxury and extravagance, were induced to compound with a power they had not the means to destroy.

From these causes may be traced the circumstance that, for a long series of years, many of the provinces, particularly those of Asia Minor, were wrested from the Porte, or merely held in nominal allegiance to it, by the strength of successive chieftains of powerful Turkman tribes, called "Darah Beys," *vulgo* Darah Begs, among whom the famous family of Kara Osman Uglu, "son of the black Osman," hold a distinguished place. Cilicia has been in the same position, torn by contending factions of chiefs among the Turkman tribes which have in succession contended for the supreme authority; and I think it not irrelevant to my subject to follow up the history of some of these chieftains during the last forty-six years, which may perhaps expose in a clearer point of view the state to which the country has been reduced by the defective system of government above alluded to, and explain the effects of such a system on the provinces, better than a more studied or elaborate account.

One of these Darah Beys, Khalil Bey, better known by the name of Kutchuk Ali Uglu,[*] was in 1800 a Turkman chief of the mountains in the vicinity of Bayas (near the ancient Issus), which is now almost deserted,[†] but in his time was a populous and flourishing town, that carried on a considerable trade with Egypt, and produced annually ten

---

[*] A sketch of the life of Khalil Bey (or *Bay*, the *a* pronounced as in nay, say, may, bay-tree, &c.), commonly called Kutchuk Ali Uglu, has been published by Messrs. Mangles and Irby, and still more lately by Mr. Neale, in both cases from statements or documents obtained from my father, Mr. John Barker; but as the real facts of the case have been much mutilated at second-hand, and as I shall have to give the life of the chieftain's two sons, which are intimately connected with the history of Cilicia, a more correct and detailed history will not perhaps be unwelcome to the reader, and will serve as an introduction to events in later times.

[†] There are in the present day a group of very handsome buildings at Bayas. A spacious stone bazar, or more properly speaking, bazastain, solidly arched over, and approached by noble portals, opens at the centre, to the east, into a khan with a large paved yard, having a fountain in the centre, and the usual stables with galleried apartments above.

To the west, another passage, after leading by some massive domed buildings which constituted the public Hammam or bath, opens into a court-yard, at one end of which is a pretty little mosque (masjid) with a graceful minaret (minar), and at the other the entrance to a polygonal castle of considerable strength and dimensions. This is indeed the most complete and compact thing of its kind to be met with perhaps in the

thousand pounds of silk. Kutchuk Ali laid the foundation of his power by making nocturnal excursions from the mountains to rob the gardens of Bayas. Some gardeners, with a view to purchase exemption from his depredations, stipulated to pay him a trifling yearly tribute, or *blackmail*. Their example was followed by others, who were petty merchants, glad to secure the mass of their property by entering into similar engagements; and from a rotolo* of coffee, or a few rotolos of rice, the whole town became at length compelled to furnish a stated contribution.

This fund enabled Kutchuk Ali to support himself at the head of a band of forty or fifty robbers; and he then aspired to render himself master of the place. He began by waylaying the heads of the principal families; and in the course of a few years he succeeded in exterminating every individual of such as possessed any weight or influence at Bayas or in its territory. The last member of the most influential of these families, whose adherents he could neither subdue by open force nor corrupt by bribery, successfully contended for some time with him for the supreme authority, till at length Kutchuk Ali, having lulled his suspicions by giving him his daughter in marriage, murdered him with his own hands; and he has often been heard to warn his own children against a male infant the offspring of that marriage; advising them to crush the crocodile in the egg, lest he should one day revenge on them his father's blood.† With a very inconsiderable number of dependents, who often did not exceed 200 in number, Kutchuk Ali succeeded in impressing with terror and dismay the minds of the people by a system of cruelty, continued for many years; and he occasioned much trouble to the Porte, between whom and the rebel there existed, however, a

East. Every thing that is essential to the nucleus of an oriental city is gathered into the smallest possible compass, and is in excellent preservation.

These structures are attributed in the Mecca *Itinerary* to Ibraham Khan-Zadah, better known as Sakali Muhammad Pasha, or the " bearded pasha Muhammad," who was wuzir to Sultan Sulaiman II.

The river of Bayas flows past these buildings on the south side; and at the port, distant about a mile and a half, is a castle with a square bawn and a small village. The modern village of Bayas, where the governor resides, is about two and a half miles north, upon another and lesser rivulet; and between the two is the village of Kuratas. There is also a small village of Syrians of the Greek Church on the river, a little above the castle and khan of Bayas. This, as the site also of the antique BALÆ or baths, was certainly one of the most charming spots on the coast of Syria.—W. F. A.

* A *rotolo* is a Turkish weight, varying in different parts of the empire; in Cilicia it is equal to five and a half pounds.

† Kutchuk Ali Uglu's second son, Mustuk Bey, as we shall see by the sequel, mindful of his father's injunctions, actually put them in practice, and murdered this unfortunate individual.

reciprocal desire to be on a footing of friendship, founded on mutual advantage, and which prevented their continuing long on terms of either real or ostensible hostility.

Kutchuk Ali's territorial government was, it may naturally be imagined, such as to afford him but very slender means of drawing wealth from the impoverished inhabitants of Bayas and its environs. His revenue, therefore, in a great measure, was derived from the casual passage of travellers and caravans through his territory, and whom he laid under such contributions as he thought they would bear, rather than be obliged, by going another way, to make a very inconvenient journey. Sometimes his rapacity and naturally brutal inclinations impelled him to overstep the bounds he meant to prescribe to his own extortions, and then the Porte testified its displeasure by prohibiting travellers from passing through Bayas. As soon as the rebel found his coffers in need of fresh supplies, the Porte succeeded in forcing him to sue for pardon, which was seldom long withheld, on account of the necessity of procuring a safe passage for the annual grand caravan of pilgrims from Constantinople to Mecca, which was obliged either to pass through his territory or to make a circuitous and fatiguing journey through the mountains of Cappadocia. When the caravan of pilgrims came into Kutchuk Ali's dominions, it yielded him a very considerable revenue; for he taxed every individual according to his own caprice, but always, however, with an eye to the rule above mentioned. On the approach of this caravan to Bayas, Kutchuk Ali sent some of his household to compliment on his arrival the chief of the caravan—a personage of great distinction, who dismissed the rebel's emissaries with rich presents for him. On such occasions, the horses it was customary to present to Kutchuk Ali would be returned, with a hint that they would be preferred completely accoutred in the usual gilt and silver trappings. Much time was invariably lost in negotiating and stipulating the precise tribute required, but as invariably the measure of his rapacity was filled, the caravan was permitted to proceed.

In order the better to dispose the pilgrims to submit to his extortions, Kutchuk Ali was always careful to exhibit, as proofs both of his power and his cruelty, the spectacle of two bodies impaled at the gate of Bayas. It happened on one of these occasions, when the caravan was approaching, that his prisons were empty, and he had no victims that he could impale. He imparted his embarrassment to a convivial companion. "The caravan," said he, "will be here to-morrow, and we have not yet prepared the customary execution. Look ye, pick me out two from among my servants." His friend expostulated; and while he was endeavouring to induce him to abandon his design by the assurance that every thing would proceed in due order without the execution in question, Kutchuk Ali, still revolving the matter in his mind, and stroking his beard, exclaimed, " I have it: go fetch me Yakub the Christian; he has been four months in bed sick of a fever, and can never recover." The poor wretch was forthwith dragged out of his bed, strangled, impaled, and hung up! When it is considered that the forces of this monster did not exceed two hundred armed men, it becomes a matter of surprise, even to those who are well aware of the once existing weakness and indifference of the Sultan's government, that such a bandit could have been so long allowed to brave the authority of the Porte. But it was at that time rendered almost powerless by evils and abuses that have since, to a great extent, been remedied and corrected.

Kutchuk Ali was well aware that his usurped power rested on the tottering foundation of public opinion, and the little arts he put in practice with a view to conceal his weakness are characteristic and curious. Whenever an individual of distinction came into his territory (which was only to be approached through dense woods), in order to deceive the new comer by an ostentatious display of his forces, he disposed his men in the thickets, so as to pass and repass at several points before the traveller like soldiers on a stage; thus the reports even of an ocular witness became fallacious, and the power of Kutchuk Ali was extolled and exaggerated all over the Turkish dominions. He also erected numerous tall towers, which he scattered along the eminences of his mountains, and which from afar appeared like the turrets of so many impregnable castles. They were, however, in reality nothing more than rude edifices composed of mud and straw, and white-washed with lime, which a night's heavy rain frequently damaged.

Kutchuk Ali also occupied the narrow passage known in history, more especially in the Anabasis, as the Cilician and Syrian gates, as well as the castle of Bayas. It was at this latter spot that Heraclius in his first campaign disembarked, choosing it as the most secure spot in which to strengthen himself and concentrate his forces against the Saracens.

Cicero also apparently writes to his friend from this place : " Castra habemus ea ipsa quæ contra Darium habuerat apud Issum Alexander Imperator, haud paulo melior quam tu aut ego."

Its modern name is derived perhaps from the Turkish word *bayaz* (white), descriptive of the snow that for a great part of the year is seen on the summit of its grey mountainous cliffs, which descend abruptly towards the sea, leaving a narrow tract between its precipices and the sea.*

Kutchuk Ali was short in stature, and in 1800 appeared to be about sixty years of age; his body was thick-set and muscular, and his head disproportionably large. His face was round, bluff, and flat, and it was rendered apparently flatter by a chronic disorder which had carried away the bones of his nose, and caused him to snuffle as he articulated; and it is remarkable that his son, Mustuk Bey, speaks much in the same way, although he is quite free from any infirmity. But this is a fashionable tone prevalent among the Turks, and which they ape from one another, doubtless considering it very impressive and sonorous. Kutchuk Ali had nevertheless a very insinuating address, and often deceived by his mild and courteous demeanour those who did not discriminate his real character in the tiger-like glances of his restless eye. When he was raised to the high rank of a Pasha of three tails, he altered nothing from the rude simplicity of his way of life when only a Turkman freebooter. As an instance of this he had two wives, who so far from being secluded and guarded by eunuchs (yunuks) in splendid apartments, were in no way distinguished from the other women of his family. They made bread and fetched water from the spring unveiled, having only one distinction, that of occupying exclusively two separate rooms, which were divided by a slight wooden partition, instead of the curtain which served the same purpose in the tents of his forefathers. Whenever he intended to honour one of his consorts with his company, he sent to bid her prepare for the occasion; and the thought being always suggested when he was wholly or partially intoxicated, the poor woman had generally to watch in vain for his appearance, while he gradually sank down on his carpet in forgetfulness of everything in this world. But however deep might have been his nocturnal potations, he always rose at the first dawn of day to call his men to their daily labours, and in all seasons and in all weathers accompanied them to the field of their toils. He sat without mat or carpet on the ground to superintend their operations, which were not, as might be supposed, in the chief industry of the country (mulberry-plantations for silkworms), nor in the useful labours of rearing garden fruits and vegetables, of which he knew not the want. His habitual occupations were

* Between Bayas and Alexandretta is the river Markatz (ancient Kersus), with village and castle (Markatz Kalahsi) on its banks, and ruins towards the sea-shore; while beyond is the Macedonian relic now called Sakal Tutan,—the Bomitæ or altars of Pliny,—all comprised within the Cilician and Syrian Gates.—W. F. A.

in pulling down, rebuilding, and changing the form of the white-washed turrets and sham battlements before described, with the view, no doubt, of preventing revolt among his followers by keeping them constantly employed in hard labour.

He prided himself on the discipline he maintained. " I am not," he would say, " as other Darah Beys are,* fellows without faith, who allow their men to stop travellers on the king's highway;—I am content with what God sends me. I await his good pleasure, and, *Alhumdlillah* (God be praised), he never leaves me long in want of any thing."

Upon Kutchuk Ali's attaining the rank of Pasha it was thought indispensable that he should exchange the Turkman sash and turban for the *kaük*, a head-dress of distinction. A Tartar accidentally passing through Bayas was commissioned to bring him one, but it proved to be too small for his head: he wrote for another, but it again fell short of the proper dimensions. Disgusted at his ill-success, he gave up the attempt, coming to the conclusion, as he said, that if *kaüks* could not be made for *heads*, his head could not be made expressly for them.

In 1798, Mr. Fowls, master of an English vessel in the harbour of Alexandretta, went with four of his men to water at the Markatz Chai, a river in the territory of Bayas, at a place before alluded to, and called by sailors Jonas' Pillars. Here they were seized by Kutchuk Ali Uglu, and thrown into prison, and a large sum was demanded for their release. Before the necessary arrangements could be made for its payment, the master was driven by despair to put a period to his existence by precipitating himself from a high tower in which he was confined; and all the others perished soon after, except a boy twelve years old, named Charles Edwards, who was sent by Kutchuk Ali as a present to his friend Mr. Masseyk, Dutch consul at Aleppo. It is not known exactly what measures were taken by the mission at Constantinople to obtain the necessary satisfaction for this act of violence, but it is certain that none was ever given by the savage perpetrator.

Two years after this event (in 1800) a French ship from Marseilles, richly laden with merchandise for Aleppo, was, by the captain's ignorance of the locality, taken under the walls of Bayas, when the master, with a part of the crew, supposing that they had anchored at Alexandretta, landed in search of the consular establishment, and were conducted to the governor, who received them with every mark of hospi-

* Chiefs of Turkman tribes, and self-appointed governors of districts in Turkey, whom the Porte used to find it necessary to confirm in their posts, and even to load with presents and raise to various dignities, in order to obtain through their means a portion of the contributions which they levy,—having no better means to enforce obedience.

tality; but while he was entertaining them with a sumptuous repast, his men were occupied in taking possession of the vessels. This accomplished, he immediately unloaded and sunk the ship, sending the crew by land to the French consul at Alexandretta. Remonstrances were made to him on this act of violence by all the consular authorities at Aleppo, and in particular by his intimate friend the Dutch consul, to whom he replied in these terms :

" My dear friend,—You know very well that consistently with the friendship subsisting between us, property and life itself are indifferent matters. Nay, I swear by God, that for your sake I would sacrifice my son Dada Bey; but I entreat you not to drive me to the extremity of denying you what it is impossible for me to grant. My dear friend, place yourself in my position. I am in disgrace with my sovereign, without having given him any just cause for this displeasure ; I am threatened with attacks from the four quarters of the earth ; I am without money, I am without means; and the ever-watchful providence of the Almighty sends me a vessel laden with merchandise ! Say, would you in my place lay hold of it or not ? I know very well the Franks will claim restitution of the property from the Sublime Porte, and that is precisely what I want, because an opportunity will then be offered to me of negotiating my pardon."

On the receipt of this letter all hopes of recovering any thing by amicable means were given up in despair, and the French consul made application to his superior at Constantinople, and obtained several imperial commands on the subject. Three Turkish caravallas (ships of war) were sent to Bayas to enforce obedience to the orders of the Porte. Kutchuk Ali retired to his mountains. The caravallas fired a few guns against empty houses and dilapidated fortresses, and in a very short time, having consumed their stock of provisions, the officers and men on board were glad to accept such as were liberally tendered them by Kutchuk Ali, who soon obtained, through the customary means of bribing with French watches and fine French broadcloth, the good will of all the commanders of the ships sent against him. So great was their astonishment and satisfaction at the rebel's princely magnificence, that they contracted with him solemn engagements of private friendship, and promised him their intercession in his behalf with the Porte on their return to Constantinople. The dignity of an additional *tail* was obtained for him on this occasion, with an imperial firman *pro formá*, ordering restitution of the property. In compliance with this order, Kutchuk Ali addressed a letter to the French consul at Aleppo to announce that he was ready to obey the commands of the sultan, but the cargo of the ship in question having been *converted to use*, he offered as an equivalent to make over to the proprietors of the goods sundry plantations belonging to him in the territory of Bayas. The merchants of Aleppo rejected with scorn the proposal, as adding insult to injustice; particularly as they considered that the environs of Bayas are unhealthy, and their agents would be liable to take the malignant fever of the place whilst directing such an arduous enterprise as the cultivation of land. The neighbourhood was also reputed dangerous; and the poverty of the inhabitants was supposed to render it impossible for them to sell any produce for a quarter of its value. Yet the merchants could not obtain any other redress.*

In the beginning of 1801, Mr. John Masseyk, Dutch Consul-general in Aleppo, was arrested by Kutchuk Ali Uglu, as he was returning from Constantinople, although furnished with an imperial firman for the exercise of his official functions, at a period when the Porte was at peace with Holland. The proceedings of Kutchuk Ali on this occasion will serve to elucidate his character, which will be exhibited in a curious light when it is considered that there had for many years previous to the detention of the Dutch consul existed between him and the pasha, as has already been observed, habits of the most cordial friendship and interchange of gifts, according to oriental custom.

On the arrival of the consul at Bayas he was immediately thrown into prison, bound with chains, and stripped of everything except the apparel he wore. But the pasha, with great circumspection, avoided all opportunities of being thrown in contact with his prisoner; for it is a peculiarity worthy of remark, that this tyrant, whenever he ordered a bad action to be committed, kept himself personally aloof from the scene of its perpetration, from an idea that it would lower his importance to assume the office of executioner to his own orders, or perhaps in this instance from very shame for thus ill-treating an old friend. The sum fixed for the consul's ransom was 25,000 piastres of those days (about 2000*l.*); but being unable to produce more than 7500, Mr. Masseyk underwent during the period of eight months every species of ill-usage. Every means was tried to force him to embrace the Muhammadan religion, and to extort from him the money required for his ransom; to which end they would at one time confine him in a damp dungeon with-

* No doubt, fevers prevail at Bayas at certain seasons of the year, as in other parts of the coast of Syria; but the situation is open and dry, the soil gravelly yet fertile, and well supplied with clear and rapid streams. The climate is mild and serene; there is no marshy ground except at Markatz, which could be easily drained. Altogether Bayas is differently circumstanced to Alexandretta, and would appear to be as healthy, as fertile, and ought to be as wealthy, as any spot on the coast of Syria.—W. F. A.

out light, and often without sustenance for twenty-four hours. At another they would threaten him with immediate death; and once, in order to shew that their menaces were not wholly nugatory, two innocent wretches, who had been arrested under similar circumstances with himself, were impaled before him, for having delayed, as he was informed, to procure the money for their ransom.

When the news spread abroad that Kutchuk Ali had entrapped an European, the mountaineers descended in crowds to see how much humanity the tyrant exhibited; and Mr. Masseyk used to relate that being one day engaged in writing, a man who had thrust his head through the bars of his prison-window, after contemplating his person and occupation for some time, exclaimed with reproachful indignation, "What, is it possible the wretch is so lost to all sense of shame as to hold *an effendi* (a clerk) in captivity?" referring evidently to the well-known rights and *immunities* enjoyed by the learned, as well in this barbarous region as in Europe. This picture indeed resembles more the state of society in the twelfth and thirteenth centuries than that of the nineteenth; and to those who are unacquainted with Oriental ideas and customs, which have undergone so few changes for centuries past, might appear unfaithful to nature, were it not for what history has related of those dark ages.

Although Kutchuk Ali persisted in refusing to admit his prisoner to his presence, he more than once sent to him his lieutenant with consoling messages to assure him of his sympathy. "Tell him," said he, "that unfortunately my coffers were empty when his fate brought him into this territory; but let him not despair, God is great and mindful of us. Such vicissitudes of fortune are inseparable from the fate of men of renown, and from the lot of all born to fill high stations. Bid him be of good cheer; a similar doom has twice been mine, and once during nine months in the condemned cell of Abd'ul Rahman Pasha: but I never despaired of God's mercy, and all came right at last,—Alla karim (God is bountiful)."

At length, fortunately for this poor man, the arrival at Bayas of a caravan from Smyrna proceeding to Aleppo afforded Kutchuk Ali Uglu an excuse for extorting his ransom from the travelling merchants by obliging them to advance the money on the bond of his prisoner, whom he delivered into their hands as a slave sold to them for 17,500 piastres. This was a debt beyond Mr. Masseyk's means of discharging at once, but he paid it off by instalments, not without the hope that the Dutch Republic would come to his assistance. This it did in part, but he never recovered the whole amount. The restriction placed on his person proved, however, beneficial to the consul in one respect, inasmuch as he was by means of the rigid prison fare entirely cured of the gout, to which he had been much subjected previous to his incarceration; and he has frequently remarked to his friends, that Kutchuk Ali had in this respect unwittingly conferred on him an almost priceless favour, and had proved himself a better physician than friend.

The Porte at different times sent several pashas with considerable forces against this rebel; but whether owing to the natural defences that abound in the precipitous mountains, covered with forests into which he retreated, or to the system of compromise already described, the Sultan was never able to subdue him during forty years' existence in open defiance of his authority.*

Such is the individual whom Mr. John Barker, then British Consul at Aleppo, to whom I am mainly indebted for the foregoing facts, had the address to propitiate, in order to facilitate the transmission of despatches from the East India Company, which passed through his hands; and his influence with the rebel was so great, that he once induced him to give up goods to the amount of 6600*l.*, belonging to British merchants, which he had seized along with other property.

* My readers will perhaps be startled on hearing that, in the beginning of the present century, there was so little personal security even in the vicinity of a well-frequented harbour like that of Alexandretta, that the crews of two European vessels could have been subjected to such treatment, or that such an affront as the incarceration of a public officer could have been suffered to pass without redress of any kind having been obtained from the Porte. Let us hope, however, that as time has wrought many changes in Turkey since the establishment of the Nizam, or regular troops, by Sultan Mahmud, by which some of the chief rebels have been crushed and piracy put down in the Mediterranean, that a new turn to this state of things has been now definitively brought about, and that the light which is dawning even in the benighted East will prevent the recurrence of such scenes.

CHAPTER VIII.

DADA BEY, SON OF KUTCHUK ALI UGLU—HIS PIRATICAL EXPEDITIONS—REPELS THE ATTACKS OF THE TURKS—IS TAKEN BY STRATAGEM—IS BEHEADED AND BURNT—HISTORY OF MUSTAFA PASHA—KEL-AGA KILLED BY HAJI ALI BEY—DERVISH HAMID—STORY RELATED OF HAJI ALI BEY—CONQUESTS OF IBRAHIM PASHA—MUSTUK BEY PLACED IN POWER—COMPARISON BETWEEN THE EGYPTIAN AND TURKISH GOVERNMENTS.

IN 1808 Kutchuk Ali Uglu died, and was succeeded by his son Dada Bey. Mr. Masseyk, while in prison, having gained the goodwill of Dada Bey, conceived the hope that he might be induced to make him some reparation for the ill-treatment he had met with at his father's hands; and he wrote him a letter of condolence on his recent bereavement, in which he took occasion to remind him of the reprobation he had always expressed of his late parent's cruelty, and in a particular manner of his injustice to himself. Dada Bey received Mr. Masseyk's application with the usual tokens of sympathy and affection, but replied, "My dearest friend, you know very well that were I called upon to make restitution of all the money my late father (God have mercy on his soul!) unjustly acquired during a long life, all the stones of the mountains of Bayas converted into gold would not suffice."

Dada Bey was of large stature, and had an expressive countenance and a fine full black beard: he was about thirty years old when he succeeded to his father. He had not, however, the same tact and cunning, as he evinced in the circumstance of his being unable to keep out of the grasp of his enemies for more than nine years; and during this period he encouraged his people in all kinds of piracy, and his boats infested the coast, attacking vessels at anchor off Alexandretta, and among others a large ship belonging to Abdalla Bey, son of Abd'ul Rahman, Pasha of Baylan.

An individual still living, who formed one of an expedition undertaken to carry off some ships at Kaisanli, the roadstead of Tarsus, related to me the following fact:

"We were twenty-two in number, and started one night from Kara-Tash (Black Rock, ancient Mallus and Megarsus,) in a small boat. We found eleven small brigs of the country moored at Kaisanli, loading and unloading. We attacked them one by one with as little noise as possible. As they were not armed, and were taken by surprise, we had no difficulty in binding such of the crew as made any resistance; and having cut the cables, we made use of the lads on board to manœuvre the vessels, which we brought safely to Bayas, where they were detained till their proprietors sent large sums to ransom them."

Amin Pasha Chiapan Uglu, who governed at Uzgat, received an order from the Porte to send the head of Dada Bey to Constantinople. The Turkman chief of Uzgat sent 2000 irregular troops of those days to accompany an expedition which he ordered to be assembled from among the various Turkman tribes in the district of Tarsus and Adana: Kurmud-uglu Ali Bey, Kalaga, Bashaga, Tur-uglu, and Takal-uglu, from the territory of the former; and Osman Bey Jarid (son of Hussain Pasha), Malamangi-uglu, Kara Hajili, Karagiya, and Hamid Bey, father of Haji Ali Bey, from that of the latter. These chiefs collected about twelve or fifteen thousand men, and encamped on the sea-shore near Bayas for many days, without being able to make up their minds what plan to adopt in attacking the lion in his den; at last they agreed with Abd'ul Rahman Pasha of Baylan, and Chulak-uglu of Mar'ash, to fall upon him on all sides at the same time.

Dada Bey, who had more friends than enemies in this motley band, composed of all his neighbours, being informed by his spies of the position of the tent which contained the ammunition of the troops, sent a boat in the night, with two cannons of wood filled with powder and old nails. These were disembarked by some of his men, who having succeeded in placing them near the tent, set fire to the match and retreated to the boat. Only one exploded, and it had no other effect than that of awakening the astounded chiefs, who the next morning gave orders for a general attack. Dada Bey wished for nothing so much as to try the mettle of his men against a multitude of peasants, who he knew were assembled against their inclination to make war on a person whom they considered invincible. He posted Jin Yusuf of Karatash and a few men in the fort, with strict orders not to fire till the enemy arrived so close that every shot might tell, and to wait the signal of a discharge of two cannons from the turret above. He himself, with about 100 picked horsemen, fell on the troops in the rear; while Jin Yusuf, on the first volley, killed forty men; and the roaring of the cannon from above, the shot of which came over the heads of the dismayed Turkmans, sufficed to inspire all the terror he could desire. In half an hour there was no one to oppose him in the field, from which the soldiers retreated to Adana, and the Turkmans dispersed to their respective homes. Thus it constantly happened before the institution of the Nizam, that when any of the Turkman chiefs revolted, the Porte had no effectual means of compelling them to obedience, but was obliged to have recourse to the neighbouring tribes, who were unwilling to excite a lasting feud among their relatives (as they all intermarry), and only made a *feint* of attacking them. Thus the government was obliged to conform to their desires by coming to a compromise, wherein the outward dignity of the Porte was only consulted, whilst all the interests of these petty rebels were attended to, inasmuch as they were only submissive as long as it suited their purpose.

That which could not be effected by open violence was, however, effected by treachery. Mustafa Pasha, son of Abd'ul Rahman, Pasha of Baylan, Dada Bey's neighbour and personal enemy, seized on an accidental opportunity of destroying him. During four years that Mustafa had been pasha at Adana, he had endeavoured, by influence and intrigues at Constantinople, to obtain from the government an order that the whole of the country as far as Baylan, his native town, should be placed under his orders. Having accomplished this object, the first thing he did was to summon Dada Bey to submit to his authority, which of course the latter refused to do. Whereupon Mustafa Pasha sent his brother Ismail Bey, with four or five thousand men, to Bayas. Dada Bey, happening to pass alone at this time through a village close by, was betrayed by an old woman into the hands of a Baylanli named Tal-ughi, who chanced to be there. This man, with the assistance of a few others, succeeded in taking Dada Bey by surprise, when they bound him and took him prisoner to Adana. The people of the country had such an instinctive dread of Dada Bey, that it is reported that even the pasha refused to see him till he had been heavily chained. Dada Bey retorted upon his exulting enemy in terms of indignation all the insults he had received, and expressed infinite contempt for "a wretch who could so abuse the power which chance had given him over a *fallen lion*." His head was nevertheless cut off and sent to Constantinople, and his body was burnt in the court-yard under the windows of the palace, and the ashes scattered to the winds. Such was the insatiable feud that existed between these families!

Mustafa Pasha had in earlier years killed his brother Mulla Bey, in order to become master of Baylan; but another brother, Abdullah Bey, raised the populace against him and drove him away. He proceeded to Constantinople, where he obtained the pashalik of Adana, which he held seven years; he was then sent to Erzerum, and afterwards to Aleppo, where he remained two years. From this place he went to Acre, to attack Abdullah Pasha of that place; and he acted as lieutenant to Durwish or Dervish Pasha, commander-in-chief of the troops. He then returned to Aleppo for another year and a half, and was thence removed to the governorship of Damascus; and when at that place, he laid Jerusalem under heavy contributions. He was afterwards transferred to Bosna and Kurk-Kilisa, and subsequently he obtained the command of some troops, with whom he treacherously attacked the Russians in time of a truce or peace. On the Russian mission representing this perfidy to the Porte, he was, in *outward* appearance, disgraced and sent to Brusa, where he was lately living, as a private individual, in the enjoyment of his ill-acquired wealth, the reward of his crimes and cruelties. Few such adventurers, however, meet with such good fortune. They rarely escape the intrigues entered into against them, and generally return to the same state of obscurity as that from which they emerged, unless possessed of extraordinary ability, or of means to bribe their way to other employments as lucrative, by large sums which they have had time to amass during their stewardship. When well supported, they frequently secure the pecuniary assistance of their Armenian bankers (*sarraffs*), which they repay with an interest of 50 per cent.

People may have read in the newspapers published at Constantinople of such an effendi, to whom every virtue is attributed, having been promoted for his *patriotic* conduct to a post of distinction, and might have been led to imagine these men to be something above the common order of Turks; whereas those who, like myself, have had opportunities of knowing the truth, are aware that they were generally chosen from among the *servants* of older pashas.

On the death of Dada Bey, A.D. 1817, his brother Mustuk Bey, then twelve years old, took refuge in Maraash with Kalandar Pasha, and with whom he remained for some years, till after the departure of Mustafa Pasha; and during his minority of ten years, his uncle Zaitunuglu governed for him.

On his return to Bayas in 1827, Mustuk Bey was attacked by Haji Ali Bey;* at the same time that a certain Kel-Aga, chief of the Turkman tribe of Kugiuli, whose residence was in the mountains to the

* This man had constituted himself master of Adana and independent of the Porte's authority, and he had driven Muhammad Pasha (who had bought the post of governor of this province, and was on his way to take possession of his government) back from Kulak Bughaz. Muhammad Pasha was by this flagrant act of rebellion reduced to the necessity of returning to the capital, where he complained of his having been sent to occupy a post, which had cost him a large sum, of which he could not take quiet possession; and the pashalik of Erzerum was assigned to him to compensate him for his loss. After the usual delays in nominations of this kind, he was installed governor of that district.

north-westward of Taurus, and who had become absolute master of this last-mentioned town, thinking this a favourable moment to take Adana, had proceeded against that town with a large body of followers. Haji Ali Bey, hearing of this movement, made peace immediately with the young Mustuk Bey, and by a forced retrograde march reached Adana; and coming suddenly upon the encampment of Kel-Aga at night, and in the outskirts of the town, he surprised the chief, who was found dead drunk, and had his head cut off on the spot.

The father and grandfather of Kel-Aga both lost their heads in rebellion, the one by means of the bands of Tur-uglu, and the other by Sadik Aga; and Durwish Ahmed, son of Kel-Aga, is not an unworthy descendant of such ancestors. As a young man, Ahmed held the government of all the villages to the westward of Tarsus, in which Mursina and Kaisanli are included. Being related to most of the influential families of the country, he did what he pleased with impunity, abandoning himself to all and every imaginable excess. A dozen horsemen accompanied him wherever he went, and were made the ministers of his pleasures and vices by dragging instantly to his presence any woman or child he might call for in his drunken fits. The inhabitants of the villages in his district were obliged to submit to his heavy impositions, and to furnish the sum requisite to complete the taxes due from nearly a thousand persons whom he exempted from all contributions, because he shared with them the produce of their lands. This system of "protection," as it is termed, used to be very general in the Ottoman dominions; the ayans or nobles of all the large cities appropriating to themselves a large tract of country by sharing the produce with the proprietors, who give up a third or fourth of their income for the advantage of being exempted from paying the dues to government. This exemption the nobles were enabled to afford them, being members of the council of the city, to whom all political affairs were referred in conjunction with the pasha. The pasha himself was generally, if not invariably, won over to their party, for without their participation he could not hope to carry on public business. Thus they contrived to protect each other's interests, and the whole weight of taxation fell on the poorer classes and those who had not the advantage of an "ayan's support." This system resembled in some respect the feudal, and took its origin when the country was ruled by rebel chiefs, whose partisans were respected by their independent colleagues in return for the same courtesy mutually shewn to one another.

Intrigue and the love of power perpetuated this state of things after the cause which had given rise to it had vanished, and it was carried on in miniature in all the villages, each elder having his *protected*. Durwish Ahmed had led this dissipated life for some time after his father's death, when his cousin, Mustafa Aga, was induced to bribe the governor of Tarsus with 15,000 piastres to appoint him instead of Ahmed; and he was accordingly summoned to Tarsus, where he agreed to appear at the governor's house, on the guarantee of his father-in-law and chief of the Zaims (Turkish irregular troops). On this occasion, an account of the revenue that had passed through his hands was demanded of him, and he was brought in a debtor to the government of 95,000 piastres. Ahmed evaded paying any portion of this by privately bribing the governor with a sum *for himself* of 30,000 piastres; and he might, probably, have been re-established in his post, had not the governor been shortly afterwards recalled.

But to return to Haji Ali Bey. A year after the death of Kel-Aga, (A.D. 1828,) Hussain Pasha, general-in-chief of the army sent into Syria against Ibrahim Pasha of Egypt, arrived in Cilicia at the head of his troops. Haji Ali Bey, unable to resist so overwhelming a force, was compelled to dissimulate; and therefore, putting on the semblance of perfect submission, he went as far as Kulak Bughaz to meet the commander-in-chief, and busied himself in procuring means of transport for the army, at the same time furnishing the troops with provisions of all kinds. Hussain Pasha, acting under the orders, doubtless, of the Porte, was glad of an opportunity of destroying a Darah Bey who had become so formidable and independent as to have refused to receive a pasha sent by the Sultan to his district, and who might cause some uneasiness by tampering with the Egyptians. He accordingly resolved to manage matters so as to induce him to go to Constantinople; and in order to lull his suspicions, treated the Turkman chief with marked distinction until the army had passed the formidable pass of the Cilician gates, when the pasha having no further need of his services, he exhibited a firman he pretended to have just received, but which he had had long by him, wherein Haji Ali Bey was ordered to proceed to Constantinople, and promised that *there* he should be preferred to great honours for his late services. The Turkman chief fell into the snare, and on his arrival at Constantinople he was put under arrest, and soon afterwards disappeared, in the same way as many others have done before him.

As the head of Haji Ali Bey was exacted from his keeper, that of some other man, who may have died about that time, was procured; and the escape of the Haji having at the same time been connived at, he found his way from a Turkish bath, disguised in a Frank dress, on board a vessel then setting sail for Italy. The bribes requisite for this manœuvre had completely stripped him of every thing of any value, and he was maintained by the government of the Pope, as a convert to the Catholic religion, under the name of Signor Giovanni, on an allowance of a dollar a day.

His family, hearing of his escape, sent an old Christian servant who had brought him up to see and identify him, and if possible to persuade him to return. The man came back with assurances that Haji Ali Bey was really alive, and passing under the assumed character of a Christian in Europe; but that he refused to return to his country until his great enemy old Khusru Pasha should be no more. It was further reported that Haji Ali Bey, during the long period of his exile, had once visited the province in European costume, and that a Turk who saw him at the French consulate in Tarsus was observed to say, "That Frank, sir, is so like Haji Ali Bey, that were it not for his being in this dress, and his ignorance of Turkish, I should have no doubt it was he, in spite of his being reported dead."

When the army of the sultan was routed by Ibrahim Pasha in 1832, Mustuk Bey did not fail to conciliate the favour of the conqueror by pillaging the vanquished, and he was confirmed in his government of Bayas, which he kept for several years; but he could not bear the restraint of the regular and strict discipline of the Egyptian soldier, and he retired to the territory of Marash. Ibrahim Pasha, however, finding it difficult to maintain order among the turbulent factions of the Turkmans, who were continually in revolt and committing all kinds of disorders, and his time being too much taken up with more important matters to admit of particular attention to the mountain of Bayas (over which he was obliged, however, to lead his forces twice in person, to reduce the turbulent mountaineers both of Amanus and Taurus to obedience), he thought it expedient to invite Mustuk Bey to return, and resume the direction of the thirty Darahs of whom he is the chief, and over whom he has much influence.

When the Egyptian army evacuated Cilicia, Mustuk Bey did all he could to restrain his people from plunder until the troops had passed the strait of Bayas, in order that the army might not be provoked in its passage to lay waste a country which he felt was more particularly returning under his own immediate control; but as soon as the army had passed his own domain he fell on its rear, robbing all the loiterers and runaways.

It is but justice to Ibrahim Pasha to say here, that the affairs of the province of Cilicia were ably and efficiently administered in his time by Selim Pasha and Hamid Minikli. These worthy individuals

GOVERNMENT OF IBRAHIM PASHA. 91

did an immense deal of good in being the first to introduce the administration of justice into the province; and they are still much regretted, although the people suffered considerably in their time from military conscriptions.

Ibrahim Pasha is said to have maintained at one time as many as 20,000 men in this province out of its own revenues, and yet to have saved money. He re-opened the long-closed mines in the Taurus; he exported to Egypt vast quantities of timber from Mounts Rhosus, Amanus and Taurus; he introduced the sugar-cane, and favoured agricultural pursuits; and he founded in the gates of Cilicia, at Kulek Boghaz, a line of defences which were constructed with great engineering skill, but which were blown up by the army previous to their retreat.

SACCAL TUTAN.

A ruin at a place near Alexandretta, known by sailors as "Jonas's Pillars," and supposed to be the gates mentioned by Xenophon, and called by him the gates of Syria and Cilicia; they are on the battle-field of Issus, and from the top of these Alexander may be supposed to have witnessed the retreat of Darius's army before his brave troops.

CHAPTER IX.

MUHAMMAD IZZET PASHA—A PRETENDER TO THE TURKISH THRONE—HIS STRANGE HISTORY AND RARE ACCOMPLISHMENTS—DISAPPEARS AT KUNIYAH—AHMED IZZET PASHA—GRANTS PERMISSION TO MUSTUK BEY TO MURDER HIS NEPHEW—SULAIMAN PASHA—DURWISH AHMED'S EXPEDITION AGAINST MUSTUK BEY—HIS CHIEF OFFICERS TAKEN AND STRIPPED—BAYAS CAPTURED AND SACKED.

I NOW proceed to the history of the last five pashas who have successively governed the province of Cilicia since the evacuation of the Egyptians in 1840, and to narrate the various facts of note that have taken place since that epoch.

Muhammad Izzet was the first appointed by the Porte to preside over this province. He is one of the *employés* of the Porte that I have known who most deserves well of his country. This worthy man filled his post with dignity and honour, and combined much of the munificence of the "old school" with the simplicity of the new. This good man fell into disgrace without meriting it, and remained some time neglected, until he obtained, through the greatest pecuniary sacrifices, the post of governor at Uzgat, where he died. He was so much beloved, that on his leaving Adana the people actually wept at the loss they were about to sustain; and this is a fact for which I can vouch as an eye-witness. But perhaps, although I would not detract from his merit, this mildness of temper was owing in a great measure to the times he lived in as governor of Cilicia; because as he was the first appointed after the evacuation of the Egyptians, he would no doubt have had particular instructions to be extremely lenient.

It was during the administration of Muhammad Izzet Pasha that an event occurred in Cilicia which I must pause to relate, for the facts are as extraordinary as they are inexplicable.

In February 1843, an individual calling himself Nadir Bey, accompanied by an amiable young Englishman of good family and education, whose parents live in London, arrived at Tarsus. The former (Nadir Bey) appeared to be little past thirty, of a very prepossessing cast of

NADIR BEY AND HIS PRETENSIONS.

countenance and engaging manners, highly accomplished, and acquainted with fourteen languages, which he appeared to know as well as a native of the countries whose language he spoke.

He had been in the service of Ibrahim Pasha, under the assumed name of Murali Mahandas (Grecian engineer), and was well known to the inhabitants of Tarsus and Adana. Indeed, he seemed to know every body all over the Levant. It was remarked that on his former visit to Tarsus, while in the Egyptian service, he used to gamble a good deal, and often lost of an evening all he had about him, frequently large sums, upwards of 20,000 piastres (200*l.*); and the next day his purse would be replenished as usual. He had, however, maintained his incognito generally, and only confided to a few of his private friends his real history, which was that "being the son of Sultan Mustafa, and the elder brother of Mahmud, he was the rightful heir to the throne." His knowledge of English was perfect, and he sang Italian music like a vocalist of that country; and I have since been informed by his companion that he had at Palermo a palace filled with a large collection of first-rate paintings of the old masters, chosen by himself, and "a live portrait" of a young and beautiful Circassian whom he looked upon as his wife. He had passed in all the courts of Europe under an assumed Italian name, Count Ricchi of Corfu, and was much respected and beloved by all who knew him. Indeed, his companion has since assured me, that one day having called unexpectedly on the brother of the King of Naples, who was at dinner, that prince rose from table to receive him with more *empressement* than even the greatest courtesy could exact or court etiquette allow. As I cannot doubt the veracity of my friend the young Englishman, who has since informed me that he believed Nadir Bey was allowed 5000*l.* a year by the Emperor of Morocco, I am at a loss how to proceed in my history, as I have to state that these two gentlemen arrived in Tarsus without any pecuniary means whatever, and on the wildest of all imaginary schemes!

Nadir Bey applied to a friend in Tarsus for a small sum in order to obtain a suit of Turkish clothes, as he was dressed in the European costume. Having obtained what he desired, he departed for Adana the third day of his arrival, leaving his friend in Tarsus; and the latter has repeatedly declared that he was only his travelling companion, and had no idea of the rash step Nadir Bey was about to take, or he certainly would not have allowed him to go, as he was very much attached to him.

Nadir Bey had two private interviews with the former governor of the city, who had been Mutsillim, or town-governor, in the time of

Ibrahim Pasha, and who it seems knew him well. They agreed to go to the Mufti's; and the next day, on presenting themselves there, whilst smoking the first pipe, and before they could enter on the subject of Nadir Bey's views, the Tufankji Bashi, or chief officer of police, summoned them to appear before the pasha in council, where they found all the ayans (nobles) assembled.

When Nadir Bey entered, he proceeded to take his seat next to the pasha, and began a discourse in Turkish, saying that he felt it a duty he owed his country to take the present step, inasmuch as his heart bled to see it suffering under the present tyranny, and that if they would rise and declare him sultan, he would make them all his ministers; "for," said he, "you must know that I am the rightful heir to the throne, being the son of Mustafa V., the elder brother of the late Sultan Mahmud. On the murder of my father, my mother escaped on board a Russian vessel, and I was born a few months after her escape to her family in Georgia." He had subsequently been sent to Russia, where he was educated. To support his claims, he shewed them a letter addressed to him by Muhammad Ali Pasha of Egypt, wherein he is styled "Effendim Sultanim," and recognised as the lawful heir to the throne.* The pasha observed that his proposed enterprise could only be undertaken with a large body of men, and much money would be requisite. To this he replied, that if they would only promise to rise, he would engage that early in the spring there should arrive 25,000 men on the coast, and that pecuniary means should not be wanting. The Nakib then observed, "Our pashalik is small, and we think you had better go to Kuniyah and have a conference with the pasha of that place, whose district is much more extensive. Yes," said the pasha, "that is the best place; so you had better retire to the coffee-room" (where the principal attendants of the pasha remain in waiting, and which often serves for a more honourable confinement to a person of distinction than a public prison), "until two Tufankjis (military police) can be got ready to accompany you."

* I cannot suppose this letter authentic, because I must also note that he had last come from Egypt, which country he and his companion had been obliged to leave so suddenly on board an Egyptian frigate bound for Tarsus, that the latter had not time to apprise his friends of his destination, and he had to wait some time before he could hear from them and receive remittances. The officers of this Egyptian man-of-war have often asked me very anxiously concerning him, and acknowledged that he had confided his secret to them during the passage. They appeared to idolise his memory, for he contrived to engage the affections of every one wherever he went; but I cannot help thinking that his sudden departure from Alexandria was in consequence of Muhammad Ali's determination not to be compromised personally, though he allowed him to try his luck, or rather risk his life, in attempting to raise the people elsewhere.

Nadir Bey remained twenty-four hours under this arrest, weeping, and vouching for the truth of what he advanced, and saying that now his life would be the forfeit of his patriotism. " Yes," he exclaimed, " I am a sacrifice for my poor people; still my rights shall be recognised." He then would cheer up with the delightful prospect with which his madness deceived him, that he would obtain justice eventually, and then again he would relapse into despair.

Mounted on a bad horse, he set off the 4th of March, 1843, under the escort of two armed men, to Kuniyah. Before leaving the town, he called at the house of a French resident at Adana, and without being allowed to dismount, asked him for a little money and a cloak to screen him from the inclemencies of the season. Having obtained the latter, he then begged him earnestly to send a portfolio he had taken the precaution to confide to his care previous to his entering on this mad enterprise, to the English consul at Tarsus, with a request that he should take notice of the papers contained therein, and immediately inform the British embassy of his position, " that, if necessary, the ambassador may intercede to save his life, as he had already done once before."

This is in allusion to a statement which is also current, that Nadir Bey had been a great favourite with Sultan Mahmud, who entrusted him with the government of a province in Europe, where he tried to excite a conspiracy, and being brought to Constantinople would have lost his life but for the humane intercession of his excellency.

I have seen the contents of this portfolio, wherein there is no paper of any consequence except a very urgent one from the Emperor of Morocco to the late Sultan Mahmud, recommending Nadir Bey very strongly to his kindness, as " his nephew and own flesh and blood." This letter I have perused with great attention, and have no doubt of its authenticity; but I have not heard how or by what means of persuasion it was obtained.

Here I should mention, that when Nadir Bey was seized by the pasha, the British consular agent at Adana thought it his duty to claim him as a person furnished with a passport, and consequently under his jurisdiction; but the pasha smiled and said, " No, no, we know this man well; his name is Ahmed, and we have all along been on the look-out for him." Nadir Bey reached Kuniyah in safety, and a European, who had been apprised by letter of his coming, immediately went to the palace of the governor to inquire after him. He was informed that such an individual had arrived, and had prosecuted his journey to Constantinople.

The people of the country, who all took interest in his fate, said that at Kuniyah he had been recognised by the Mullah Khunkar, or chief of the dervishes, on whom devolves the duty of buckling on the sword of every newly-elected sultan, and that he was presented with a good mule, and furnished with money and servants to proceed to the capital as became his rank. Be this as it may, nothing more has ever been heard of this mysterious young man. Two or three months after this event, the British vice-consul at Samsun, who had been informed of what had occurred in Cilicia, taking a ride, saw a horseman who answered the description given of Nadir Bey. He was in Egyptian clothes,* and was whistling as he rode before him into town an Italian air with the greatest correctness. The resemblance of this man to what he had heard of Nadir Bey did not at the time strike Mr. C——; but he had scarcely reached his home before the thought occurred to his mind that this might be the same individual, and he immediately sent people to all the public khans and coffee-houses, and to every place where he could suppose it possible he could go, to find him out; but although the town is small (not containing 6000 inhabitants), he was not able to discover any person agreeing to the description he gave of the individual he had met that afternoon! This is all I have been able to ascertain and collect regarding this extraordinary character, who has interested me exceedingly, and the more so as I found that he was universally beloved and esteemed by all who have known him personally. I regret that I did not see him (being at the time confined to my room by fever), to be enabled to give a more particular description of his person. There appeared, some days later, an article in one of the Constantinople papers saying that an impostor had been seized in Tarsus who pretended to the throne, and that he had been sent to Constantinople, where he was daily expected; but his arrival there was never announced.

But the circumstance of his appearing in Cilicia as a claimant to the throne of Constantinople *alone* and without funds, to create a revolt in a country where he was well aware the natural feelings of patriotism are unknown, and where the inhabitants are driven like sheep by the strongest or by those who pay them, at the best, can only be reconciled to common sense by supposing that he must have lost his senses before entering on his project: for what reasonable hope could there be of exciting a sympathy or enthusiasm in a population reduced by poverty to the last stage of indifference, and that too in the character of a man who had passed the greater part of his life among infidels, the

* Like those purchased by Nadir Bey at Tarsus, previous to proceeding to Adana on his inexplicable undertaking.

enemies of their religion and nation, himself tainted by the odium of having been allied to the hated Jawurs, and hence unfitted for the sacred office of defender of the faithful,—a prejudice impossible to eradicate from the minds of those who aspire to be strict Mussulmans, and who form by far the great majority of the population? Politically speaking, the attempt was madness; and we are lost in a maze of conjecture when we reflect on the infatuation of this individual, who was well acquainted with the country and people, and who in all other respects excited the astonishment while he captivated the hearts of all who knew him.*

The second pasha who was appointed (12th May, 1843) to govern Cilicia after the evacuation of the Egyptians, was Ahmed Izzet Pasha,† son-in-law of old Ali Pasha of Bagdad. Ahmed was jealous of the influence which the Muhassil (financial agent of the Porte) Abdullah Rushdi exercised, and by which he could appropriate to himself all the emoluments arising from bribes. He therefore persuaded Mustuk Bey to quarrel with the Muhassil, in order to frighten him out of his post. The pasha hoped thus to get a more complaisant Muhassil, who would allow him to take into his own hands the advantage of directing through him the financial government of the Porte in the country. Mustuk Bey accordingly seized the earliest opportunity of quarrelling with the Muhassil, and which presented itself as they were seated during Ramadan at the door of a large caravansarai, enjoying the coolest place they could find in that sultry town. Mustuk Bey began by threatening to take away the Muhassil's life, and made a shew of drawing his pistols for that purpose. But the Muhassil, so far from being intimidated, wrote to Constantinople, and had, it appears, sufficient influence to get the pasha dismissed.

In the meanwhile, however, before an answer could come from Constantinople, and it could be known which influence would ultimately prevail, Mustuk Bey had nothing to fear from the resentment of the Muhassil; but as family matters called him to Bayas, he took his leave of the pasha at Adana and returned home, whilst the latter set off in a contrary direction for Tarsus, " to make hay while the sun shone," that

* I must also add, for the satisfaction of the reader, that his friend and companion, before leaving Tarsus, did not fail to pay whatever debts Nadir Bey had incurred during his passage through Tarsus. See Appendix.

† The Porte had been for some time uneasy about old Ali Pasha of Bagdad, not knowing whether he would submit or throw off his allegiance. This man undertook to persuade Ali to be faithful to the Sultan, and proceeded to Bagdad, where he ingratiated himself so completely in the old man's good graces that he gave him his daughter in marriage, and, as a proof of his obedience to the Porte, agreed to give up his post and accept the pashalik of Damascus, in order to spare the bloodshed of the faithful, consequent on civil war amongst Muhammadans.

is, to profit by his position and make a tour among the Turkman tribes, from each of whom it was customary that every new pasha should receive one or more horses, valued at from 10*l.* to 20*l.* sterling, the number of which in this province generally amounted to a hundred given to each pasha. These horses were afterwards taken away to be sold, in the interior or at Constantinople, by the pasha when he was recalled, and thus the country was drained of all its best steeds. The money to purchase these horses was raised by contribution from the inhabitants of the district the pasha visited, and they were charged by their chiefs *at twice* their value!*

Ahmed Izzet Pasha had just arrived at Tarsus, when he was astonished to see Mustuk Bey make his appearance there, at a time when he thought him at Bayas. I happened accidentally to be present at their meeting, and witnessed the embarrassment of the pasha, who was persuaded that something very serious could alone have brought him thus suddenly to Tarsus. He was soon, however, relieved from his anxiety to know the cause of this sudden visit, by Mustuk Bey's informing him privately, that he was come to obtain his sanction to make away with his own relation, who had conspired against him during his absence from Bayas, whilst paying his court to the pasha at Adana. Mustuk Bey obtained the permission he had come to solicit and returned home, where, the better to cloak his design, he soon after made peace with his nephew Hassan Aga Zaitun Uglu, the very individual against whom his father had warned his children, and whose father, as has already been stated, Kutchuk Ali Uglu had murdered. Mustuk Bey accepted from his nephew a dinner of reconciliation, and went with his followers to visit him. Soon after dinner Mustuk rose to depart, and ordered his nephew's followers to escort him, leaving his own to finish their meal; and when the master of the house, who is required by the etiquette of the East to be the last to rise from the table, had just got up, and was in the act of washing his hands, his cousin Osman Aga shot him with a pistol, and the rest despatched him with their swords, after which they mounted their horses to follow their master. The dying man is said to have exclaimed, "Is such treachery possible?" referring to the maxim common to all nations, that there should be " honour among thieves."

Mustuk Bey resembled his father; his face was large and flat, with rather a scanty beard, becoming grey. He also spoke through his nose

* When a new pasha arrived, all the local officers employed by his predecessor were expected to make him a present of greater or less value, according to the importance of their office, in order to be continued in their posts, which was generally done till the pasha had had time to look about him, when he took occasion to turn them out, and place in some of his dependents.

like his father. His conversation was pleasing, his manners very polished, and he treated all travellers who visited him, particularly the English, very kindly, and with much respect. He occupied a little palace above Bayas, which his predecessor Rustam Bey, the governor appointed by Ibrahim Pasha, had embellished after the Turkish fashion.* His great generosity reduced him to be often in want of the necessaries of life; and the debts he contracted towards the government by reason of his munificence afforded an opportunity to his enemies wherewith to work his ruin.

The moment Ahmed Izzet Pasha had lost his post through the superior influence of the Muhassil Rushdi Effendi's friends and supporters at Constantinople, the latter availed himself of his power to bring Mustuk Bey into disgrace.

Sulaiman Pasha, who succeeded Ahmed Izzet Pasha in the month of November 1843, was, under the advice of the Muhassil, induced to summon Mustuk Bey to appear in Adana. He replied, that he was ready to obey as soon as the Muhassil should be recalled, or else to enter the city with a suite of 500 horsemen; whereupon the Muhassil took secret measures to induce the Porte to believe that Mustuk Bey refused to pay the tribute he owed to the government, the greatest of all crimes in the estimation of the ministry.

In order further to excite the government against his enemy, the Muhassil gave private orders to the Tartar bearer of letters from Damascus to Constantinople not to pass through Bayas, but to take a boat and go across the Gulf of Alexandretta to Kara-Tash. The post having thus been delayed in its progress, the Muhassil had a pretext for accusing Mustuk Bey of interrupting public communication, although caravans and passengers were never in the least molested, and although that *very week* two Hajjis arrived from Syria, after having been treated on their way by Mustuk Bey with his usual hospitality.

The Porte, giving ear to these insinuations, issued an order to attack Mustuk Bey. Two conscripts, one on foot, the other on horseback, were exacted from every village; and such, of course, were sent as could best be spared from agricultural labours. These were therefore boorish shepherds, many of whom had never used any other arms than those given them by nature, unless it were a club or stone against the wolves that attacked their sheep, and were equally unacquainted with riding. Each man was also furnished by the village to which he be-

* He was in great favour with the first two pashas after the evacuation of the Egyptians, and was honoured with a Nishan Iftichar, and the title of Kapitchi Bashi, by the Sultan,—an honorary grade given to governors of towns and chiefs of Turkman tribes who render themselves useful to the Porte.

longed with a hundred piastres for his expenses during the campaign, a pound of powder, and four leaden bullets. In this manner five or six thousand men were collected outside the gates of Adana, where biscuit and barley were the only things provided by the government for the use of their levies. On the other hand, 1800 cartridges were discovered in the corner of some magazine, and were broken open in order to distribute the powder therein contained to the Turkmans by the handful. No chief would at first condescend to lead such a rabble; and this honour was finally reserved for Durwish Ahmed, son of Kil-Aga, who was the only man who had the courage to march against the redoubtable Mustuk Bey.

For more than a month the conscripts were still assembling, and the encampment had been transferred to Kurt-Kulak, twelve hours' ride from Adana.

In the meanwhile the caravan of Mecca was approaching; and the Tufankji Bashi and Oda Bashi, or chamberlain, resolved to advance with about sixty followers, with the impudent boast of their doing so in order to protect the caravan. Mustuk Bey received their valiant onslaught with a handful of his followers, took them all prisoners, and ignominiously stripped them of their clothes, sending them back with a message to the effect that he would not make them pay with their lives the insult they had offered him, and that the only thing he would retain would be their horses, in part payment for a herd of cattle which the enemy had a few days previously carried off. These fellows, ashamed and disgusted, returned to Adana. The caravan passed with all due honours, and the chief undertook to intercede at Constantinople for Mustuk Bey, and to explain the exact state of things. Mustuk accordingly, satisfied with the hopes which the promises of the Suramini had inspired, and unwilling to be the cause of the effusion of "Muhammadan blood," as also not to implicate himself still further, retired to his mountains, a'though he could, as the people expressed it, "*have eaten them up all at once.*"

As soon as Durwish Ahmed heard of Mustuk's retreat, he fell on Bayas, and pillaged and burnt every thing that came in his way, even to the wood for building belonging to merchants of Adana that happened to be on the sea-shore ready for embarkation. Neither the sex nor the rank of one of Mustuk Bey's harim, who remained behind, saved her from being stripped and ill-treated—an act unprecedented in the annals of the East, as women are always respected by the most barbarous. Mustuk Bey went to Mar'ash and afterwards to Aleppo, where he was hospitably received by the pasha, who took him with him to Beyrut, and thence to Constantinople.

CHAPTER X.

ANECDOTES OF SULAIMAN PASHA—GIN-JUSIF, REBEL OF KARA-TASH—ARIF PASHA—MURDER OF A PASHA—HASAN PASHA—ANECDOTES OF THE COUNCIL—CHRISTIAN MEMBERS OF COUNCIL—EMPLOYÉS OF THE PORTE—TOLL AT KULAK BUGHAZ—HATI SHERIFF—COURTS OF JUSTICE.

DURING this period, as I have already stated, Sulaiman Pasha governed Adana. This old man was of all pashas the most stupid, except in matters relating to money, the sound of which alone could awaken his attention. During his government, an oke of sugar as a bribe would not be refused by him or his officers when nothing more valuable could be had.

On his arrival to take the reins of government, this pasha told me that he had been named for his peaceable disposition, in opposition to that of his predecessor; and in *this* the Porte really shewed great discrimination. He was rich, although he maintained a whole troop of women servants, together with a wife. On the landing of the latter at Mursina, the wife of the doctor of quarantine called to pay her respects. To excuse her very ordinary apparel, and the tattered garments of her children, she said, "Pray do not look at these clothes; I have some with four fingers' width of gold lace on them." But this was not likely, as, contrary to our customs, the people of the East always travel in their finest and newest apparel.

When Sulaiman Pasha first arrived at Mursina from Constantinople, he was also met on the sea-shore by the director of the quarantine, who caused a sheep to be slaughtered in honour of his disembarkation, lodged his excellency with all his suite for the night, giving up to him his own apartment, and standing before him all the while to serve him, &c. The next day he accompanied him to Tarsus, to swell the number of his *cortége*. After remaining twenty-four hours in attendance, as the pasha was to proceed to Adana, he came forward to take his leave; and kneeling down, kissed the hem of his garment, requesting permission to return. Will it be believed, that the pasha actually asked him who he was?

The power of the Porte was much shaken in Kara-Tash about this time. Yusuf, son of the man whom we have seen defending the castle of Bayas under Dada Bey, had killed his brother and usurped his post. This man was a peasant of the Ansairi tribe, but he had no particular religious belief. His domestic establishment was composed of seven women, among whom were the sister and mother of his wife! He collected all the rogues he could, by screening them from the pursuit of justice; and Kara-Tash was fast passing from under the jurisdiction of the pasha, when Jin Yusuf was enticed to Adana and put into prison. But as the government thought he might one day be required for the purpose of setting him against his other brother Mustafa, his life was spared. Tired of such restraint, Jin Yusuf sent one of his followers to shoot Mustafa, knowing that he would then be necessary to government at Kara-Tash. It turned out as he expected: Mustafa died of the wound he received from a bullet, and the pasha being about to quit Adana in disgrace, was glad to take 10,000 piastres (equal to about 90*l.*), which Jin Yusuf paid him for his release, and which sum he soon after recovered, levying it by contributions on the villagers in his district of Kara-Tash; and Jin Yusuf is at this moment the right-hand man of one of the ayans of Adana, and the pasha, in a letter to me, styles him *kiz-agasi*, a title equivalent to lord-lieutenant of a county.

Old Sulaiman Pasha having been a sufficient time at his post to make up more than the sum he had defrayed to obtain it, he was recalled A.D. 1844, and Arif Pasha was named to succeed him; but the pride of this man soon led to his downfall.

Kuzan Uglu, chief of the Turkman tribes that dwell near Sis, and a friend of Mustuk Bey, had been summoned to Adana; but he refused to appear, suspecting Abdullah al Rushdi, the muhassil, of treachery. On the guarantee of the Armenian patriarch, he ultimately consented to answer the summons; but on his arrival he was treacherously put under arrest. The mountaineers hearing of this breach of faith, prepared to attack the city, and would certainly have pillaged it, had not the pasha invested Kuzan Uglu with a pelisse of honour, and sent him back to quell the insurrection. The Turkman tribe of Kuzan Uglu has always been, to a certain extent, independent alike of Ibrahim Pasha and of the Porte.

Shortly after this, a pasha of Mar'ash (a young man whose name I have forgotten) was killed by some of the *Aushir* tribes, neighbours of Kuzan Uglu; for having gone among them to levy tribute, and with a dozen of his followers he fell a victim to his imprudence. Arif Pasha, in consequence, made some demonstration of his intention to invade the Kuzan Tagh, which constitutes a portion of the Taurus mountains; but the demonstration came to nothing.

The unsettled state of the country was indeed at its height during Arif's government. He actually refused to convict a thief without competent witnesses, although some of the stolen property was found upon him, because this individual had powerful friends, and bribed the cadi with 500 piastres.

Abdulla Rushdi at last fell into disgrace; but he contrived to leave Adana with upwards of a hundred horses and forty-two panther-skins, together with several thousand purses (of 5*l.* each) wherewith to intrigue for new honours. He was succeeded by another intriguer, who had united with the chiefs of the country to get Arif Pasha dismissed.

In 1846 the Porte, having been repeatedly petitioned by these people, and worn out by their importunities, as well as tired of their complaints, determined to make a complete change in the officers of the pashalik of Adana; and Hassan Pasha was deputed, with a suite of fresh-imported *employés*, to fill up the various vacancies.

This fat illiterate man was one of the Janissaries of old, who had, in the time of the reformation of Sultan Mahmud, willingly submitted to the new discipline called Nizam, and was consequently spared the fate of his companions in arms. His stupid, coarse manners corresponded with his appearance.*

Mustuk Bey, who had been to Constantinople with his patron Waji Pasha, availed himself of the change of ministry at Adana to return, and he accompanied Hassan Pasha in the Turkish steamer. On their arrival I took occasion to recommend Mustuk Bey to him, on the ground of his being the only man who could keep the Turkmans in order; for the roads had been infested with robbers during his absence, which was never the case when he was at the head of his tribe.

Hassan Pasha contemptuously answered, "that neither Mustuk Bey nor any one else, not even himself, could presume to consider that he was indispensable to the Daulat il Aliyah (Sublime Porte), whose breath

* An Arabic story is told of a governor, who surpassed his father and grandfather in tyranny, going out in disguise one day to hear what people said of him. He was surprised to find that an old woman alone, out of all his subjects, prayed God to prolong his life,—"Alla yitawall amru." He accosted her, and entering into familiar conversation, desired to be told why she prayed for the prosperity of a tyrant hated by every body. She informed him that "the grandfather of Effendina was tyrannical, his father still more so, and Effendina was worse than both; should God Almighty, therefore, in his vengeance deprive us of him, he could at *this rate* send us none other than Eblis (Satan) himself 'Azlam,' more just than Effendina (our lord), whom God preserve: and that is why I pray for the long life of Effendina, as we can only change for the worse."

alone supports or exterminates all men!" I could not help smiling at this assumption of grandeur, having been witness of the little power of the government he so much lauded only a few days previously, when the Turkmans had carried off with impunity between two and three hundred head of cattle within half an hour's ride of Adana. Arif Pasha, with a spy-glass in his hand, had actually seen from his window some travellers stripped on the other side of the river, and dared not afford them assistance; nor could the post ever pass without an escort of Dali Bashis ("mad heads," irregular cavalry).

But the weakness of the Cilician governors is in some degree excusable when we consider that they are thrown in a strange land without sufficient means to enforce their authority, being scarcely allowed the pay of fifty saimans (irregular troops). They are thus placed at the mercy of the chiefs of the country, who offer them the option, viz. on one side the opportunity of becoming rich, and on the other, opposition in every thing, which would completely cripple their power; and they are induced, by want of principle, to choose that which is most conducive to their private advantage.

It sometimes happens that, in consequence of the mutual jealousies of the members of the council, they submit to receive a Mutsallim, or governor, among them: but this man, as well as his master the pasha, with whom he shares his profits, becomes a tool in their hands; and as soon as one of the members contrives to get the ascendant of the rest, the Mutsallim is set aside without any scruple or ceremony. This is perhaps the case in this province more than in any other, the members of the council being chiefs of Turkman tribes supported by 2000 or more followers, who are encamped within call at a few hours' ride from the towns.* Thus we see that this pashalik is governed only nominally by the *envoyés* from the Sublime Porte, and that the real authority is in the hands of the ayans, who retain the power of levying the *Saliyan*, an arbitrary tax originally paid by the people for the purpose of defraying the travelling expenses of Pashas, Kapitchi Bashis, and other officers of the Porte, while resident in the towns, and which has continued in force, although since the financial reforms of the sultan it has been fixed on more regular principles, and the reasons for its exaction have long ago been cancelled. This tax is levied twice a year, and from the uncertain nature of the sum, holds out a wide field for peculation. It is divided into so many portions, generally double the sum required by the Porte, and it is exacted from the chiefs of the several

* Some of the tribes are much more powerful. Malamanji Uglu could unite from 800 to 1200 guns.

districts, villages, or departments, who in their turn also speculate on its advantages to their own profit; so that the poor villagers have to pay three times what the Porte receives, and they are also the greatest sufferers, as the ayans contrive to exempt their own people; and this tyranny falls so heavily on the villagers, that they often find no other chance of escaping the exactions of the ayans than emigration, which takes place to a great extent,* although a husbandman is not allowed by law to quit his district; so that when unable to pay the dues fixed upon them at the capricious option of the chiefs, they wander about from place to place, and leave their children to the mercy of strangers.†

This system is also put in practice in its several ramifications by the sheiks of the villages, who mimic their superiors in the council; and they enjoy the same immunity from punishment. Nothing can be more detrimental to the public weal than this combination of six or ten persons who act in concert. The more individuals in power, the more channels of extortion, and the more subjects exempt from taxation to the prejudice of the rest of the community.

This council, presided over by the Pasha and Muhassil, is composed of the Mufti, Cadi, Nakib, and some of the chiefs of the Turkman tribes, who, by the venal means above alluded to, have contrived to establish an influence indispensable (without regular troops) to the collecting of the taxes. These keep up a good understanding among themselves as to what regards their individual interests, and cede by turns to each other every advantage they can avail themselves of to monopolise and

* Karadughar (Anchiale) and Kaisanli, formerly two flourishing villages, were in 1847 nearly deserted, in consequence of the heavy exactions of the government-people, who, seeing a populous village, fixed a sum to be paid in Saliyan far beyond the means of the poor inhabitants, who, having been reduced to sell every thing they had to satisfy the extortions of their petty tyrants, and their lands proving barren in consequence of the want of rain, were all dispersed, each seeking refuge in some distant place,—some going to Cyprus, and others to Syria, while those who had any relations in the country were too happy to become their servants in the culture of the ground, to obtain food for themselves and their distressed families. Happy it is that such a state of things is rapidly going by!

Out of some forty families in Karadughar, only six families remained; and these being required to pay 18,200 piastres of the Saliyan of the village when it was populous, tried to run away to Syria by embarking in a small boat at night. The number of the families at Kaisanli was seventy, and they were reduced by desertion to a dozen, in the same state as those of Karadughar; and many other villages, such as Karajillas, Nisani, &c., were reduced to the same condition. All these villages were peopled with Ansairi peasants, a quiet and laborious race of men.

† This is certainly a remains of the feudal system; and I have repeatedly heard of two neighbouring chiefs quarrelling, and reclaiming from each other the taxes due by their several serfs, who had taken refuge and been received by another chief from his neighbour's territory: and often these individuals are compelled to return to their former place, and submit to the still greater exactions of their exasperated chief.

extort, allowing to the Pasha and Muhassil a fair portion of the booty for their co-operation.

The introduction of Christians into the councils, as ordained by the Porte, has not in Cilicia as yet gone beyond the summoning of some illiterate follower of the Messiah, who sits on his knees near the door, and never opens his mouth but with low obeisances to confirm their nefarious decrees. He is generally a servant of the Mufti, and officiates as Sarraff or banker of the government, a lucrative employment, which throws much floating capital into his hands. He is supposed to be the most respectable of his co-religionists; but the Turks pay little regard to the rank he holds as representative of the Christians and *member of the council*, for he often gets the *bastinado* to quicken his accounts.*

In this council all the "appaltos" (monopolies) of the government, which have not been abolished, are sold yearly, although in the treaty with England a heavy duty of twelve per cent is established by the last tariff on condition of their being set aside; and here I may notice, that from time immemorial it has been observed that in Turkey a new tax very seldom cancels old ones, but is added to them, in spite of all arrangements to the contrary. The Pasha and Muhassil buy in the name of their servants the most profitable monopolies, without any one outbidding them, as they distribute to each of the members a sufficient number of such "appaltos" as regards their various districts. Last year a present or bribe of 25,000 piastres (250*l*.) was offered to the Muhassil to allow the monopoly of tobacco to be sold freely, but he preferred keeping it to himself. This dignitary, by this one fraud alone, collected yearly several thousand pounds sterling. I perfectly recollect the first arrival of Abdalla Rushdi Effendi in Mursina, where he had occasion to accept of my hospitality. The first question he asked was, whether there were any dresses to be had *ready-made* at Adana! He had actually arrived at his post without a change of clothes; and yet on dismounting from his horse at Adana he found a house furnished for him with such magnificence, that he was enabled to treat those who called upon him with pipes and coffee in cups set with diamonds, and

* A remarkable instance of this took place on the arrival of Arif Pasha, who, on inspecting the public records, found a deficit of about 300*l*. to 400*l*., and required its immediate payment. The money was not owed by the sarraff of Tarsus, but by the effendis of the council, who had each taken what they required; and yet the sarraff was afraid to explain this knotty point, and at first received 500 bastinados, and was afterwards obliged to disburse the money out of his own purse. He had even to pretend that the money was due by different Christians, friends of his, who acknowledged the debt, which was paid by the sarraff, in order to conceal the tricks of the ayans, who are always trifling with the public revenue.

which had been prepared for him by the officious ayans. We have seen how he left Adana after three years' residence there. The Cadi of 1844, on his arrival to take possession of his post in Adana, had not wherewith to pay his horse-hire from Mursina to Tarsus!

Very large salaries have of late been paid to all the *employés* by the Porte, in the hope that this may induce them to give up their habits of venality; but unfortunately the instability of their appointments, at least in Cilicia, renders them anxious to profit by the opportunities afforded them, in order to be enabled by their ill-gotten wealth to bribe in their turn their superiors at Constantinople when they are recalled,—an event which takes place every few months, in consequence of the many complaints that reach Constantinople of their venal practices, and which is generally brought about by one intriguing against the other. By this constant change of oppressors, the people are always falling into fresh hungry hands, which must be satisfied, lodged, and maintained; and although very strict commands are issued from time to time by the Porte to prevent these irregularities, in distant provinces like Cilicia little or no attention is paid to the wishes and good intentions of the government.*

But the great source of local mal-administration is the influence of the members of the council, whose whole energy is directed to the support of its members and dependents at the expense of the Porte and people. An useless, unprincipled, and in most cases an ignorant oligarchy, ruinous to the country and to the treasury of the Sultan; and until some very effective measures are taken to crush the power it has usurped, no hope can be entertained of any amelioration in the legislature. Individual despotism is always to be deplored; but an oppressive oligarchy is the perfection of tyranny.

It had been agreed upon between the Porte and the European powers, that there should be no more monopolies; still these exist in full force: and the Bage or toll levied at Kulak Bughaz is not one of the least

* At Antioch the tax-gatherers used to exact the tithes in *money*; and as they fixed a larger sum than even the produce of the land, the villagers found it so ruinous, that they preferred leaving a great portion of their grounds uncultivated, and actually cut down their trees. This came to the cognisance of the Porte, and a firman was issued to forbid such abuses; and it was therein clearly specified that the tithes should be always collected in *kind*: and each of the Ayans of Antioch, who are not, like those of Cilicia, supported by Turkman tribes (not belonging to any), was himself compelled to read in his district this firman before the assembled people, for the purpose of giving due publicity to the intentions of the Porte. That year some attention was paid to this order: but they soon returned to their original mal-practices; and the tithes are now actually paid in *cash* at a price double the value of what the produce could be sold for in Antioch. But great changes are taking place for the better every year even in these remote districts; none more important than the abolition of the Saliyan in 1846, which has not been renewed since that period.

onerous. Three piastres per load, and one oke* in kind, is exacted in soap, coffee, tumbac, &c., which makes the *road-tax* amount to more than 12 per cent. The Muhassil, who has the chief interest in this oppressive toll, gives it his energetic support, and has not allowed it to be suppressed, in spite of many orders from the Porte obtained by the French and English ambassadors for that purpose.

Although the Porte had declared that personal taxation should be abolished, and a tax on property be established in lieu thereof, this has not taken place, at least in Cilicia, where the members of the council being almost the sole landed proprietors, they would have been the chief sufferers; and as the executive power is in their hands, they have not allowed such an innovation to come into force.

Nor have many advantages accrued to this province as yet by the *Tanzimat Khaïriyah*, or Hatti Sheriff of Gulhana, so deservedly applauded as a charter granted by the Sultan to his subjects. The people, at least in Cilicia, are under the same tyrannical subjection, and are exposed to the same rapacity of their governors as ever they were; the latter never fail to avail themselves of the slightest excuse that can be found to put them in prison, whence they are never freed, however innocent, before they have paid a sum in proportion to their means, which imposition they call *expenses of the prison*, and which is fixed at the arbitrary caprice of the Tufankji Bashi. The Cadi also takes advantage of his position to carry on measures of intrigue very foreign to his station and profession. The great license allowed by the Turkish law, the facility of procuring false witnesses, and the difficulty of appealing to Constantinople for redress, enable him to carry through, by the connivance of the council, any measure, however detrimental to the public weal. Indeed, the whole administration of justice, if such it can be called, may be summed up in the great facility of procuring false witnesses, and the extraordinary article in the Turkish code of condemning individuals sued against, *however false the accusation*, to pay the costs. Innumerable instances may be brought forward of innocent persons prosecuted *solely* from motives of ill-will on the slightest pretences, to oblige them to pay the costs; and the officers of law, to whose profit this system accrues, give naturally encouragement to such mal-practices. These abuses, and many more, are adopted by the pasha and officers of police, in order to make up for the loss of the privilege they formerly enjoyed, of imprisoning a man known to be rich, for the avowed purpose of making him pay an arbitrary tax for the private use of the pasha's kitchen. In order to render the present plan *as lucrative* as the old one, it is in too many instances made

---

* Two pounds and three-quarters English.

MAL-ADMINISTRATION OF JUSTICE.

as general as possible, by encouraging the population to complain one against the other; and although a person is falsely accused, the accuser is not punished, nor do the costs of the suit, as I have already observed, fall upon him, as they should do. If any sum is recovered, the creditor pays seven to ten per cent, besides what is given to the constable for his trouble by the latter, and what is secretly paid by the creditor to the judge, generally about a third of the sum.

I trusted to be able to conclude the present chapter with more consolatory words of hope to the friends of Turkey, of which, notwithstanding its faults, and the difficulties the Porte has to fight against, I may truly say that I rank as one, and indeed as a most zealous well-wisher. It has been my endeavour throughout these pages to lay before my readers only simple facts which speak for themselves, to enable them to judge of the actual state of a province so remote and so peculiarly circumstanced as Cilicia. Nearer to Constantinople, the Turkish government is enabled to carry into more effective operation the many excellent regulations that are daily issued at the Porte for the benefit of the people.

PLAIN OF ANTIOCH—OVERFLOW OF THE ORONTES; MOUNT AMANUS IN THE DISTANCE.
(From a Sketch by C. F. Barker, Esq.)

MISSIS.
(From a Sketch by Edward B. B. Barker, Esq.)

CHAPTER XI.

GEOGRAPHY OF CILICIA—TARSUS AND ADANA—MISSIS (MOPSUESTIA)—SIS (PINDENISSUS)—BAYAS AND THE COAST—PYLÆ CILICIÆ—POPULATION OF CILICIA—EUROPEANS AND THEIR INFLUENCE DESTROYED—CONSULS AND THEIR AUTHORITY—ENGLISH CONSULS ALLOWED TO TRADE—CLIMATE—STAGNANT LAKE (RHEGMA)—MARSH OF ALEXANDRETTA—COUNTRY-HOUSES—NIMRUD—SEA-PORTS—KAISANLI—MURSINA AND ITS ROADSTEAD.

HAVING traced the history of Cilicia down to the present day, I propose now to say a few words on its geographical position, statistics, commercial resources, natural productions, and antiquities. The so-called pashalik of Adana, which corresponds pretty nearly to ancient Cilicia Campestris, is comprehended in a plain that extends from Sulufska (Seleucia,) to Ma'rash, in a north-easterly direction, about 120 miles between the Taurus and Jawur or Giaour Tagh, which last, running north and south, forms with the sea a triangle in which the province is composed, and which is called by the Turks Chukur Uvah, and corresponds to the Aleian plain of old. Tarsus is situated on this plain, at the foot of Mount Taurus, about twelve miles from the sea, and a branch of the river Cydnus passes through the city, taking its rise in the adjoining chain of mountains, and emptying itself into the sea about twelve miles from Tarsus. Adana, fabled by Stephanus to have been founded by Adam (vide *Ainsworth's Retreat of the 10,000 Greeks*), stands to the north-east, and is also on the plain at the foot of the Taurus range, and about thirty miles from the sea. It has another and larger river, Saihun, ancient Sarus, passing by it, which, running parallel to the Cydnus, empties itself near the mouth of the latter.

Missis, anciently called Mopsuestia, is said to have been founded by Mopsus, a celebrated prophet, son of Manto and Apollo, during the Trojan war; he had three daughters, *Rhoda*, Meliade, and *Pamphylia*. It is now a ruined village about twenty-five miles north-east of Adana, and through it flows the Jaihun (Pyramus), a river still larger than the two last mentioned. The Pyramus springs from the other side of Ma'rash, whence it passes winding along the plain to Sis and Missis, and finishes its course in the Bay of Ayass (Ægæ), which is opposite Alexandretta.*

Sis (Pindenissus) is to the north of Missis, about sixty miles distance, at the foot of Taurus, which the people of the country call at that point Kusan Tagh, after the name of the tribe of Turkmans who inhabit the district. At this place is a monastery of great antiquity, the residence of an Armenian patriarch, who has some influence in the country, but who, notwithstanding his high rank, when he comes to Adana to visit the pasha, is as obsequious to the Turks as the rest of the oppressed Christian subjects of the Porte. A view of Sis, with the Armenian patriarch in the foreground surrounded by his bishops, is given in the frontispiece.

Bayas (Issus) is on the gulf of that name, sixty miles to the south-east of Missis. Alexandretta is sixteen miles more to the south-east, at the foot of the Jawur Tagh, which rises almost perpendicularly behind it, constituting the farthest limits of the pashalik at *Bailan* (Pylæ Syriæ), where the confines of Syria begin in a very tortuous and difficult pass.

Arsus (Rhossus) is to the south of this town; it has the sea on one

---

* This place, that is, Ayass, is remarkable for its extraordinary number of sea-turtle, which are very easily caught as they come out on the sea-shore in the night to lay their eggs in the sand. Fish is also very abundant; but when taking it with a seine or *draw-net* the turtle fill up the sack; so that before it can reach the shore the fishermen have to go into the sea, which is not deep near the beach, to take them out, two or three times successively. On one occasion (May 1842) the crew of H.M.'s steamer *Hecate*, Captain Ward, took more than 150 turtles in less than twenty-four hours.

side and Mount Rhossus towering above it on the other.* The latter projects into the sea, and forms Cape Khanzir, or Wild-boar Cape, (Scopulus Rhossicus), so formidable to sailors in leaving the Bay of Alexandretta. Karatash is a village opposite Arsus, on the extreme side of the gulf, and has a little harbour affording a precarious shelter to small boats of the country, and is about sixty miles east by south of Tarsus.

At Kulak Bughaz (Pylæ Ciliciæ) is the pass into this province to the north-west from Anatolia, which is the most convenient road for beasts of burden, and was that principally used in all the military expeditions of the ancients. It was repaired by the Romans so as to admit of their chariots passing, but being neglected, has fallen to ruin, and in the narrow part you have now to pass through a stream two or three feet deep for more than a hundred yards. But I must, for a more minute description of this celebrated pass, refer to Mr. Ainsworth's work entitled *Travels and Researches in Asia Minor, Mesopotamia, Chaldea, and Armenia*. It was here that Ibrahim Pasha caused to be conveyed to the crest of the pass some very fine pieces of artillery of such a size that the present government have not been able to bring them down, and have been obliged to content themselves with twenty-eight small pieces of brass artillery, which they sent to Constantinople to be melted down into bishlics (five-piastre pieces of the country), worth something less than a shilling. At the same time six vessels of 250 tons were laden for Constantinople with powder and military stores, which had remained and been overlooked by the Egyptian army at the moment of departure, although by order of Ahmed Minikli Pasha some of the magazines were blown up. This shipment was made, not only to turn to account the leavings of the Egyptian army, which would have been useless in Adana, but also to keep such dangerous articles out of the people's reach. Ibrahim Pasha had had constructed at Kulak Bughaz by a clever Polish

* Arsus is now a small village built on the site of ancient Rhosus; and in the vicinity are many fragments of walls, arches, and some remains of a temple with Corinthian columns. The most remarkable ruin in the neighbourhood is, however, an extensive aqueduct carried on arches, and which formerly brought water direct from the mountains to the town, although a rivulet of clear water flows through it.

Nothing indicates that this town, whither, according to Plutarch, Demetrius repaired from Seleucia Pieria, was ever an extensive site. It is, however, a spot still much frequented by Syrian Christians, with whom its church is in great sanctity; thus preserving, to a certain extent, the ecclesiastical importance which belonged to it in the middle ages, and which enabled it to send its mitred representatives to the Christian Synods of the East. Eusebius, it is true, only notices Rhosus as a parish; but Socrates (iii. 25) mentions Antipatrum as Bishop of Rhosus; and it is also noticed as an episcopacy in the *Acts of the Synod*. The name is variously rendered Rhosus, or Rosus, by the Greeks and Latins; the *Acts of the Synod* have it Rhosopolis, and the *Theodosian Tables* Rhosus. W. F. A.

BIRD'S-EYE VIEW OF ALEXANDRETTA AND THE PASS OF ISSUS, WITH THE CILICIAN TAURUS MOUNTAINS IN THE DISTANCE.
TAKEN FROM THE SUMMIT OF MOUNT RHOSSUS, FROM A SKETCH BY C. F. BARKER, ESQ.

engineer, Colonel Shutz, fortifications which were intended to repel an invader, and at the same time serve as a model to instruct officers in every branch of fortification. These works were executed by the Colonel, but they were in great part destroyed by the Egyptians on their retreat, before they were completely finished, after having cost immense sums of money and eight years' constant labour of 10,000 men.

The population of this pashalik amounts to about 300,000 souls; but it is not easy to make an exact calculation, as the reports of the Turkmans are either false or exaggerated. Adana contains 18,000 inhabitants; Tarsus, 6000: of this one-third are Mussulmans, more than a third Ansayrii or Ansarians, generally Deists, and the rest Armenians and Greeks. There are more than 300 villages on the plain, which average 200 souls each, and the inhabitants of which are for the most part Ansayrii, and a few Muhammadans. At Sis the population is almost entirely Armenian, and numbers about 2000. Missis and Bayas contain 200 to 300 inhabitants altogether, and Alexandretta and Arsus as many.

The Turkman tribes, who dispersed in the plains, valleys, and mountains of this province, feed their flocks in the pasturages of the Jaihun, Saihun, and their tributaries, in winter, and repair to the uplands of Taurus in summer, make up the sum of the rest of the population, as above stated. There are at Tarsus a few families from Cyprus, who lead the same monotonous existence to which they are accustomed in their native town of Larnika. The few Europeans who inhabit Tarsus live a life of great privation, devoid of all intellectual society; they appear to exist only in the hope that some day or another the relative commercial advantages of the place will at length be fully appreciated and settled; they will then be the first to profit thereby.

There are English, French, Russian, Dutch, and Neapolitan consulates established in Tarsus. The English system of allowing a consul to trade is very disadvantageous to commercial interests, and frustrates the very intention for which he is appointed—that of encouraging British commerce. It brings him into constant personal collision with the local government, and detracts from his respectability and authority. Besides, his position gives him such an advantage over other merchants, that few Englishmen can settle in any place where such is the case; and therefore, as I have just observed, the desire and interest of England to extend her commerce is thus counteracted for the saving of a few hundred pounds a year of salary. This is particularly the case in Tarsus; and indeed we may observe, that in few places in the Levant where a British consul is allowed to trade have we any commercial houses, and this fact speaks for itself: although consuls have been appointed in those places for many years, and although a good deal of real business might be carried on by the means of English houses of commerce, were their interests properly supported by disinterested individuals.

The climate of Cilicia is not more unhealthy than the rest of Asia Minor, but the air of Tarsus is very much so, particularly during the months of July and August, when the town and its environs are subject to exhalations productive of putrid and intermittent fevers. The principal cause of this evil is a stagnant lake about thirty miles in circumference, now a few miles from Tarsus, which formerly communicated with the sea, but which is now separated from it by a sand-bank. This is the harbour mentioned by Strabo, which he says was the port of Tarsus (and that there were in his time the remains of the arsenal). Indeed, its position leads us to infer that the sea once came up to Tarsus; but as the alluvium of the river has raised the ground considerably, it would be easy to dry this lake by drains, which would not cost more than 200l., and the deleterious state of the atmosphere would be permanently obviated; and not only would many diseases be prevented, but the ground would become well adapted to the cultivation of sesam, cotton, and wheat, and its incomparable fertility the first year would no doubt repay a thousand-fold all expenses.* This lake lies between Tarsus and the sea, and thus its putrid exhalations are conveyed to the town by the sea-breezes. It is the opinion of medical men, that the pores of the skin being opened by the great heats of the day, are much influenced by the damp and cold wind of the mountain at night; and this combined with the malaria above mentioned occasions congestions of the brain, and hence bilious and gastric fevers, which, if not properly treated by bleeding and other active remedies, will carry off the patient in three or four days, as the fever soon ceases to be intermittent and assumes a malignant type.

Ibrahim Pasha caused the small lake of Alexandretta to be drained at the suggestion of M. Martinelli, as also subsequently of Mr. Hays, her Majesty's consuls there, and for two or three years afterwards no deaths took place, whereas previously there were accidents occurring every few months. The canal for carrying off the water has, however, since unfortunately been allowed to fill up, and Alexandretta is now the tomb of all who inhabit it for any length of time without change of air.

* A few years ago, in consequence of a great dearth, part of this lake having dried up, the people of the adjoining village sowed and reaped melons twice in one season, the seed of the second crop being from that of the first, and the quality produced was most excellent.

The inhabitants of Tarsus and Adana go to the mountains to pass the summer, at a place called Nimrud, sixty miles distant, where there is a castle which they attribute to Nimrod and call it after his name. There are evident traces of its having been built at three different periods, and it was at one time in the possession of the Crusaders. It is built on the summit of a hill, which I should calculate to be certainly 3000 feet above the level of the sea, and it is not commanded by any of the adjoining heights. It was probably here that Syennesis first retired on the approach of Cyrus to Tarsus, B.C. 401 (vide Ainsworth's *Travels in the Track of the Ten Thousand Greeks*). The country around Nimrud is arid, with scarcely any running water; but the water of the wells is not bad and is abundant, and the air is fine. Each habitation stands in a little vineyard, and this extends the cultivation of the mountain for many miles; and the luxuriance with which the vine, cherry, and walnut-trees grow is very remarkable. All who come up here lead a life of perfect indolence, and the poor man will sell any thing he may possess rather than fail to take his family to the mountain during the summer months. This constant shifting of residence prevents the inhabitants from building good houses either in Tarsus or in the *Yaila*, as they call their summer quarters. The merchants of Tarsus and Adana are chiefly strangers, and during the hot season they visit their families in Kaisariyah, and in the other towns in the interior of Asia Minor, whence they return in the months of September and October.

Kaisanli is a village containing about a hundred families, established in the point of the bay nearest to Tarsus (about twelve miles distant). It is in this place that Arab lombards come from Syria to load and unload; but on the slightest appearance of bad weather they are obliged to take shelter at Mursina (Zephyrium), more to the westward of the bay, about eight miles further, where the roadstead is excellent, and, according to some captains, is preferable as a safe anchorage to that of Alexandretta or any other on the coast of Syria.* Two French vessels and some Arabs have been driven on shore; but in every case the fault has been from their chains or cables breaking, and not from bad bottom in the anchorage, English vessels, at the same time and in the same storm, sustaining no damage whatever. The only inconvenience they experienced was that their crew were prevented from communicating with the sea-shore for three days till the storm had subsided; but this is of very rare occurrence, and generally speaking, morning and evening the business of embarking and disembarking is not inter-

* The sea-breeze is stronger here than any where else on the coast; hence its ancient name perhaps. I had a beautiful brass medal struck here, which I have mislaid.

rupted. About midday there is a little swell, and the want of a small pier alone prevents the working of merchant-ships' boats all the year round. This could be easily made for the trifling sum of 50*l.*; but the governors of the country, although in landing to take possession of their posts they have often got wet, always *talk* of having one made; as soon as they reach Adana, their head-quarters, they forget entirely that such a place as Mursina exists. Mursina is a name compiled from the Greek, μυρσίνη, *myrtle*, because formerly immense bushes of that plant were the only characteristics of the place.

When I first went to Tarsus, in 1838, there was only a small magazine and a few miserable huts at this place, and the bales of cotton were left out under the rain until French vessels came to ship them for Marseilles. In the hope of drawing the commerce of the interior and rendering this a place of transit for such produce as is usually conveyed overland to Smyrna, I built large magazines capable of holding the cargoes of fifteen vessels at one time. As I had anticipated, this convenience, so much wanted previously, induced people to avail themselves of them, and deposit therein goods which were shipped to Europe and Smyrna. Commerce taking a new course, three other magazines were built, and other persons settled there.

ALEXANDRETTA AND CAPE KHANZIR.—(From a Sketch by C. F. Barker, Esq.)

CHAPTER XII.

ADVANTAGES AND DISADVANTAGES OF TARSUS IN A COMMERCIAL POINT OF VIEW—TABLES OF NAVIGATION—TABULAR VIEW OF THE TRADE OF THE INTERIOR OF ASIA MINOR—TABLE OF EXPORTS—TABLE OF IMPORTS— STATE OF AGRICULTURE IN CILICIA— PRODUCE OF THE COUNTRY—COTTON— WHEAT—BARLEY—LINSEED—WAX—FRUIT-TREES—SILK—OLIVE-TREES —PAY OF A DAY-LABOURER—PASTURE OF LAND—TENURE OF LAND— TIMBER AND WOODS—GEOLOGY AND MINERALOGY—EXTRACTS FROM MR. AINSWORTH'S WORK: PLAIN OF TARSUS—FALLS OF THE CYDNUS—FIRST, SECOND, THIRD, AND FOURTH RANGE OF HILLS—MINES OF IRON AND LEAD —ARGENTIFEROUS GALENA—REVENUE OF THE PASHALIK.

TARSUS being the nearest port to the several large towns of Asia Minor, —Adana, Maraash, Nighdah, Kaisariyah, and others,—it would seem to be the best adapted to embark goods from; but the inhabitants of the interior have long been accustomed to go to Smyrna and Constantinople by land (five times further off), where they have the advantage of finding more buyers who are ready to compete with each other in the purchase of their merchandise, whereas in Tarsus the competition is trifling, as there are few if any merchants; and these only acting as factors, they cannot make large purchases without consulting their principals, who are too far off to allow of any activity in their operations. For these reasons Tarsus will remain for many years in the background: but attention to the causes of malaria would soon eradicate the greatest evil, and then many respectable merchants with their families would be induced to reside in Tarsus, otherwise not a disagreeable residence, and one of the most fertile spots in the world; and they would profit by the advantage of its vicinity to the interior of Asia Minor, inasmuch as goods can be shipped twenty per cent cheaper here than by taking them overland to Smyrna, where the produce of the country now chiefly goes for want of a nearer *mart*, and to reach which place on camels' backs, wool and madder-roots are deteriorated in quality by being exposed to rain on the road; but the merchants of Anatolia do not mind that, as *the weight is thereby increased!*

Albertus Aquensis, according to Cellarius, talks of 3000 ships sailing from the port of Tarsus at one time (vide Ainsworth's *Asia Minor*, p. 83). At present its commerce, although increasing within the last eight years, is confined to twenty or thirty Arab vessels, that come successively to load here for Syria, bringing a little soap, coffee, and English manufactures for the consumption of the pashalik. About twelve French vessels also load sesam and wool for Marseilles yearly: one or two Austrian and Sardinian. An English vessel may visit this roadstead in the course of the year to take up a *part* of her cargo for Leghorn or Smyrna, which they get in Alexandretta. A few Greeks also from Cyprus keep up a traffic in the products of their country, taking wheat in exchange. Steamers have been put on this route from Smyrna two or three times; but in consequence of the irregularity of their arrivals and departures no dependence could be placed on them, and nothing was done satisfactorily. (See the accompanying Table on the Trade and Navigation of Tarsus, No. 1.) Tarsus might, at least for the present, serve as a convenient depôt for the produce of the interior, were the agents there more to be depended on; but what man would live there who could gain his bread elsewhere, particularly as the means of business are less than any where else, and the disadvantages of ill-health and difficulties of getting and executing orders greater than any where else? But in order to give some idea of the impulse that might be given to the trade of Asia Minor through Tarsus were the difficulties alluded to removed, I shall accompany this notice with a report or table of the trade of Anatolia as regards Kaisariyah and the towns of Asia Minor, which I drew up from researches on the spot and upon the best authority. (Vide Table in the Appendix.)

The principal exports, a table of which I also adjoin in the Appendix, consist in cotton, wool, wheat, barley, wax, sesam-seed, and linseed from the interior, from whence might be brought Caraman madder-roots in great quantities, Persian yellow-berries from Kaisariyah, buffalo-hides and cow-hides, and all the minor produce of the country.

All kinds of imports, such as English manufactures, sugar, coffee, indigo, cochineal, soap, and Persian tobacco, are brought from Syria; but the want of cash in the country renders the sale precarious. The seller is compelled to wait months for payment, and frequently money is lost by the failure of the buyers, who are as insolent as they are needy. The import trade is very discouraging; but in exports sometimes a good profit is to be obtained, particularly in wheat, which is remarkably cheap: often it may be had at a price that enables the buyer to deposit it in the London Docks at 20s. the English quarter.

During Ibrahim Pasha's administration, the government was put to the deplorable necessity of pressing the population into military service, by seizing the strong and able-bodied, in order to recruit his troops in Syria. As he could not well do this in the border territories, from an apprehension of their deserting, he made the latter labour at public works, and this interrupted the course of agriculture. Grain was in consequence dear, but since the departure of the Egyptians the people do not suffer from this grievance, and being more at leisure, have applied themselves to the culture of the land, which is extremely fertile; and were it not for the fatality which seems to be attached to this ill-fated province, brought on from mal-administration, this might be the happiest instead of the most miserable district of the Ottoman dominions.

Its chief produce is cotton, of which 20,000 cantars, of 180 okes, are annually produced, and sent chiefly to Tarabuzun (Trebizond) and Erzerum by caravans. It is inferior to Egyptian cotton, and not well cleaned. The cotton costs about three piastres, or $7\frac{1}{2}d.$ the oke (of $2\frac{3}{4}$ lbs.). In 1845 the crop failed entirely for want of rain.

More than 400,000 quarters of wheat are produced annually, half of which is exported to Syria; the current price is sixty to eighty piastres per quarter, which the people call kilu or kaily, equal to eight measures of Constantinople. A soft kind of wheat comes from Karamania, the flour of which is whiter, and is sold at 100 piastres the kilo, same measure as barley.

More than 150,000 quarters of barley are grown yearly, which barely suffice for the consumption of the country, many making bread of it when the price of wheat rises, which it invariably does toward the end of the season. The current price is from 40 to 60 piastres, same measure, weighing 130 okes.

Of sesam are annually produced 15 to 20 m. kilos, of 130 okes weight, of which the current price is 200 piastres. The quantity produced is yearly increasing, as people find it gives better returns than any other agricultural product, and it obtains the readiest sale, as merchants make advances for several months to obtain it.

Of linseed, about 40 m. okes are produced. I was the first person who introduced this seed on trial; but as it was sown by the farmers too late in the season, the plant was burnt up by the heat of the sun, two years successively, before it all came to maturity, and the farmers were discouraged from attending to it: price current, 40 paras or 1 piastre the oke.

Of wax, scarcely more than 8 to 10 m. okes are produced; but the quality is good and the price moderate: 18 piastres the oke.

I also introduced the best kind of Muscatel grapes, peaches, and apricots with a sweet kernel, and the finest cherries; as also the *tomato* or love-apple, the French bean, and the artichoke, which were previously unknown to the inhabitants. Generally speaking, I found the gardeners prefer *not* having any superior kind of produce to distinguish their gardens, because it attracts the attention of the ayans (nobles), who are then induced to visit them daily, and with their horses and servants commit depredations, for which they never think of making any remuneration to the proprietor. There are a great many magnificent mulberry-trees, which serve as trellises to support a kind of grape which does not ripen till Christmas; but very few silk-worms are brought up, because the heats come on too soon, and kill the worm before it begins to spin. The people of the country wind it off with their hands, using small pebbles to prevent it entangling, and it comes out very coarse, which they like, as they work it out in pieces for silk shirts.

The sloping sides of most of the hills in the province are planted with olive-trees, which no doubt were universally cultivated by the ancients, especially between Tarsus and Sulufka, along the shore, for a distance of 120 miles in length and several miles in breadth. All these trees were in full bearing in the time that the Genoese were masters of the country; but having since been neglected, they are overgrown with brush-wood, and in many instances lost in a forest of pines. Many old trees were also cut down, but new branches have sprung up from their roots, which now bear a small wild olive used by the Turkmans. In some places there are as many as several thousand trees upon each acre of land, and it would be extremely easy and profitable to restore them to their pristine state; but the want of hands is one of the many drawbacks in the East to improvement. A labourer in the harvest-time is paid 2s. a day, besides his food; and people often come from Cyprus and Syria to avail themselves of such high wages for a season, returning to their homes to restore their health, which is invariably impaired by hard labour in the great heats.

The Turkmans who gather the cotton take one-tenth for their trouble; the man who separates the cotton from the seed takes another tenth; the government takes also a tenth; added to which is a very heavy duty of 27 piastres on its value, which goes under the head of customs!

The occupation which attracts more particularly the attention of Turkmans is the pasture of their cattle, inasmuch as it is the easiest kind of work. The produce of their dairy is excellent and abundant, although their animals are remarkably small, except their sheep, which are magnificent, and have extraordinary large tails, all fat, and which, when melted down, is used instead of butter in cooking. The wool produced yearly in this province amounts to from 600 to 1000 cantars, of 180 okes each cantar, of which one-third is white and two-thirds black or grey. The texture is fine, but it is generally very dirty, and if washed would lose forty per cent in weight.

Europeans find no difficulty in buying land, as they can legally purchase it in the name of females, either really appearing or represented by proxy, all women born in the country being regarded as Rayas in the eye of the law; or rather I should say, that the property of the harim is considered so sacred, that any European stating that such property belonged to his wife, no questions would be asked of what nation she were, or if she even existed at all. Title-deeds thus obtained in the name of any female of the country are then made over to the purchaser, in token of a bond for a supposed debt, and this effectually secures to the European purchaser every right to the property.

The land may be cultivated by taking into service farmers of the country, whom it is usual to interest by granting a quarter, or a third share, or a half, according as the case or agreement may be. On my arrival in this country, I had purchased some land advantageously situated near the sea; and I caused it to be cultivated by the villagers whom I established on the estate; and I induced them to turn their attention principally to the produce of vegetables and fruits for the use of the shipping. I also erected in the magazine a machine for pressing wool and cotton, and I omitted nothing that could assist in facilitating commercial operations; but the extreme apathy of the people renders it very difficult to change the course of things, or to introduce any innovations in the habits they have had handed down to them from their forefathers. In this province remarkably fine timber for building purposes is produced, chiefly fir. The oak is also very common near Arsus. Timber is cut of all sizes, and exported from Alexandretta, Bayas, and Arsus to Egypt. Ibrahim Pasha used to have more than 10,000 magnificent trees cut every year, which he sent to Alexandria for the use of the arsenal. To the north-west of Mursina a smaller kind is cut, which serves for the building of Arab bombards in Tripoli, on the coast of Syria. The people also trade in boards, which the Turkmans bring from the mountains, and which are sawn by their women. These are sent to Syria, and cost on the average one piastre and a half per board, and are of all sizes and thickness. The smell of turpentine contained in the pine-wood is supposed to be an antidote to bugs; in Tarsus they are seldom seen, except when imported from Cyprus, and even then they speedily disappear, being destroyed by the obnoxious smell of the turpentine.*

Mount Taurus presents a rich field for the researches of the mineralogist. Three hundred specimens of stones and minerals were collected by the mineralogists appointed to work the lead-mines by Ibrahim Pasha, some of which were very beautiful, and some very interesting. I have by me some specimens of metals which I procured at Kulak Mäaden. Here I cannot do better than quote from Mr. Ainsworth's work before mentioned.†

"*Plain of Tarsus.*—From within three miles of Adana to beyond Tarsus, in a westerly direction, the plain is composed of humus and alluvia, which have an average depth of from twenty to thirty feet, and repose upon rubbly limestone. These plains are mostly cultivated, and villages are numerous.

"*Falls of the Cydnus.*—The country to the north of Tarsus rises gradually up towards the Alpine region of Cilician Taurus, remarkable at this point for its bold precipices and rugged grandeur of scenery. The falls of the Cydnus and the grotto of the Seven Sleepers are in an out-lying range of supra-cretaceous limestone and limestone conglomerate.

"The river issues through deep ravines, with perpendicular walls of limestone, and on entering the plain falls over a ledge of rocks of limestone breccia, about forty feet in width and eighteen in height.

---

* The forests of the Cilician mountains consist chiefly of pines (*Pinus maritimus* and *Halepensis*) and Balanea or Valonia oaks (*Quercus ballota, ægilops,* and *infectoria*). The mountain-peaks are clad with the gloomy foliage of the cedar-juniper (*Juniperus excelsior*). In the yailaks, or mountain-pastures, we find thickets of dwarf holly-oak (*Quercus coccifera*), berberry, and yellow jasmine. The low hills are covered with myrtle, arbutus, Daphne, Phlomis, Styrax, Cistus, and Lentisk. The Eleagnus, the oleander, the chaste-tree, and colutea, are the most conspicuous shrubs on the borders of the plains. Christ-thorn (*Paliurus*) abounds in sterile places, especially in the rock of Anazarba. The waste ground is studded with bushes of juniper (*Juniperus Phœnicea*), spiny burnet (*Poterium spinosum*), spiny cichory (*Cichorium spinosum*), and Lithospermum hispidulum. On the sands of the sea-shore, the Tamarisk attains almost the port and bearing of a tree, and great bushes of tree-spurge (*Euphorbia dendroides*) are mingled with more humble, but more gaily-flowering, phænogamous plants.

In the highlands of Cilicia there are plantations of walnut-trees, apples, apricots, cherry-trees, Lombardy-poplars, and pollard-willows. The Oriental planes are not so common or so large in Cilicia as in other parts of Asia Minor; but the number of carob-trees in the plain of Adana is remarkable. The dark cypress not only adorns the cemeteries of the Mussulman, but also grows wild in the ravines. The almond and manna-ash also grow wild among the rocks, and the bay and Judas-tree in the ravines. Mr. Barker has alluded to the fine groves of oranges, lemons, and pomegranates. The palm-tree also adorns the gardens of Adana; and a few specimens of this tree, probably the refuse of gardens, are also met with on the shore near the Cilician and Syrian gates. W. F. A.

† *Researches in Assyria, Babylonia, and Chaldea,* p. 327.

"*First lowest range of hills.*—Proceeding to the north-east, the outlying and lowest range of hills is composed of marles and gypsum in the lower beds; and superimposed upon these are beds of brecciated rocks. The gypsum is snow-white, granular, or lamellar. This range is divided from the second by level, low, and often marshy plains.

"*Second range of hills.*—The upper beds are composed of coralline limestone—grey, friable, fracture uneven—almost entirely composed of stony polypiferous masses with stelliform lamellæ, or waved laminar furrows.

"The lower beds consist of green marles and greenish-white calcareous marles; the first are argillo-calcareous, earthy, friable, greenish, brownish-green, and yellow; the second are compact, even, non-fossiliferous.

"This second range consists of low hills, rounded or of a conical form, frequently cultivated, with little wood, but often villages on the summits.

"*Third range of hills.*—The upper beds consist of ostracite sandstones, compact, earthy, friable, frequently divided on the surface into polygonal and rhombic masses, like a tessellated pavement. Ostraceæ (ostreæ and aviculæ) are very abundant. An ostrea, probably not different from ostrea gigantea, attains sometimes from a foot to eighteen inches in length.

"The lower beds are composed of ferruginous sands, yellow and red, and sometimes of pink-coloured sandstones.

"Beneath these are argillaceous limestones, alternating with marles (valley of Yani Kushlak) and with slaty beds (hill of village of Yuruks).

"*Fourth range of hills.*—The upper beds consist of blue anthracitous limestones, compact, fine granular, glistening fracture, blue and dark-blue colour. The lower beds are white limestones, compact, fine granular, or more cretaceous, with chalk fossils. Both beds appear to belong to the chalk formation.

"*Mica schist with limestone* (Cipolin of Alex. Brongniart).—On the summit of this range, not far from an ancient Roman arch, and by an antique causeway, a formation is met with of mica and argillo-calcareous schist, sometimes forming a solid schistous rock.

"The limestones after this begin to form a truly Alpine country, sometimes towering up in lofty and perpendicular precipices upwards of 1000 feet in height; at others forming lower and rounded hills, covered, when not lofty, with shrubbery and forest-trees, but when lofty, with oak and pine alone. Sometimes the cliffs are tomb-excavated, as at Mizar-lik; at other times, isolated knolls of limestone bear castellated ruins.

"*Kulak Bughaz.*—The formation downwards, from Kulak Bughaz to the plain of Adana, presents pretty nearly a similar succession of deposits as above Tarsus.

"*Tertiary deposits.*—At Khan Katlah Uglu, a travertine formation covers a marley and limestone deposit.

"At the village of Durak, granular gypsum occurs in ferruginous sand and common clay. The sand and clay alternate beyond the sandstones, slaty, ferruginous, coarse-grained, in thin strata, and very determinate rhombic cleavage.

"Polypiferous or coralline limestone succeeds to the rhombic or ostracite sandstone, the litture polypi occurring in groups, or at other times forming the whole mass of rock. The formation also contains botryoidal hæmatites.

"The coralline limestone, or coral rag, alternates in its lower part with dark-coloured clays, which are replete with bivalve shells belonging to the genera tillina and lucina.

"At Khan Kusan Uglu, ferruginous sandstones and sandstone conglomerate underlie the clays and polypiferous limestones. Below Khan Sarashi, cirithia and conide limestone succeeds to the central chalk formation, and between the two formations is a deposit of limestone, breccia, and argillaceous shale.

"In the valley of Khan Kusan Uglu, the conide limestone descends in precipitous cliffs to the south-east, which cliffs are deeply fissured, and wrought into fantastic forms.

"To the north, the limestone is capped by ferruginous sandstones, above which again are coralline limestones; while to the south, beneath the coral rag and sandstones, are sandstone conglomerates. The friable nature of the last three formations has given rise to many curious effects of denudation; tall columns and masses, in various fantastic forms, rising up in picturesque confusion.

"The chalk formation of the central chain is almost every where the same, a hard and compact limestone containing few organic remains, and rising up in bold precipitous rocks, with castles on their summits; or sweeping circularly, as if to block up the road with their gigantic gates, called those of Taurus or Cilicia."*

Mines.—Above Adana, in that part of the Taurus which is occupied by the tribe named Karasanti-Uglu, there are *iron mines*, which are

* The formations here described evidently correspond to our Eocene formations: chalk or new Alpine limestones; plastic clay, sandstones, with lignite; London clay and calcaire grossier; siliceous limestones, gypsums (in large beds at foot of Mount Casius), and marles. These are the beds in which large and thick oysters occur in wondrous abundance; some weigh at least twenty pounds. Sandstones and sands above the gypsum, fresh-water deposits, coralline rag, &c. These beds are full of organic remains, and would furnish a rich harvest to a geologist who had time and opportunity to explore the country, especially between Tarsus and Kulak Bughaz, leisurely and carefully. W. F. A.

worked by the people of the country on their own account, and with very little difficulty. The quality is more esteemed than Russian iron, being softer and more malleable ; it is sold at two piastres the oke.

Near Kulak Bughaz there are *lead mines,* which are worked for account of government. The samples I possess of this mineral in its pristine state are extremely rich. It has lately been discovered by an Italian mineralogist, M. Boriani, that together with this lead there is a good deal of silver, and he extracted a small quantity in proof thereof. The local government is not aware of this, and very possibly regular veins might be easily discovered. Towards Sis there are also many mines of great value; but the Turkmans there used to hide them, in order not to be interfered with by the local authorities.*

The revenue of this pashalik exceeds 10,000,000 piastres, and is collected in the following manner :

Saliyan	3,500,000
Kharaj (personal tax on Christians only)	5,000,000
Spinji (ditto ditto, 3 piastres per head)	4,000
Miri of the Fallahs (Ansayriis)	5,000
Customs (lately increased to 1½ millions of piastres)	1,200,000
Monopoly of tobacco	68,000
,, ,, snuff	30,000
,, ,, spirits of wine	30,000
,, ,, the manufacture of candles	2,000
,, ,, the burning of coffee	3,000
,, ,, auctions	17,000
,, ,, salt	15,000
,, ,, dues exacted at Kulak Bughaz, 5 piastres per head (*worth much more than*)	70,000
,, ,, tax levied on the Turkmans that come down to the plains in the winter	5,000
	10,024,000
The expenses of the Government are for the Pasha alone	600,000
,, ,, for the Muhassil	144,000
,, ,, for the Governor of Tarsus	60,000
,, ,, for the fourteen members of Council	140,000
,, ,, for the chiefs of the Turkmans	100,000
,, ,, for the subalterns	100,000
	1,144,000

---

* At the time that the Euphrates Expedition was at Suwaidiyah, an Englishman arrived, who had been invited to the country by Ibrahim Pasha to work the mines of argentiferous galena, near Sis. The unfortunate man, however, soon fell a victim to the climate. W. F. A.

Besides, no doubt, a large sum which the pasha contrives to pass in his account for the maintenance of *troops that never existed*.

The rate of twelve per cent duty to be paid to custom-houses was calculated in Constantinople on merchandise of first-rate quality; but although the produce of the provinces often only costs half the price of that quality in the capital, still the same fixed duty is exacted; so that the merchant of the interior, paying a duty calculated by the same tariff, actually pays often as high as twenty-five per cent instead of twelve per cent as intended. This has considerably retarded the activity of commercial interests and relations, as no article can properly bear such a high duty. The better to illustrate this subject, I shall add a table, wherein the value of each article, and the per-centage duty to be paid is noted; and from which it will be seen how much the commerce of these countries lies under a disadvantage by being obliged to pay so much per cent duty more than what merchants in Constantinople pay. This was a mistake of such as had the establishing of the rates of the tariff, and who fixed each quota according to what the article was worth in their market, and not by an average value of the whole, which would have facilitated commercial operations.

It is impossible to impress the people of the East with a conviction of the salutary effects of a quarantine establishment: they cannot divest themselves of the idea that it is only a pretext of the government to enable it to pry into private relations and interfere with the personal liberty of the subject, at the same time that it is another excuse for raising money. They are the more readily led to this conclusion by the shameless conduct of the *employés*, who exact all manner of presents to exempt the donors from *various kinds of restraint*, such as being confined in the most *filthy holes*, and to be eaten up by vermin of all sorts. When a man desires to perform the *spoglio* (which is done by passing through water and putting on *uncontaminated* clothes), he gives secretly a suit of clothes to the chief "*guardian*." The next morning this man brings the bundle, and cries out, "Mr. A. or B., your friend sends you this packet of clothes: come and perform the *spoglio*." Generally speaking, an oke or two of every article that enters the quarantine magazine is *abstracted*, and the merchants in vain call for redress. I have seen notes made out by the merchants wherein their sacks of soap, coffee, &c., had been specified as found wanting ten per cent in the weight by going through the hands of the quarantine; and when bales of goods are opened, generally a piece or two of stuffs disappear.

One of the magazines built at Mursina serves for a quarantine establishment, although in the *centre of the place*. But the pilgrims coming overland are obliged to perform quarantine in tents at Adana, exposed to all the inconveniences of the weather; but to that they are accustomed.

If two persons present themselves at the gate of Adana, the one with a teskere or passport from Aleppo, and the other from Alexandretta or Bayas, as an inhabitant of the latter places, the former is put in quarantine for fifteen days, while the latter is admitted to free "pratique," although they have been journeying on together for the last three or four days, and been in constant communication. What are the people of the country to think of such a quarantine?

CHAPTER XIII.

IL LAMAS (LAMUM)—KURKASS (CORYCUS)—ASKI SHAHIR—SOLI, AFTERWARDS POMPEIOPOLIS—GREAT MAUSOLEUM AT TARSUS—STRABO'S DESCRIPTION OF THE COAST OF CILICIA—HIS ACCOUNT OF TARSUS AND NEIGHBOURING TOWNS.

ANTIQUITIES.—As this province was on the high road between the great contending powers of ancient times, the Greek, Roman, and Persian empires, it has passed and repassed into many hands; and this may account for the very few perfect remains of art which are to be met with, the country having suffered greatly by the inroads of troops with almost every successive generation.

There are several castles built on eminences by the Persians, Saracens, Crusaders, and Genoese; but although the Turkmans continued for some time to make use of them, they have gradually fallen into ruin, as doubtless the jealousy of the Porte does not care to allow such facilities of defence to exist among people always disposed to rebel.

IL LAMAS.—At Il Lamas there is an aqueduct of some extent, which conveyed water from a distance of eight or ten miles through hills and across valleys to Kurkass Castle, which is on the coast between Selefkeh and Mursina. This castle is built on a rock in the sea, and is of a very ordinary style of architecture, as are all the ruins that are to be seen on the coast. The aqueduct is now dry, and in some places impassable, as the damp of the mountain above oozes, and forms, drop by drop, as it were, icicles of petrified water (travertino). The waters that formerly ran through it are now lost in a little stream which runs into the sea at a short distance from their source, where Admiral Sir Francis Beaufort's boat took in water. Near the entrance of the aqueduct are still to be seen the remains of a Saracenic tower, which no doubt was built to defend it from invasions of pirates.

Above the aqueduct at Il Lamas, and at a distance of three miles inland, a rocky mountain rises perpendicularly to the height of about 3000 feet. In the centre of this precipice, half-way up, may be observed, out of the reach of man, two cannons in bronze, that sparkle in the morning sun, deriding for centuries past the vain efforts of the Turks to bring them down; and the marks of many bullets may be seen, fired at them by Arnaut troops as they have passed the spot. They are in a *port-hole*, as it were, the one almost erect, but in an oblique position, and the other protruding horizontally. They appear to be about sixteen feet long; the bore, perhaps, a foot in diameter. They were probably placed there to defend the aqueduct; and it is very likely that there is behind them an excavation in the mountain th   served for military stores. A part of the mountain having fallen down, the ancient road to them is thus cut off, and they have remained isolated and inaccessible to any one using ordinary means.

A road might be cut to them with very little expense, or a person might be let down from above; but the latter would be a dangerous experiment, as the rock projects above, and it would be requisite to swing the rope backwards and forwards till the person hanging at the end could catch at the port-hole and enter. This place unfortunately was not visited by Admiral Sir Francis Beaufort, otherwise the jolly tars of old England would certainly have 1 ought them down.

Strabo says of Coracesium (prese t Kalaht Kurkass), that it is situated on a rock close to a small bay, which forms a small harbour for boats of the country, having an entrance on each side of the castle; and he adds, that Diodorus, surnamed Tryphon, made use of it as a place of defence, and a depository for arms, when he detached Syria from the power of the Seleucians. He was so formidable as to pretend to the throne of Syria, and maintained himself with various success, drawing his resources from Apamea and its surrounding towns, such as Larissa Cassiana (his native place), Megorus and Apollonia, until Antiochus, son of Demetrius, compelled him to take refuge in a fort, where he killed himself.* It was this same Tryphon who first gave the Cilicians the idea of organising a company of pirates, in order to take advantage of the weakness of the different princes who reigned in succession at this epoch over Syria and Cilicia; being the first to rebel, and with so much success, that others followed his example. As to the ruling princes, says Strabo, " we may remark, that discord having broken up the union in which brothers ought to have lived, placed the country at the mercy of any one who chose to attack it." But what principally encouraged crime and plunder, were the great profits that accrued in the sale of persons reduced to slavery. Independently of the facility of making slaves, the robbers had the advantage of being near a place of

* Vide Appian de rebus Syriæ, cap. 67, 68, and Justin. lib xxxvi. cap. 1.

commerce of some importance, viz. the island of Delos, which was rich enough to receive and send off to various places several thousand slaves per day; and this had suggested the proverb, "Merchants anchor and discharge, for all is already sold," referring to the facility of meeting with a good market in this island. The Romans also contributed to these lawless deeds by the encouragement they gave in the purchase of slaves, who had become a matter of necessity to them; the destruction of Carthage and Corinth having rendered them so rich, that they accustomed themselves to be served by a great number of slaves; and the pirates profiting by this opportunity of administering to their luxury, wandered boldly forth to pillage and seize all whom they met.

The kings of Cyprus and Egypt also contributed to the encouragement of these pirates, by reason of the hatred they had of the Syrian princes; and the inhabitants of Rhodes, a maritime power that could have suppressed these lawless brigands, being jealous of the Syrians, did not choose to come to their assistance. Add to this, that the Romans at this time did not care much for the countries on the other side of the Taurus. It is true that Scipio Æmilius, and after him other officers were sent to visit these countries; and they soon discovered that the cause of these robberies proceeded from the cowardice of the successors of Seleucus Nicator; but they did not choose to interfere with them, or deprive them of a government which they had themselves guaranteed to the family of this prince. The weakness of these kings, says Strabo, was the cause that Syria fell under the domination of the Parthians, who became masters of the country beyond the Euphrates, and after them the Armenians pushed their conquest beyond the Taurus as far as Phœnicia, exterminated the kings and their race, and left the sea open to the depredations of the Cilicians.

The Romans, who had not *at first* taken energetic measures to stop the progress of the Cilicians in their lawless conduct, were obliged to have recourse to armies of considerable force, in order to destroy the power of the pirates. But Strabo excuses the Romans by saying, that they had at home so many things of greater interest to look to, that it is not to be wondered at if they neglected what was passing at a distance from the metropolis.

POMPEIOPOLIS* (SOLI).—On the coast, five miles to the westward of Mursina, are the ruins of Pompeiopolis. They are in a delightful situa-

* See Dr. Holt Yates's description and plan of the ancient ruins, from Captain Prissick's report, which will illustrate my remarks; *Modern History and Condition of Egypt, &c.* (Smith and Elder). We have already quoted Admiral Sir Francis Beaufort's admirable account of these ruins from his *Karamania*, pp. 249, 259 et seq.

tion, but at present deserted. Here and there a little plot of ground is cultivated; the rest is overgrown with pines and brushwood. The only public buildings that can be distinguished out of such a heap of ruins are, 1st, the place of the amphitheatre, which was built of white marble, and had at the top all round a cornice with wreaths in alto relievo, between each of which was sculptured a tragic mask. In this place was found the centre part of a Venus of full size, in white marble. 2dly, Some hundred columns, forty-two of which are still standing: they are composed of several pieces, and are about thirty feet high. Their capital above is ornamented with sculptured heads of Venus, Hercules, &c. There are six fluted columns, which stand out beyond the others. The whole are of very inferior work and taste. It is supposed that these columns served for an aqueduct, because it is difficult to explain exactly for what other object they were erected. Sir Francis Beaufort states that possibly the whole colonnade was once a covered street. The people of the country call Pompeiopolis *Aski Shahir*, "the old town:" Mazatli is a village higher up inland. There is a tradition that Soli was built by "*Hakmun*," a Jew, who erected for his daughter "*Hind*" a castle two miles above the town, which is still standing on the banks of the river, but in ruins, and appears to be of Saracenic origin. 3dly, and that which attracts the attention of the antiquary above all other remains, are some tombs which have certainly a very ancient origin. One that is out of the town to the eastward, near the river, in a field, has been opened. It contained two large sarcophagi, more than twelve feet long; one is overturned, and the other still in its place. They are of marble, without any ornament, not having been

SARCOPHAGUS AT SELEUCIA PIERIA, OPENED BY MR. W. B. BARKER.

intended to be seen, but to be completely buried in the masonry. They have been originally covered all over by a composition formed of pebbles, sand, quick-lime, and pieces of brick, which has become petrified. Some inquisitive persons have succeeded in detaching this composition from the sarcophagi when opening the tomb, and they are now quite empty.*

Another tomb, which has not been opened, lies in the town to the west of the amphitheatre towards the sea, and is overgrown with brushwood. It appears to be eight times the size of the last described. The French consul some years back tried to force it open; but although he cut the monument nearly half through at the centre, as he did not happen to light upon either of the sarcophagi, they have remained enveloped in their pristine mass of mortar.

Judging from what we see here, I conclude that the great monument at Tarsus, which so highly deserves the antiquary's attention, and which has frustrated every historical inquiry as to its origin, contains similar sarcophagi. It is of the same epoch and composition as the last mentioned in Pompeiopolis, but at least one hundred times larger. It has two parallelograms that may be about 80 feet square each; they are at a distance from one another of about 200 paces, surrounded by a wall of the same composition, which is 30 feet high and 22 broad. To the north are two similar walls parallel to the monuments; and a third that was begun and remained unfinished, because (I suppose) it was not required to contain any more sarcophagi.

1. Here a large hole has been made, but nothing found.
2. Vain attempts at an opening.
3. Here a tunnel was made sideways in the monument at the base till it reached the centre, and then the French consul dug down perpendicularly till he came to water, without finding any thing in this conglomerated mass of lime and pebbles, except the first and second fingers of a man in marble, of gigantic size, joined together, but not as if they had belonged to the hand of a statue, but a finished work in itself.
4. Here are holes in the wall made to support beams, which must

* Here I may mention having opened two similar sarcophagi of very massive stone at the ancient Seleucia Pieria near Suwaidiyah, or Suedia, a few years back. There was this difference, that these sarcophagi were of a yellow stone, and had a bas-relief ornament in the shape of a garland of ordinary work on their side and on the lids, for they were at first intended to be exposed to view, and not buried in any mortar whatever. The cover or lid was so large, that although it had been broken in several pieces, it required some trouble to move the fragments. Both these sarcophagi were found empty for about a foot, beyond which there was a layer of clay three inches deep; then below this were several large stones regularly built in, like the building of a wall; and where the right ear should be, we found a small jar of very ordinary terra-cotta work in each. The only difference between these two sarcophagi was, that in one the ashes of the dead were collected in the little jar; but in the other the jar was empty, and the ashes were strewn between each layer of the stone masonry built in the sarcophagus. On one were the remains of a Greek inscription quite illegible. See the sarcophagus in the preceding page, as well as the one in page 35.

ANCIENT TOMB. 133

have been placed against it to form shelter for some Turkish cavalry in modern times. The whole of what is now standing is, as it were, only the *interior* of a wall, the facing, composed of large fine marble stones

WALL UNFINISHED.

WALL 30 FT HIGH 22 BROAD

WALL 30 FT HIGH 22 BROAD

WALL 30 FT HIGH 22 BROAD

MODERN GARDEN.

CUT BY THE TURKS TO INTRODUCE THEIR CAVALRY

1

2

3

4

WALL 30 FT HIGH 22 BROAD

MODERN GARDEN.

2

2

2

2

WALL 30 FT HIGH 22 BROAD

GROUND-PLAN OF THE GREAT MAUSOLEUM AT TARSUS.

has all been taken away and used elsewhere. I imagine that these walls also contain sarcophagi of some branch of the family of an ancient king, and that they were laid in the walls and filled up and covered with the mortar as the persons died; for the last wall to the north has remained unfinished for want of tenants. In the centre there was space reserved, as it is said, for Sardanapalus himself, who, however, could not have required this mausoleum, having destroyed himself by fire in his palace at Ninus. Some assert that he was buried in a similar monument at Anchiale on the coast, and that, in conformity to his desire, an inscription was erected over it commemorating his having built Tarsus and Anchiale in one day, as a trophy of his greatness and power. Where Anchiale stood, there are now the remains of such a monument; but it is insignificant compared with this one. Many vain attempts have been made to open this monument; and it remains a question worthy the attention of antiquaries, inasmuch as it has hitherto frustrated the investigation of the learned; and all hypotheses formed upon its pristine object and the date of its construction are as vague as any proposed concerning the pyramids.*

Strabo, remarking upon this portion of the coast, says, that Cape Anamour (Anemurium) is the nearest point of the land to Cyprus, being 350 stadia; and he calls the distance from the frontiers of Pamphilia to this cape 820 stadia along the coast of Cilicia. "The rest of the coast, of about 500 stadia, terminates at Soli." Strabo further observes, that some persons considered Cilicia to begin at Celenderis (Kilindriya), and not at Coracesium (Kurkass); but this is no doubt in reference to those who divide Cilicia into two, Campestris and Trachea; Celenderis belonging to the latter, and Kurkass to the former.

Strabo mentions two philosophers among the illustrious men born in Seleucia, Athenæus and Xenarchus. The former, he says, was friend of Murcia, who had revolted against Augustus, and fell into disgrace, having been taken prisoner with his friend; but having proved his innocence, was set at liberty by order of this prince. On his return to Rome, being cross-questioned by some persons who met him, he replied, desirous of avoiding any political discussions, "I have just

* The people of the country call it Dunce Dash—*Pierre renversée*—and foolishly imagine that it is a temple turned upside down, with its foundations upwards! W. B. B.

We have seen in a note upon Selinus, afterwards Trajanopolis, that Admiral Sir Francis Beaufort identified a low massy edifice of seventy feet by fifty, composed of large well-cut blocks of stone, and containing a single vault, with the tomb or mausoleum of Trajan. Mr. Barker describes similar remains at Soli or Pompeiopolis. These appear to be the massive mausolea in which the sarcophagi of the great were imbedded before and at the early part of the Christian era. May not the great mausoleum at Tarsus be the tomb of Julian, with which others have been afterwards connected? A mausoleum of similar characters, but of later date, has been joined to that of Trajan, on one side of which is a sepulchral inscription to Chrestion, the son of Rhæstus. The existence of more than one mausoleum within the precincts of Julian's tomb would not thus militate against the validity of the identification. W. F. A.

left the residence of the dead, and been freed from the gates of the lower regions." He was killed by the fall, during the night, of a house which he inhabited. Xenarchus passed his life chiefly in Alexandria and Athens, and the latter part in Rome. He enjoyed the friendship of Areus,* and afterwards the good will of Augustus; and was much respected to the last, dying in an advanced age, after having lost the use of his sight. Strabo does not omit to say that he had been one of his disciples, "*and followed his lessons.*"

Strabo says that at the extremity of the Taurus ridge, high up, was Mount Olympus, called, no doubt, after the Olympus of classical celebrity, whereon was a castle of the same name, and from whence you might see Lycia, Pamphilia, and Pisidia, and which served as the stronghold of the pirate Zenicetus. This must be a way of speaking allegorically to express the great height of the Taurus near the sea at this place; for Strabo could not, had he ever been there, make this assertion, as the mountains to the north of Sulufska, and which run along the coast, intervene between the eye and Lycia. The ridge is here sufficiently high to see therefrom the island of Cyprus, or some sixty miles off; but it cannot overtop the mountains that intervene between it and Lycia.

This country was much fortified, as may be seen by the many remains of old castles all along the coast, many of which have been repaired by the Genoese, and adapted to resist the attacks of modern warfare. Strabo says, that the Romans considered it too unsettled and too much exposed to be attacked both by sea and land, to undertake to govern it themselves by means of officers or proconsuls, and that they preferred it should be governed by kings, who might be always present to suppress any insurrection or incursion of pirates; and they " gave Cilicia Trachea to Archelaus, who already possessed Cappadocia."

The pirate Zenicetus, Strabo tells us, burnt himself and his whole family in his castle, when Publius Servilius, surnamed *Isauricus*, became master of the mountain. He was at the time also " master of the Cape Corycus, and of the town of Phaselis and other places in Pamphilia, which were all taken by the general previous to Pompey's occupation of the country" (year of Rome 674, c. 679).†

Next to Lamus (the present Illamus) comes Soli, whence begins Cilicia Proper (Campestris). It was founded by the Acheans and the people of Rhodes, from the town of Lindus; and when Pompey subdued the pirates, as the number of inhabitants was much reduced, he established therein such of those whom he had conquered as he

* See Plutarch in Anton. § 81.   † Vide Eutrop. lib. vi. cap. 3.

deemed worthy of pardon, and changed the name of the town, calling it Pompeiopolis, after himself.

The illustrious men of Soli enumerated by Strabo are, Chrysippus, a Stoic philosopher, son of an inhabitant of Tarsus who had settled in Soli; Philemon, a comic poet, and Aratus, author of a poem entitled *The Phenomena.*

There were two capes that bore the name of Zephyrium, one near the Calycadnus river of Sulufska, and the other in sight of Anchiale. Near this latter is the present village of Mursina; at its extremity are the ruins of an ancient building, which the people of the country have dubbed with the title of Church of St. George; and the Christians repair thither once a-year and pay their devotions under a large tree, which they have consecrated in their minds. The whole of the hill at this cape was covered with the foundations of ancient buildings, most of which I caused to be excavated, to build therewith a large magazine and house, which commands the finest prospect on the coast, and are both a kind of landmark to vessels approaching the roadstead of Mursina. The people of the country not being allowed the use of bells, which only Europeans may have or ring, there being a Mahomedan prejudice against them, arising from a notion that the idol worship of Baal is attached to them, I recollect one day being specially requested to allow my dinner-bell (which was a large ship's bell) to be sounded in order to inspire extra devotional feelings in those who had assembled near my house to pay their devotions to St. George on the day set apart for that saint according to the Armenian calculation.

At Anchiale (the present Karadujar), says Strabo, citing Aristobulus, was the tomb of Sardanapalus, and a statue of stone representing him snapping his fingers, with this inscription below it: "Sardanapalus, the son of Anacyndaraxes, caused the town of Anchiale to be built in one day, and also that of Tarsus. Passer-by, eat, drink, and divert thyself; for every thing else is not worth *that*" (meaning a snap of the fingers). The poet Chæribus mentions also this inscription, which is no longer in existence. But there is an old ruin, the mortar of which is petrified, and which may stand for the supposed tomb above mentioned.

To the north of Anchiale was a fort, called by Strabo Cynda, where he says that "the kings of Macedonia deposited their treasure,* and which Eumenes carried off when he rebelled against Antigonus."

Forming a triangle with this fort and Soli, at the foot of the Taurus

---

* Strabo, it appears, looked upon the generals of Alexander of Macedon as Macedonians, and therefore gives to Antigonus this title, although he was master chiefly of Asia Minor as far as Syria.

was *Olbus*. This town had a temple to Jupiter, founded by Ajax, son of Teuca; and the priests of this temple, says Strabo, were formerly masters of Cilicia Trachea, which is very expressive of the influence of the priests in those times, considering the difficulties of the road, and the distance from their temple into another province so much separated by nature as Cilicia Trachea and Campestris. Later, continues Strabo, the country was taken possession of by marauders, and converted into a stronghold for brigands. When they were destroyed, " which took place in our time," this province took the title of Principality of Teucer, and even " Priesthood of Teucer;" and the greater part of the priests of the temple bore the name of Teucer or Ajax. " Alba, daughter of Zenophanus, having married one of the Teucer family, took possession of this province, which had been under the regency of her father. She was confirmed in her rule by Antony and Cleopatra; but afterwards, at a later period, she was dethroned, and the government restored to the family."

" Next to Anchiale," says Strabo, " is the mouth of the Cydnus, at the place called Rhegma, which is a lake, and where you may still see the remains of stocks for building of ships. Into this lake the Cydnus falls." The river at present circumvents the lake, which is a marsh of about thirty miles in circumference. The modern Tarsus is watered by a canal from the Cydnus, and this, after passing through the town, used to fall into the marshes; but the Mufti, at my suggestion, caused a road to be cut for it to return into the river, in hopes that the waters of the marsh would diminish, and, in case there was no spring in the lake, that it might eventually be dried up, which would make the residence much more salubrious. At present, the exhalations from the marsh, which are blown over the town by the sea-breeze, render the place most unhealthy; and the fevers that are engendered thereby are of the most pernicious kind, often carrying off the persons attacked by them in three days.

As I have observed in another part of this work, the lake had been at one time drained, and the remains of a canal to carry off the waters and turn them into the Cydnus may be seen close along the shore at the mouth of the river. I also believe that this lake was once a port, and communicated with the sea through a passage which is now but slightly blocked up by the sand. Strabo confirms this idea by adding: " This river has its source in that part of the Taurus which is above Tarsus, and it traverses this town (the ancient Tarsus, on part of which only the present town stands) before reaching the lake; *so that this latter serves as a port to the town.*"

Strabo tells us that "Tarsus was founded by Triptolemus (a priest of Argos) in his search after Io;" and there were at Tarsus and Antioch monuments to prove that Io had been in their neighbourhood, and that they were colonies of Argos.*

Strabo further says, that as the sources of the Cydnus are not far from the town which it traverses, directly after leaving a deep valley, its waters are cold, and the current strong. "These," he adds, "are considered good for persons or animals suffering from sprains or inflamed limbs;" as if the good effects of the cold water, which we fancy to be a discovery of modern times, were known and had recourse to in his time.

Strabo proceeds to say, that the inhabitants of Tarsus had distinguished themselves so much by their application to philosophy and literature, that this city in that point surpassed Athens, Alexandria, or even any other town where schools and colleges were to be met with directed by philosophers and learned men. "The only difference is, that at Tarsus those who apply themselves to literature are all Tarsiots, and that it is visited by few strangers; even those who are born there do not remain in this town, but leave it to go and perfect themselves elsewhere; and they remain away from home willingly, except a small number, who return to their country. This is quite the contrary in the other towns that I have referred to above (except Alexandria): many strangers go there to study, and fix themselves in them, whilst few of their inhabitants leave their town out of love of science, or seek to instruct themselves at home—two things that take place in Alexandria, whose inhabitants receive many strangers in their schools, and send a great many of their young men to the schools of other towns."—"Tarsus possesses schools for every kind of instruction. It is furthermore populous and powerful, and must be regarded as a capital."

Of the illustrious men whom this city has produced, Strabo mentions Antipater, Archimedes, and Nestor, Stoic philosophers, and the two Athenodori. Antipater was disciple and successor of Diogenes, the Babylonian (not the cynic of Sinopi, but the disciple of Chrysippus), about 80 B.C. according to Lempriere; but Smith places him 144 B.C. Feeling his deficiency in the powers of disputing verbally with his opponent and contemporary, Carneades, he confined himself to writing, whence he was called *Kalamoboas*. Cicero praises his acuteness, and Plutarch speaks of him with Zeno, Cleanthes, and Chrysippus, as one of the principal Stoic philosophers.

* Vide Smith's Dic. of Greek and Rom. Biog. and Myth.

I find no particular mention of Archimedes and Nestor in Smith's *Biography*; but of the Athenodori we find that the first was called Cananites, from a town in Cilicia, although he was a native of Tarsus; and Cicero calls him Athenodorus Calvus. He was in great favour with Augustus, whose government became milder in consequence of his attending to his advice, and the young Claudius was instructed by him. He retired to Tarsus, where he died at the age of 82, much beloved and respected in his own native city, of which he has written an account, as well as other works.*

The other Athenodorus, surnamed Cordylia, was also a native of Tarsus, and a Stoic philosopher. He was keeper of the library at Pergamus; and in his anxiety to preserve the doctrines of his sect in their original purity, used to cut out from the works of the Stoic writers such parts as appeared to him erroneous or inconsistent. He removed from Pergamus to Rome, and lived with M. Cato, at whose house he died.† Strabo enters into a long account of the first-mentioned Athenodorus, how, on his return to Tarsus, finding Boëthus and his faction intractable, he availed himself of the power confided to him by Augustus, and banished them. This same Boëthus, Strabo tells us, was as bad a citizen as a poet, and maintained himself in power over his fellow townsmen by flattering Antony, whom he compared to Achilles, Agamemnon, and Ulysses, in his verses, which he had the impudence to insinuate were like those of Homer.

"These philosophers," says Strabo, "whom I have mentioned, were Stoics; but the sect of the Academicians has furnished us in our days with one other distinguished man, Nestor, who was preceptor to Marcellus, son of Octavia, sister of Augustus. This philosopher was at the head of affairs in Cilicia, after Athenodorus, whom he succeeded, and he enjoyed to the end of his days the esteem of the governors (sent from Rome) and that of his fellow-countrymen."

As to the other philosophers "*whom I know and specify by their names*," says Strabo, quoting this line of Homer, "there are two, Plutiades and Diogenes, both among those who pass from city to city, to shine in society by making their talents appreciated. Diogenes possessed, moreover, the power of improvising, like a man inspired, on all kinds of subjects—poems, for the greater part, of a tragic turn."‡

This Diogenes mentioned here is not, I should suppose, the Diogenes Laërtius, the historian of philosophers, although it is remarkable that

---
* Vide Hoffman Dissert. de Athen. Tarsensi, Lips. 1732; Sevin, in the Mémoires de l'Acad. des Inscr. xix. 14.
† Vide Smith's Myth. ‡ Vide Laertius, lib. iv. sigm. 58.

he is also one of the celebrated men of whom Cilicia can boast, as he received his surname from being a native of the town of Laërte in Cilicia.

Of Plutiades I found no mention elsewhere, except that Smith seems to think him to be the same as Plution, who was a celebrated teacher of rhetoric; and Westerman places him in the period between Augustus and Hadrian.

"The grammarians that came from Tarsus," says Strabo, "are Artemidorus and Diodorus. This town also produced Dionysides, an excellent tragic poet, and one of the seven who composed what is called the *Pleiad*." This Artemidorus is supposed to be the same as the grammarian of that name surnamed Aristophanius, from his being a disciple of the celebrated grammarian Aristophanes of Byzantium, at Alexandria, who had also another disciple named *Diodorus*, and who may be, perhaps, the person above referred to by Strabo.

There was in the time of the Emperor Valens a person of this name, who was appointed Bishop of Tarsus (A.D. 378) by Melitus, the Bishop of Antioch. Diodorus attended the Council of Constantinople (A.D. 381), at which the general superintendence of the Eastern churches was entrusted to him and Pelagius of L odiceia.

Of Dionysides nothing further is known than what Strabo says above, that he was one of the best of the composers of the *Tragic Pleiad* of the Alexandrian grammarians, and regarding whom historians are not so well agreed as regarding their number. Hephæstion the scholiast makes them contemporary with Ptolemy Philadelphus, and calls them Homer (not the author of the *Iliad*), Sositheus, Lycophron, Alexander (cited by Strabo in more places than one), Œantides, Sosiphanes, and Philiscus. Others place *Aratus, Apollonius, Nicander*, and *Theocritus* at the head of the list, although none of these poets wrote any tragedies.

"It is particularly in Rome," continues Strabo, "that we may procure information regarding the great number of men of letters produced by Tarsus; for it is full of learned men from that city, as well as from Alexandria. But," he concludes, "*this is enough regarding Tarsus*."

From this Strabo passes on to the Pyramus, which, he says, comes from Cataonia, and he refers to his account of this river, where he describes the country whence it takes its rise, alluding at the same time to the deposits of mud which this stream makes, and which, he says, gave rise to an oracle, which declared "that the time would come when posterity would see the Pyramus reach the island of Cyprus, by means of its deposits on the continent;" and, indeed, the sea is rather shallow at the mouth of the Pyramus: when the drag-nets are thrown, the men have to wade in the water for a quarter of a mile, as ropes of a general length are too short to reach the shore; and what is remarkable is, that such is the abundance of turtle on this coast, that they fill the sack of the net, and have to be extracted therefrom three times before the net can reach the shore, by which time, however, it is generally found abundantly provided with fish.

The mention of the mouth of the Pyramus naturally leads Strabo to notice Mallos, now a little ruin, and which, he tells us, was founded by Amphilochus and Mopsus. The latter, however, remaining master of the place on Amphilocus's voyage to Argos, refused to admit him to share in his authority on his return; on which a mortal combat ensued, wherein both perished; and they were buried at a distance from each other, so that the tomb of the one could not be discerned from that of the other, " in order that their enmity should cease after death."

Strabo also mentions two fables regarding the death of Calchas, the greatest of the Grecian soothsayers at Troy. "Hesiod," says he, "arranges this fable in the following manner. Calchas proposed to Mopsus this enigma: 'I am astonished at the quantity of figs on this wild fig-tree; could you guess the number of them?' Mopsus replied, 'There are ten thousand of them, which make a *medim* measure, and there remains one over; and this you are not capable of understanding.' Thus spoke Mopsus; and the measure having been found complete (or correct), the sleep of death closed the eyes of Calchas.

" But," continues Strabo "according to Pherecydes, the subject of the enigma was a sow with young. Calchas asked Mopsus how many pigs it bore. Mopsus replied three, and one of which a female. Calchas, finding Mopsus right, died of grief. Others say that he proposed the enigma of the sow. and that Mopsus in his turn proposed that of the fig-tree; and that Calchas, not having been able to guess rightly, died of vexation, as it had been predicted to him by an oracle. Sophocles, in his 'Vindication of Helen,' says that the oracle had declared to Calchas that he was destined to die as soon as he met with a soothsayer cleverer than him. This same poet places this dispute and death of Calchas in Cilicia. But this is enough," says Strabo, " of these ancient fables."

"Mallos" (or Mallus), says Strabo, "was the birth-place of the grammarian Crates, of whom Panœtius tells us he was a disciple." This Crates was son of Simocrates, and lived in the reign of Ptolemy Philometer, and was contemporary with Aristarchus. This would give us some clue to the epoch in which his disciple lived, and regarding whom there is some uncertainty as to the year of his birth or death.* Crates was brought up at Tarsus, and afterwards removed to Pergamus, where he founded a school about the year 157 B.C. He was sent by Attalus ambassador to Rome, where, having by accident broken his leg, he was compelled to lead a sedentary life, and this enabled him to find time to hold frequent grammatical lectures. This, says our historian, is all that is known of the life of Crates.

We are told by Strabo that, whilst Philotas conducted the cavalry of Alexander through the Aleian plains—taking, no doubt, the route which is the high road of the present day through Adana and Missis—the latter conducted the infantry from Soli along the coast to Issus. He must, of course, have passed by Mallos; and Strabo says that it was reported that Alexander offered libations on the tomb of Amphilochus, in consideration of their common origin from the city of Argos.†

After mentioning different places on the coast, such as Ægeus (Ayas), the Pylæ Amanidæ, Issus, Rhosus (Arsus), and the Pylæ Syriæ, he says that the first Syrian town on leaving the latter is Seleucia Pieria, the Suedia described in this work, "near which the Orontes river discharges its waters. From this town to Soli the navigation in a straight line is about 1000 stadia."‡ He then concludes with the following passage regarding the origin of the Cilicians:

"As the Cilicians of Troy whom Homer mentions § are very far from the Cilicians of Mount Taurus, some people pretend that the latter issued from the first; and they shew places bearing the same name as those of Trojan Cilicia, such as Thebes and Lernassus in Pamphilia. Others, on the contrary, consider the Cilicians of Troy to be descended from those beyond the Taurus, and equally point out among them a plain which is called Aleium (after that in which is Tarsus)."

* Vide Smith's Myth. † Vide Arrian de Exped. Alexand. lib. ii. cap. 5.
‡ I have crossed it by a sixteen hours' sail in an open boat.
§ Iliad, lib. vi. vers. 395-397.

LARES AND PENATES;

OR THE

HOUSEHOLD GODS OF CILICIA.

LARES AND PENATES.

CHAPTER I.

INTRODUCTORY.

LARES and PENATES were the names of the household gods of the ancients. Many derivations have been found for both: the Lares from their descent from Lara; but the most likely is that given by Apuleius (*De Deo Socratis*), from *lar*, familiaris. The Penates appear to be essentially of Eastern origin, and the etymology of the word, it has been said, must be sought in the Phrygian; although Cicero and others have given it a Latin origin, *quod penitus insident*, or again, *quia coluntur in penetralibus*, "because they are worshipped in the innermost recesses of the house."

A mythology or pantheism of this kind dates from the most remote antiquity; it is probably one of the first soothing fictions by which the great Deity was brought into immediate contact with persons and actions. The Egyptians had their four gods, for example, who presided over the birth of children — Genius, Fortune, Love, and Necessity. These were subsequently called PRÆSTITES,

"Quod præstant oculis omnia tuta suis"—OVID. *Fast;*

and were supposed to take care of particular houses and families. We trace the same faith lingering in poetic rather than admitted notions of angelic and saintly interference in our own times.

The Penates were divinities, or household gods, who were believed to be the creators or dispensers of all the well-being and gifts of fortune enjoyed by a family, as well as an entire community. It is not clear whether all or which of the gods were venerated as Penates; for

L

many are mentioned of both sexes, Jupiter, Juno, Minerva, Vesta, Neptune, Apollo, &c.; but every family worshipped one or more of these, whose images were kept in the inner part of the house, the *tablinum*, situated beyond the atrium. They are represented in various ways on coins and medals. Mr. Rich gives an example in his *Illustrated Companion to the Latin Dictionary and Greek Lexicon*, from the Vatican *Virgil*, in which they appear as old men, with their heads veiled like priests officiating at a sacrifice. The occurrence of such an illustration would tend to throw some light on the bearded and hooded figures met with in the Tarsus collection, and the origin of which will be afterwards discussed under various points of view.

The Lares, as tutelary spirits, were also sometimes confounded with the souls of deceased persons. Thus Apuleius tells us that the private or domestic Lares were no more than the souls of departed persons who had lived well and discharged the duties of their station; whereas those who had done otherwise were vagabond, wandering about and frightening people under the name of Larvæ and Lemures. The Lares were supposed to exercise a protecting influence over the interior of every man's household, himself, his family, and property; and yet they were not regarded as divinities like the Penates, but simply as guardian spirits, whose place was the chimney-piece, and whose altar was the domestic hearth (focus) in the atrium, and where each individual made offerings of incense to them in his own home. Many illustrations of these descriptions of private or domestic Lares occur in the Tarsus collection.

According to Ovid there were but two Lares; and these, like the Penates, were worshipped in the form of little figures or images of wax, earthenware, or terra cotta, and of metal, more especially silver. They were dressed in short habits, to shew their readiness to serve, and they held a sort of cornucopiæ in their hands, as the emblem of hospitality and good house-keeping. Rich says they are constantly represented in works of art as young men crowned with a chaplet of laurel leaves, in a short tunic,[*] and holding up a drinking-horn (*cornu*, not the *cornucopiæ*,) above their heads; and he gives an example from a bas-relief in the Vatican, under which is the inscription, "Laribus Augustis."[†] Examples are met with in the Tarsus collection.

---

[*] Succinctis Laribus. *Pers.* v. 31.

[†] The Lares were also represented as young boys, with dog-skins about their shoulders, and with their heads covered, which was a sign of that freedom and liberty which men ought to enjoy in their own houses; their symbol was a dog, to denote their fidelity, and the service that animal does to man in preserving and watching over

The accessory of the drinking-horn has induced many antiquaries to take these figures for cup-bearers (*pocillatores*); but the inscription just mentioned is sufficient evidence of their real character, and they are repeatedly seen on the walls of the Pompeian houses, in kitchens, bakehouses, and over street-doors, standing in pairs, one on each side of an altar, in the same attitude and drapery. Great houses and persons of wealth had their Lararia, a sort of shrine, small chapel, or apartment, where the statues of the Lares, as well as of other sanctified or deified personages, were placed and worshipped.* Tatius, king of the Sabines, is said to have built a temple to the Lares.

Plutarch distinguishes the Lares, like the Genii, into good and evil; and there were also public and private Lares. The public Lares were sometimes called *Compitalis*, from *compitum*, a cross-way; and *Viales*, from *via*, a way, or public road, as being placed at the intersection of roads and in the highways, and esteemed the patrons and protectors of travellers. The Romans also gave the name *Urbani*, that is, Lares of the cities, to those who had cities under their care; and *Hostilii*, to those who were to keep off their enemies. There were also Lares of the country, called *Rurales*, as appears from several ancient inscriptions; and also Lares called *Permarini*, who, it is probable, were the Lares of ships; nor is it unreasonable to suppose that these floating houses should have their tutelar deities as well as others. They had even their grunting Lares; the Lares called *Grundiles* having, according to tradition, been instituted by Romulus, in honour of a sow that brought forth at one time thirty pigs. The name *Grundiles* was given to them *a grunnitu*, from grunting.

When the Roman youths laid aside the bull (a golden ornament shaped like a heart, but hollow, which they constantly wore till fourteen years of age), they consecrated or hung it up to the Lares. Slaves likewise, when they obtained their freedom, hung up their chains to these deities.

The Romans at first offered young people in sacrifice both to the

---

the places allotted to their charge, on which account the dog was particularly consecrated to them. The number of heads, and other portions of "deified boys," in the Tarsus collection, is quite remarkable, and would tend to shew that the intention of these figures was the same in Cicilia as it was at Rome. Figures of dogs are not so common, but several instances occur, sufficient indeed to lead us to believe that the same tradition with regard to these faithful domestic animals as obtained among the Romans was also accepted by the Cicilians. They appear to have been the hoarders up of the mythological traditions of almost all the countries by which they were surrounded, or by which they were successively conquered.

* Lamprid. *Alex. Sev.* 29, 31.

Lares and Penates; but those barbarous rites were ultimately superseded by more harmless offerings,—hogs in public, and wine, incense, heads of poppies, bandages of wool, and images of straw in private; they also crowned them with flowers, particularly with the violet, myrtle, and rosemary.

The term Lares, according to Mr. Bryant's mythological theory, was formed from *laren*, an ancient word by which the ark was represented; and he supposes that the Lares and Manes were the same domestic deities under different names, and that by these terms the Hetrurians and Latins denote the Dii Arkitæ, who were no other than their Arkite ancestors, or the persons preserved in the laren or ark, the genius of which was Isis, the reputed parent of the world. He observes further that they are described as dæmons and genii, who once lived on earth, and were gifted with immortality. Arnobius styles them, *Lares quosdam genios et functorum animas*; and he says that, according to Varro, they were the children of Mania. Flutius* adds, that Mania had also the name of Laranda, and she is styled the mother of the dæmons. By some she is called Lara, and was supposed to preside over families; and children were offered at her altar in order to procure her favour. In lieu of these they in after-times offered the heads of poppies and pods of garlic.

This accounts somewhat for the discrepancy of the ancients as to their origin. For example, Varro and Macrobius say that they were the children of Mania; Ovid makes them the issue of Mercury and Lara or Larunda; Apuleius assures us that they were the posterity of the Lemures; Nigridius, according to Arnobius, made them sometimes the guardians and protectors of houses, and sometimes the same with the Curetes of Samo-Thracia, which the Greeks call *Idæi dactyli*. Nor was Varro more consistent in his own opinions, sometimes making them the manes of heroes, and sometimes gods of the air. In Cilicia we have a faint tracing of the admixture of Egyptian and Samo-Thracian mysteries in the national Pantheism, in the existence of a terra-cotta crocodile, a crocodile river, Kersus of Xenophon, Andricus of Pliny, and a " Mons crocodilus."

With respect to the Penates, they were of three classes: those who presided over empires and states, those who had the protection of cities, and those who took the care or guardianship of private families; the last were called the lesser Penates. According to others, there were four classes: the celestial, the sea-gods, the gods of hell, and all such heroes as had received divine honours after death.

* Demonst. prop. iv. p. 139.

Authors are not agreed about the origin of the Dii Penates, which are generally admitted to have come originally from Asia, and were known as the tutelary gods of the Trojans. Dionysius Halicarnassus tells us that Æneas first lodged these gods in the city of Lavinium, and that his son Ascanius, upon building the city of Alba, translated them thither, but that they returned twice miraculously to Lavinium. The same author adds, that in Rome there was still seen a dark temple, shaded by the adjacent buildings, wherein were the images of the Trojan gods, with the inscription " Denas," which signifies Penates. These images represented two young men sitting, each of which held a lance. I have seen, says Dionysius, several other statues of the same gods in ancient temples, who all appear like young men dressed in the habit of war. Varro brings the Penates from Samothrace to Phrygia, to be afterwards transported by Æneas into Italy.

It is a popular question among the learned, who were the Penates of Rome? Some say Vesta, others Neptune and Apollo; Vives says Castor and Pollux, with whom agrees Vossius, who adds, that the reason of their choosing Castor and Pollux in the quality of Penates might be the important service they rendered the Romans in some of their wars. When Macrobius says that Jupiter, Juno, and Minerva were the Penates of the Romans, it does not follow from that that they were the Penates of Rome. It seems, indeed, to have been in the option of every master of a family to choose his Penates; and hence it was that Jupiter and some of the superior gods were often invoked as patrons of domestic affairs.

The positive domestic and public deities selected by a country or province and its inhabitants were, perhaps, never before so fully illustrated as in the instance of the remarkable collection now brought to light, discovered also in a country of great antiquity, and which perhaps, more than any other in the East, forms the connecting link between Assyrian and Greek mythology, and with Lycia between Assyrian and Greek art. The light they may yet be made to throw upon these relations will, in all probability, be found to be very considerable, and to present a field of investigation as yet almost untouched.

The Assyrians of old recognised in the stars of heaven golden chariots of heavenly hosts.* Zeus or Baal, as the most perfect leader of the most perfect chariot, was drawn by the finest and largest horses of Asia; while the god of the sun had only one single Nisæan horse, or was represented

---

* Grotefend on the *Mythology of the Assyrians, according to the Sculptures of the Palace at Nimrud.*

upon a winged horse, whose image Layard* found embroidered upon the garment of the king.†

Like the tradition of Bellerophon and Perseus, whom, according to Herodotus,‡ the Persians declared to be an Assyrian, the designation of this horse by the name of Pegasus seems to be of Assyrian origin, especially since Tarsus, whose inhabitants, according to Dio Chrysostomus,§ worshipped Perseus, together with Hercules or Sandon,|| and the tridented Apollo, is said to have been built by an Assyrian king.¶

We have here, then, at once accurate legendary information as to the Penates of Tarsus, and tolerably satisfactory testimony as to the Assyrian origin of some of them. Perseus himself has been recognised in this collection; and it has been ingeniously suggested that Tarsus winged, feathered, pinioned, may have reference to the conqueror of the Gorgon. Reasons have been elsewhere given for a preference to an etymology which brings Tarsus more into connexion with the story of Bellerophon, and the frequent fragments of horses' feet have been suggested to have some reference to Pegasus; while the circumstance of the Apollo of Tarsus being winged might be made to bear reference to either or both of these local traditions. We may observe that Apollo was the chief object of superstitious worship at Tarsus; that his image was no doubt in every house; that his remains are more numerous than the other objects of heathen idolatry; and that he is represented in many various ways.

We have also a head of a horse which, it has been suggested, may be one of the horses of the sun; a surmise which is further said to be sup-

* Vol. ii. p. 461, fig. 84.

† Grotefend describes, from Layard, a slab at Nimrud upon which is sculptured a flying horseman, who bore a helmet with curved crest. The Persians themselves, Layard remarks, vol. i. p. 443, may have recognised the Assyrian source of their religion, when they declared Perseus, the founder of their race, to have been an Assyrian. Herodotus, i. vi. c. 54. The head of Perseus occurs on two of the Babylonian cylinders engraved by Mr. Cullimore for the Syro-Egyptian Society.

Some traditions made this Perseus a great astronomer, who instructed men in the knowledge of the stars. Περσευς ὁ Ἡλιος. Perseus is the sun, says the scholiast in Lycophr. v. 18. According to some, he married Astarte, the daughter of Belus. All these traditions point to his Assyrian origin.

I only find in Layard, vol. i. p. 376, mention of a horseman wearing a helmet with a curved crest, pursued by two Assyrian warriors; but in vol. ii. p. 461, is figured the winged horse, "so closely," says Layard, "resembling the Pegasus of the Greeks, that we can scarcely doubt the identity."

‡ Herodotus, vi. 54.

§ *Orat.* xxxiii. init. and p. 407, ed. Mon.

|| Compare Raoul Rochette, *Mémoire sur l'Hercule Assyrien*, p. 489 et seq.

¶ Ammianus Marcellinus writes of Tarsus, xiv. 8, *Haud condidisse Perseus memoratur, vel certe ex Anchi(al)o profectas Sandon quidem nomine, vir opulentus et nobilis.*

ported by another fragment existing in the collection which shews the head of a second horse coupled to it as if attached to a chariot, and also by the many votive memorials of horses' limbs before alluded to.

We have in the collection several heads of Hercules, one of which is radiated, and figures of Hercules with the mace. The Assyrian Hercules, Sandes, Sandon, or Sandok,* but more properly Dayyad the Hunter, was represented on a colossal winged figure holding a mace, and also as bearing a stag on one arm, and a flower with five blossoms in the right hand. It does not appear that this latter form of the divinity was accepted by the Tarsians.

It is sufficient, however, that we certainly find traces of Assyrian mythology interwoven into a compound worship—the Egyptian, Syrian, Grecian, and Roman characters of which are elsewhere developed,—and which combination has been justly pointed out to have arisen from the local position of Tarsus and its commercial connexions. "I believe," remarks Mr. Abington, " that there has never before been presented to this world so striking a proof of the easy plastic character of the old mythology as we find in this precious collection of antiquities." A further development even to this view of the matter is given when we add an Assyrian origin to the most characteristic of the Tarsus divinities, and to the before-mentioned Egyptian, Syrian, Grecian, and Roman combinations.

It need only be added, that some further curious and remarkable illustrations of the same affinity—that is, of Cilician and Assyrian mythology—will be found in the chapter devoted to the description of certain gods, demi-gods, and heroes represented in the Tarsus terra-cottas, and which arrived in this country, and were described, at a period subsequent to the examination of the first portions of the collection.

* Tacitus, An. xii. 13.

CHAPTER II.

DISCOVERY OF THE TERRA-COTTAS — LARES AND PENATES OF CILICIA — EVIDENCES OF PROMISCUOUS WORSHIP — APOLLO OF TARSUS — PERSEUS, BELLEROPHON, AND PEGASUS — RADIATED APOLLO — IDENTITY OF PHYSIOGNOMY — UGLY FACES — DEIFICATION OF CHILDREN — DEIFICATION OF PRINCES — DEIFICATION OF LADIES — CHARACTER OF CILICIAN ART — PROGRESS OF CHRISTIANITY — DESTRUCTION OF THE LARES AND PENATES — ATYS — APOLLO, THE SYRIAN BAAL — CYBELE, CERES, AND ISIS — ELEUSINEAN MYSTERIES — CYBELE AND ATYS, ISIS AND OSIRIS, VENUS AND ADONIS — THE CAT, DOG, AND HORSE — HARPOCRATES AND FLORUS — ISIS AND THE NELUMBIUM — SACRED BULLS — EGYPTIAN ART — MORPHEUS.

"The incarnations, which form the principal subjects of sculpture in the temples of idolatry, are above all others calculated to call forth the ideal perfections of the art, by expanding and exalting the imagination of the artist, and inciting his ambition to surpass the simple imitation of ordinary forms, in order to produce a model of excellence worthy to be the corporeal habitation of the Deity; but this no nation of the earth, except the Greeks, and those who copied them, ever attempted. Let the precious wrecks and fragments, therefore, of the art and genius of that wonderful people be collected with care, and preserved with reverence, as examples of what man is capable of under peculiar circumstances, which, as they have never occurred but once, may never occur again."—R. P. KNIGHT on the Symbolical Language of Mythology.

IT has been my good fortune to discover such remains as are above alluded to in the extract from Mr. R. P. Knight's learned and interesting work. During a residence of eight years in Cilicia, I was, in the year 1845, at different intervals, presented with one or two of these terracotta heads by an Armenian, who passed a great part of the day rummaging among old ruins, which is frequently the case with lazy fellows, who pass for moral men or "saints" of the modern Eastern population, and who have an ulterior object besides that of seclusion: the desire of discovering hidden treasures, or of imposing on the credulity of their countrymen, by pretending to supernatural knowledge in the secret of finding the same. I had in vain questioned him regarding the place where he had found these objects. He had naturally an interest in avoiding to satisfy my curiosity, as I paid him handsomely for every thing he brought me; and he pretended that he used to write magical words on pieces of paper, which he would throw up in the air, and then he would dig in those places whereon they fell! Such is the kind of nonsense which he no doubt endeavoured to impose on his credulous neighbours.

One day a friend observed the Armenian scratching the earth on the slope of a hill at no great distance from my residence. He suspected what the man was looking for, and on informing me of the circumstance, I proceeded to the spot, where I discovered the rich mine from which I have drawn the whole of my collection. Having set workmen to clear away the rubbish, I collected all I could get, and these are the objects of which I now offer sketches to the public. These drawings I have taken care should be done as correctly as possible; yet such is the artistic merit of the originals, that no one can do them sufficient justice. Still I have endeavoured to give such an accurate delineation of these objects as shall bear the closest critical inspection.

On the ancient wall of Tarsus a hill leaned (if I may be allowed the expression), which must have been many centuries there, inasmuch as on its summit, and towards its base, there exists a fabric, the foundations of which are of Roman cement, which was used for the interior of walls, and which, petrifying, becomes a conglomeration of mortar, sand, and pebbles, of different sizes, and harder to break up than the rock itself. The inhabitants of the present town do not trouble themselves to go to the mountains to cut thence the stones they may require for their buildings; they prefer using such as those who lived in the same spot before have left them; and they carry away, wherever they find them, all the large square stones they require. After using up all that they could find on the surface of the ground, they dug up the foundation of the old city of Tarsus. This foundation is now as low down as forty feet under ground, such being the speed with which alluvial deposits accumulate in a country so near to the high ridges of the Taurus, and in a city on which several towns have been built in succession. In the course of time the wall on which the hill *leaned* was thus carried away stone by stone, and a *secant* of the hill left exposed to view. In the centre of this secant it was that I first discovered these precious objects; and by beating the earth down the hill, I had it well examined, and carried off, as I imagined, every thing worthy of notice, until no more objects were exposed to view by working in the hill. The curiosity excited by this discovery was naturally great, and it was impossible to prevent the inhabitants from crowding to the spot. They were all much pleased with the lamps found among the rubbish, all of which were more or less perfect, and in a state ready for use; these I could not prevent them carrying off; but as they took no interest in any thing else (heads being perfectly useless to them), and as they were aware that I would have purchased all that were presented to me, I have every reason to believe that nothing of any consequence escaped me except these lamps, of which, however, I secured a great many, rejecting such as were of common workmanship, or devoid of interest, from their having no *basso relievo* or inscription to recommend them to notice.

It was thus that I obtained this unique collection of ancient Ceramic art.

At first I imagined that I had lighted upon the site of a Ceramicus, and that the mound might have been formed of the waste of a manufactory, or what is technically called "sherdwreck," many of which are now accumulating, and will disclose their secrets to some future generation. But on further inspection of the articles themselves, I have no doubt that Mr. Abington's[*] suggestion will be found correct, that these precious vestiges are the Penates of the ancient Cilicians, and consequently of a much more interesting character, inasmuch as they bear witness and testify to the triumphs of Christianity over the superstitions of the Gentiles. The following are some of the reasons that lead to this conclusion.

1st. None of the articles appear to have been rejected by the maker on account of defective workmanship; though the work of some of them is very slight, yet even these have evidently been in use; they had been sent out by the manufacturer as finished; had been applied to the purposes intended, and subsequently broken, either by design or accident; "and if they had been used," Mr. Birch observed, before he had seen

[*] Here I am happy in an opportunity of expressing publicly my great obligation to Mr. Leonard J. Abington, of Hanley Potteries, Staffordshire, for the valuable information he has furnished me with; indeed, without him, I question if I should have been able to bring these valuable remains of antiquity into notice. He not only mounted each piece on a pedestal adapted to it, and thereby presented the object in the most advantageous position to be viewed, but he addressed to me a series of remarks doubly interesting: first, as coming from a person who seems at home on every subject, ancient and modern; and second, as emanating from one who could speak artistically as well as scientifically, he being connected with one of the largest establishments of China pottery in England. These observations are incorporated in the following remarks, and form the basis of what I would turn the attention of the reader to, leaving (as I have already observed) to others to work upon the subject, which is of great interest, and affords matter for many volumes by more able pens.

the objects, "they would have been covered with lime, and painted in fresco, traces of which must be sought upon them." Now they have all been painted; indeed, some of them have been painted more than once: see the head of Pan, No. 1, which had been painted blue, and afterwards with a thick coat of red; many were painted in party-colour—the flesh and the garments different. In a mounted headless bust of Apollo Belvidere there are two or three spots of the colour remaining; the body was red, and the garments green; and a careful examination of many of the pieces, after breathing upon them, will discover traces of colour which would not be suspected on a cursory view. The rays upon deified figures are generally painted blue, and sometimes the eyes are of the same colour. The head of Pan, No. 1, was not thrown aside because of any defect making it unsaleable; except a little damage to the edge of the garland with which it is crowned, it is as perfect as when the maker sold it. The mortar, which still remains, by which it was fixed upon the stile which supported it, proves that it had been put up in the place which superstition had assigned to it, and from which it was afterwards deposed and cast out. This remaining mortar or cement proves further, that it had been applied to the purpose for which the heads of Pan and Bacchus usually were, in woods, pastures, and vineyards: it escaped the destruction which came upon its fellows by reason of its solid and almost spherical form.

NO. 1.—HEAD OF PAN.

NO. 2.—INCENSE-BURNER.

2dly. The Incense-Burner, No. 2, has not been rejected by the maker on account of any failure in the workmanship. It had left the manufactory, and been in use in the worship of some household idol; this is certain, by the carbonaceous stain still remaining in the bottom of the crater. This piece, therefore, after having been consecrated to religious use, was afterwards broken and thrown out, either by accident or design.

3dly. The same argument may be drawn from the Lamp, No. 3, which had been long in use. The stag upon it suggests the thought

NO. 3.—LAMP.

NO. 4.—HEAD AND STATUE OF DIANA.

that it has been used to burn before an image of Diana, whose head we have, No. 4, and who was honoured in Lesser Asia.

Another Lamp is entire, and fit for service; and it was not likely to have been thrown away as rubbish. The symbols upon it indicate that it has been used for religious purposes. Such articles would certainly be rejected, as contaminated by the use for idol-worship, on the owners embracing the "glorious Gospel of the blessed God." The circular arched form of the lamps would enable them to bear considerable violence without breaking, and would account for such a number having been found whole and perfect, although subjected to the same intentional destruction which the rest of the pieces of the collection have experienced.

4thly. Some of the fragments are votive offerings, consecrated to the honour of the gods, and attesting their condescension to suffering humanity, and their power to help. To damage or remove such would have been considered the highest act of desecration. The most wicked man would have been shocked at such a crime. What, then, could have caused such a sweeping act of sacrilege? Here lie the prized memorials of relief obtained from the gods in time of trouble, and the very gods themselves lying in the same indiscriminate ruin. There lies the Olympic Thunderer with his jaw broken, No. 5, and the head of his saucy wife for a companion, in the dirt, No. 6. His wings could not save the patron, No. 7, a *winged* Apollo,

NO. 5.—HEAD OF JUPITER.

NO. 6.—JUNO.   NO. 7.—APOLLO WINGED.

the honoured of Tarsus, from the general break-up; nor even the honesty of little Mercury, No. 8, exempt him from the common lot.

There is no fact in history to account for this sacrilegious devastation, but the resistless progress of the Gospel in apostolic times.

NO. 8.—MERCURY.   NO. 9.—HEAD OF MESSALINA, THE FIFTH WIFE OF THE EMPEROR CLAUDIAN.

5thly. The age to which we must attribute the production of these works of art coincides with this supposition. Additional confirmation of this is afforded by some coins found with them, and which are known to date no further back than a century and a half to two centuries B.C. The fashion of the hair in the head No. 9 will admit of our fixing the date of the destruction of these objects in the first century. I am not aware that we have any account of the introduction of the Gospel, or of its triumphs at Tarsus; but it is not unlikely that this rejection of the objects of superstitious reverence might have taken place before the close of the first century: and doubtless St. Paul would have been anxious for the conversion of his immediate friends and re'ations; and if he could not have superintended it in person, he would have early sent his most able and efficient disciples to carry on this work of grace.

This question now meets us, Was this casting away of idols the act of private individuals, clearing their habitations of these abominations, at the risk of persecution from the authorities, and burying them outside

DESCRIPTION OF FIGURES FOUND. 159

the gates? or was it a general cleansing of the city by the force of public opinion, such as is described in Acts xix. 18-20? In either case we find here accumulated every variety of idol, including the compound worship (which had been carried on for years) of Assyrian, Egyptian, Syrian, Grecian, and Roman mythology,—this combination no doubt arising from the local position of Tarsus and its commercial connexions; and if some person competent to the study would take up the subject, I feel persuaded that much might be elucidated of further interest to the archæologist and to the divine, which would bring us to the firm persuasion, that their being purposely mutilated and thrown away was to be attributed to the influence of apostolic missionaries of the Christian faith in the first century of our Lord.

A proof of the promiscuous worship of the people of Tarsus, and a picture of their religious superstition, before the establishment of Christianity, is afforded by the accompanying list of some of the figures found, which will shew how comprehensive their religious faith must have been: here we have

Apollo.	Adonis.
Isis.	Atys.
Venus.	Bacchus.
Jupiter.	Pan.
Serapis.	Horus.
Mercury.	Apis.
Diana.	Anubis (the Egyptian
Juno.	Mercury).
Pallas.	Typhon.
Pluto.	Iris.
Eros.	Æsculapius.
Fortune—Victory.	Phre—(the Hawk, the Egyptian
Hercules.	Sun).

and a multitude of deified men, women, and children, to whom it is impossible even to assign names.

The religious system, therefore, prevailing at Tarsus must have been a compound of all the creeds existing at that epoch. Such a combination was perhaps common to the cities of Asia Minor; but was more likely to be found at Tarsus, it being a place of resort from all the surrounding countries, on account of its schools, as well as of its commerce. It has been before remarked, that there has never been presented to the world so striking a proof of the easy, plastic character of the old mythology as we find in this precious collection of antiquities. Unlike Christianity, which treads alone in all the rigid inflexibility of eternal truth, and will not amalgamate with any thing earthly or of man's device, we find ready adoption of any thing or every thing likely to fascinate the people, and to bring traffic to the temples.

In order to read these vestiges intelligibly, it will not be uninteresting that we should review the peculiarities of the place of their discovery. Tarsus was "no mean city;" its foundation was in the earliest antiquity; and when it came under the power of the Romans it was made a metropolis, as appears on its coins; its schools rivalled those of Athens and Alexandria, to which it often furnished professors in eloquence and philosophy. One of the supposed derivations of its name may have been from the Greek. The most fanciful derivations were certainly sometimes represented in works of art. Have the wings any thing to do with *Perseus*, who has a great place in Tarsian mythology? Tarsus, says Mr. Birch, is an old name, certainly as old as the twentieth Egyptian dynasty, or fourteen centuries B.C. "Tarsus" signifies winged—feathered—pinioned, which the following observation on one of these relics, a sketch of which is given under No. 7, elucidates, and affords a solution to a great mystery.*

---

* Ταρσός is used by the writers of old not only to express a wing, but also the palm of the foot and hand. In anatomy *tarsus* is distinguished as belonging to the foot, *carpus* to the hand. Dionysius, surnamed Periegetes, from his poem of *Periegesis*, or "Survey of the World," refers the name of the city of Tarsus to Pegasus having landed Bellerophon there, leaving the mark of his hoof, or foot, in the ground. The passage runs as follows:

> Κύδνου τε σχολιοῖο μέσην διὰ Ταρσὸν ἰόντος,
> Ταρσὸν εὐκτιμένην, ὅθι δή ποτε Πήγασος ἵππος
> Ταρσὸν ἀφεὶς, χώρῳ λίπεν οὔνομα, τῆμος ἀφ' ἵππου
> Ἐς Διὸς ἱέμενος πέσεν ἥρως Βελλεροφόντης.

There are here three Tarsuses, a play upon words, which may be freely rendered:

> "Tortuous Cydnus, through Tarsus' centre flowing,
> Well-built Tarsus; where once most truly Pegasus
> Placed its foot: leaving it thus a name. There 'twas
> That Jupiter caused the fall of Bellerophon."

Avienus, who is distinguished for his ingenuity displayed in varying the expression of the constantly recurring ideas of the Alexandrian, thus records the same myth:

> "Cydnus item mediæ discernit mœnia Tarsi.
> Pegasus hoc olim suspendit cespite sese,
> Impressæque solo liquit vestigia calcis:
> Esset ut insignis revoluta in sæcula semper
> Nomen humo. Clari post ultima Bellerophontis
> Hic cespes late producit Aleius arva."

The fall of Bellerophon here alluded to is not contained in Apollodorus, nor in all the versions of the legend; but it is in Pindar, with the variation of Pegasus being stung by a gad-fly, and hinted at by Horace:

> "Et exemplum grave præbet ales
> Pegasus, terrenum equitem gravatus
>   Bellerophontem."

APOLLO. 161

The figure is rayed, and probably crowned with the symbol of fecundity, which would give it an Egyptian character; but what gives this piece its singular interest is the fact of its being "*winged.*" Apollo was the tutelar god of the place; here, then, we have him in character as *the Apollo of Tarsus*, "*the winged.*" A coin of Tarsus has Apollo standing on the back of a lion; he holds a lamp in his hand (the lamp of science?), and has wings to his shoulders. These attributes had never been sufficiently explained; but the accompanying figure now renders their signification evident. There is also another symbol confirmatory of this view. There hangs upon the wing a cluster of grapes; grapes were used in the decoration of the great temple of Baalbec, and on the images of Baal (the Sun) grapes are hung round the neck. The grapes, therefore, shew the Syrian cast of the mythology of Tarsus, and identify its Apollo with Baal, as No. 22 connects him with the Osiris of Egypt. The fluted chalice in which this head terminates was probably intended

NO. 22.—APOLLO AS OSIRIS.
(With the Nelumbium.)

Homer also represents Bellerophon as wandering over the Aleian plain on which Tarsus stands:—

"Forsook by heaven, forsaking human kind,
Wide o'er the Aleian field he chose to stray,
A long, forlorn, uncomfortable way!"

Stephanus, speaking of Tarsus, also says that it was so called ἀπὸ τῆς τοῦ Βελλεροφόντου πτώσεως, from the fall of Bellerophon; adding, τῆς ἐκείνου χωλείας ὑπομνήμα ποιουμένων τῶν ἀρχαίων, in reference to the lameness produced by the fall, and which is alluded to in Pindar's version of the fable. Cellarius also says, "A Pegasi, *ungula* quam ibi amiserit, nomen urbis fingunt, quia Ταρσὸς etiam *planta pedis* est."

Scenes of the story of Bellerophon, it has been justly remarked by Dr. Leonard Schmitz, were frequently represented in ancient works of art. His contest with the Chimæra was seen in the throne of Amyclæ, and in the vestibule of the Delphic temple. On coins, gems, and vases, he is often seen fighting against the Chimæra, taking leave of Prœtus, taming Pegasus, or giving him to drink, or falling from him. But until the recent discoveries in Lycia by Sir Charles Fellows, no representation of Bellerophon in any important work of art was known; in Lycian sculptures, however, he is seen riding on Pegasus and conquering the Chimæra. The several pieces of Cilician art in this important collection made by Mr. W. Burckhardt Barker, will suggest a reference to this same story with many; and it is not a little singular that among these works of art a great number of single horses' feet were found, which upon this fabulous origin of the name of Tarsus, as here given, being communicated by me to Mr. W. Burckhardt Barker, that gentleman ingeniously suggested might not impossibly have reference to the very point in question. The more ancient fable of Bellerophon's fall from Pegasus at that spot may just as well have been represented in Cilician works of art as that which refers to Perseus. W. F. A.

to contain incense or lustral water. Mr. Birch calls this the head of Isis; but whether it be Isis or Apollo, it still proves the existence of Egyptian worship in Cilicia.

Here I must refer to another head, No. 23, which Mr. Birch has

(This is mentioned by Mr. Birch as Apollo represented on the Colossus at Rhodes.)

NO. 23.—HEAD OF APOLLO RADIATED.

recognised as the same as that upon the gold and silver coins of Rhodes. He says it is the Apollo (Helios), or the Sun, and is a copy of the Colossus at Rhodes. It is radiated. This radiation was not usual with the Romans and Greeks; but in the present case it admits of an easy explanation. Tarsus, bordering upon Phœnicia, and having ready access to Egypt, would have its mythology tinctured with that of its neighbours. Baal of the Phœnicians, Osiris of Egypt, and Apollo of the Greeks, all embody the myths originating in the worship of the sun. This peculiarity in the figure before us quite accords with the locality where it was found. There is a coin of Tarsus on which Apollo is seated upon a mount, with a lyre in his hand, indicating the presiding influence of that deity at the schools. It is believed that Apollo had an oracle in that place. Of this god the collection offers many specimens, all more or less diversified by some peculiarity or other.

A large portion of these terra-cottas are of a sacred character, but they are not of a magnitude or material to make us suppose that they could have had a place in the public temples. They must have been for use in domestic *lararia* or *chapels*, or rather *oratories*.* It is likely

* Lares, the presiders over housekeeping affairs, occupied a place in the house by the fire-places and chimney-corners. Penates were the protectors of masters of families, wives, and children. Lares had short habits and cornucopias in their hands, symbols of servitude and hospitality. Ovid says, " two Lares with a dog at their feet." Plutarch, "good and evil Lares, or Genii, also *public* and *private* lares." Apuleius says

DEIFYING MEN.

that the owners did not restrict the honour of a place there to one or two deities, but that people of opulence had a collection of such as had been duly consecrated by the priest, which were all honoured in turn, or as their special help was required.

Alexander Severus is said to have preserved the images of all the great men who had been raised to the rank of the gods, and rendered divine honours to them in the same manner as to the most holy souls. Among these he had Apollonius Tyaneus, Jesus Christ, Abraham, Orpheus, Virgil, Cicero, &c. &c.

The *lararia* of private persons could not have been so well furnished, and the common people must have been content with still less.

Before these idols it was the custom to light lamps, to burn incense, to offer flowers, fruits, meat, and wine; also votive memorials of benefits received were consecrated to them: many such small *ex votos* we have in this collection. See No. 32, p. 175, which is selected out of a great many, and which I imagine to be of this description, and devoted to Apollo.

The custom of canonising or deifying men seems to have arisen from the idea that all which made them eminent for their talents or actions proceeded by emanation from the Divine Essence. Hence the simple rites which express veneration for the dead grew into direct and explicit acts of worship to the shades of renowned men: these splendid qualities, dazzling the minds of inferior men, soon obtained for them divine honours, as having exhibited and exercised the attributes of the gods upon earth. These deifications multiplied greatly under the Macedonian and Roman empires; and many worthless tyrants were by their own preposterous pride, or the abject servility of their subjects, exalted into gods, Nero himself not forming an exception.

The most usual mode of expressing this deification was by representing the figure *naked*, or with the simple chlamys, or cloak, as often given to the gods. The head, too, was *generally* RADIATED, and the bust placed upon a square inverted obelisk. The *cornucopia* was often given as a symbol to the statue.

The loose and indeterminate system of ancient mythology presented

---

the Lares represented the souls of departed persons who had lived well and done good. Lares are also called Penates, images of silver, wax, and earthenware. Public Lares were called Compitales, from *compitum*, a cross-way; and also Viales, from *via*, a way or road. These public Lares were placed at meetings of roads, as protectors and patrons of travellers. There were also Urbani, *i.e.* Lares of cities, as well as the country. The Lares were also genial gods, having the care of children from their birth. Bryant holds the Lares of Egypt and Rome to have been the same. Titus Tatius, king of the Sabines, built a temple to the Lares. The custom was observed of burial in the highways; a hog was offered in sacrifice. Lara was the mother of the demons; children were offered in sacrifice to her.

very feeble barriers to the innovations and mutations which were constantly taking place, through intercourse with nations following different practices and other fables.* This collection affords ample proof of this plastic character of the mythology of Tarsus, and of the medley of Grecian, Syrian, and Egyptian worship which went to form it. Every man felt himself at liberty to honour those whom he loved with his adorations and offerings, without waiting for a public decree of canonisation. The object of his admiration, gratitude, or esteem might receive any religious rites, provided they did not disturb others, or do any thing in violation of the established forms of religious worship. This consecration, however, was not properly a deification, but what the Romish Church still practises under the title of canonisation, the object of it being considered rather a saint than a god; wherefore a deified Roman emperor was not called *deus*, but *divus*.

These facts will explain many of those difficulties which present themselves on a view of this collection; such as heads which have no trace of the orthodox form or ideal beauty of the deities whose attributes and symbols they bear; but which, on the contrary, are unquestionably portraits of mortal men and women, and give us illustrations of the practice of conferring divine honours upon magistrates, philosophers, priests, and relatives, as the feelings of respect or affection might suggest.

To exemplify this remark we have nineteen heads bearing the same expression of face, but with different attributes. Most of these heads have striking resemblance; they all have the hair knotted in the orthodox fashion distinguishing the figures of Apollo. But this deity is almost always characterised by unearthly ideal beauty of form: these are remarkable for gross sensuality. Such overfed, bloated faces, with an expression of merriment and cunning, would, with tonsure and cowl, have made excellent monks.

It seems that it was no unusual thing to make the gods in the likeness of mortals. The emperors, ladies of high rank, and priests of the chief order, were thus complimented. Is not No. 24 a chief priest, thus in divine character? and it has the

NO. 24.—PRIEST WITH ATTRIBUTES OF APOLLO.

---

* See quotation from R. P. Knight, prefixed to this chapter.

attributes of Apollo more fully preserved. Here is the wing, the torch, the painting, &c.; but the leering of the eyes and the elevation of the corners of the cunning and merry mouth are any thing but divine, and as far removed from that calm repose by which the ancients always sought to characterise their gods as it is possible to conceive. Whether this was done during the life of the priest, or whether it was only a compliment paid to him after his death, we have not at present the means of knowing.

In Josephus* we find a story which shews the depravity of the priests of Isis at Rome, and which caused Tiberius to destroy both them and their temple. May we not imagine that we see these rogues in some of these heads?—a *family* likeness, no doubt.

Several other heads are of this family, and are worthy of careful study; they all represent the same individual, though they have been wrought by different hands. Some are a piratical copy of the others. Such a piracy indicates that the demand for the figure must have been great. The hair is knotted on the top of the head, in the mode peculiar to Apollo, and shews that the person had been deified; yet there is nothing mythological in the face, which is that of a bloated sensualist. As such, it would do well for Vitellius; but I do not think that he had the honour of apotheosis, though he was rather popular in Asia Minor. The men of Tarsus were very prone to flatter the Roman emperors, and often changed the name of their city in compliment to their imperial masters. After the great earthquake, A.D. 17, Tiberius gave relief to the unfortunate cities of the province of Lesser Asia, for which their gratitude would be due. When Tiberius died, he was raised to the rank of the gods; and that these heads represent a deified emperor there is no doubt. If it is Tiberius, it must be his likeness after his mode of life and debauchery in the island of Capri, and not as he appears upon the medals struck of him. As such medals of him in his deified character would not be made until after his death, such a difference in the likeness might be expected.

Or we may take another view of the question. It was not unusual to pay divine honours to the images of the emperors which were erected in the cities of the empire during their lifetime. The city of Tarsus may have honoured one of its masters by an image in which he was flattered by being invested with the attributes of Apollo, their tutelar deity, before he was dead; and in that case we may imagine these to be cheap copies for the use of the *million*. Every way they are of much interest; and it would be desirable to have the opinion of more compe-

* Antiquities of the Jews, book xviii. chap. 3.

tent judges in the investigation, which, by publishing drawings of some of these, and others in this collection, I hope to afford persons the opportunity of making, who may not be able to see the objects themselves.

It was usual at the birth of a child to name it after some divine personage, who was supposed to receive it under his care; but this name was not retained beyond infancy, when the *bulla* was given up; after which a name was given expressive of some quality or peculiarity of body or mind, or after its kindred. If the child died in infancy, parental affection would indulge itself in the worship of the idol of the heart, under the character of that god to whom it had been consecrated: the image would be formed with rays, &c., the sign of its exalted state, and honoured accordingly; nor is it unlikely that parental fondness might in some cases be carried as far, even before death. With this view I lay before the reader Nos. 25 and 26. Here we have a beauti-

NO. 25.—EROS WINGED.   NO. 26.—HEAD OF A CHILD.

ful head of a boy (Eros), with the arm turned over it. Does not this indicate heavenly repose? And the fact of similar other figures being rayed, would go to prove the supposition of deification having been added to the endearing epithets of the departed spirit. People very commonly worshipped the manes of their ancestors, supposing them to have influence in heaven, and cognisance of human affairs.

The devices which were stamped upon the coins of ancient nations were of a religious character, and held so strictly sacred, that the most proud and powerful monarchs never ventured to put their own portraits upon them, until the practice of deifying them, and giving them the title of divine, was begun. Till after the time of Alexander the Great, neither the Kings of Persia, Macedonia, nor Epirus, nor even the tyrants of Sicily, ever took this liberty; the first portraits which we find upon money being those of the princes of the Macedonian dynasties, whom the flattery of their followers (in imitation of Eastern pomp) raised to divine honours. The artists had, indeed, before this, found a way of gratifying the vanity of their patrons without offending their piety; which was by blending their features with those of the deity whose image was to be impressed on the coin. This artifice was practised on the coins previous to the custom of putting portraits upon them. The coins of Archelaus, Amyntas, Alexander, Philip, and Seleucus I., &c., all have different heads of *Hercules*, which seem to represent those of the respective princes. The earliest instances of this practice are found in Egypt, in sculptured representations of the divine Triad, Amun, Maut, and Chons, or Osiris, Isis, and Horus, found in the temples; which were sometimes made so as to immortalise the Pharaoh by whom the temple was built. The countenance and figure of the king were given to the supreme god, that of the queen to the divine female, and the likeness of their son and heir to the third of the Triad. This practice was carried by the Romans to the greatest lengths; so that private families indulged in this feeling of personal ambition, by employing modellers to form their visages in the character of the gods; and these facts will doubtless go far to explain the very evident mixture of human and divine expression in many of these heads, especially those which are of a Roman character, both male and female.

We find, in the first place, the head of one of the Roman emperors, No. 27 (perhaps Commodus), represented as Hercules, crowned with a

NO. 27.—HEAD OF COMMODUS AS HERCULES.

NO. 28.—HEAD OF A LADY WITH ALL THE ATTRIBUTES OF JUNO.

wreath of laurel. It bears, by the way, a remarkable resemblance to the head of Napoleon Bonaparte.

In the second case, we have No. 28, the head of a lady, with all the attributes of Juno; and I possess more, all of equal interest, and characteristic of the above peculiarity, which would prove that the ancients represented the goddesses by the features of the empress, or of some favourite lady of the day, out of compliment to them, just as we might represent the goddess of song by the personification of a Jenny Lind or a Grisi. Although they have different features, they are all adorned with the veil and the symbols of Juno, either in the diadem or otherwise.

No. 29 is decidedly of a Roman character, and probably represents some lady high in station—perhaps the wife of an emperor who had bestowed favours upon the city of Tarsus, or was popular in the empire. Some person acquainted with Roman antiquities may probably supply the name. This head is well modelled.

Referring back to No. 6, we have another beautiful representation of the goddess Juno, with the diadem and veil, but with different features. This is one of the fine pieces of the collection, and would appear, from its perfect state, to be more modern, were it not for the great beauty of its execution.

NO. 29.—HEAD (REDUCED) OF A LADY, TEMP. EMP. CLAUDIAN.

When persons of high rank were invested with divine honours, the *cornucopia* was placed in the hand, as in No. 28.

"Reviewing the whole collection," says Mr. Abington, "there is a strange incongruity of high artistic excellence and bad workmanship, such as we find in the plaster images of the Italians, which are moulded from good originals, but made by men of very inferior skill. The trade of figure-making was chiefly in the hands of the Greeks, and the magistrates permitted them to take casts of statues of the gods, which were public property, in order to promote domestic religion, by giving a plentiful supply of copies. There was a figure of Mercury in the Ceramicus at Athens, which had been so often moulded, that it was saturated, and shone with the oil used in the operation. The practice was so general, that the Greek figure-makers pirated the works of all the great artists wherever they could get access to them, and got wealthy by their impositions upon the rich Romans, who wished to make a display of taste in their mansions, but were unable to discriminate between an original and a base copy.

"The greater part of the moulds, however, were of clay. The fragments of lamps in some instances were made by casting, *i.e.* by pouring clay in a thin fluid state; the plaster-mould absorbs the water, and gives

MAKING CASTS.

a more regular thickness of clay than is seen in those articles which were made by pressing clay into the mould with the fingers. I might add other remarks upon this subject, but they would be of no interest to any but a potter.

"On comparing these remains with modern figures, we see what benefit the arts derived from the use of plaster, of which moulds are now made, which being run in a fluid state, sets hard like a stone, giving an accurate counterpart of the model, with joints or seams which fit perfectly close. The ancients generally made their models of clay, which would be difficult to press up to the recesses of the mould, and could never give close joinings, and would certainly be distorted in pulling off. Clay moulds would also shrink greatly in burning; this would occasion a rapid reduction in the size of images which were copied from one another, and bring down a life-size to a miniature very soon.

"Apply these remarks to No. 15. This Hercules is a copy of a well-known but much larger figure. The beauty of the original is seen

NO. 15.—HERCULES.   NO. 12.—PALLAS.

even through the disguise which bad workmanship has thrown around it: the same may be said of No. 12, and many others.

"But when the modeller at Tarsus had to produce an Apollo in character, as the tutelar deity of that city, he was thrown upon his own resources; and the result is, that No. 7 is far inferior to No. 23, which was a piracy from the work of a superior artist, but to which rays were added to adapt it to the traditional form worshipped in Asia Minor.

"The defectiveness of the mould caused very thick and ugly seams where the two sides of the mould are brought together.* These have not been taken off, as they would be by an artist, and indicates that they were sold at a low price.

"These specimens also shew that the ancient potters were unacquainted with the use of sponge in their operations. You may perceive, on the back sides, the impress of the workmen's fingers in forcing the clay into the moulds; if they had beaten the clay in with a ball of sponge, the noses, lips, and eyelids would have been perfect. We receive this indispensable article (sponge) from the Levant, where it grew almost at the doors of these terra-cotta image-makers, without their being aware of its value."

That the ancients were well acquainted, however, with the art of making fluid plaster, and images of the same material, there is no doubt. This is confirmed by what Pliny says,† whereby it would appear that in his time the art was of great antiquity, more so than brass-founding. He says:

"Hominis autem imaginem gypso e facie ipsa primus omnium expressit ceraque in eam formam gypsi infusa emendare instituit Lysistratus Sicyonius, frater Lysippi, de quo diximus. Hic et similitudinem reddere instituit; cum antequam pulcherrimas facere studebant. Idem et de signis effigiem exprimere invenit, crevitque res in tantum, ut nulla signa statuæve sine argilla fierunt. Quo apparet antiquiorem hanc fuisse scientiam quam fundendi æris." But plaster is so prone to absorb moisture and to return to powder, that it is not to be wondered at if we had no practical demonstration of the knowledge of this art, until the four specimens in this collection were first discovered. Of these I give one drawing (No. 30), which doubtless represents the head of Venus. Mr. Abington says : "I am persuaded of the value of these heads, and look upon them as objects not to be matched by any collection. The heads are hollow, proving that they were cast in a mould, in the same manner as practised by the Italians.

NO. 30.— PLASTER OF PARIS HEAD OF VENUS.

"The ancients used gypsum or alabaster, the stone from which plaster is prepared for purposes of sculpture and ornament; but I have never before met with any evidence of their having prepared it by calcination for the casting of figures. These specimens, however,

---
* Which may best be seen on examination of the objects themselves.
† Natural History, lib. xxxv. 153.

render the fact indubitable." However numerous their works in plaster may have been, it is not surprising that such poor remains as these should be unique, for no material is so destructible. Water dissolves it rapidly; frost also destroys it. In a European climate such remains must have perished utterly; and their preservation can only be accounted for by the dryness of the place in which they were entombed, and which I have described as above the present level of the ground, and about sixty feet above that of the ancient city of Tarsus, on the sides of a hill that covered these monuments for some thirty more feet with dry sandy rubbish.

"They do not seem to have been very skilful," continues Mr. Abington, "in the management of this plaster: the moulds, which the potter made of plaster, were such as I would not tolerate in a manufactory. The plaster was run upon the model to make the mould in such an unskilful way that the air was shut in the deep parts of the work, forming bubbles in the mould. This, when the clay is pressed in the mould, occasions those bead-like protuberances which disfigure the work, and prove that the mould was plaster, and not burnt clay.

"These specimens may now be considered of much interest, inasmuch as they appear to be the unique remains of an art evidently well known to the ancients, but of which only an account has come down to us in history. The Assyrians and others carved gypsum in its natural state; but the art of calcining and grinding, and then restoring it to a stony state, by renewing the water of crystallisation, is a very different thing; and it would appear further, from a part of a wainscot ornament executed in calcined gypsum, that it was the habit of the plasterers of those days to use this ingredient as in later times—that is, to form the ornament in a mould, and then to fix it in the place intended."

With regard to the date to which we should attribute these interesting remains, I must remark, that as the coins found with them were struck from 150 to 200 years B.C., and as we see from No. 29, where the female figure bears the hair dressed in the fashion of the Augustan age, we must conclude that they existed between these two epochs, and may therefore give a difference in date of upwards of three centuries between some of these various fragments. In No. 29, the very artificial and elaborate manner in which the hair is dressed shews that it was probably of the Claudian period. Messalina, the fifth wife of this emperor, is represented with her hair in this same fashion. The great ampux or frontal, with which the head is crowned, is characteristic of the same age. It is rather the effigy of some great lady of the empire than a divinity—possibly an empress who might have rendered the province some service, or was a native of it. It is plaited in the elaborate manner practised by the Roman ladies, and which is censured by the Apostle Paul and by the Roman satirist, on account of the sacrifice of time which it occasioned. It may represent the head of Juno, and be the resemblance of the favourite female of the day, as has already been remarked.

In order to form an approximate idea of the time when these Penates were destroyed, I must now quote from Neander's *Church History*, as elucidative of the supposed introduction of Christianity into Cilicia, of which we have no positive mention in general history: "The easy means of communication within the vast Roman empire; the close relation between the Jews dispersed through all lands and those of Jerusalem; the manner in which all parts of the empire were linked with the great capital of the world; the connexion of the provinces with their metropolitan town, were all circumstances favourable to the diffusion of Christianity. These cities, such as Alexandria, Antioch, Ephesus, Corinth, were centres of commercial, political, and literary correspondence; and hence became also the principal seats chosen for the propagation of the gospel, where the first preachers tarried longest.

"As a general thing, Christianity at first made progress in the cities, for it was needful above all to gain fixed seats for the propagation of the gospel; the first preachers, passing rapidly over the country, had to propose their message first in the cities, whence it might be afterwards more easily diffused by native teachers.

"In the New Testament we find accounts of the dissemination of Christianity in Syria, in Cilicia, probably also in the Parthian Empire, at that time so widely extended; in Arabia, in the Lesser Asia, and the countries adjacent, &c. But we are greatly deficient in further and credible accounts on this subject; the later traditions, growing out of the eagerness to trace each national church to an apostolic origin, deserve no examination."

It is certain that Christianity was early diffused in Cilicia, though it is not until A.D. 160 or 170 that we find indications that the king was a Christian.* He forbade the mutilation connected with the worship of Cybele; and it is on the coins of this prince that the usual symbols of Baal worship of this country are for the first time found wanting, and the sign of the cross appears in their place. In the year 202 the

* Abgar-Bar-man. There is another king of the same name, said by the Armenians to have sent persons to Christ to ask for his portrait, which the Saviour granted him by placing a handkerchief on his face that bore miraculously the impress of his features; and this is why the Armenians admit of paintings in their churches, while sculpture is excluded, as in the Greek Church.

Christians had already a church built, as it seems, after the model of the Temple of Jerusalem.

The theory of these fragments of household gods having been thrown out of the city in consequence of the introduction of Christianity, we may regard as admitted and settled. But the problem now is, when this took place. The last extract from Neander would seem to suggest an examination of the coins of Tarsus, and to see when they ceased to bear the symbols, &c. of heathen worship. But this examination of the coins of that city would not decide the question, as it might have done if Tarsus had been an independent kingdom; but being a provincial city, its imperial masters would continue the fashion of the coinage long after the acceptance of the gospel by the inhabitants of this distant city. We know that, in many cases, the inhabitants of cities renounced the worship of idols, and suffered persecution for it, long before their governors followed their example. The learned author of the life of St. Paul has not been able to find any thing decisive upon this question. We may therefore conclude that there is nothing remarkable in the records of history relating to it. His conjectures are very reasonable and well-founded, no doubt; still they are but conjectures.

The question, therefore, must be left open. Were these remains—these mutilated, dishonoured images—once the objects of religious regard, thrown out of the city in consequence of a movement produced by the missionary visit of Paul and Silas?

The authors of the life of St. Paul seem inclined to this solution of the query. The act appears to have been sudden. The clearance of the *lararia* of a few families of respectability would furnish all that have been found. Such a movement would be analogous to the sacrifice of valuable books made in consequence of the preaching of the apostles. Such a rejection of idols was, in many instances, followed by persecution; and this conflict was severe in many parts of the empire before Christianity was finally established. It may, therefore, be admitted as possible, that these memorials indicate the earliest triumphs of the religion of the cross, and the suggestion already made be confirmed, that they need not be considered of later date than the close of the first century, or beginning of the second.

In Bulwer's *Rise and Fall of Athens*, in the chapter on the Religion of the Greeks, after speaking of various theorists, who refer the origin of the Greek mythology to Northern Thrace or Phœnicia, or the Hebrews, or India, or Egypt, he says, " Accept common sense as our guide, and the mystery is less obscure.

"In a deity essentially Greek, a Phœnician colonist may discover something familiar, and claim an ancestral god. He imparts to the native deity some Phœnician features; an Egyptian or an Asiatic succeeds him, discovers similar likeness, and introduces similar innovations. The lively Greek receives, amalgamates, appropriates all; but the aboriginal deity is not the less Greek. Each speculator may be equally right in establishing a partial resemblance, precisely because all speculators are wrong in asserting a perfect identity.

"It follows as a corollary from the above reasoning, that the religion of Greece was much less uniform than is popularly imagined.

"1st. Because each separate state, or canton, had its own peculiar deity.

"2dly. Because in the foreign communication of new gods, each stranger would especially import the deity that at home he had more especially adored. Hence, to every state its tutelary god, the founder of its greatness, the guardian of its renown. Even each tribe, independent of the public worship, had its peculiar deities honoured by peculiar rites.

"The Grecian mythology differed in many details in the different states; but under the development of a general intercourse, assisted by a common language, the plastic and tolerant genius of the people harmonised all discords. I think it might be abundantly shewn that the Phœnician influences upon the early mythology of the Greeks were far greater than the Egyptian, though by degrees, and long after the heroic age, the latter became more eagerly adopted, and more superficially apparent."

These observations are written as if the present collection of terra-cottas were before the learned writer. The amalgamation of the Phœnician Baal with the Grecian Apollo, and the other mixtures which have already been referred to and brought to light, have in the above quotation a commentary prepared for them and written before their resurrection from their tomb!

In exemplification of this, I will now cite such as most conduce to the confirmation of this reasoning, and then proceed, as far as the limits of the present work will admit, with an account

[NO. 31. — YOUNG ATYS.]

of such of the remaining pieces of the collection as may appear to merit special notice.

No. 31. These two fragments, when reunited, give us a very fine model of a boy. Mr. Birch thinks it was intended to represent Atys, a celebrated shepherd, of whom Cybele was enamoured, and who afterwards became her high priest: after his death, Atys received divine honours, and temples were raised to his memory, particularly at Dymæ, a town of Achaia. Others have thought this represented Mercury in his youth.

He would thus appear in his character of a herdsman, with a hooded cloak and the *pedum*, or crooked stick, in allusion to his exploit in stealing the flock of King Admetus, when intrusted with it by Apollo.

This is a beautiful piece of modelling; the soft folds of the drapery are admirable, and the reason for giving it precedence to all the others is —first, because I consider it one of the choice pieces of the collection; and secondly, because, as it has a cap not unlike the Phrygian cap, it might be considered also as representing some of the deities of this nation, and thus form a connecting link between the Egyptian and Cilician mythology: as the Phœnicians must have carried into Greece, with their learning, the mythology imported from the Egyptians; and Phrygia was colonised by the Greeks, receiving its name from the Bryges, a nation of Thrace and Macedonia, who came to settle there. In confirmation of Mr. Birch's observation, I will remark that Cybele was the chief deity of the country, and her festivals were observed with great solemnity by these people, who, residing on the same peninsula imparted their religious creeds to their neighbours, the Cilicians, who must have also had frequent communications with them by sea.

No. 32. These two fragments, which, like the rest, appear to have been purposely broken by the new converts to Christianity, as having been contaminated by being in juxtaposition with idol-worship, have now been united after a separation of nearly eighteen centuries. They give us the leg of a horse; the truncated part of the thigh shews that it is complete in itself, and that it never formed part of an entire figure. Apollo, as worshipped at Tarsus, partaking of the attributes of the Syrian Baal, was the patron of horses, and horses were sacrificed to him. This is most likely a votive

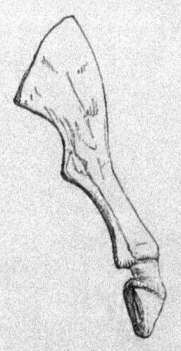

NO. 32.—LEG OF A HORSE (VOTIVE OFFERING).

memorial of a cure obtained for a horse from some lameness or disease of the leg, and which was presented to the deity to record the gratitude of the owner.

The mysteries of Cybele certainly originated among the Egyptian priesthood, although in later ages the Phrygians seem to have introduced the worship of this deity, *Mater Dei et hominum*, on the continent of Asia; hence we see in this collection many pieces in commemoration of this goddess: one of the finest specimens is the head, No. 33. This beautiful head is crowned with corn, as Ceres is sometimes represented. The features are not in such high relief as the rest of the specimens, in consequence of the workman not having pressed the clay close into the mould; but even with this defect, it is an interesting head. Cybele was generally represented as a robust woman, far advanced in pregnancy, to intimate the fecundity of the earth. Here at Tarsus she is identified with Ceres, who is the same as the Isis of the Egyptians, whose worship was first brought into Greece by *Erechtheus*. The Eleusinian mysteries, which descended from the Egyptian secrets of initiation, have left their traces in Asia Minor; and to this day we have several tribes who live quite distinct from the others, in separate villages chiefly, and to whom are falsely attributed all the vile practices of which their forefathers were accused, in consequence of their persisting in keeping secret their religious rites. Among these stand pre-eminent the Fellahins of Syria, the Yezidi of Asia Minor, and the Ali Illahi of Persia,—all three sects closely connected, and who still keep up a kind of freemasonry, which affords certain privileges to the initiated descendants of *Ansar*, their chief. I have lived much among these people, and will bear witness to their morality and the chastity of their women. Their religion, from all I could learn, was a kind of Deism, which enabled them to distinguish the errors of their neighbours, and kept them, by their horror of idolatry and superstition, from amalgamating with the many tribes who have vanquished them, without subduing their judgment; and on the whole, I consider their morals superior to those of their

NO. 33.—HEAD OF CERES.

neighbours, even the benighted erring Christians of the East, who have, alas, but a faint glimpse of true Christianity.

Mr. R. Payne Knight observes, that Isis is frequently confounded with the personification of Fortune and Victory, each having the crown or chaplet of immortality. I have many specimens in this collection which may bear on this subject, and represent Fortune.

No. 34 has both the radiation and the diadem, with which Juno is often represented; but as there is no sign of any veil, I do not imagine that this goddess was intended to be represented by this beautiful fragment, although we may evidently trace on the top of the sceptre, which the figure held in its right hand, and leaning over its shoulder, a crown often forming the acme of this ensign of royalty.

The Greeks and Romans, who adopted the worship of Isis, varied these figures very much from the original Egyptian type, introducing different symbols to signify the various attributes of universal nature. In this character Isis is confounded with the personification of Fortune or Victory, which in reality is no other than Providence. The modius upon the head is also found on the head of Pluto, Serapis, and Venus. All the heads with the modius are probably intended for Isis, in those modifications of figure, and also of worship, above referred to. The bow, which seems to form an arch over the head of No. 20, and of which there are only two specimens in this collection might suggest the

NO. 34.—HEAD WITH THE ATTRIBUTES OF JUNO.

NO. 20.—IRIS.

NO. 35.—COMIC MASK.

178   LARES AND PENATES.

idea that they were intended to represent *Iris*; and as the figures of this goddess were gaudily painted, it might have been done in water-colours, which have disappeared through age, whereas those that were painted in fresco, with a layer of lime, still retain strong marks both of the lime and the body-colours used. See particularly No. 35, which is a fragment of a large comic mask that seems to have been fixed to a wall at a considerable height, as the eyes are looking downwards. The ear is bored, probably for the purpose of fixing it more firmly. It was perhaps part of a decoration of a theatre, and was covered with a thick coat of paint, and must have been rejected as an *image connected with idolatry*, by those who condemned it to take place with the rest of the pieces of this collection, and been cast out from the temples and private residences of the Cilicians on their conversion. It is natural to suppose that all figures would share the same fate, by reason of the zeal of the new converts to a faith that as yet could scarcely be expected to be sufficiently understood, to admit a distinction being made between a mask and an image of a deity. This is, doubtless, why we find it here, as well as No. 36, which is remarkable for being radiated,—why, it

NO. 36.—COMIC MASK (SMALL).   NO. 16.—ADONIS AS APOLLO WITH THE CLOAK AND BROOCH.

would be difficult to guess, unless we may trace out an idea from its resemblance to *Silenus*, who, as the preceptor of Bacchus, stands as a demigod, and who received after his death divine honours, and had a temple at Elis, the present Belvedere, which was a large and populous city in the time of Demosthenes, though it did not exist in the age of Homer.

Adonis (No. 16) is also represented by the Greek artists as *androgynous*. He was especially honoured in Syria, the supposed scene of his death by the wild boar; and being a special favourite of Apollo, who was so particularly revered at Tarsus (in which latter conclusion we are confirmed by the great many representations we find this god to possess in this collection of the Cilician Penates), it is not astonishing to find him here in company with the other objects of worship: we may observe that he has a cloak and brooch, with which his patron, the Apollo de Belvedere, was represented. He is the Tammuz of Ezekiel, viii. 14. In Egypt, the tales of the loves and misfortunes of Isis and Osiris are the counterpart of those of Venus and Adonis. Adonis or Adonai was an oriental title of the Sun, signifying Lord; and the boar, which was supposed to have killed him, was the emblem of Winter. After his death, he passed six months with Proserpine, six with Venus; signifying the increase and decrease of solar influence (will this connect him in identity with Apollo?). Byblus in Syria was the chief scene of his rites; there the women annually mourned his death, and celebrated his renovation. These mysteries were held by the uninitiated in the same estimation as those of Ceres and Bacchus at Eleusis (already referred to), and Isis and Osiris in Egypt. The Phrygian tales of Cybele and Atys seem to be another version of this same fable. One specimen has been painted with a ground-colour of blue, and then red, or probably flesh-colour, and has the stamp of Grecian art.

Mr. Abington remarks of this piece, and several others similar in the collection:—"They are all of high art; it is not too much to say that, as sculptures, they are of great value." No. 16 exhibits the human form in the very perfection of human symmetry—no wonder that Venus fell in love at first sight. The artist has done his part well in this beautiful conception of the adored Adonis. The ivy chaplet shews the relation there was between the rites of Adonis and those of Bacchus; both embodied the same mystic signs, and out of compliment to Apollo.

Among the animals that denote the link in the remains of Egyptian worship, we have the representation of a cat, symbol of the Moon, on account of its faculty of seeing in the dark, or rather by night. The Egyptians worshipped the Moon under this figure, which denotes fecundity; and their reverence for cats is peculiarly demonstrated by the many thousands of their mummies which are found preserved with the same care they bestowed on the bodies of their nearest and dearest relations, and on the ibis, a bird sacred to the goddess Isis.

We have also representations of a dog, the patient expression of which is very characteristic: the animal seems as if he were waiting for his master to take him out. It is a symbol of Hermes, Mercury, and the Anubis of the Egyptians. When Osiris went on his expedition into

India, Anubis accompanied him and clothed himself in a sheep's skin. In this collection we find him represented as a dog of the woolly species. Some make him the brother of Osiris, some his son by Nepthys. We must not therefore wonder at seeing him in such company. This piece had a hole below the right ear, probably to hang it by. For what purpose these two pieces, representing dog and cat, were used, it is difficult to guess, but it was most probably connected with some religious rite.

There is also a head of a horse, sculptured very rudely in tufa limestone, and painted with a colour which has penetrated and given a very hard surface to the stone. There is a cavity in the lower jaw—a mortice, to receive a support, upon which it was elevated. The horse was one of the Roman ensigns. They were carried upon poles, which branched in some instances like a Y or Y at the top, to support the horse, boar, &c.

If this was the symbol of Roman power, it must be very ancient, as quadrupeds were laid aside in the consulship of Marius (B.C. 104), and the eagle alone retained.

But if admitted to be the symbol of Roman dominion, we cannot suppose that it was carried with the army, but was, perhaps, erected over the entrance of some public place, court, or head-quarters of the garrison; and, being considered as an image forbidden by the Christian religion, shared the same fate as those which had been really objects of worship. The same observations may be applied to No. 37, which demonstrates a knowledge of anatomy that would do credit to any epoch.

The city of Tarsus owed a debt of gratitude to Alexander for having delivered it from the Persians at the moment they were going to burn it. A city was built by Alexander in honour of his favourite horse: has this fragment any relation to this place? or is it not natural to conclude, from the many remains of horses we find in this collection, that the inhabitants of Tarsus regarded Bucephalus with a favourable eye as the bearer of his master in their salvation from thraldom? Or another guess may be allowed: Is this one of the horses of the Sun, connected with the worship of Baal or Apollo? Such a surmise is supported by another fragment existing in this collection, which shews the head of a second horse coupled to it, as if attached to a chariot, and also by the

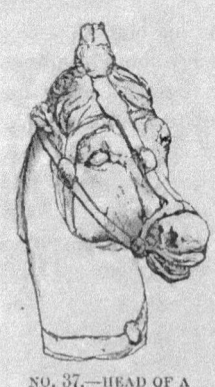

NO. 37.—HEAD OF A HORSE.

many votive memorials of horses' limbs. The horse is a device found on the medals of many Greek cities.

We have also the snout of a hippopotamus. The Egyptians represented Typhon by this animal; and upon his back they put a hawk fighting with a serpent. This is one of the many proofs of the prevalence of Egyptian superstitions at Tarsus, owing to the intercourse between the learned men of the schools at Tarsus and those of the schools at Alexandria.

Out of many beautiful specimens, I have selected one (No. 38), which Mr. Birch has denominated Harpocrates, who was the same as Horus (of the Egyptians), son of Isis. By the Romans he is represented as holding one of his fingers to his mouth, intimating that the mysteries of religion and philosophy ought never to be revealed to the people.

As a further illustration of the spread of Egyptian worship, I will observe, that I possess a small brass image of this god, which was found in the plain of Babylon, and which I bought on the spot from one of those who, after a heavy shower, scour the ruins, in order to pick up what cylinders and other curiosities the rain may have exposed to view by washing off the dust. I was there in February, and witnessed the interest taken by the inhabitants of the villages in the environs of the ruins of this celebrated city, which has for years yielded up, and still continues to furnish, on such occasions, many a valuable remnant in confirmation of the wonderful accounts of its ancient splendour. I must here add, that some of these heads have been considered by connoisseurs to represent Isis herself, the face being more like that of a female, and bearing the Nelumbium* on the head; whereas others have more the

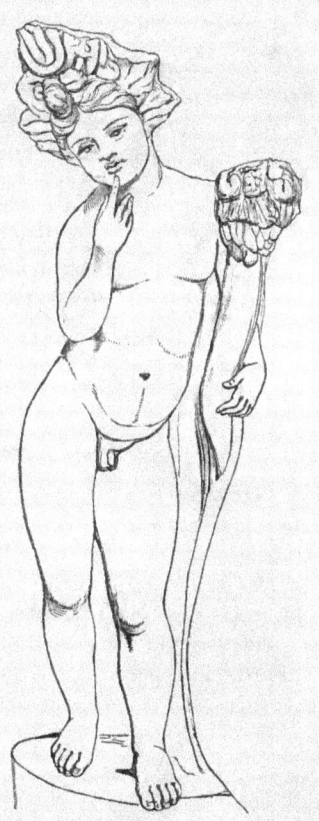

NO. 38.—HARPOCRATES.

* The sacred Egyptian bean is the fruit of the *Nelumbium speciosum*, which grows

features of a youth, and may be supposed to represent her son; but on this I will presume to form no decision. Indeed, it would be impossible to do more than throw out such hints as may lead the learned to express opinions based on more scientific reasons and further research, which I am far from being prepared or competent to do.

In further confirmation of an undoubted fact of the Egyptian mythology having been cultivated at Tarsus, we have many heads of bulls representing either Mnevis, the celebrated bull, sacred to the sun, in the town of Heliopolis, and regarded as the emblem of Osiris, or else Apis, No. 19, and into which the soul of Osiris was supposed to have passed. The hole in the forehead might have been for the purpose of fastening a disc of some other material, probably gold. The head was painted red. The mildness of the expression would induce us to identify it with the Grecian *Io*, which was but a modification of the Egyptian myth.* If we prefer the idea that No. 19 may be Jupiter in the form assumed for the rape of Europa, it suits the poet's description very well:

NO. 19.—APIS.

"Large rolls of fat about his shoulders slung,
And from his neck the double dewlap hung;
Small shining horns on his curled forehead stand,
As turned and polished by the workman's hand;
His eyeballs rolled, not formidably bright,
But gazed and languished, with a gentle light."

There are several beautiful specimens, representing the ox, in basso-relievo, among which is one on a lamp, where may be seen portrayed a sacrifice to Apis, the sacred bull of Egypt. The bull has the sun between his horns. The priest has the lotus ornament on his head, and holds in his right hand a basket: a festoon is suspended over his head. The altar has a fire burning: the scene is a temple.

Further, we have part of a vase, round which were represented, in relievo, heads of an ox, surrounded by a festoon of flowers which divided

---

in the waters of the Nile. Linnæus calls it *Nymphæa Nelumbo;* a common name applied to it is *Lotus*, or Egyptian water-lily: it is the seed-vessel which is used in mythology. The fruit of the plant contains a number of seeds, which are not shed when ripe, but germinate in their cells, the parent fruit affording them nutriment until they are of a magnitude to burst their way out, when they release themselves and sink to the bottom, where they take root, and become independent plants. It was therefore chosen as a symbol of the reproductive power of nature. The Hindoos, Chinese, Tartars, Japanese, &c., all use it to express the same idea. Their deities are seated on a lotus flower.   * See Ovid. i.

each head. This vessel was doubtless used in some of the libations during the ceremonies of the priests, or carried in honour of Apis.

I will conclude these remarks, which have been suggested by the inspection of such pieces as I thought implied the close analogy of the Egyptian worship with that of the Cilicians, by referring to another piece, which seems to be of totally different manufacture from any of the others, and was not improbably brought from Egypt, and found its way to the outer gates of the city, from having been in company with the other objects of worship.* It is crowned with the lotus, and round the full head of hair there appears to be a chaplet of ivy. It is a young face, and of an Egyptian cast altogether. I have set it down as Horus, the son of Osiris and Isis.

I can only discover a few specimens which would indicate that the worship of Neptune was not entirely neglected. This is remarkable, as I should have expected to have seen many more signs of this god; the Cilicians having been decidedly a maritime nation, they would certainly have propitiated in their favour the god of the sea. In the first, we have an interesting piece of pottery. "It is," says Mr. Abington, "a fragment of a shallow bowl or dish, five and three quarter inches in diameter, made for the service of Neptune or some sea-god. If the centre had been left, it would have contained some symbol which would have decided this. The edge is worked into waves, and the cavity of the bowl is impressed with lines forming fish-scales. This kind of ornament could not be continued to the centre, as it would have converged into confusion; there must have been a central panel or compartment. It is made of coarse clay, and, after it was turned on the wheel, it was dipped into a slip of white clay, containing a large portion of lime, to make it still whiter. The scales were then impressed, and ornamented by a pencil dipped in a thin ochreous clay, which gives the reddish-brown stains. It was then burnt."

In another, we have the tail of a fish, probably half-man.†

The only sign of Morpheus, the god of sleep, that I have discovered, is No. 39, the head of a lad half asleep; it is of beautiful workmanship, and would prove that they were *not* a sleepy nation who could model such a head!

NO. 39.—SOMNUS.

* On a closer examination of this collection, it will be found that many Indian gods bearing the features of the Budists and Bramins had accumulated in Tarsus before the introduction of Christianity.
† See the tale of Ovid, "Mariners transformed to Dolphins."

CHAPTER III.

APOLLO—APOLLO BELVEDERE—CARICATURES OF MIDAS—APOLLO OF TARSUS—SENATOR IN THE CLAVUS LATUS—LION ATTACKING A BULL—TELEPHUS OR MERCURY?—CERES—VICTORY—DATE OF DESTRUCTION OF THE LARES—METAMORPHOSIS OF ACTÆON INTO A STAG—REMARKS OF MR. BIRCH.

I WILL now proceed to note some observations regarding Apollo, who appears to have been the god most in favour among the Cilicians. We have copies of the admirable statue of the Apollo Belvedere, so called from having been placed in the Belvedere of the Vatican by Pope Julius II.; it was found in the ruins of Antium, in Italy, in the fifteenth century. It is supposed to have been executed by an Ephesian artist, for one of the Roman emperors—some think Nero. These miniature copies, found in a distant province, shew how popular that beautiful figure must have become immediately after its production. One of these, which is better executed than the others, shews traces of the painting—a speck of red on the flesh, and the cloak has some remains of green, and much of the red paint remains on another. There are a great many fragments representing Apollo in various ways, and we must conclude this idol was the chief object of superstitious worship at Tarsus; his image was no doubt in every house: for this reason his remains are more numerous than the other objects of heathen idolatry. There is one of good Grecian work, which appears to have been diademed. It has very much the expression of the Apollo Belvedere, though the hair is not knotted. The dignified repose, and the scornful look of the mouth, seem to identify it with the slayer of the Python. But one of the most certain of the identifications of Apollo is where he is represented with a crown of rays on his head, being often taken for the Sun, Phœbus, and Hyperion.

As this god was so much in repute at Tarsus, we should expect that out of compliment to him caricatures of Midas, with lengthened ears,

BEAUTY OF THE SPECIMENS.

would abound; hence we find several, among which I have singled out No. 40. It is remarkable for another singularity; the head never belonged to any statue, but was *detached*, standing upon special pedestals, one of which was found, and although it did not actually belong to No. 40, I have adopted it in order to exemplify a singular peculiarity. These were not intended as Lares, but probably, on the contrary, made to be scoffed at; and we perceive that the heads of Pan, the rival of Apollo in the art of music, in this collection, are in the same shape. Other heads there are with only a bust, as, for instance, one representing a young woman in a tunic, well modelled, with a jewelled necklace, such as we see in the British Museum.

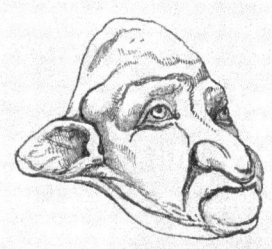

NO. 40.—MIDAS.

Hitherto I have endeavoured to bring to the reader's notice such pieces as I thought might best explain the nature and intention of the whole collection. I have also endeavoured to afford an idea of the very great variety of the objects; but here I must confess that I begin to despair of being able to convey an adequate idea of the whole, unless a drawing of almost every piece should be made, which is beyond the limits of the present publication. I have by no means chosen the most beautiful pieces; indeed, some of the choicest remain to be described: and I fear the artist will despair of being able to delineate their beauty with sufficient accuracy. Mr. Waldon tried to express the beauties of one piece (the head emblematical of the city of Tarsus, see vignette in title-page), in coloured lithography; and although he exerted every possible faculty of the artist and the lithographer, he has confessed that he came far short of the original, the beauty and grace of which are inimitable, and apparent in spite of the destroying hand of time. Mr. Abington says of this piece: " It has suffered more from age than many of the others, in consequence of its having been but imperfectly burnt by the potter. Enough of its excellence remains to make us wish that more of a figure in such good drawing could be obtained. Every position in which you view this fragment calls forth our admiration." Alas, I found no duplicate of this gem!

But setting aside the beauty of many of the pieces which deserve to stand forth as perfect gems, I will now proceed to note a few more, on which certain observations have been suggested, which, although unconnected, I think will afford sufficient interest to the reader to require no further apology for my introducing them without any other ulterior object. Indeed, the whole nature of the collection is such, that I question if any possibility of identification of each piece could be arrived at; and nothing more than *suggestions* can be expected, at least not without a much deeper study than I am prepared, or even competent to give to the subject.

With these remarks I proceed, first, with No. 41, which is one of the most precious pieces, inasmuch as it gives a clear solution of a question which has been hitherto undecided. The image is that of a senator or magistrate of high rank : he wears the toga, and over it a kind of belt or scarf, fringed at the ends and embroidered, which is unquestionably the clavus latus,—an article which has given rise to much difference of opinion among modern writers. Ferrarius supposed it to be a band thrown over the shoulders, the ends hanging down in front, as in fact it is. Others say that it was a round loop or buckle, resembling the head of a nail, fastened to the dress in front of the chest. Others, again, that it was an ornamented hem sewn on to, or woven in the dress, or that it was figuring upon the dress itself. Dr. Smith, or rather Anthony Rich, B.A., who supplied the article in Smith's *Dictionary of Antiquities*, 1842, says: " it is a remarkable circumstance that no one of the ancient statues representing persons of senatorian, consular, or equestrian rank, contain the slightest trace in their draperies of any thing like the accessories above referred to ; some indications of which would not have been constantly omitted if the clavus latus had been a thing of substance." He therefore comes to the conclusion that it was merely a band of purple colour upon the garment, which the *painter* could depict, but which for want of substance could not be shewn in sculpture. This shews how erroneous theories may sometimes bear the appearance of truth, and carry conviction almost against the actual demonstration. This fragment affords conclusive evidence, and supplies what has hitherto been sought for in vain. The clavus is a separate article (as the band of the Order of the Bath), worn over the toga, and exhibited with some satisfaction by the wearer, as seems by the handling of it by the figure before us. The clavus was introduced at Rome by Tullus Hostilius ; and iti s certainly remarkable that Rome, with its rich stores of sculpture, should not furnish one example of such a valued and coveted mark of distinction; but that the doubts concerning

NO. 41.—IMAGE OF A SENATOR WITH THE CLAVUS LATUS.

it should be cleared by a terra-cotta fragment found in a distant province of the empire.

No. 42. A Lion attacking a Bull, unique in the collection. This is

NO. 42.—LION ATTACKING A BULL.
(Subject of a reverse on a Cilician silver coin.)

one of the most interesting and valuable fragments in the collection: it is a work of high art, from the hands of a first-rate artist; the rage of the assailant and the agony of the victim are brought out of the material with wonderful effect. The tale which it tells is more historical than mythological. A country symbolised by a bull is conquered by another power represented by the lion. The same symbols are found sculptured at Persepolis; and in Conybeare and Howson's *Life of St. Paul*, now publishing, we have (p. 24) a coin of Tarsus with the head of the Emperor Hadrian on one side, and on the reverse is this very symbol, in the same drawing, as if it had been designed by the same artist. The author says, "This coin was struck under Hadrian, and is preserved in the British Museum: the same figures of the lion and the bull appear on a series of silver coins assigned to the period between Xerxes and Alexander." The symbol therefore commemorates the conquest by the Persians of the country bounded by Mount Taurus, and when Persia was subjugated by Alexander, he adopted it, and it was used by his successors; hence we find it on the coins of Macedonia, though the drawing is quite different. After the Romans, in their turn, had subdued Greece and Asia Minor, Hadrian having rebuilt Tarsus, issued a new coinage for it, with the old mythological types. "I consider this fragment," says Mr. Abington, "as the most choice morsel in the collection; its artistic excellence is equal to any thing among the terracottas in the British Museum, and it affords the finest example of the heraldry of antiquity that can be conceived."

Before we proceed further, it is requisite to refer back to another exquisite "morsel" given in this work under No. 8. Mr. Birch calls it Telephus the son of Hercules and Auge the daughter of Aleus, who, dreading the anger of her father, exposed him at his birth on Mount Parthenius; but his life was preserved by some shepherds, who caused a goat to suckle him, and hence his dress as a shepherd-boy. Mr. Birch adds, that if it be young Hermes, it is probably from a terminal figure wrapped up in his chlamys. Mr. Abington remarks on this piece, " This is a very clever miniature figure of the boy Mercury (Hermes being the Grecian appellation). To appreciate the merit of this choice morsel, we must look at the character of this divinity, whose counterpart we may find in every house of correction. Mercury is represented under several different characters; as the boy he is wrapped in a close cloak, tied or held fast under the chin; he is often represented without feet, as in this case, to shew that the power of speech can effect its purposes without limbs for its assistance. As soon as he was born he began to indulge his craft and acquisitiveness, and his cloak enabled him to carry off the plunder. He stole sheep the day after he was born: he stole Neptune's trident, the girdle of Venus, the sword of Mars, Vulcan's tools, and Jupiter's sceptre. The subtle innocence of the little thief is admirably expressed by the artist, though there is not much finish in the model. It should be prized as a gem. Mercury, as the god of speech and eloquence, was honoured in such a city, remarkable for learning, though I cannot refer to any evidence of the fact."

This, like No. 43, is one of the pieces in the collection of which there is no duplicate. Mercury was the patron of travellers and shepherds; and Cilicia being on the high road between the eastern and western nations, it is remarkable that no more images of this god should have been met with.

No. 43. A beautiful and simple head of a lady, not unlike the one representing Ceres: it was probably intended to represent the same person in her private capacity of a daughter or a bride.

NO. 43.—HEAD OF A LADY.

Mr. Abington says of this piece, " The artist has represented nature with the most perfect truth in the front view and in the profile. It was made out of a plaster mould, as may be seen by the bleb in the corner of the mouth; but the joining of the mould was very imperfect, as shewn by the thick clumsy seam."

Looking to No. 14, which is a figure of Victory, with the palm and crown, and of which we have a great many representations in

VICTORY AND ACTÆON.

this collection, by different masters, I must note, that there was a great battle fought in Asia Minor between Septimus Severus and his rival Piscennius Niger, in which the inhabitants of that province took great interest. If these figures could be proved to refer to the triumph

NO. 14.—VICTORIA ALETA.

NO. 44.—ACTÆON.

of Severus, it would bring the time in which these valuable remains were destroyed to the close of the second century, and as some of the pieces must have existed at least one century B.C., they must have remained stored up in the houses of the people who set a value on them, as Lares and Penates, beyond that of common sculptures.

No. 44. From the great variety of lamps in all kinds of shapes, and all offering, in basso-relievo, subjects of much interest, I have singled out No. 44, which represents the metamorphosis of Actæon into a stag, as is seen by the horns branching off from his head.

> . . . . . . " The man began to disappear
> By slow degrees, and ended in a deer:
> A rising horn on either brow he wears,
> And stretches out his neck, and pricks his ears."

Here we see him attacked by his dog, without *apparently* being able to offer any resistance, and thus he was devoured by his own hounds for his presumptuous curiosity in prying at Diana and her attendants while bathing at Gargaphia.

I must here beg leave to insert Mr. Birch's able and succinct account of these monuments of antiquity, to illustrate which it has been deemed expedient to introduce only some woodcuts, as it would be impossible to have cuts of all the pieces referred to by him.

"An examination which I have recently made of a large collection of terra-cotta figures, consisting of above 1000 pieces, found on the site of the ancient Tarsus by Mr. Barker in 1845, is so instructive to the history of that city — celebrated for its connexion with the Assyrian Sardanapalus, the Apostle Paul, and the apostate Julian — that I think it important to place my observations upon record. As in the case o the collection from the island of Calymna,* the mere inspection of so large a number of pieces leads to a correcter knowledge of the employment of terra-cottas, of those *types* which prevailed on the spot, and of the time at which they were made. Hence the collection of Mr. Barker, although containing several repetitions of the same figures, and almost all in a mutilated condition,† is a most instructive comment on the local history of the city. In style of art, too, many are of exquisite taste and feeling, — some the most charming fragments of terra-cotta which I have seen. These objects were found in the midst of an ancient mound or rubbish-heap, one of the *monti testacei*, as they are called at Rome, which leaned on the old city-walls, the stones of which, having been carried away by the modern inhabitants, exposed a section of the hill: in the centre were the terra-cottas. The whole collection had been anciently thrown away as rubbish, all the figures being found, not only broken but incomplete; while proof existed of the former use of the utensils, such as the lamps and vases. The figures also had certainly been prepared for sale, as many exhibited traces of the colours with which they had been painted; consequently they could not have been the sherd-wreck or refuse of a potter's establishment. Mr. Barker is disposed to think that their destruction was caused by the progress of Christianity, the new converts having destroyed and mutilated their former penates and idols; but it is evident that terra-cotta must have been constantly destroyed by accident, and conveyed to the rubbish-mounds. In the temples, the great accumulation of votive figures was

* See *Arch. Zeit.* 1848, p. 277.
† Since Mr. Birch saw these pieces they have been restored by a first-rate sculptor, who has done great justice to them, and renewed to life the dead and departed spirit of the Lares, who now stand forth in all their pristine elegance and beauty.

perhaps cleared out, and the fragments thrown away. I shall proceed to describe them in the following order:—I. Figures. II. Vases. III. Miscellaneous objects.

I. Figures. These objects, chiefly the πήλινοι θεοί of the Greeks, and *sigillaria* of the Romans, are principally figures of deities. They have all been broken, especially the heads, of which a great number are in the collection. They are made of a remarkably fine clay, either of a pale straw or of a red colour, the difference of which is owing to the degree of heat to which they were subject. All of them were made in moulds, *typi*, and hence their name of *ectypa*, or *sigillaria*. Mr. Abington, himself a potter, remarks, that their technical defects are owing to the use of moulds of clay, which shrunk in the baking, distorted the original figure, and reduced it in size. Owing also to their not joining accurately, large seams, which were not pared away, were left in the places where the moulds united. The figures also, on account of the ancient potters not using the sponge, which presses the clay into all the finer parts, are not so sharp as they should be. The marks of the potter's fingers are still discernible in many specimens. They were probably retouched, as in the Æsopian fable (cccix. κεραμεύς τις ἔπλαττε πολλὰς ὄρνις ἐν τῷ ἐργαστηρίῳ) the potter is described as modelling birds.* The figures were then coloured with a fresco, having first been washed all over with a white ground of lime. The crowns and rays of some figures were blue; the faces and bodies red, and the garments green; the eyes sometimes blue. The figures, when complete, were represented standing upon oval or circular pedestals, sometimes with a moulding; and one bust was on a round moulded pedestal, very like those of marble. From this it is evident, that many were ruder copies of statues, probably of those in the temples. Some few heads, grotesques, or caricatures, have holes for plugs to fit them to some other material: these were probably toys. Few of the figures exceed the height of nine or ten inches; but part of the crowns, and the imitated *pschent* of the Greek figures of Harpocrates, were found, which shew that some of them must have reached between two and three feet. The first subject of remark, indeed, is the prevalence of the Isiac worship. Busts of Serapis, with the modius, others perhaps intended for Isis (No. 11),

NO. 11.—ISIS.

* See also Lucian, Prometheus, s. 2.

192   LARES AND PENATES.

and distinct busts of Harpocrates (No. 38), as he appears at the time of the Roman Empire, wearing on his head the crown called *pschent* and a laurel wreath, holding the index finger of his right hand raised to his mouth, and holding in his left hand a cornucopia, often occur repeated, although no one figure is complete. Once he was represented leaning against a column. Considerable respect appears to have been paid to this exotic cultus, which divided with that of the Ephesian Diana, the Samian Juno, and the Phrygian Cybele, the Pantheism of Asia Minor, and even Rome itself. Of these two other cultus no traces occur; but several busts from figures, which either represent the turreted head of Cybele, or of the city of Tarsus, as it appears on the silver autonomous

HEAD OF CYBELE.   NO. 45.—TUTULATED HEAD.

currency,* are among them; and one or two of Atys wearing the cidaris, draped in the full garment, and holding in his left hand the pedum. In connexion with these are several tutulated heads (No. 45), from figures which, when complete, appear to have been winged, and to have held a cornucopia, a wreath and palm-branches, and probably represent the Tyche or Fortune of the state.

In connexion with these are also several female heads, wearing the stephane, or sphendone, and veiled, and part of a more perfect figure, holding in the left hand a cornucopia, consequently also a form either of Hestia or Cybele (No. 28). Some of these are fine and spirited, and may have composed parts of the figures of Venus, portions

* See Coombe, Mus. Hunt.

of whose form are in the collection. Of the usual Hellenic divinities of Olympus, and of the secondary gods of Greece, several examples are found, but always under their later types. Thus a veiled head of Chronos or Saturn (No. 46); one or two busts of Zeus; others possibly of Hero (No. 47); and several of Athene wearing a Corinthian helmet. Of this latter goddess one remarkable type occurs thrice. The goddess is standing armed with the usual Corinthian helmet, her whole form is enwrapped in the peplos, her face only partially revealed. Torsos and parts of figures of Mercury, wearing the chlamys, are comparatively rare. Those of Venus,

NO. 46.—CHRONOS OR SATURN.

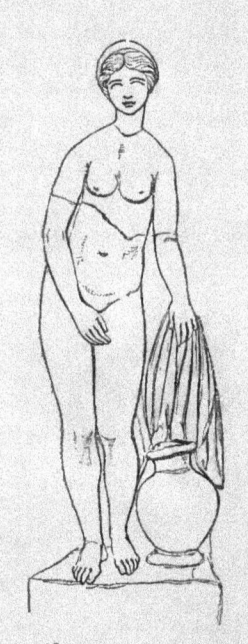

NO. 47.—HERO.   NO. 48.—VENUS AT THE BATH.

whose worship was universally diffused in Asia Minor, are more abundant; and several types of this goddess, representing her as draped, and holding a pigeon in her left hand, like her figure* in the old hieratic form, or as she appears upon the coin of Cos, naked and at the bath (No. 48), her right

* Gerhard, über die Venusidole, Taf. iii. 4.

o

hand concealing her nakedness, her left hand placed upon some drapery, which covers an unguent vase—the sentiment repeated in the Capitoline Venus—probably the goddess bathing prior to revealing her charms to Paris. Another figure with the same motive had the left hand placed under the breasts, the right concealing her nakedness, and at her side a vase; another wearing the stephane, naked, her right hand upon her breast. Probably certain figures of a female wearing a stephane, and covered with a peplos, which she unveils, are intended for the same goddess. The Erotes, or Cupids, whose multiplied forms became so Pantheistic at the time of the Roman Empire, appear to have been abundant at Tarsus, although few of their figures are perfect. Either he holds up fruit, like Priapus or one of the Seasons; or is on horseback, or holding by both hands a conch-shell, as he appears at the Bath of Venus; or holding the dove, or throwing his hand over his head, in the same gesture as the Bacchante of Scopas. Almost indistinguishable from the Erotes, are the fragments of boyish figures, of fat proportions, which may be intended for the youthful Dionysos, especially those which wear an infibulated chlamys, or have suspended round the neck the Roman bulla, or where the boy, like Telesphoros or the young Hermes, is enveloped in a cloak (No. 8, p. 158). Several heads of other figures of this god, either with the hair divided at the forehead, or else wearing a wreath, as in the head of Cupid or Eros (No. 49); and others with the lock plaited on the head, or even plain, were found.

NO. 13.—EROS.

NO. 49.—HEAD OF CUPID OR EROS.

Of the Delian deities, Apollo and Diana, few, if any, specimens occur. Some heads crowned with laurel-wreaths, and some legs crossed, from figures in that attitude, may possibly represent the Apollo (No. 10), Citharœdus or Lycius. One head only can be assigned to Diana. The Apollo, Phœbus, or Helios, as he appeared on the celebrated Colossus at Rhodes, is, however, among the collection; his head surrounded with

FIGURES OF APOLLO AT RHODES.

rays, which are placed upon a nimbus, or disk, in bas-relief. This head bears a remarkable likeness to that of the god as he is seen upon the coins of Rhodes, and on the handles of the Rhodian amphoræ;* and the appearance of this god at Tarsus may be accounted for by the universal diffusion of Rhodian commerce, and the increasing respect paid to the god Helios in the days of the Ptolemies and under the Roman Empire. In the collection is a perfect figure of that god, of singular type: the head is in the radiated crown; the body is naked; the arms and legs have never been complete, the one terminating at the thighs, the other in the thick of the arm, and in them are holes, which do no go through the substance of the figure, for fitting on the fore-arms, and feet, and legs in some other material, like the neurospasts or dolls, or the acrolithic statues. The whole of the figure was coloured yellow, in allusion to the golden shower which fell in Rhodes — the great

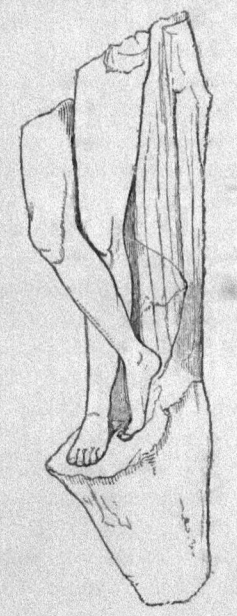

NO. 10.—PART OF A STATUE OF APOLLO.   NO. 18.—BACCHUS.

encomium of the city.† Few figures of the Muses, which are of such frequent occurrence in terra-cotta collections, are found in this.

* Transactions of the Royal Society of Literature, New Series, vol. iii. Pl. I.
† See Rhetores Græci. 8vo.

female amply draped, her head laureat, and leaning her elbow on a square pilaster, resembling the supposed Polyhymnia, was perhaps one of the Pierian quire. From the great gods, of which the cycle is so incomplete, it is necessary now to pass to the demigods, the first of whom, in rank and power, is Dionysos, whose worship in Greece was universal at almost all periods, and whose companions, the Sileni and the Nymphs, presented such a field for the plastic art—so many *capricij* for the imagination emancipated from the hieratic style. In some cases, the artist chose the youthful infantine form, or else the naked youthful god, holding the thyrsus in his raised right hand, while his cloak is thrown across his left arm, in the hand of which he holds the cantharus by one handle (No. 18), or else his head bound with the credemnon, while the nebris is thrown over his form. Some heads and fragments of Sileni, one of remarkably fine expression (No. 1, p. 155), crowned with a wreath of the leaves and flowers of the ivy, are complete in themselves, but with holes for plugs beneath to insert them to the figure. Scarcely more than traces of Bacchantes exist, and those only shewn by some uncertain heads and parts of one or two figures, the attitudes of which recall the χιμαιροφόνος, or goat-slayer of Scopas. A few figures of Hercules, whose worship did not enjoy that early local preference which that of Bacchus had, as appears from the early coins of the city, were found. There are some heads, one from a group in which the hero as the Callinicos was crowned by victory, or else crowned with the poplar (No. 27, p. 167), referring to the branch of the silver poplar which he brought from Hades, which was afterwards the emblem of the Olympic victor,[*] or in laurel-wreaths; besides which are torsos and other parts of his form, with the club, and the lion's skin thrown over his left arm (No. 15, p. 169). One fragment of a figure of Æsculapius standing upon a pedestal, with part of his drapery, and the serpent coiled round the staff at his feet, was found. There are several figures of Victory, which were probably made and sold at the time of the different Roman conquests. The goddess is either advancing forwards, holding a crown and palm-branch (No. 14, p. 189); or else with a palm-tree behind her, alluding to the conquest of Judæa, or holding in each hand a palm-branch, both of which meeting, form an arch or festoon above her head (No. 20, p. 177). In all examples her hair is parted, and rises up in a double curl at the centre of the forehead; in one instance, like Tyche or Fortuna, she holds a cornucopia. To Somnus may be attributed the head of a sleeping boy, with his eyes closed, broken off from a figure (No. 39, p. 183); and to one of the Seasons a child holding

---

[*] Theocrit. Idyll. ii. v. 121. Schol. ad eund.

grapes. Of heroes there are Perseus* killing Medusa, and the head of the Medusa, from a group; a heroic head in a pilos (No. 50); and the naked torso of a female, possibly Venus. More uncertain are the head of a youth wearing a wreath; a Phrygian bearded head in a cidaris (No. 51); and an old Phrygian, bearded, carrying a lamb; a female

NO. 50.—PERSEUS.   NO. 51.—PHRYGIAN HEAD.

head with dripping locks, perhaps of a Nereiad or Naiad; a hand holding an apple, detached and perfect; part of a figure holding an inverted torch; a hand holding a lyre, placed upon a Corinthian capital; and a draped figure, holding over the left hand and arm a narrow fringed

---

* We have, it appears from Mr. Abington's researches, several representations of Perseus among the Oriental cylinders published by the Syro-Egyptian Society. In one he is represented capturing Pegasus. He is altogether Babylonian; his bushy hair and beard trimmed and dressed in a style worthy of the son of Jupiter. His wings, and breastplate, and falchion, all agree with the character, only differing from later sculptures in its quaintness and great antiquity. On another cylinder we have a four-winged figure dressed like persons of royal rank in the Assyrian sculptures, except the breastplate, which seems to be jewelled, and consists of twelve compartments, like the breastplate of the Jewish high-priest. He is very closely girded with a close belt round the loins, and altogether like the Assyrian figures, except in the want of a beard, which fact, together with his wings, marks him as a divine person, or a demi-god. He has captured two ostriches; and Mr. Abington very ingeniously and plausibly suggests that this may refer to the great exploit of Perseus—the taking off Medusa's head, which is fabled to have occurred in the Libyan desert, which the ostrich might well represent. On another cylinder we have the representation of a figure seated on a throne, holding a symbol of authority in his hand. He is addressing a man (Perseus?) who has his back turned to him, as if going on some mission, for which he has received his orders. A bird is following him, having a remarkably long neck, apparently an ostrich, and indicating beforehand the country to which he is repairing. Mr. Abington also thinks that a representation of a man with four wings contending with two gryphons, on another cylinder, refers to the same hero of mythology. The deciphering of the inscriptions on the cylinders will one day assist materially in determining the Oriental origin of a great number of these classic stories, giving to them their true parentage, their real country, and their original meaning.

sash, the supposed clavus latus; a hand holding a tympanum; a hand holding a rhyton, terminating in a male head; the arm of a boxer, the hand loaded with leads; a hand holding a basket; and a large wing. Several heads bore distinct proof of being portraits of persons living at the time of the Roman Empire, from the time of the Flavii to the Antonines. Among them were a head resembling that of Otho or of Titus; others of ladies who wore the head-attire seen on the coins of Julia, the sister of Titus and Domitia (Nos. 9, p. 158, and 29, p. 168); another laureated head resembling Domitian. Three other little heads of exquisite finish, also of the same time, represented personages living under the Roman Empire. Other subjects were taken from the circus, such as a horseman, and the head of another; the same, holding a palm; from the bath, as the head of a slave; or from the theatre, as a comic actor, the davus seated on a cube, with his hands folded (No. 52); and another of the Satyric cast, like the figures represented in the New Comedy, which appear from the vases of later date to have approached the broadest style of caricature.* Several heads only, with pointed ears, and plug-holes beneath, to adapt them to bodies of some other material, and one with a helmet apparently also comic, and supposed to have been a lamp, were also either taken from the stage or from those obscene dwarfs and moriones, which are so often found represented in bronze at the Roman period. With this list closes the torso of a figure wearing the paludamentum, probably from the figure of an emperor. A considerable number of animals were found, and among them a spirited group of a lion attacking a bull, upon which he has sprung (No. 42, p. 187), a subject found on the coins of Cilicia.† A panther, several fragments of horses, some caparisoned or votive; parts of bulls, probably dedicated for the preservation of cattle; a dog, emblematic of Hecate; and a small cat, having a cord tied round its neck, from which is pendent an inverted crescent, shewing that the animal had been sacred to the moon, recalling the collar placed round the neck of the stag of Mount Cereynitis. Among them was also the skin of an animal tied up like an askos.‡

NO. 52.—DAVUS.

* Wieseler, Theatergebäude. Gotting. 1851, Taf. ix. 9.
† Duc de Luynes, Suppl. Pl. iv. Gaos.
‡ It is known that the water is carried in skins. Mr. Bonomi has engraved in

VASES. 199

This closes the list of sigillaria, which forms the most important portion of this collection, and which throw considerable light on the state of the arts in Tarsus, certainly not inferior to those in Italy. Many of the heads, although of small size, have a wonderful power and expression, and the arts were generally in a high state at the period. This seems to have been towards the close of the Cæsars, to which period the female head-dresses point.

II. UTENSILS. Few vases were found. The most remarkable of these was an œnochoe, quite plain. Several pieces of red glazed Roman ware, not the supposed Samian, but of the class called the false Samian by the English and French antiquaries, distinguished by not being of an

NO. 53.—A BASSO-RELIEVO GEM WITH A WREATH: PRIESTESS EXAMINING THE OPENING OF A FLOWER.

equal colour throughout, and not stamped with the names of potters inside. On the bottom outside of one cup is the letter T, in bas-relief, but not stamped, as the usual potters' sigillum. Two pieces of cups in

his excellent work, *Nineveh and its Palaces*, p. 182, from the monuments discovered by M. Botta at Khursabad, the figure of a sack or rather skin, and water-bearer with a leather helmet on his head, and also of a clasp by which his outer garment was fastened—a peculiarity of costume that leads to the surmise, he adds, that these people are from the coast of Cilicia, and may be called Milyæ, who, Herodotus tells us, wore helmets of leather, and who had their vests confined with clasps. It is not a little curious, and corroborative of the fact, that the Assyrian water-bearers were strangers, possibly some conquered people from Cilicia or the neighbouring Taurus, that the water-bearers in large towns are generally a peculiar people : thus the Sakkas of Constantinople are Armenians from Armenia Proper and Kurdistan—not Armenians of Constantinople; and the water-bearers of Paris are Auvergnats.

this collection I consider the finest of any which I have yet seen. One (No. 53), part of a cylindrical cup of fine ware, of a pale straw colour, has, in delicately raised relief, the bust of a draped female figure, apparently Venus, in a talaric tunic, placed between two festoons of wreaths, a subject which has been repeated round the cup. The other, from a bowl of a remarkably fine light-red clay (No. 54), has, in a slight bas-relief, as if impressed from the mould of a fine gem or cameo, the bust of a Bacchante, her head bound with a wreath of ivy, her form clad in a nebris, and a thyrsus thrown over her shoulder—a subject already known from some gems. Of inferior workmanship are parts of a cup, with wreaths and *bucranea*. One piece alone, ornamented with feathered ornaments on a maroon ground, belongs to painted vases. Neither of these pieces were of glazed or polished ware; but half of a patera had in the inside, in bas-relief, a female hand, placed amidst

NO 54.—BASSO-RELIEVO GEM, A BACCHANTE.

foliage resembling that of the ivy; and several vases with a small handle, in shape of a rude antifixal or helix ornament, with scoral handles made separately, and ready to attach to others, were found; with them was part of a cantharus, or cup, of late black polished ware, the side ornamented with ivy-leaves (*hederata*), completely resembling similar canthari found in France and England. The number of lamps which were found, according to Mr. Barker, amounted to upwards of 3000; and of these he selected for his collection only the most important, allowing the country people to carry away those which were not ornamented with subjects in bas-relief. This find may be compared with that mentioned by Avolio in his Argille, p. 117. The lamps found at Tarsus were very different from those from Italy or Greece. They are of a fine straw colour, of small size, circular, and with one nozzle, and generally without handles. One lamp, which is only ornamented with an egg and tongue moulding, has the remains of the wooden candelabrum still adhering to it below. None of these lamps have the names of makers, one alone being impressed below with a thunderbolt and cross. The nozzle of many had been burnt, shewing that they had been used. Many are perfect, and by no means worn out. Their subjects are, a goat, emblem of Dionysos and Priapus; a wild boar; Selene in a car drawn by two buffaloes, holding in each hand a torch; Isis, whose worship has been already traced in the city, holding a situla, on her head the usual ornament, before her Apis as a buffalo, having on his head a star, advancing to a lighted altar behind a temple; Actæon attacked by one of his dogs (No. 44, p. 189); a Nereid traversing the sea upon a hippocampus; a hare; a gryphon; Cupid riding upon a lion; two Cupids, one leaping over a lion: a dolphin; a bunch of grapes and vine-leaves; a crater or cantharus; an instrument; a crown, altar, and laurel-branch; a bunch of grapes, leaf, and wreath of laurel on the base ΔO; a river-god, probably the Cydnus, reclining, holding a reed in the left hand, a cornucopia in the right, at his elbow an urn, Victory hovering in the air, and crowning him; head of Minerva, full face, with the triple crest to the helmet;[*] a dolphin; head of the Medusa, the mythos of whom was intimately connected with the city founded by Perseus; a stag advancing to the right. A small lamp; one fragment of a circular lamp of a hollow band, which had held four wicks, closed this list. Distinct from these, and probably of an earlier age, are two shoe-shaped lamps with handles, of coarser red ware, one entirely plain, the other having the oriental subject of a goddess holding up two lions by their tails.

III. MISCELLANEOUS OBJECTS. The number of miscellaneous objects of terra-cotta was by no means great; and what is the most startling is the total absence of all architectural fragments, which generally form an important portion of similar collections. The few objects of this nature which were found were chiefly models, such as a Corinthian column quite detached. Some lion's claws, with mortaises apparently for a throne of a small figure. Several oscillæ or masks, with hollow eyes, which appear from the mural paintings at Pompeii to have been suspended by cords between the intercolumniations of the

---

[*] Duc de Luynes, Essai sur la Numismatique des Satrapes. Suppl. 4to. Paris, 1846. Pl. xi.

columns, were found, either scenic masks, either tragic or comic; the head of a bull. Besides these are fragments of a kind of calathus in open work, a pecten shell, a stud, a cylindrical object excised at one end Z H, resembling those found at the Polledrara of Vulci, and apparently bobliquets, or curling-pins for the hair. Some hollow altars, supposed by Mr. Barker to be censers, with evident marks of burning; an object in shape of a cubical seat or altar, with a slit above, supposed to be one of the boxes for money which the gladiators carried round;* and two large disks or medals about three inches diameter, with a hole to suspend them, on one an A, on the other a B; and last, although not least, a plain flat disk of terra-cotta on which is incised in cursive characters, the name Ἀπολλως; this is a remarkable name, being that of the Alexandrian coadjutor of St. Paul.† The inscription is written like a memorandum on the disk. Few objects not of terra-cotta were found; but among these were a bust placed upon a table with four legs, the head broken off, which had been used as a knife-handle of dark steatite, and three flat circular stones, which are supposed to have been used for polishing vessels placed on a lathe, or tools. The most interesting, however, of these objects are parts of some figures cast in plaster of Paris or of a coarse gypsum burnt,‡ and which recal to mind the architectural mouldings of a tomb found at Kertch, and now in the British Museum. Those in Mr. Barker's collection are a female head wearing a sphendone, having the hair gathered up at the sides; a head of Harpocrates, the face coloured red; a head of Hercules in the lion's skin; an eagle; and two architectural mouldings.

* See Seroux d'Agincourt Recueil, and Caylus Recueil.
† Acts xviii. 24, xix. 1; 1 Corinth. iii. 6, 22, iv. 6. Suidas voce.
‡ Pliny, Nat. Hist. xxxv. 153.

CHAPTER IV.

ON CERTAIN PORTRAITS OF HUNS, AND THEIR IDENTITY WITH THE EXTINCT RACES OF AMERICA.

MONSTROUS HEAD IN A CONICAL CAP—PORTRAIT OF A HUN (?)—IDENTITY WITH AMERICAN SCULPTURES—EMIGRATIONS OF ASIATIC NATIONS TO AMERICA—TESTIMONIES FROM STEPHENS, SCHOMBURGK, HUMBOLDT—ANALOGIES OF LANGUAGE—EVIDENCES FROM KLAPROTH AND D'HERBELOT.

Mr. Abington's observations on this piece (No. 55), a head of most monstrous form, in a conical cap, are of so remarkable a nature that I must be permitted to publish them here, and I will add what I have had time to collect from Humboldt and others in confirmation.

Mr. Abington says: "This is the most extraordinary thing in all the collection. On the first view, I was struck with the identity of its strange profile with the figures sculptured upon the monuments and edifices of an extinct people in Central America.* Many of Stephens's engravings represent the same faces exactly.

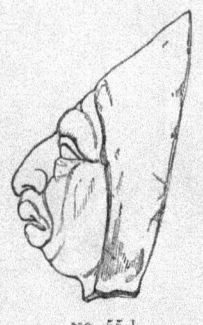

"But what possible connexion could there be between the people of Asia Minor and that far-distant race? This is a question for the Ethnographical Society, and I hope you will lay it before them.

"In the meantime, I will venture a thought upon the subject. Is it not a faithful and correct portrait of a Hun? Humboldt, on the authority of Klaproth, I believe, says that the Hiongnu belonged to the Turkish, and the Huns to the Finnish or Uralian race. We know that

---

* See Stephens's Incidents of Travel in Central America and Yucatan.

the latter were driven by the former, who had been repulsed from the walls of China and roamed westward, upon their neighbours, with whom they are mixed in the relations of their inroads on the south of Europe.* By Huns I do not mean the modern Magyar race, which is of other blood, but the ugly race, whose inhuman faces and horse-like heads, terrified the inhabitants of southern countries, when that Scythian flood rolled in upon them.

"One division of their tribes went eastward, sweeping all before them as far as China; and the great wall was built to keep them out of that kingdom. It is ascertained that some bodies of the Mongol, Kalmuck, and other Tartar tribes crossed to America.†

"Hitherto the sculptures of Central America have only been wondered at, but not explained. Does not this head of yours identify them with the Huns, and thereby let light in upon a dark mystery? It is a subject I should like to follow up, if I had the means within reach. I can only indicate the direction in which others may follow the matter; and I am very much mistaken if it does not richly reward them. Dr. Pritchard would have been the man to submit it to; but he is, alas, no more. For an account of the migration of the Huns, and their policy in levying a tribute of beautiful women in all the conquered countries, by which their own ugliness was rapidly mitigated, see Gibbon's *Decline and Fall.*

"The following sketches of the sculptures in Central America, taken from Stephens's plates and the *Quarterly Journal*, will shew that my notion of the matter is not a mere fancy.

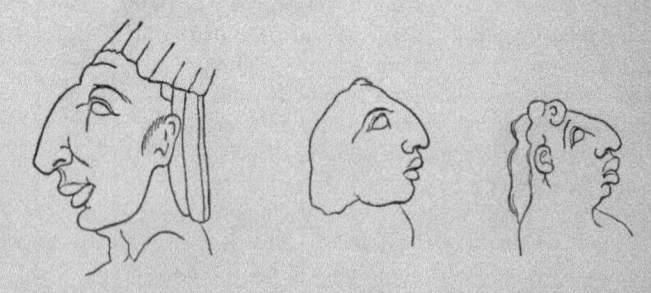

"Heads so very unusual, not to say unnatural, though found in such distant places, must surely have come from the same stock.

* The Οὖννοι are first noticed by Dionysius Periegetes in the time of Augustus; and Ptolemy writes the word Χοῦνοι, strongly aspirated, which may be found again in the geographical name of *Chunigard*.
† See Quarterly Journal of Science, vol. iii. 1828; Dr. Ranking's paper.

THE HUNS AND AMERICANS. 205

"We have *written* descriptions of the inhuman appearance of the Huns who devastated the nation; but I never met with any representation of them either pictorial or sculptural. Perhaps you have the gratification of first bringing before the world a true and exact representation of that once terrible but now forgotten race, and that too by an illustration probably *unique;* also of removing the veil which has hitherto concealed the mysterious origin of the men who have left the memorials of their peculiar conformation upon the sculptured stones of America, but who have been long extinct."

Sir Robert Schomburgk, in a letter he addressed to Humboldt, says, "The hieroglyphical figures are more widely extended than you had perhaps supposed. . . . . They extend, as ascertained by actual observations, from 7° 10' to 1° 40' north latitude, and from 57° 30' to 66° 30' west longitude. Thus the zone of pictured rocks extends, so far as it has been at present examined, over a space of 192,000 square geographical miles; comprising the basin of the Corentyn, the Essequibo, and the Orinoco; a circumstance from which we may form some inference respecting the former amount of population in this part of the continent."

I find confirmation of Mr. Abington's idea in Humboldt's *Aspects of Nature*, and will proceed to quote his remarks that bear the most on this subject in his *Annotations*, p. 176. He says, "I regard the existence of ancient connexions between the inhabitants of Western America and Eastern Asia as more than probable; but by what routes, or with what Asiatic nations the communications took place, cannot at present be decided. Our knowledge of the languages of America is still too limited, considering their great variety, for us as yet entirely to relinquish the hope of some day discovering an idiom which may be spoken, with certain modifications, at once in the interior of South America and in that of Asia; or which may at least indicate an ancient affinity. Such a discovery would be one of the most brilliant which can be expected in reference to the history of mankind."

I am aware that the analogy of one language to another must be sought in the organic structure, and the grammatical forms resulting from the workings of the human intellect and character. Still, when we have no opportunity of following up such research, as in the case of the Americo-Indian languages, it is interesting to trace the similarity of sound in the words which are handed over to us.* For instance, I

* I have a catalogue of many words that resemble each other in different languages. I found, however, so many in the German and English having evidently the same origin, that I forbore collecting them, as they would form a little volume in them-

find *itz-cuin-tepotzotli* to signify a humped-backed dog. Now *itz* I trace to *eet*, the Tartaric appellation of a dog: *cuin* is the Turkish for a *sheep;* therefore *itz-cuin* would be a sheep-dog, or shepherd's dog: *tepotzotli* I take to be the same as *teppeh*, the Turkish for a hill; and the terminative particle *li* or *lu* is quite Tartaric, and always used to express a property or possession: thus, *topal*, lame; *topalli herif*, a lame man; *cör*, blind of one eye; *cörli avret*, a one-eyed woman. I find, moreover, that, some miles from the Encaramada, there rises in the middle of the Savana the rock Tepu-Mereme, or "painted rock." Observe here the similarity of tépu to téppe, and the construction so *Semitic*, having the substantive first; here is still greater affinity; for the "me" may be the same as the "mu" in Arabic; and be the form used to express the adjective. You would in Arabic, using the word *naksh*, paint, say jebel *munaccash*, a rock painted. But what I find contradictory is, that the construction of this word is more Semitic than Hindo-Germanic; for we find the substantive to *precede* the *adjective*, and we have dog-shepherd; humped-back, and not *humped-backed shepherd-dog*. The Arabic form would be *kelbun rayee-un ahdab*, precisely like the Americo-Indian. Would this lead us to trace an affinity between the two, and to suppose that a Semitic tribe traversing through Asia on its way eastward, adopted words from the people with whom it came in contact, and which it afterwards perpetuated in America, preserving, however, its original Semitic construction?

I find further, that some etymologists have thought they recognised in the American word *camosi*, the sun, a similarity to camosh, the name of the sun in one of the Phœnician dialects, and to Apollo, Chomeas, or Balphegor.

Humboldt's further remarks are most interesting, and bear on this ethnological subject. He says: "In looking at Peruvian carvings, I have never remarked any figures of the large-nosed race of men so frequently represented in the bas-reliefs of Palinque in Guatemala, and in the Aztec paintings. Klaproth remembered having seen individuals with similar large noses among the Chalcas, a northern Mogul tribe. It is well known that many tribes of the North American red or copper-

---

selves. The resemblance between many words of the German and Tartaric language was more interesting; and I have a list which would in itself alone prove the connexion between the Alcmagui and the tribes in the east, were such proof requisite, or were the fact at all doubted. But what astonishes me is to find a great many words in German that appear certainly to possess a Semitic origin. These words must have been adopted in consequence of the communion between the wandering tribes in earlier times, who, it will be observed, kept to their *own construction*, although they borrowed the use of words or sounds.

coloured Indians have fine aquiline noses, and that this is an essential physiognomic distinction between them and the present inhabitants of Mexico, New Granada, Quito, and Peru. Are the large-eyed, comparatively fair-complexioned people spoken of by Marchand as having been seen in 54° and 58° lat. on the north-west coast of America, descended from an Alano-Gothic race, the Usüni of the interior of Asia ?"

It is very interesting to read the above question in connexion with what we now have in hand. Following up this idea, I find further, that " the southern Huns or Hajatelah (called by the Byzantines Euthalites or Nepthalites, and dwelling along the eastern shore of the Caspian), had a fair complexion. They cultivated the ground, and possessed towns. They are often called the white or fair Huns; and D'Herbelot even declares them to be Indo-Scythians. For an account of Panu, the leader or *tanju* of the Huns, and of the great drought and famine which, about 46 A.D., caused a part of the nation to migrate northwards, see Deguignes' *Histoire Gen. des Huns, des Turcs, &c.* 1756, t. i. pt. i. p. 217; pt. ii. pp. 111, 125, 223, 447. All the accounts of the Huns taken from the above-mentioned celebrated work have been subjected to a learned and strict examination by Klaproth. According to the result of this research, the Hiongnu belong to the widely-diffused Turkish races of the Altai and Taugnu Mountains. The name Hiongnu, even in the third century before the Christian era, was a general name for the Ti, Tukui, or Turks, in the north and north-west of China. The southern Hiongnu overcame the Chinese, and in conjunction with them destroyed the empire of the northern Hiongnu: these latter fled to the west, and this flight seems to have given the first impulse to the migration of nations in Middle Asia." Might not some families of these tribes have embarked in some fishing-boats, and been cast on the western coast of North America, in the inhospitable climate of from 55° to 65°; and civilisation thus introduced, like the general movement of population in America, have proceeded successively from the North to the South ?*

* Humboldt, *Relation Historique*, t. iii. pp. 155-160. At Weston-super-Mare, in Somersetshire, have lately been found, outside a Roman camp, the bodies of three men of rather a large size by persons excavating. The heads seemed to have been forced in between two ricks, and to have sustained some injury from violence. The crania were examined and compared with Mr. Lawrence's work on the species of man, and no similarity could be traced between them and any of the crania described in that work, except to the head of the Caribbean Indian. It is supposed that these must be the remains of some of the tribes of the Huns that found their way into Britain, as they had done into Rome, marking their progress by acts of cruelty, and causing, by their extreme ugliness, horror to those they vanquished.

CHAPTER V.

ETHNOLOGICAL SUBJECT OF THE HUNS CONTINUED.

"THE UGLY HEADS" OF THE COLLECTION—STANDARD OF BEAUTY—MONUMENTS OF CENTRAL AMERICA—PARALLEL CASE IN HAYTI—THE HITTITES OF SCRIPTURE—REFERENCE TO EGYPTIAN SCULPTURE—EFFECTS OF THE EGYPTIAN INVASION OF CILICIA.

ON a first examination of a few of the ugly, monstrous heads of the collection, I had imagined that they represented Midas. Apollo being a great favourite at Tarsus, it was natural to conclude that Midas would be there jeered at and caricatured. But, at a later period, when Mr. Abington had pointed out the extraordinary resemblance he had traced between No. 55, p. 203, and the heads sculptured on the rocks in Central America, I was led to look closer into the subject; and by setting apart all the heads of that kind, I found a family likeness to prevail through the whole lot, which consists of upwards of fifty heads, that justifies me in coming to the conclusion that they are the representatives of a nation or tribe, if not of a single family, such is the likeness that prevails among them.

These heads have, for the most part, been radiated. The female heads bear the same form of head-dress as that given by the Cilicians to heads representing persons they deified; as if the chiefs of the conquering tribes, hearing that it was customary in the country to have such a compliment paid to the rulers of the land, and to include their ladies, insisted on their being represented by the same effigy. That this was done may be ascertained by an examination of the other heads in the collection, wherein the Junos are represented with the features of the favourite empress of the day; or, to reverse the case, the features of the ladies of that period may be seen bearing the attributes of Juno, Venus, Cybele, Ceres, &c. And on many of these heads may be traced the head-dress of Apollo, with the hair knotted in front,—of Jupiter, with the radiation, &c. Now it is not at all likely that any of the monsters of Grecian mythology would have that compliment paid them; and certainly Midas, who would rather be an object of derision, could never be thus represented.

Now it would seem that when the power of these tribes passed away, the artists, as if ashamed of their subserviency to the people who had ejected them, carefully cut off all the rays on the heads; and only one male and two females have remained perfect enough to tell the tale of their fellows, who are only mutilated about the forehead.

Let not their extreme ugliness be considered a reason why they should not have been deified by the Cilicians or by the people of America. What shall be imagined to be the standard of beauty which shall be acknowledged by all people? The negro is shocked at the first sight of a European. The thin lips, the narrow lengthened nose, oval face, and long hair, are so far from all his notions of beauty as to be ugliness unmitigated. The ugly fellows, whose likenesses we now possess in this collection, would not be ashamed of their peculiarities, nor take offence at their true effigies, any more than the Chinese would be offended at being represented with their ugly cheek-bones, oblique pig-eyes, and Tartar noses, even a little exaggerated. One of these, now in London, is so monstrously ugly, that it would be difficult for a modeller to shew him up worse than he is. How hideous are the heads and faces of many of the holy fakirs of India in the present day! And I have no doubt but that we might find rivals to the ugliest of these heads among many people both in the East and in the West.

Further, the monuments of Central America must be looked upon as bearing a mythological character, and representing objects of adoration—persons who conferred benefits on their fellow-creatures by the introduction of civilisation; holy men, priests, and priestesses, whom the sculptor would not wantonly degrade by giving them features to cause them to be treated with derision; yet we find them characterised by ugliness of the superlative degree. We must not, therefore, be surprised at finding such features radiated with the same glory which is applied to Apollo, the perfection of the Circassian type of beauty. If men of one tribe were eligible for divine honours, others of tribes less favoured in physical beauty were equally so. The deification was for other qualities than personal beauty, and that too judged of by an arbitrary standard. These priests, conquerors, or chiefs of the people—call them what you please—pretended no doubt to be versed in the doctrines of astrology, divination, mesmeric arts, and wonders; their ugly countenances would serve to increase the distance between them.

and the people; there would be nothing to prevent the modeller from even exaggerating this difference; and the priesthood would never take offence at it, if it tended to make the deluded multitude stand in awe of them as beings of another and higher order.

We have a case in point to refer to, in modern times, which bears on this question. The Emperor Soulouque of Hayti has caused Corradi to take portraits of himself and all his family and government, civil and military. However desirous the artist might be to flatter his imperial highness, the latter would not be pleased or accept of his likeness, if he were represented with Grecian features, but would rather insist on the delineations being as nearly like to nature as possible. He might consider himself and family a great deal handsomer than the European; and an exaggeration of his ideal beauty, although a monstrosity in our sight, might only be complimentary to him.*

As yet I have called the people represented by these heads *Huns*, to use an appellation known to all; but I believe that their original name was Khita—perhaps the Hittites of the Scriptures,—a people who were aborigines of Asia Minor, if not of the province of Cilicia itself, and whose chiefs were taken into captivity by Rameses III.

In Rossalini's great work on Egyptian Antiquities there are represented four bodies kneeling, with their arms tied behind them; each has a line of hieroglyphics stating who he is. The first says, " This is the vile slave from Tarsus of the Sea ;" its features are unfortunately disfigured, but alongside there is another captive whose features are complete. The hieroglyphic writing of this says, " Phoor khasi em Khita en Sacca enk,"—" The chief of the Khita as a living captive." Now the fact of these two figures having stood in such propinquity on the monuments in Egypt, erected doubtless to commemorate the conquests of the Egyptian king over the nations of the north of Syria, and the coincidence of the heads found in Tarsus resembling so much the second as to identify them with the same race at least, if not the same individual, would lead to the conclusion that if the Khita were not the inhabitants of this city, they were some of its immediate neighbours, and that it was their chief who had been carried into bondage by the Egyptian conquerors of the country.

I will leave this point to be discussed and settled by more competent judges; and will only add, in support of my conclusion, that directly I exhibited the head, No. 55, to Mr. Birch, he exclaimed at once, and

---

* These portraits have been published in a handsome lithographed album, and a full account of them will be found in an extract from the *New York Herald*, in the *Times* of Oct. 14, 1852.

CONNEXION WITH EGYPT. 211

without hesitation, "I will tell you what people this head represents;" and he turned immediately to the plate in Rossalini's work beforementioned.

Indeed, if we admit similarity of features as a guide in discerning the difference of races, there can be little doubt on the subject. It might be imagined that these two heads (No. 55, p. 203), and the one copied out of Rossalini's work herewith introduced, not only represented the same race of men, but were even intended to portray the same

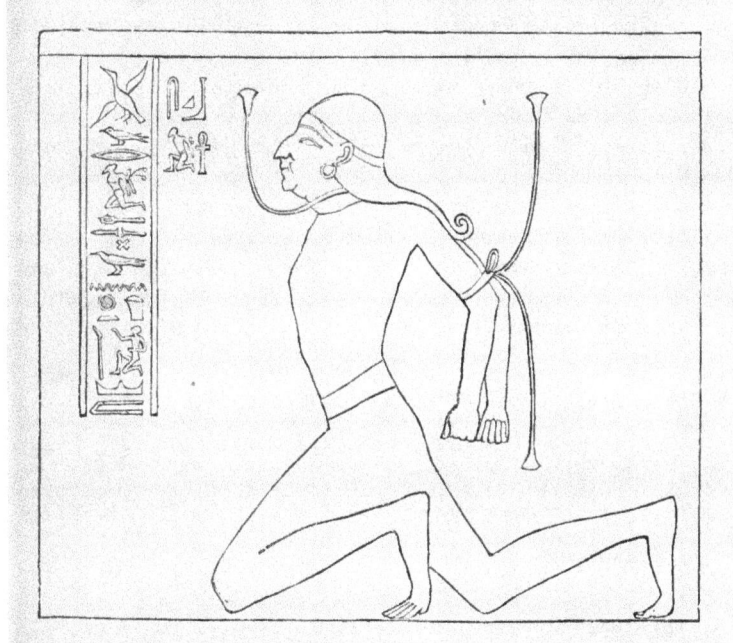

A KNEELING CAPTIVE—FROM ROSSALINI.

individual, with some twenty years' difference in age, only such as he would be at forty and at sixty.

Rameses III. was of the 18th dynasty, and must have effected his conquest 1200 or 1500 years B.C.: my Lares and Penates have been proved to have been destroyed about the year 70 of the Christian era; so that if these heads represent the Khita, as I have no doubt they do,*

* Mr. Layard discovered in the mound of Nabbi Yunus, or of the Prophet Jonah, near Mosul, a head carved in a yellow silex (Eisen Kiesel ?) with singularly grotesque features, which he considers to belong to the later Assyrian period, and an imitation

they had been accumulating in Tarsus, together with many other gods and idols of all nations from the East and West, which were found with them, upwards of 1200 years.

How interesting is this fact! and what light may not these monuments throw on ancient history, on times of which we have now no written records; on times when sculpture formed the basis of the means for perpetuating historical events; and how precious will be such memorials —how useful in the hands of the learned archæologist, who could find leisure to devote a little attention to a closer scrutiny of them!

The Cilicians at a later period became a mixed race, and lost their resemblance to these horrid faces, who, as I have already observed, were possibly tribes that conquered them; but if these were the aborigines of Cilicia or Asia Minor, what was the effect of the Egyptian invasion and conquest? Did it disperse them? Were they the stock from which the ancient Scythians descended? Or were they all from one common origin? How did these wandering tribes, who fought and conquered the West, find their way eastward to America? Can we infer that the American monuments are of a higher antiquity than heretofore supposed? These are all questions to which, at present, we are obliged to "pause for a reply."

of the head of the Egyptian deity, which some believe to represent death. (Layard's *Nineveh*, vol. ii. p. 214; Wilkinson's *Ancient Egyptians*, plate 41, vol. iv.)

This head is now in the British Museum. It has an inscription in cuneiform letters in the crown and back; it might otherwise, Mr. Layard says, be mistaken for a Mexican relic! Mr. Birch suggests that, as a similar head is frequently represented on Egyptian monuments, on vases brought as tribute by an Asiatic people; and is, moreover, found on the Phœnician coins of Abusus, as that of the deity; it may be the Semitic Baal or Typhon.

There is a representation on one of the Babylonian cylinders, engraved by the Syro-Egyptian Society, of a female divinity of horrid aspect, and very slightly clothed: she stands upon a dragon, and holds three articles in her hands, which, if keys, Mr. Abington remarks, would mark her as the Cybele of the Babylonians. There is something round her cap, which, if intended for oak-leaves, would also distinguish her as that goddess.

CHAPTER VI.

ADDITIONAL WORKS OF ART. GODS, DEMIGODS, AND HEROES.

APOLLO—MERCURY—HERCULES—BACCHUS—SILENUS—FAUNS AND SATYRS—PAN—MINERVA—VENUS—CUPID—EUROPA—MARSYAS—LEANDER—LAOCOON—ÆSCULAPIUS—FORTUNE—CAIUS CALIGULA ?—PRIAPUS—HARPIES—MARSYAS—ABRERIG OR NERGAL ?—SUMMARY.

WE find from the discoveries of Layard and Botta, that the god of the sun was represented by the Assyrians as an eagle-headed or vulture-headed human figure. It is one of the most prominent sacred types in the earlier Assyrian monuments, and was, according to Dr. Grotefend, the tutelar divinity of the nation. "This figure may also," says Layard (vol. ii. p. 459), "be identified with the god Nisroch, in whose temple Sennacherib was slain by his sons (2 Kings xix. 37); for the word Nisr signifies, in all the Semitic languages, an eagle."

Josephus[*] calls this image Arascus; Isaiah, Asarak or Nisroch (xxxvii. 38); Jeremiah (vii. 18), Nit; the Septuagint, Μεσοραχ. It was also written Asarax, Esorac, Nasarac, and Mesarac. The distinguished French archæologist, Lajard, has traced the Mithra of the Persian system, the same as the Nisroch of the Assyrians, through its various transformations to the Απολλων of the Greeks, and Apollo of the Romans. We have the authority of Herodotus, and other of the ancient historians, for the identity of Apollo and the Egyptian Florus; and we have seen in the course of this work that Apollo was not only the favourite deity of the Cilicians, but, as Tarsus the winged, he was in fact the tutelary divinity of the city. It appears from additional terra-cottas obtained since Mr. Birch's descriptions were penned, and which have been described by Mr. Abington with his usual taste and discrimination, that we have representations of the same deity in other forms among these truly interesting relics.

[*] Antiq. Jud. i. c. 1.

One of these formed part of a basso-relievo of bold projection: the brooch by which his pallium is buckled in front has been made by the impress of a punch much too large for the purpose.

There is also a very finely modelled face of apparently the same divinity. In this face the eyes are remarkably expressive, and the mouth diminished so as to give a good example of the sublimated or ideal beauty which the Greeks aimed at. The hair is bound by a fillet into a knot on the top of the head, in the style usually given to Apollo.

There is also in the collection a little figure of Horus or Harpocrates, with its finger to its lips, excessively slight and rude.

Also a head, trunk, and right thigh of Harpocrates (No. 38). The youthful rotundity and fleshiness of the body and thigh are well expressed. The head has the hair knotted on the top, is radiated, and surmounted with the sacred Egyptian emblem, and the finger on the lip places, Mr. Abington remarks, the designation of the figure beyond dispute. The left arm supports a horn of plenty filled with fruits.

"It is to be regretted that this figure came so late, as it affords a correct key to very many fragments which we have had before by piecemeal. It is most valuable in every point of view. We have many youthful heads with the same Egyptian symbol of the Nelumbium on the top: are they all to be referred to Harpocrates? If so, he must have been the most popular of the divinities at Tarsus, if we may judge from the number.

"I have before noticed the identity of Assarac, Horus, and Harpocrates, as the incarnation of deity through a female divinity, Isis. It may be asked, when the Roman empire began to resound with the testimony of the Apostles, that the long-expected Messiah of the Jews was incarnate, did the priests of the old mythology bring out more fully to popular notice, and in opposition to the Christians, their ancient mystery of the incarnation of the son of Isis? If this policy was resorted to—and it would seem under the circumstances very natural—it would explain the fact of the representation of Horus being so multiplied at that period.

"It would be their policy to persuade the people that the wonderful tales respecting the birth of the Messiah were but stolen from the system of religion maintained by them and their fathers, and therefore an innovation to be rejected."

Another small head in the collection, similar to the foregoing, has a circlet of flowers as a crown, with the sacred bean in front.

Another larger head has a diadem of flowers similar to the preceding, but surmounted by a radiation, with the Egyptian symbol in front.

Another head similar to the one with the hair knotted on the top, but without any radiation; behind it rises a kind of shell-work or plaiting.

The origin of Mercury, known as the Hermes and Cyllenius of the Greeks, the Anubis of the Egyptians, the Theutates of the Gauls, and Woden of the Saxons, has been sought for in Phœnicia; the image of this god being the symbolical figure of the ancestor and founder of the kingdom. This, however, is mere speculation, and further research will no doubt shew that some of the many forms of this many-symbolled god were as common to the Assyrian and Hindu forms of idolatry as to the Egyptian and Phœnician.

Among the different forms in which this deity is represented in the Cilician terra-cottas, is one which Mr. Abington calls the ancient Pelasgian Mercury, in which he is usually represented terminating in an inverted obelisk, cloaked, and with a phallus. Several examples of the same kind are met with in the British Museum.

Hermes, under various forms, seems to have been much honoured in Cilicia. Among the terra-cottas is a head with a cap, which seems to be intended to represent a young Mercury. The expression of the features is very pleasing, both in front and profile. There is also another, with a curly head, more plump and infantine than the preceding.

There is also among the terra-cottas another bonneted head of the same character. It is of childish age, but bears a strong family likeness to some heads of Apollo, &c., modelled from the countenances of priests, or persons of rank; very fat and luxurious-looking. It will be curious if this should be a youth of the same family, who sat to the artist for a study of young Hermes.

Also, a winged boy in the act of flying; he has the hair knotted over the forehead, a Phrygian bonnet, and loose drapery, fastened by a fibula on the breast, but flying open in front. It is a very good figure.

Mercury, as the messenger of the gods, is most usually represented with a winged cap, and wings to his ankles; but in this case the wings are fixed to the shoulders. Apollo, as sculptured by the Greeks and Romans, has no wings, but at Tarsus he was winged! So that it does not appear that we can urge this fact of his being winged against the idea of its being the young postman of Olympus. We know that there were so many different legends concerning these deities, and so many different tales of their origin, descent, &c., that they are quite confusing. There are no fewer than six or eight different Mercurys, concerning whom we have accounts. The early traditions would vary in the various lines through which they were transmitted; and priests and poets, by the exercise of a liberty which was unrestrained by any real reverence for such objects, have added to the confusion.

There is also among the terra-cottas a face and neck of a very good figure, similar to those just described. It is the plump, healthy countenance which we cannot look upon but with pleasure.

The legends of this hero were well known to the Phœnicians, and also to the Far East. His labours are engraved on some of the Babylonian cylinders. The tales handed down to us by the Greeks were drawn by them from the tradition of the East. This, independently of the Assyrian origin of the deity, would account for such numerous fragments of this demi-god being found at Tarsus.

Among these is a restored figure of the hero, nearly complete, except the head. It is of good execution.

In another head and bust, the breadth of shoulders and fulness of muscle at once declare it to be Hercules. The radiation of the head also shews that it is one honoured by apotheosis.

There is also a head of plaster, which appears to represent the same demi-god.

Also a terminal figure of an old man dressed in a lion's skin. Is this an oriental form of Hercules? We know from the cylinders that the Babylonians had their Hercules.

Also, a left hand of a Hercules holding his club; the lion's skin falling over it. The Assyrian Hercules was also represented holding a mace in his hand.

It is remarkable, however, that among the many and various representations that occur of Hercules among the Cilician terra-cottas, we do not find any of the representations precisely identical with that of the Assyrian Hercules, Sandon or Sandok, also called Dayyad "the hunter."

One head of Hercules is radiated: it is a magnificent head, and the profile is like the finest figures of that deity which have come down to our times; nor will it suffer by comparison with any of them, making allowance for the material.

Among the Cilician terra-cottas are two heads in the act of kissing; the female seems to be crowned with ivy, the crown of the other is obliterated. These may not improbably re-

NO. 56.—HEADS OF ARIADNE AND BACCHUS.

present Bacchus and Ariadne. The ivy forbids us calling it Cupid and Psyche.

There is also a fragment of a vessel worked into the head of the Indian Bacchus. Also a remarkable fragment of a figure in bold relief: a naked, old, fat, ugly man, bald-headed, bearing a thyrsus and a wine-cup, which he seems to have been making free use of.

It will be remembered that Bacchus brought his thyrsus, surmounted by the pine or fir-cone, from the East, when he returned from his Indian expedition; and this is probably an Indian, or, at all events, an Oriental Bacchus.

M. Lajard has shewn in an elaborate essay* the connexion between the cone of the cypress and the worship of Venus in the religious systems of the East.

Layard hesitates to identify the object held by the winged figures of the Assyrian monuments, and evidently, from their constant occurrence, most important objects in the religious ceremonies of the Assyrians of old, with the fruit of the fir or cypress; and he adds, " Any attempt to explain their use, or their typical meaning, can, at present, be little better than an ingenious speculation." (See vol. ii. p. 471.) The handing down of the same tradition through long spaces of time, its diffusion over vast spaces geographically distant, and the permanence of forms in art, possess, however, an interest of their own, both artistic and psychological, independent of the true or corrupted meaning of the thing.

It is not impossible that the origin of the veneration for the fir-cone has been its aphrodisiacal properties. In the celebrated Bishop Berkeley's work called *Siris, a treatise on Tar-Water*, the learned author argues, that as the elemental fire, which he identifies with animal spirits and natural life (paragraph 277), may not inconsistently with the notions of that philosophy which ascribes much of generation to celestial influence, be supposed to impregnate animals and plants; so the benign spirit of the native balsam of pines and firs may, by invigorating the said elemental fire, increase the power of fecundation. The Hera of the Assyrians, who, like her prototypes Isis, Astarta, Mylitta, and Venus, presided over generation, is, we see, represented bearing the cone, as are also her priests and priestesses.† The infamous law which, according to Herodotus, marked the rites of the goddess at Babylon, is generally known, and deservedly condemned in the apocryphal book of Jeremy.

* Nouvelles Annales de l'Institut Archéologique, vol. xix.
† Although unseemly symbols are rare in the Assyrian monuments, still enough exists, as Layard has shewn, to attest that such a worship did exist even under its most degrading forms.

What could be a more fitting accompaniment of Bacchus than the same emblem which he carries on his thyrsus?

Bishop Berkeley furnishes in his pages abundant proof that the virtues of the pine and fir were known to the ancients. Pliny tells us that wines in the time of the old Romans were medicated with pitch and resin; wherefore but for their aphrodisiac qualities? Pliny also records that it was customary for the ancients to hold fleeces of wool over steam of boiling tar, and squeeze the moisture from them, which watery substance was called *pissinum*. Ray will have this to be the same as the *pisselæum* of the ancients; but Hardouin, in his notes on Pliny, thinks the *pisselæum* to have been produced from the *cones* of cedars. No doubt the effect of both was the same. Bishop Berkeley acknowledged that he was ignorant what use the ancients made of these liquors, but the whole evidence can suggest only one conclusion. It was used as an aphrodisiac; and so powerful is this property, that Jonstonus, in his *Dendographia*, observes that it is wholesome to walk in groves of pine-trees, which impregnate the air with balsamic particles. The Eleusinian and Axio-Kersian mysteries appear to have peculiarly affected pine-groves; and satyrs and fauns, that dwelt in woods, were notorious for their libidinous propensities.

The drunken follower of Bacchus, Silenus (No. 57), is represented in a very fine fragment of his head, in which only the middle part of the face remains; but quite enough to make us regret that there is not more. There is also in the collection part of a bold relief figure of the same rollicking demi-god.

NO. 57.—HEAD OF SILENUS.

As illustrative of other followers of Bacchus we have the head of a young faun or wood demon, with the wattles under his throat like a goat. It is a good thing, and worthy of care. The top of a satyr's head, large size, and the lower part of a faun's head, with a characteristic sensual grin.

Among the terra-cottas is also a head of Pan, or of a satyr, with a crown of fir-leaves and cones. It is a work of high art, and exhibits a freedom and facility of touch which could only come from the hand of a first-rate artist. The expression of the lower half of the face is admirable, and the sensuality of the mouth, &c. &c., is wonderfully characteristic. It is seen to great advantage on the three-quarter face, with the right cheek presented to the spectator. There is also the base of a figure of Pan; all that remains is the end of his crook. Also a very excellent head, the expression of the mouth shewing it to be a Pan or wood demon. There are also the lower part of the face of Pan, and a small head of the same character.

We have among the Cilician terra-cottas a figure of Minerva as Pallas, in white clay; a work of art in which there is much graceful ease, though the facial angle is remarkably round. And it may be remarked here, in connexion with the Lares and Penates of cities, that as Pallas was essentially the city guardian and protector, so the Palladium, an image of Minerva, which gave security to those cities in which it was placed, was emblematic of the great fact that those kingdoms and cities flourish and prosper where wisdom presides. Also a figure of the same goddess, holding a ram; the ram was sometimes represented on her helmet, together with the sphynx. There is also another head with the fore part of a helmet remaining, apparently the same deity. The workmanship is tolerably good.

Among the terra-cottas is a fragment of a female figure, only the thigh and left fore-arm remaining. She has taken Cupid captive, who is struggling to escape. It does not appear certain whether this was a figure of Venus or of a Nymph, who, having captured Cupid, is scourging him. The portion of drapery remaining is stiff and formal.

Among the numerous figures of Cupid that are met with in the Tarsus collection is one winged, bearing the club of Hercules. This was a not uncommon form among the Egyptians, where Horus was in like manner represented, according to the custom of the Neomenia, with different attributes, sometimes with the wings of the Etesian wind; at others with the club of Hercules and arrows of Apollo; and at others riding on a lion, driving a bull, or tying a ram. The powerful child, celebrated for disarming both gods and men, is often represented with some trophy of this character, such as the helmet of Mars, &c. &c., to denote the triumphs of love over the strongest of men.

NO. 58.—CUPID AND SWAN.

Another Cupid (No. 58) occurs, caressing a swan; the head is radiated.

It is a pleasing group: the association of Cupid and the swan was very common. It is altogether a sweet little piece, both in composition and execution; but the neck appears to be too short to represent a swan's, and what corroborates the doubts entertained on this subject is, that Mr. Major, of St. John's Wood (Abbey Road), possesses a dozen terra-cotta images, found in Italy, of great beauty, among which there is a similar form of a bird, the neck of which is quite as short, and of which Mr. Major has kindly allowed a copy to be taken. It is of very superior

finish, and must be of the time when the Romans had arrived at their highest degree of perfection in the art of sculpture. Here we have the neck quite as short, although most graceful, and it certainly seems to be intended to represent a more ignoble bird than the swan.

We have in the same collection a fragment which represents Europa riding upon Jupiter in the form of a bull. A portion of the bull's head remains; he is turning and rubbing his neck against her foot. Several fragments of bulls appear also to have formed parts of illustrations of the same popular fable.

The well-known fable of Marsyas was not passed over by the Cilicians. Several illustrations of this strange and ungodlike story are met with. In one of these Marsyas is represented bound to the tree and flayed alive. This favourite subject was never better expressed than in this particular fragment. The anatomy is perfect, and must have been carefully studied from nature; and the agony of the face, as the head sinks upon the right shoulder, shewing the approach of death, is most impressive. This fragment must take its place in the first class for excellence:—

> "The satyr's fate, whom angry Phœbus slew,
> Who, raised with high conceit, and puffed with pride
> At his own pipe, the skilful god defied.
> Why do you tear me from myself? he cries.
> Ah, cruel! must my skin be made the prize?
> This for a silly pipe, he roaring said;
> Meanwhile his skin from off his limbs was flay'd
> All bare and raw, one large continued wound,
> With streams of blood his body bathed the ground.
> The blueish veins their trembling pulse disclosed,
> The stringy nerves lay naked and exposed.
> His guts appeared, distinctly each express'd;
> And every shining fibre of his breast."
>
> OVID. *Met.* vi.

Upon another very remarkable anatomical figure of Marsyas being flayed alive and holding something, possibly his flute, in the hands, which it clasps to the breast, Mr. Abington remarks, that "it is but a sketch with very little finish, but of the highest merit. The marking of the bones, though not exactly correct, is very striking: the brim of the pelvis and the trochanters of the thigh-bones are very well displayed. The head and right breast form a very bold relief. The skin is flayed off the face and turned back over the scalp, and its cut edges are seen covering the hair. The expression of agony is so intense as to make it a model for study: the staring eyeballs, the swollen corrugations of the eyebrows, and the distressing spasmodic action of the muscles of expression on the face, strike us with horror, while they so fascinate by the interest felt in so much suffering, that we can hardly turn away from the sight." Another fragment of a very stout athletic figure, bound by the middle and kneeling, is supposed by Mr. Abington to represent Marsyas supplicating Apollo previous to his being flayed. Four other fragments are described by the same distinguished artist and antiquary as belonging to the same subject.

In the same collection is a remarkable fragment representing a man swimming on his back; he is in the act of drawing his legs up to strike, or tread the water from him, while he is dashing the water open with his hands. Only one-half the figure is left; the head and hands are wanting. Also the right arm and part of the body of a man swimming. He is in the act of scooping the water back with his arm. It is slight, but very expressive. There are other fragments relating to the same subject. It would appear, from joining some of these pieces together, that the subject is Leander swimming the Hellespont.

NO. 59.—LEANDER SWIMMING THE HELLESPONT.

"Alone at night his wat'ry way he took;
About him and above the billows broke;
The sluices of the sky were open spread,
And rolling thunder rattled o'er his head."

Another interesting fragment represents the body of Leander thrown up by the billows upon the shore. The wave which has cast him on the land is retreating in a volume from the dead body, leaving

"His floating carcass on the Sestian shore."—VIRGIL.

We have also in the Tarsus collection the lower part of a figure of Laocoon, or of one of his sons; and also a very beautiful figure of Esculapius. The dignified ease of the attitude agreeing so well with the repose of the face, is much to be admired; the softness of the drapery is well expressed.

Also the foot of a figure of Fortune standing upon an orb. And then, again, the fragment of a winged figure; only the right arm remains, and drapery falls from the shoulder. The feathering is remarkably bold; which would also seem to belong to the same subject. Also the left arm of winged Fortune holding up a wreath. The figures of Isis we have seen, however, have often been confounded with those of Fortune.

Among the terra-cottas are also fragments of bodies clothed in the lorica or corselet of scale-armour as worn by generals and superior officers, both Greeks and Romans, subsequently to the Homeric period, and more or less ornamented. Now, it is not a little remarkable that the Emperor Caius Caligula, when he had reigned with moderation for about two years, took a fancy for honours of a higher kind, and ordered his statue to be erected in all the cities of the empire. Josephus gives a full account of the inflexible resistance of the Jews, and of the dangers incurred by it, and of their happy deliverance by the death of the tyrant. The commander who was entrusted with the carrying out of this edict came from Syria, and it is not likely that he would find the priests of Antioch and Cilicia quite so scrupulous upon the subject.

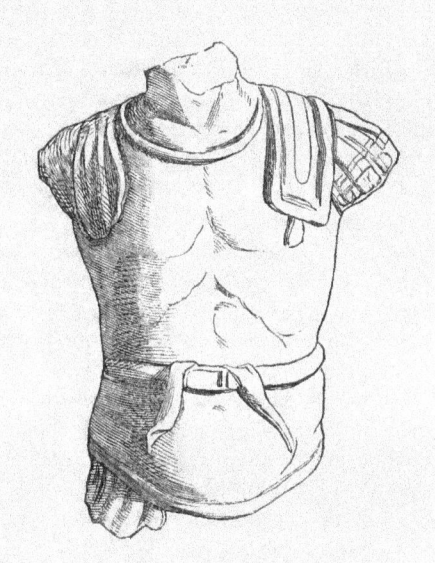

NO. 60.—BUST OF CAIUS CALIGULA WITH THE LORICA.

Images of Caligula must have been in great demand during the short-lived divine honours which were universally paid to him throughout the provinces of the enslaved empire. And it is not totally impossible that these figures of a deified person in Roman armour, or, at all events, of a Roman armed chief, admitted among the Lares and Penates of Tarsus, may have some reference to the canonisation of Caius Caligula.

LARES AND PENATES.

We come now to a more delicate subject, but one which is so intimately interwoven with all the ancient religious systems of the East, that a mere mawkish regard for modern prudery should not exclude its consideration from our pages. It is part of the great philosophy of nature, and reappears in a hundred different forms in the Pantheons of Assyria, Babylonia, India, and Egypt, and at all the first cradles of thought, sentiment, and worship. In the Cilician forms we find the rudest representation of the mysterious principle of fecundity mixed up with that of the well-known fish-god of the East—the Dagon of the Philistines, of Ashdod, and the Annedoti of the Babylonians, which Layard found as a man-god (Oannes?) at Khorsabad, and the worship of which was afterwards associated in one common form of icthyolatry in Derceto or Atergates. To the present day we see fish venerated in the East, just as the crocodile was for similar reasons in Egypt and elsewhere, and familiar examples of which occur at Urfah, ancient Ur, and Edessa; at Tashun, in Luristan, and at other places.

Among the Cilician terra-cottas there is a phallus broken from a figure with which it was connected, the body of which formed into a fish. This combination was very common, and not unfrequently the fish alone was used to express the same idea of fecundity. There is also in the same collection the lower portion of a female figure in full drapery, the left hand of which holds the symbol of the fish and phallus.

In the Bacchanalian orgies the women carried this symbol in their processions. Such facts illustrate St. Paul's testimony in the epistle to the Romans, 1st chap. v. 18-32, and in Ephesians, v. 12: "It is a shame even to speak of the things which are done of them in secret."

The most extraordinary work of art, however, that comes under this strange category is the head and upper half of a figure closely draped; the head at first view seems to be covered with a helmet drawn over the face. But the extraordinary character of this symbolical figure appears on further examination, and is apparently unique. The head is a phallus!

Layard, it may be observed, discovered at Nimrud (ancient Athur) a broken earthen vase, on which were represented two Priapean human figures with the wings and claws of a bird, the breast of a woman, and the tail of a scorpion, or some similar reptile. (See vol. i. p. 128.)

There is also among the Cilician terra-cottas the figure of a naked man bearing a huge shell on his shoulder; he has a wild expression; and we have before remarked upon the shell being appropriated to Priapus. There occurs also in the collection the following fragments, having reference to the same worship: the middle part of a female carrying the phallus; she has two large bosses on her shoulders. Another also bearing the phallus. A phallus, simply and *bonâ fide* such; as also another, with the body of a fish,—a very common way of bearing it. Further, part of a Priapean figure bearing a pitcher; and lastly, a mask representing a female head of monstrous features, surmounted by a phallus. Here also we have the two bosses at the side of the head, such as we find on the foreheads of certain priests, to be hereafter described, and which identify them as connected with the same obscene rites.

The Harpies appear to have had their original in Egypt. That country being very subject, during the months of April, May, and June, to vicissitudes of weather and the visitations of noxious insects, the Egyptians of old gave to their emblematic figures of these months a female face, with the bodies and claws of birds. The strange forms that the poetic and artistic mythology of Greece and Rome attached to these imaginary demons or genii were as numerous as they were fantastic.

Among the Cilician terra-cottas we find a harpy, the lower part of the body of which is vulture-shaped, with wings, the extremities of which are wanting. The face is very expressive of the horrid nature of these fabled beings. It seems in the very act of uttering its cry. Another fragment represents the head and wings of a harpy, which seems to have formed the angle of an altar of incense, or some such article. The head bears a sort of capital, which probably supported the moulding forming the summit.

On a fragment of a vessel in the shape of a trough or shallow laver, in the same collection, and the sides of which are formed of rows of leaves, the end is supported by a harpy. There are also in the same collection a harpy in relief, and a harpy which has been the handle to some hollow vessel.

In describing this portion of the collection, it may perhaps also be noticed, that the ancient Assyrians, according to Dr. Grotefend, recognised in the stars of heaven golden chariots of heavenly hosts. They imagined a supreme ruler dwelling in the centre of all the revolutions of the stars; the most perfect leader of the most perfect chariot. The seven bright stars in the north (the Great Bear) were compared to a four-wheeled chariot, drawn by three fiery horses, upon which the Creator was riding in eternal rotation.

We apparently see a trace of the same tradition in the Cilician terra-cottas in the figure of a man in the act of riding a bear. He has the dress of a charioteer, his loins girded with straps; his right hand seems to hold a whip, with which he is urging the animal forward; the left

226   LARES AND PENATES.

hand holds a rein connected with a collar round the neck of the beast. As Baal or Zeus rode the pole-star, this must have been an inferior deity. Possibly Abrerig, Nerig, or Nergal, the shining Bar, god of the starry skies and tutelar deity of the Assyrian monarchs.

NO. 61.—MAN RIDING A BEAR.

We find from this examination of a second group of the Lares and Penates of Tarsus, that although in early times an Assyrian city, the Assyrian character is very little preserved, and that only in a partial degree. There is no member of the Assyrian Pantheon, in the whole collection, simple and undefiled by more modern traditions and more recent art innovation. The reason of this is well explained by the fact before debated upon, as to their having been blended with others or modified in form by their transition with respect to place and time. In the Babylonian cylinders we have Hercules in the earliest representation of that hero which the world perhaps possesses. We have also the thyrsus of the Indian Bacchus as preserved in the hands of the winged figures of Assyria; the mythological figure of a charioteer riding the bear; the female figure with conical cap, like the Diana of Assyria; the worship of the fish-god; the lion of Rhea; the winged horse, the Pegasus of the Greeks, which we have seen so identified with the story of Tarsus, and which is also found among the emblematical forms and types of Assyria.

We have also illustrations of the story of Perseus. According to Herodotus (lib. vi. c. 54), a great astronomer who instructed men in the knowledge of the stars, and according to the scholiast in Lycophron,

MYTHOLOGY OF TARSUS.

v. 18, the same as the sun, and all the traditions connected with whom, more especially his reputed marriage with Astarte the daughter of Belus, Layard points out (vol. ii. p. 443) to have reference to his Assyrian origin. We have Asarac or Nisroch, the same as Horus and Harpocrates, viewed as the incarnation of a deity through a female divinity—Mylitta or Isis—one of the oldest and most important traditions of the East, viewed in all its bearings. We have also the Ras Majusi, or head magi of the Persians, transmitting an original Babylonian and Assyrian form, just as Mithra effects the transition of Nergal to Apollo; and Layard has shewn that the Assyrians knew also the obscene rites of Priapus.

The collection, taken in all its parts, truly shews that the mythology of Tarsus was (as indeed might have been anticipated from what is known of its history—its boasted Assyrian origin—its mercantile renown—its connexion with Greece and Rome, and its celebrity as a school of philosophy and religion) of such a mingled character, Assyrian, Egyptian, Indian, Syrian, Greek, and Roman, that it will always be difficult to unravel it. Yet in this very fact consists in a great measure the value, the interest, and the great peculiarity of this remarkable collection.

62.—ATYS.   63.—ANOTHER REPRESENTATION OF ATYS.

CHAPTER VII.

SIBYLS AND DOLPHINS AND THEIR RIDERS.

SIBYLS—AN AFRICAN SIBYL—HEAD-DRESS OF THE VIRGIN PROPHETESSES—A MATRON SIBYL(?)—DOLPHINS AND THEIR RIDERS—APOTHEOSIS OF DECEASED CHILDREN—STORY OF ARION—RADIATED HEADS—THE BULLA.

IT is not surprising that the Cilician terra-cottas, which, we have seen, embrace so large a field of Oriental, Egyptian, Greek, and Roman mythology, should also contain illustrations of oracular beings and virgin prophetesses, who played an important part in the rise of Christianity; whose books were largely used by the ancient fathers of the Church, as Justin Martyr, Athenagoras, Theophilus of Antioch, Tertullian, Lactantius, Eusebius, St. Jerome, St. Austin, and others, against the Pagans, and whose prophecies did not fall before the light of a new religion for nearly four centuries after the advent of Jesus.

Among the various female heads, for example, which adorn this interesting collection, is one (No. 64) with African features, broad nose, and projecting jaws. It is a female of rank. The hair is well dressed, and formed into a circle or crown of plait on the top.

Of this head Mr. Abington remarks: "It is remarkable as being one of a class of heads of which there are several examples, having a hole in the basis of the cranium to receive an axis for its support. There is no appearance of their having been in any way connected with a body, unless it was in the manner in which the Chinese heads upon their figures of Mandarins, &c., which are centred upon an axle, to which is appended a balance to counterpoise the head. By this the head has the free motion which makes it nod and bow to a spectator on the slightest agitation being communicated to the image. The head

NO. 64.—AFRICAN SIBYL.

in question might be some priestess or sibyl of African origin and of celebrity; and it remains a matter of conjecture if such heads were not used, as above described, for purposes of divination."

The same remarks apply to a female head chiefly differing from the former in the prolongation of the nose. It is crowned with a kind of cap made of plaited work, with an arch or bow on the top. Such a face, pretending to the possession of sibylline foresight, would have great influence with the multitude.

The following also possibly come under the same category: 1st, a female head, with the hair in great profusion, worked into plaits, which are doubled and crossed on the top of the head, so as to form a noble tiara. The face is pleasing from its tranquillity, though not of the first order as a work of art. Another female head, with the locks of hair twisted and carried back, so as to be bound together behind the head. This style of twisting, instead of plaiting, is partly seen in the preceding head. Also, another head of a lady crowned with a very graceful headdress or turban, which is formed of materials folded and bound together. It is a very pleasing face, though much damaged. Again, the head of a lady in fine red clay; the ears are ornamented with large pendants, and the head covered with hair-work, which may probably be artificial, finishing with a rosette on the top: altogether it is a very pleasing figure. We have also other heads and busts of ladies, who cannot but be classed in the category of sibyls. In one of them the hair is dressed so as to spread very fully round the face, and gathered into a knot behind; over the forehead is a jewel which supports what appears to be a further expansion of the hair. The ears are decorated with large spherical pendants, probably pearls. In another the hair is elaborately dressed in front and plaited behind. The bust is beautifully modelled, and the head gracefully set. Jewels adorn the ears. It is a well-proportioned and pleasing figure. Also the bust and right arm of a female in relief. She is holding some object in her right hand, which she is looking at with earnestness and complacency. Her hair is plaited, and a jewel in the ear; but there is not enough of the subject to found more than a conjecture. Also, the head of a lady with a tiara, and her hair full dressed; there are jewels in the ears. The right side is in the best preservation, and gives a very pleasing expression. There is also another female head of the same family likeness in the nose and mouth. She wears a bonnet or small cap much ornamented. Further, a woman's head with a high cap, conical in the front, and flattened at the sides. The round masses with which it is decorated are perfectly plain, as if they were globular buttons; but not a touch of the tool to give them the expression of roses or any other flower, nor is there the least bond of connexion between them to give the idea of "chaplets." Lastly, we have a small female head with a tiara, the hair turned back in the style of the figures of Pallas. It is much polished, as if it had been moulded from. And the face and bust of a matron, full-faced and plump, crowned with a tiara, the hair arranged in curled rolls, different from any we have yet seen. The ears have jewels pendent from them; a robe is drawn closely over the shoulders. Could a sibyl have been a matron?

A very interesting illustrated work on the various modes of dressing the hair, as practised by the ladies of old time, might be written from the Tarsus collection of Cilician sibyls, and the other female heads in the collection.

We also find in the Tarsus collection a remarkable number of illustrations of dolphins and their riders, which, as in the instance of other works of art, are studied to the greatest advantage, taken, not singly, but in an order of connexion with each other.

This group comprises nearly thirty pieces, among which are no fewer than five heads of dolphins, all of them most effectively modelled; two parts of the bodies and two tails.

One, the posterior end of a dolphin, having the tail perfect, has also connected with it the right arm of a boy riding the fish and holding a ship's rudder. Another, the tail end of a dolphin, has the right thigh of a youth riding it. A third, the middle part of a dolphin, with the right leg and thigh of the naked young rider. A fourth, the same on a smaller scale. On a fifth, the leg only of the rider remains. A sixth is the tail of a dolphin held by the right hand of the rider; but in what attitude he was placed it is difficult to imagine. A seventh, the head of a dolphin with a boy riding. He has a rein in the fish's mouth, which he holds tightly. Only the leg and forearms of the rider remain. This

NO. 65.—BOY AND DOLPHIN.

appears to have been a lamp, the snout of the dolphin being formed into a spout to carry a wick. Lastly, the body and arm of a boy (No. 65), with part of the head of a dolphin, to which he holds on as he rides.

Nine other examples have been previously described.

In the whole of this series of figures mounted on dolphins, all the riders, it is to be observed, are children; and the placing of figures upon a fish, especially the dolphin, was a sign of apotheosis, or that consecration of deceased children which prevailed in Cilicia, to which we have so often had our attention called. There are in the collection a number of these deified little ones, which, from their attitude and the position of their arms, appear to have been riding the dolphin. Several of them wear the *bulla* round the neck, and all are radiated. We should not have suspected their having been connected with the symbol of the dolphin but for the clue afforded by the preceding fragments.

Another fragment presents the right arm and part of a figure in drapery, with the hands resting upon the head of a dolphin. In this interesting work of art, the arm seems to be that of an adult and not of a child; the drapery is also in a different style from all the rest. It does not seem to sit on the fish upon whose head the hand rests. It is possibly a fragment of the beautiful story of Arion, who, after having charmed the dolphins by his music, leaped into the sea to escape from his murderers, and was conveyed by them safe to land.

In the same group is the head and bust of a chubby boy, wearing the bulla, and in the same attitude as the rest; but instead of the head being radiated, it is crowned with the stephanos, which was worn by persons engaged in sacrifice. Little boys were employed to hold the incense-box, and the crowns and garlands used at sacrifices; the same as children are employed for similar duties at the Mass in Romish churches. This head is that of a deceased boy who had been so officially employed, probably the son of a priest; his attitude indicates that, like the rest, he was riding, and, from the analogies, it may be presumed that it was on a dolphin.

The figure of another radiated boy differs from the others by having a broad girdle or belt round his middle. It is not certain if this figure was not mounted on a horse, as there is some appearance of a mane before him; but the work of that part is too defective to be read intelligibly. It also differs from the others in the attitude, the face looking back over the right shoulder. We shall describe other examples of deified children in the chapter devoted to the description and general illustration of human figures.

CHAPTER VIII.

MAGI AND MONKS.

AMONG the more remarkable relics which assist in illustrating the transition of Oriental systems into Greek and Roman mythology are the evidence, in the existence of two miniature figures of Magi (No. 66), of the wise men of the East having formed part of the Cilician Pantheon. These figures are bearded, and dressed in close round cloaks, with a hood or mitre, all in one piece, which must have been put on like a blouse.

The Chaldean magi enjoyed a long period of prosperity at Babylon. A pontiff appointed by the sovereign ruled over a college of seventy-two hierophants. They were also established at Memphis and at Tibet, where the costume is preserved by the priests to this day; they also extended their influence and doctrines into Etruria. When the Medes and Persians overthrew the reigning power at Babylon, they put down the old mythology, and set up their own religion. The Chaldeans, to recover their lost influence, brought in one of their own number, Smerdis the magian, as king; but the imposture was detected, and he was slain. After this they revolted in the absence of the Persian king, and set up a Babylonian of their own choice; but Xerxes returned, the city was taken and sacked, and the people slaughtered (B.C. 487). The defeated Chaldeans fled to Asia Minor, and fixed their central college at Pergamos, and took the palladium of Babylon, the cubic stone, with them.

NO. 66.—A MAGUS.

Here, independent of state control, they carried on the rites of their religion, and plotted against the peace of the Persian empire, caballing with the Greeks for that purpose. They brought forward Alexander as a divine incarnation, and by their craft did as much as the Greeks by their prowess to overthrow the Persian power.

These figures will render good service in the study of the mythology of Tarsus, and will account for the mixture of Eastern superstitions with those of the West.

These suggestions are, however, only thrown out for the right use of them; but there is every reason to believe that these two little figures will be found to be keys to a rich store of treasures of thought and of discovery.

The words magi and magii, it may be added, no doubt, originally carried with them a very innocent, nay laudable meaning; being used purely to signify the study of wisdom and the more sublime parts of knowledge. But in regard as the ancient magi engaged themselves in astrology, divination, and sorcery, so, apart from the consideration that the vulgar looked upon the knowledge of the most skilful mathematicians and philosophers of the age as supernatural, they were also, by their very arts, entitled to be looked upon from a very early period more or less in the light of necromancers and practisers of occult science.

The Egyptians, as well as the Chaldeans and Assyrians, believed in magii and in dæmons; and these superstitious notions, which had spread all over the East, the Jews imbibed during their captivity in Babylon. Hence we find them in the writings of the New Testament attributing almost every disease to which they were incident to the immediate agency of devils. Many of the same impious superstitions were brought from Egypt and Chaldea by Pythagoras, and transmitted by him and his followers to the Platonists in Greece. This was at the time that magic still cherished its mysteries in the caverns of Dakki, Akmin, and Dumdaniel, or shadowed forth its secrets in the mysteries of Isis, the practices condemned by the Jewish prophets, the Samo-Thracian orgies, and those in vogue at Delphi, and in almost every pagan temple throughout the world. Modern mesmerists or magicians would have us believe that "the powers with which the early race of man was endowed seem never to have been entirely lost." (See Warburton's *Crescent and the Cross*, vol. i. pp. 148-50.) Such is also the basis of the doctrine of apostolic inheritance.

> "Oh! never rudely will I blame his faith
> In the might of stars and angels: 'tis not merely
> The human being's pride that peoples space
> With life and mystical predominance."—SCHILLER.

It would be curious to know in which light, that of learned and pious teachers, or that of practisers of occult arts, the Cilicians admitted the magi among their Lares and Penates. Their dress would seem to indicate a foreshadowing of that system of monasticism which both in Europe and Asia, under Christianity and Buddhism alike, has always been something exclusive and mischievous,—something that cloaked and hooded itself, and has ever shunned the light of day.

In connexion with the subject of monasticism, it may be remarked on another perplexing head among the Cilician terra-cottas, that we have the head and shoulders of a man exactly like one of the bonzes of Japan; his head plucked clean of all its hairs, Tartar features, with long moustaches hanging from his upper lip, and his shoulders covered by a robe. The question arises, how came such a figure at Tarsus?

This cannot be very satisfactorily answered; but a few thoughts may be ventured on the subject. It is now pretty well understood that at Babylon, the cradle of superstition, all the idolatries of the world had their origin. There was a pontiff, orders of men bound to celibacy, and devoted to a religious life. The divinity was represented as a Triad: the eternal father, Mylitta the female, and Assarac the incarnate son. Mylitta we have in Syria as Astarte, in Egypt Isis, in Greece Aphrodite, and Assarac as Horus and Harpocrates. We have this Triad all through the East, under other names; and it is to be apprehended that the more this is studied, the more clearly it will appear that all the diversified forms of superstition are from one source. All have the same monkish orders, set apart for the benefit of the rest. Whether we know them as bonzes, lamas, talapoins, fakirs, derwises, monks, or friars, all are found to bear the same character, and came from the same common source.

When the Medes and Persians introduced another religion into the great empire of the East, this rascality was after many plottings driven out, and found a refuge in Asia Minor, which became their head-quarters. Their holy brethren in all quarters would keep up correspondence with them, and cause a strange mixture of heads. It is also not a little curious to observe that these heads are shaven, just like the other monkish orders, with the exception of the Christian monks, who affect to retain a memorial of the crown of thorns, by leaving a circle of hair. It is not unlikely that at the time these figures were made, there was a closer community of feeling and of interest among all the diversified orders of holy men than we are aware of; and the seat of their authority being shifted from Babylon to Pergamos would cause a great resort of them to Asia Minor.

The problem is—" why do we find bonzes, fakirs, &c. &c. at Tarsus," and why they should seem to be objects of religious respect?

That in their dispersion they found refuge and a safe asylum in Asia Minor is an historical fact, and that they brought their own mythology with them is equally clear. This mythology was essentially the same as that of Egypt, Baal for Osiris, Mylitta for Isis or Aphrodite, Assarac for Horus or Harpocrates. The priests of Isis were a profligate, sensual lot, notwithstanding their shaven crowns and vows of celibacy. It would appear that many of the bare-heads in the Tarsus collection represent these priests of Isis; and that they were not natives of the country, but men of the east, preferred for their sanctity and great powers. Such men were proficient in many occult arts, and strange things were done by them in that day. Versed in the doctrines of astrology, divination, mesmeric arts and wonders, their ugly countenances would serve to increase the distance between them and the people. There would be nothing, as I have already observed in chapter v., to prevent the modeller from even exaggerating this difference, and the priesthood would never take offence at it, if it tended to make the deluded multitude stand in awe of them as beings of another and a higher order.

We have in the Tarsus collection what appears to be a perfect head of a Buddhist bonze. It might have been recently brought from Japan! As also numerous heads of religious devotees, such as are to be seen daily in India by the road-sides. For this unexpected and perplexing enigma we want a solution. The only one which can well be imagined is, that though there is *now* a great gulf of separation between those people and the western countries, there was at, or before the Christian era, a wide-spread diffusion of these monkish fellows through all the heathen countries; but that, through the influence of Christianity, their occupation was gone, and they disappeared, or made their exit from a stage no longer suited to their action. May these very tribes not be represented by our gypsies as their descendants, who practise similar arts as far as the manners of the age permit, and are of unquestionable antiquity, and of Oriental descent; many of their words being known to be pure Sanscrit?

"In Antioch, the Oriental element of superstition and imposture was active. The Chaldean astrologers found their most credulous disciples in Antioch. Jewish impostors, sufficiently common throughout the East, found their best opportunities here. It is probable that no populations have ever been more abandoned than those of the Oriental Greek cities under the Roman empire; and of these cities, Antioch was the greatest and the worst. . . . . Juvenal traces the superstitions of heathen Rome to Antioch."*

This quotation is given here as bearing upon the matter of our inquiry; for whatever may be said of Antioch may be applied to Tarsus.

In an account of Pococke's *India in Greece*, given in *Blackwood's Magazine*, it is said, " By an original method of interpretation, applied to documents existing in the Greek and Sanscrit languages, the author has discovered important facts, illustrative of the most obscure periods in ancient universal history. The interpretations introduced consecutively into this work, and accompanied by the true Sanscrit text in lieu of the corrupt Greek version, produce abundant and interesting results, especially in relation to early Grecian history, of which results the following is a brief summary.

" In the great conflict between the Brahminical and Buddhistic sects in India, the latter being defeated, emigrated in large bands, and colonised other countries. It is demonstrated in this work that the principal locality from which this emigration took place was Affghanistan and North-western India; that the Indian tribes proceeding thence, colonised Greece, Egypt, Palestine, and Italy; that they also produced the great Scandinavian families, the early Britons inclusive; and that they carried with them to their new settlements the evidences of their civilisation, their arts, institutions, and religion."

Surely this goes to confirm the fact of a connexion between the East and West in old time, and to support the opinion as to the great value of the Cilician or Tarsus collection, as containing some hidden mysteries in history, which will be opened in due time by some one competent to the work.

The contest between Brahma's disciples and the followers of Buddha is a dark page in history, but the issue of it in the dispersion of the latter is a known fact. If we must go to the Sanscrit for the solution of these things, we shall find a new field opening before us, the results of a thorough exploration of which it would be difficult to anticipate.

* Conybeare and Howson, Life of St. Paul, 135.

CHAPTER IX.

MONSTERS AND IDIOTS.

AMONG what may truly be termed the curiosities of the Tarsus collection are many heads of monsters and idiots, among the first of which we may describe a small head (No. 67), much damaged, but still retaining all the horrible expression of its original state. The brows are enormously swollen, and the eyes seem starting from their sockets; the mouth is in keeping with all the other ugly features. It has a chaplet round the head, binding two large round tufts to it for ornament; but what they were formed of, or intended to represent, we cannot distinguish, as they are only marked by the impress of a small square punch. Is this, it might fairly be inquired, male or female, human or divine? It is horrible enough for Typhon himself, or one of his ministers. Then, again, we have the aquiline nose and hairy upper lip of a monstrous face; the view of the left side shews the strange outline most strikingly. There is a work called the *Magus, or Celestial Intelligencer*, in which are heads of spirits, one of which has a nose and lip just like this.

NO. 67.—HEAD OF A MONSTER.

In the same category is a fragment of the lower part of a nose with the upper jaw. The nose is turned up, as if by the expression of scorn and hatred; the lip rises in harmony with that feeling, laying bare the teeth. It is made of red clay, and the teeth have been painted white.

Also, more or less associable with the same order of ideas, and yet in another category, is a head with strongly-marked features, having a kind of cap upon it. It is loose, having, like others, a hole for an axle. It is of the same class with many others as to beauty. The expanded ears, long nose, and slavering mouth, give it much of the expression of an idiot, which also agrees with the miserably-contracted cranium. Was this image sarcastic? or were idiots, as in modern times in the East, looked upon as sacred or mysterious beings; beings labouring under an occult dispensation, and more particularly taken under divine protection? However bad superstition may generally be, whoever first promulgated this, although in some instances public nuisances are entailed, secured kind treatment among a semi-barbarous people to an afflicted humanity.

Among the same group is a very remarkable head (No. 68) with African features, and large thick ears; the cranium is of an extraordinary length from front to back. This appears to be a head of the Macrocephali, a tribe of Asia Minor, who took liberties in shaping the heads of their children as the Chinese do with their ladies' feet.

NO. 68.—A MACROCEPHALUS.

There are also in the collection two other heads of Macrocephali; one is remarkable for a bump above the organ of firmness; his mouth, however, seems to indicate much bodily pain, as if he were roaring.

Among the other monstrous heads is one with horrid teeth, yet it would seem to be a lady by the dress; the malignity of the eyes is most repulsive. Another monstrosity (No. 69) is the representation of a man's head with no brains, the tongue projecting from his slavering mouth; the ears project like a dog's. The expression is that of animal pain.

It would seem to be as dangerous to draw ethnological deductions from the monstrous productions of the Cilician artists, as it would for some Australian of the year 4000 to discuss our national peculiarities from the grotesque heads that adorn many of the old religious buildings, supposed, in some cases, to illustrate the spite and antagonism of rival monastic orders.

NO. 69.—HEAD OF AN IDIOT.

Among the heads of a more particularly idiotic character is one with a face with projecting chin and pug-nose, giving a very straight facial line. The mouth is monstrous, and the expression malignant.

Another idiot face has the skull shelving back where the brains ought to lie. Yet it is radiated! Was it a portrait of such a character deceased? Possibly so. We have before remarked that idiots are still looked upon in the East as beings under a mysterious dispensation and divinely protected.

Another curious head is that of a merry fool, who has been painted white and red, like Joe Grimaldi. He looks as if he could keep a regiment in good humour, in spite of his ugly face. In another, again, the reverse, or extreme bodily pain, is well expressed. It is almost enough to give one the tooth-ache to look at it. It would require a spoonful of magic embrocation to make him smile. Poor fellow! it is no sham.

There is also another ox-eyed head represented as in a woful plight. It is very rudely sketched, but tells its tale.

There is also in the collection the head and right shoulder of a figure which, like some others, indicates the lowest degree of mental debasement. He turns to look over his shoulder without any particular expression of pain or pleasure, but as if he were giving utterance to some unmeaning sound. The hair is woolly like a negro's.

Among the same group are two monstrous heads with caps, which, unnatural as they are, are doubtless correct representatives of persons then existing. Fools, dwarfs—out of the very sport of nature—were formerly kept in the establishments of great people and in king's courts. Negro servants were much employed in this country, and dressed fantastically, a century ago. Might not monstrous productions be sought out and retained about the temples?

We have also half the face of another of the same kind, and the lower face of another, but the mouth and chin of better mould. Another, again, with the chin almost *nil*; and another with a better chin. It would seem as if there had been wens upon the bottom of the cheeks, which have been broken off. If it is so, these *goîtres* would confirm the preceding suggestions, and prove that they were *cretins*. It does not appear, however, that such have as yet been met with in the mountainous districts of Asia Minor. It does not follow, however, that they do not exist in the secluded and little-frequented valleys of Taurus; perhaps near to Tarsus.

Among heads and faces of a similar character is part of one, the brows of which are contorted and indicative of much suffering, which the eyes also express; and another which is almost all face, the cranium excessively small. This, like some of the others, is thoroughly idiotic.

What were the superstitions (it may well be inquired on viewing such deified heads,) of that age respecting idiots? Were they not thought to be in more immediate connexion with the gods? If so, these may be portraits of some such unhappy beings. In the same strange category we may also place another unnatural head, with huge projecting ears, and a pinched narrow forehead, and the face utterly unintellectual. Two heads in slave's caps, not quite so monstrous as the last, but most intolerably ugly; another head of the same class, but with a sly sinister expression about the eyes, yet low intellectual faculties for want of brain; a small head of the same breed as the preceding, but somewhat better, except the chin, with a cap on painted blue; also two other heads of the same parentage; large eyes, heavy noses, thick bullock mouths, and enormous ears. One of them seems in pain; but it looks like mere brute suffering. Another, again, is a fragment of a head; the nose and mouth monstrous. It is a fact, that a small receding chin, and an open mouth with relaxed lips, as if never used but to take in food, is always accompanied by defective intellect. Look at the chins of George Washington and Napoleon, and the close grip of their lips, and contrast the chin of George III. and the mouth of the late Charles X. of France.

Another has an enormous *goître* hanging on the throat; and the little of the face which remains is in keeping with it. There can be no doubt from this that some of these idiots were true cretins.

Of another there is not much left, but enough to exhibit the maniac—the demoniac—in whom dwelt a god! Then again we have two other fragments of heads of the same description, perfect idiots. In another the cheek is hairy, and the nose and mouth extravagantly out of proportion.

Monstrous features and forms of head, or countenances of idiotic expression, are not confined to men. There is in the collection the fragment of a female head in which the nose is monstrous, the mouth, the chin, and the forehead idiotic. The hair in this figure is plaited and carried back. We have also a female head, the hair of which is dressed and the ears jewelled; but the mouth and chin identifying it with the same class.

It may be remarked upon these strange works of art, that if such characters were held in superstitious veneration, it is likely that they were supported by the temples, and used by the priests for the promotion of their own objects. The female head having a high cap or bonnet, ornamented with orbicular masses, like buttons, all over its surface, suggests curious thoughts. If she is of that class of unhappy beings referred to, may not the round projecting objects on her cap be *spherical bells?* They are all of one size, and have as great a projection as the potter's mould would allow. Such a belled cap was worn by the fools and jesters of kings, popes, and nobles in the middle ages. It is not less probable that this head may give us the only remaining memorial of the ancient and original fool's cap and bells. In this view the head is perhaps unique.

There is more disagreeably suggestive matter connected with the subject of the deification of idiots, contained in the following letter. It is, however, borne out by the well-known fact, that at the present day Egyptian fellah women will assemble and veil with their bodies, as it were, an idiot engaged in the indulgence of his disgusting sensual propensities.

Mr. Abington writes, under date of August 10, 1852 : " I have thought much on the subject of the idiot (*cretin*) heads, so numerous; and having read some papers on matters of a similar character by a learned but anonymous writer, I obtained his address, and informed him in general terms of your valuable collection ; of the articles it comprises, especially of these heads. I asked whether such unhappy beings were not supposed to be in more immediate connexion with the gods ? Whether it is likely that they might be kept and fed at the expense of the temples ; being used by the priests for their superstitious purposes, and generally for the promotion of their craft. I pointed out also the occurrence of figures similar to the Buddhist priests and the fakirs of India.

" He replies : 'I do not recollect that they were permanently attached to the temples ; but I take it that reverence was paid them as being preternaturally endowed with sensual propensities. I believe that *cretins* are much given this way. Fakirs, we all know, are wonderfully so given, inasmuch that no notice or resentment is ever shewn at any insult by them to a female, even in open daylight, or even by a husband. A military friend of mine in India, who had wandered shooting into a village about forty miles from Nypore, which no European had entered before, came suddenly upon a religious festival, at which all the maidens of the neighbourhood were assembled to wait upon and feast a set of naked fakirs, who were sitting in a circle with fool's caps upon their heads ; their carcasses were painted like harlequins. He was at once requested to withdraw ; but expresses his belief that the old rites of Astarte were about to follow.'

" All this so fully agrees with my own surmises respecting these creatures being associated with the figures of the gods, that I could not forbear sending it to you. I believe that the same remarks will apply to both sexes, where you find the cranium faithfully represented as formed almost entirely of animal propensities, without any adequate proportion of the sentiments to balance them. Certainly nothing can be imagined too gross and beastly for them to have embodied in their religion, when we recollect the free use of the obscene phallus in their public rites. But it is an unpleasant subject to dilate upon."

TOMB AT ELEUSA, FROM A SKETCH BY MR. LAYARD.

CHAPTER X.

HUMAN FIGURES.

BARDS—PRIESTS—MISCELLANEOUS—FEMALE FIGURES—DEIFIED CHILDREN—UNDETERMINED.

AMONG the fragments of human figures which do not belong to any of the categories before described, may be enumerated, in the first place, that of a bard reciting his verses. This figure is far more ancient than any other piece in the collection; he is playing on an instrument that is unknown, but of which there are two other pieces that will throw some light on this subject. These will be referred to in a subsequent chapter, where mention is made of a boy playing on a pan-pipe and of a syrinx. Next, two figures of priests bearing a basket or some vessel on their heads, to which their hands are applied for support. These figures are altogether of an oriental character. There are two bosses, or balls, on the head-dress, which help to identify them as to their occupation, which was undoubtedly in the temple or rites of Priapus. There is also a figure of another bearded man, which resembles the preceding, but has no chaplet on the head, though the

NO. 67.—ANCIENT BARD PLAYING ON SOME UNKNOWN INSTRUMENT.

hands are elevated to support a burden under which he seems to bend. Another figure represents a priest of the same order, but standing at ease; he bears in his hand something which appears like the links of a chain folded up. Was it for inflicting penance? We know that self-mortification was carried to great lengths by some orders of the ancient heathen priests, the same as is now practised in India. These figures go to confirm the previous suggestions made with regard to the connexion of the mythology of Cilicia with Buddhism.

Besides the above heads of bards and priests, we have also a man's head, probably a portrait, from its peculiar expression; the ears are remarkably long. Also a cloaked figure, the head of which is well-modelled and interesting; the hair is very ample and curly.

Then, again, we have a head painted white. There is another such on a lamp; it has a helmet; the twist of the nose and mouth in a contrary direction gives it a ludicrous appearance. This was probably a likeness of some well-known character employed about a temple. There is also the bald head of a man. It has a well-developed cranium, over which a cloth is thrown. It was connected with something on the back, which is too scanty to give any idea of what it was. One of the heads in the same group is more of a grotesque character, and from its peculiarity and natural proportions, a portion of one who was "no fool."

In the same collection we have the upper part of the body of a conquered gladiator; a relic of art so full of expression, so eloquent in its mute agony, that we have introduced it here.

Then again we have the middle part of a figure bearing a wine-sack, as if pouring it out. Part of a figure which has the thigh extended, as if sitting on a horse; the mortar by which it was fastened to the seat remains. Also the left side of a man, half naked, well modelled. The left hand of a bearded figure, holding up something which is broken off.

CONQUERED GLADIATOR.

Then part of the body of a man, having a cloak over his shoulders in the style of Apollo. Then an old man's head with a cap, very expressive; his bushy eyebrows give great force and character to it.

We have also the upper face of a man with his head bound up, as if he was sick; his eyes and brows seem to indicate the same. It is well modelled. Also a fragment of a head with a very bushy brow; there is a wen on the forehead. And lastly, the lower face of a man with a full-developed chin: indicating that he could both raise and enjoy a laugh; but the lips are gone.

The above are male: there are also fragments of female figures, as exemplified in the left arm and drapery of a female reclining. The lower limbs of a female; they are crossed, while drapery painted red falls down behind her. It has been a graceful figure, well drawn. Also a sitting figure of a naked female. The head is wanting. It has been found lately and proved that she represented a sibyl on her seat of inspiration. It was used as a fountain; the base is formed into a pipe, through which the water or wine would ascend; and the seat on which she is placed inclines downward, to give a free flow to the fluid.

Among miscellaneous fragments, we have an arm holding up a tripod, possibly part of a priestess of Apollo. Also part of a female and child. Then, again, the right half and head of a female with a tiara and veil; possibly a Venus. Also a female bust in relief, the left breast and shoulder naked; stiff and inferior. Another fragment represents the upper half of a female figure, having all the character of a divinity; but the right hand of a man is placed on her right shoulder. And another is the head of a dignified lady, the hair full dressed, standing on a pediment.

Among other fragments we have part of a circular medallion, containing a female in relief; the hand and part of the body remain, sufficient to shew that it refers to the rites or honours of Cybele. It was probably votive. Then, again, we have part of an elegant figure of a female bearing a veil, which floats in the wind. Also another pleasing head, little, but good, of a lady in full dress, with jewels in her ears. Another pretty head in a close dress, the veil hanging down full behind, and shewing the gathering of the hair at the back of the head. Again, a female divinity, with the hair knotted, and the drapery flowing. Then the bust of a female carrying a bird. Also the head of an old woman; she wears a cap most unique, ornamented with buttons or other round objects. And the lower part of a head, which is female, from the ringlet hanging on the cheek. Lastly, we have the upper part of a figure of a woman dressed in a garment which is wrapped close round her, and is drawn over her head; in her left arm she bears a naked boy. It has been painted. It would do for a Madonna, but must be of a date long prior to any such representations of Mary and her child. There are two of these, and they both appear to be far more ancient than the generality of the pieces, if we may judge from their style of sculpture, and from the blackness of the terra-cotta.

In the same category may be classed the following interesting works of art, being chiefly figures of deified children.

1. A fragment representing a child with wings, and in close drapery; the hair of the head is knotted on the top. There is connected with it an ornamented ring, apparently to hang it by. "It is possibly a memorial," says Mr. Abington, "of a deceased and deified child."

2. A boy with wings and a radiated crown, reposing, with his right arm over an object covered by a cloth or skin, which hangs in folds over it, and which has been painted blue. The crown also was painted the same colour, and the hair red. The figure appears to be slumbering.

3. The bust of a deified child, with the head radiated, and the right hand elevated in valediction.

4. A little fragment, having a winged infant, in relief.

5. Head of a deified child, bearing a vase, probably to receive libations.

There are also the following pieces. A fragment of a Bacchanalian group of boys, in high relief; one kneeling, with an armful of grapes. There appears something like a bow by the side; but it may be the trunk of a vine. Another fragment of a well-executed figure of a boy reminds us of Flamingo's models. An excellent figure of a boy looking upward. The balancing of the body is well managed; while it seems bent out of the perpendicular, it stands firm. A bust of a deified child. Upper portion of a boy; another is holding him by the chin; his eyes are shut. A boy in a tunic, as if ascending upward on wings: a memorial of the dead. Part of a boy holding a sickle, with which he is gathering grapes. A naked boy with a cock; on his left shoulder there is a foot like that of an eagle. This is possibly a Ganymede. Another winged boy, not improbably Eros. A boy closely cloaked, very imperfect, and a young child, led by a female. The head of a youth, with the left hand elevated with much energy. A boy carrying a basket of grapes on his back; he looks as if he was conscious of having stolen them. An imperfect fragment of a youth: good, but much decayed. A young student; a good study for the historical painter; it is complete except the feet. The hands of a boy carrying a goose. A youth's hands crossed in front, as if standing in the presence of his superiors. A fragment of two boys; they seem engaged in drawing a carriage of some kind. A boy's head, with the hair disposed in ringlets, in the style of theatrical masks. A small chaplet is placed on the crown, to which were attached large bunches of ivy-berries; it is surrounded by a copious radiation of ivy-leaves. The expression is peculiar, though quite juvenile. Still more interesting is a very beautiful boy's head, the hair thin and scanty, radiated. The more this is studied, the more it must be admired. Flamingo or Cipriana might have been proud of the production of it. And lastly, a trunk of a boy, naked, except a cloak, fastened by a fibula on the right shoulder; he carries in the cloak a variety of fruits, among which grapes and the pine are the most conspicuous.

There are several fragments in the collection, the character and gender of which it is not so easy to determine. Among these are, part of a figure bearing a square vessel or chest, covered with drapery. A left hand, belonging to a figure in drapery holding something like a modern book. The lower portion of a closely clothed figure, with shoes on the feet. It is remarkable that the legs are cut free behind, and the back drapery worked. It was sitting. Also three fragments of sitting Egyptian figures, apparently connected with the worship of Isis. And lastly, a number of detached arms and hands, not requiring any individual description.

Among the Cilician terra-cottas, the true character of which has not been as yet satisfactorily determined, may also be noticed a fragment of a figure in a sitting posture; only the lap and legs remain. It is closely clothed, and the left hand rests on the thigh, holding with the fingers and thumb a remarkable portion of the dress, consisting of two tablets hanging from the girdle. The style is altogether Egyptian, and if not a deity, it has been some sacerdotal officer.

Also part of a figure formed into a cup at the top, probably for the purpose of holding perfume. The head only remains, which is bonneted; the features are youthful, with curled locks, and the right hand is elevated, to hold the cup which rises out of the figure. Again, a fragment of a relief, which shews the left arm of a slave carrying fish, which are suspended in a bundle at the end of a pole. There is also another similar fragment; but instead of fish, a basket or net hangs at the end of a pole. The contents are so slightly modelled, that it is difficult to say what is intended.

We may perhaps be permitted to include in this chapter a notice of the following, among the strange fragments contained in the Tarsus collection, viz. several images of the lower human jaw, one with the symphysis marked very deep, a row of incisor teeth, and the left canine teeth. Another, with the teeth still more strongly marked, the canine tooth being much curved; and others with slight variations. All these remnants are portions of flat, circular medallions or reliefs; and all have the *ground* within the jaws, modelled to represent *flames*, and have been painted red.

Among the works of our early painters of Church legends, and of the temptations of saints, &c., we often find representations of heaven and hell. The latter is generally depicted as the wide yawning jaws of a great monster with enormous teeth, and belching out fire and flames. Do not these fragments shew us that such a mode of representing a fiery infernal region was but *traditionary*? Are they not personifications of the Tartarus of the ancients? If so, was the fact ever known before?

REPRESENTATION OF TARTARUS.

Lastly, several masks occur in the same collection. Among these is the half of the mask of a bald-headed man. Also a very expressive tragic mask. Again, a figure in a mask, excessively rude and imperfect in every point. In another part of a mask the hair is in short curls, and is dressed to a great height. A pair of wings ornamented the front of it. It has been painted. Is it Perseus? The variety of masks, both tragic and comic, is too numerous to be entered upon here, and they would require more illustrations than the nature of this work permits.

CHAPTER XI.

ANIMALS.

DOGS—OXEN—BULLS—BUFFALO—HORSES—LIONS—PANTHER—WOLF—BOAR—APE—HIPPOPOTAMUS(?)—CAT—GOATS—RAMS AND SHEEP—CROCODILE—SNAKE—EAGLE—SWAN—OSTRICH—COCKS.

BOTH wild and domestic animals have their illustrations among the Tarsus terra-cottas; some with a mythological meaning, as in the instance of the lion, the ape, the cock, and others. The meaning of others is more difficult to detect, unless as accompaniments to figures and personages wanting in the work to make it complete.

Among such is the hind half of a dog in relief, which seems to have been the top of a lamp; also the hind legs of a dog in relief, behind which is a basket.

Also, a dog sitting by the side of a figure, the foot of which only remains. This may have been Diana and a hound, as it forms the plinth of a statue.

Further, the rump of a shaggy dog in the act of running; and a dog whole length appears to be climbing; and lastly, a hound's head at full speed—good. There are also several hind-quarters of dogs, which do not require particularising.

Among these zoological fragments are also a very fine head of a young ox, and the forehead of a bull, with the hole in front by which the golden disk was fastened, shewing it to have been divine. Also, a good bull's head, one horn wanting; the expression is admirable. Another bull's head, probably a fragment of a group, with a lion on his back. Again, a head which appears to have belonged to an Indian buffalo.

The buffalo, it may be remarked, is a common animal in the marshes of Asia-Minor and Syria; and the Indian buffalo is met with on the Euphrates and Tigris. The bull may be partly illustrative of Egyptian, or also of Greek and Roman mythology.

Besides the numerous fragments of horses attached to chariots or otherwise, and the still more numerous horses' feet, the meaning of which has been previously discussed, fragments of horses and of equestrian figures are common in the Tarsus collection. Among these, we may notice as deserving of separate mention:

A boy riding a horse, of which the hind half only remains. Part of a horse with a saddle, and naked leg of a boy-rider. Also, the thigh and leg of an equestrian figure, who, by the bend of his body, would seem to be at full speed. Also, the upper part of a horseman: his loins are belted, and he seems to be racing. And then, again, part of a group of horses—the bridled head of one, and the shoulder and neck of the other harnessed. We have also, in part of a circular tablet in bas-relief, the fore-leg of a horse, and the booted leg of a man running by the side of him. By putting all these and other pieces before him, the sculptor has been enabled to restore several complete figures that are most interesting.

Among animal relics of another order, we have a small head of a lion; when viewed on the left side, the effect is admirable. It was attached to some other object on the right side, which is therefore unfinished, not being intended to be seen. Also, the head and paw of a lion's skin, hanging by the side of a throne—only one leg of which remains: it is formed of a chimæra head and lion's paw. Also, a detached lion's head, and a lion's skin, from the figure of Hercules. As also a lion with a figure riding upon it. The left arm and drinking-cup remains. And the same subject, but only the head of the lion is left.

Then, again, we have a panther, probably part of a bacchanalian group, in high relief. The head of a wolf, and the fore part of a boar wanting the snout. The figured face of an ape is a solitary instance of the kind: it has a cap on the head: this animal is rarely found in Greek sculptures, but it was a sacred animal among the Egyptians. Isis is sometimes represented riding upon a monkey. It was in some such association that this figure was used. Also, the fore part of an animal, thick, clumsy, and short-legged, which might be taken for a fragment of an hippopotamus, sacred to Typhon; and in the collection there exists the snout of this intelligent animal.

Among figures of other familiar creatures are the head of the long-eared Syrian goat; another goat's head; a fragment of the same, and a fragment of a boy riding a goat. Also, the top of the head of a ram; a ram's horn, and part of a sheep kneeling on a plinth. The ram had mostly reference to the rites of Minerva.

Among the same relics we find the mutilated or imperfect representation of the crocodile. We have had occasion to remark elsewhere, that there exists in Cilicia, a river called Andricus by Pliny, as also a *mons crocodilus*, and that both are connected geographically as well as by name. This river, now called Markatz Su, and remarkable as flowing between the walls of the antique Syro-Cilician gates, is of too small a size ever to have been frequented by so remarkable a saurian. But the same river is called Kersus by Xenophon—a word derived from a Coptic and Syriac idiom, and which refers to the ancient crocodile worship, being met with in the Axio-*Kersus* of the Samo-Thracian mysteries, and is explained by Soega and Münter, as the great principle of fecundation; and hence it was expressed by Pliny by the word Andricus, whilst the *mons crocodilus* rose up above it.

It is to be observed that the crocodile worshipped by the Syrians was also called Succoth; but the able commentators of Pancoucke's Pliny suggest an identity between the Syriac Kersus and the Egyptian Kamses, the name of a ferocious crocodile, which has been ascertained to be a different species from the sucko or succoth.

In this same class we have also a snake winding round a staff, the symbol of Æsculapius, and probably part of his statue.

There are also several fragments of figures of birds; and to take the most noble birds first among fragments of this description, there is a foot of an eagle; the ground has been painted blue. It was of great size, and probably connected with a figure of Jupiter. Also the full figure of an eagle, which has been connected with some object at the side, most likely the throne of Jupiter, to whom the eagle would then be looking up. Then, again, we have the figure of an ostrich, with a loop behind for suspension; as also of a swan, the head of which is supported by a human hand. The crane is also here represented and the dove.

Among the other ornithological fragments may be noticed three cocks, probably relating to Æsculapius; as also two cocks' heads.

Nergal, the Assyrian Abrerig, god of the starry sky, and the tutelar deity of the king, was also, it is to be observed, conjectured, according to the presumed Semitic or Indo-European origin of the name, to have reference to a fire-worship, or to that of the sun under the form of a cock.*

* See Layard, vol. ii. p. 459. It is worth mentioning, however, that being at the mines of Ishik Tagh, near Angora, in the year 1839, we were surprised one day to find a cock, in the midst of great scarcity, newly killed, yet not eaten, in front of the houses. Upon inquiry, we ascertained that the miners, who were Christians by name, of the Greek Church, had killed it in order to propitiate some genius of the mines, and that a sacrifice must not be eaten. This was evidently a remnant of the old superstition of cocks being sacrificed to Pluto for the same objects. See Travels and Researches in Asia Minor, &c. vol. i. p. 131.—W. F. A.

252 LARES AND PENATES.

We have also in the collection the figure of the hawk—a bird, like the eagle, of quite as great importance in the Assyrian pantheism as the Egyptian; and of which we introduce an illustration.

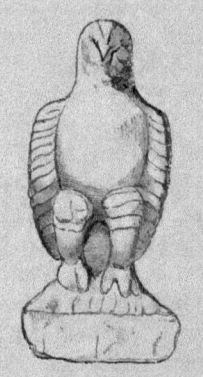

PHREE, THE EGYPTIAN SUN.

CHAPTER XII.

DOMESTIC AND RELIGIOUS ART.

CHARIOTS—VASES—BOWLS AND DISHES—WINE-JARS AND DRINKING-VESSELS —LAMPS—HANDLES—TABLE AND CHAIR—RING AND GLASS—ROUND DISC OF POTTERY—NET—BUTTER-PRINT (?).

OBJECTS of domestic and religious art are not so numerous in the Tarsus collection as might à priori be imagined. Among these are fragments of the wheel of a chariot, with the hind leg of the lion which is drawing it. It was painted red. The lion was connected with the worship of Cybele; and the goddess Rhea, with her lions, as described by Diodorus, may be recognised with similar accompaniments in the Assyrian sculptures; so also Hera, the Assyrian Venus, stands erect on a lion in the rock tablets of Pterium and those of Assyria.[*]

Also, of a more or less similar character, a chariot driven by a naked boy; the wheel is partly covered by what appears to be the tail of the animal drawing. Also the hand of a boy, holding the reins and driving a chariot; and the two hands of a boy in the same action. He holds the reins with much apparent skill and energy. And lastly, a chariot, in which sits the lower half of a boy, with a portion of drapery thrown across him. If they are horses' legs immediately before the wheel, they are very stiff and out of place. Add to which, a boy's hands grasping reins, and several detached chariot-wheels, two of which are bored as if placed free in their axles.

In the same collection are several fragments of vases, of greater or less interest both in an artistic and an archæological point of view. One is ornamented with vine-leaves and annular handles. The foot is wanting. Only one side of it is wrought, shewing that it was fixed against a wall. The cavity is shallow. It was, perhaps, used for libations to Bacchus, and was possibly placed on the head of a figure.

Another is somewhat like the preceding, but not ornamented. This

---

[*] See Layard, vol. ii. p. 456.

appears to have been borne on the head of a figure, and supported by the right hand.

Another part of a vase is of very elegant design, but slight workmanship. It is a portion of the foot only; the plinth part is ornamented with festoons of fruit, supported on ox-heads, and on the shoulders of winged boys. The cove rising to the leg of the vase is very gracefully fluted.

There is also part of a cup or vase in the Egyptian style. It is formed of two rows of lotus-leaves representing a flower, and very like the capitals of some columns of Egyptian temples. Round the bottom there is a row of animals, such as are seen on some cornices in the British Museum; but whether they are hooded snakes cannot well be made out.

There is also, among fragments of a similar character, one that presents a very graceful design for the support of a vase, or for an incense altar. It is formed of three leaves, giving it a tripod character. The intervals between the leaves are occupied by swans couching, with their pinions advanced over their breasts. This would indicate its application to the rites of Pan or Venus.

Another fragment seems to have been intended as a leg or support for some article. We have a round base, upon which is a well-formed lion's paw, which passes into the figure of a crouching man, who grasps the two handles of a drinking vase. It has very much the aspect of a Babylonian work.

Lastly, we have two vases, one between two animals. There is a hole in it, and the vase being in the shape of an amphora, indicates that it was part of a vessel to hold wine. And another with drapery thrown over it, in modern funereal style.

Among the minor objects of art having a similar tendency, and illustrative both of art and feeling, are a portion of the side of a drinking bowl in red clay (No. 54). It bears a bas-relief of the head of a Bacchante, crowned with ivy and bearing a thyrsus, that is, a long pole, with an ornamental head, formed by a fir-cone, or by ivy or vine-leaves, which was carried by Bacchus and his votaries at the celebration of their rites. The back of the Bacchante is turned toward the eye, and her face is looking over the left shoulder, from which the tunic is sliding off; nothing could be better conceived; it must have come from the hand of an artist of the first order, though it has somewhat degenerated in the hand of the potter. Altogether this is a precious fragment, and will bear comparison with any thing which has hitherto been discovered of ancient ceramic art.

Among objects of a similar character are a fragment of a Bacchanalian bowl; it has a moulding of beads and buttons round the top, under which is a border of vine-leaves and grapes. On the body is a mask, and a nymph, slightly draped, beating upon an instrument like a drum or gong. This vessel was painted red, and by its curvature must have been seven and a quarter inches in diameter.

Also a portion of a bowl of a different shape from the preceding. It was of a beautiful shape, though the ornamentation is very rude and slight. The leaves, &c. were pressed on with a die after the bowl had been *thrown* by hand upon the wheel. It is also red; the diameter is about five inches and three eighths.

Reclining on a large wine-jar or amphora is the figure of a comedian performing his part in a play. He is in the attitude of one at a banquet, has the comic mask on, and sandals (baxea) on his feet. The baxa, or baxea, worn on the comic stage,* and by philosophers who affected simplicity of dress,† are, it may be observed, sometimes indicated on the feet of Egyptian statues, and many originals have been discovered in the Egyptian tombs; some made with close sides and upper leather, like a shoe; others with a leaf, forming a mere strap, like a clog, across the instep; and others with a band across the instep, and another smaller leaf on the fore part of the sole, intended to pass the great toe through.

We have next to notice a fragment in yellow clay (No. 53), part of a cylindrical drinking-vessel, three inches in diameter, similar to our modern mugs. A relief has been made out of a plaster-mould, and laid upon it; but the body of the vessel was *thrown* upon the potter's wheel. The subject is a female, slightly clothed, holding in her hand a branch of sesamum, which she is attentively watching to observe the opening of the seed-capsules, a mode of divination often resorted to for the solution of love-questions. The modelling is very good, except the breasts, which are out of place. The back part of the vessel was decorated with ivy. This vessel might, it may also be observed, possibly, have been an oil-jar; and the female contemplating the common oil plant (sum-sum of the Arabs) be poetically emblematic of the uses of the vase. "The piece," says Mr. Abington, "is interesting to a potter, as it shews that the ancients laid reliefs upon their works in the same manner as is practised now; but the workmanship on the part of the ancient potter was unworthy of the beautiful models supplied to him by the artist, and would not be tolerated in a modern pot-work."

Among the minor objects of art in the additional collection are many

* Plaut. Men. ii. 3, 40. † Apul. Met. xi. p. 244.

fragments of lamps well deserving of mention. Among these are the upper portion of one with a bas-relief of a centaur bearing a wine-vase upon his back, and about to drink from a bowl. The modelling of this beautiful fragment is truly admirable. Another fragment of the top of a lamp has a relief representing Vulcan occupied in his workshop. He sits with one foot upon his anvil, and upon his raised knee is a shield, which he is fashioning into shape with a finishing hammer. His pincers, or tongs, are lying upon the ground. This is one of the pleasing deifications of the most humble art, ennobled in this case by the object in which the artist is engaged, and a tribute to the imaginary inventor of forges, and the first teacher of the malleability and polishing of metals. Another part of the top of a lamp is adorned with the figure of a Roman herald, bearing his staff and an ensign. This fragment is painted red, and is of inferior merit as a work of art. Lastly, another has the head of a satyr on the top, and is like the former of rude workmanship.

The designs for handles found among the Tarsus terra-cottas are sometimes very elegant. Among them may be particularly noticed a most elegant handle of a lamp: it is formed of a horse's head of first-rate execution, emerging from foliage most gracefully drawn. Also a lamp-handle very plain, but the lines graceful and well drawn; as well as the handle of a lamp with a slight relief of the conventional honeysuckle, in pure Greek style, on the triangular face of the top. There are figures of such in many works of antiquity. Well worthy of notice also is the handle of a lamp in the form of the prow of a ship; there is the figure of a bird upon it. This piece was burned so hard in the fire as to be vitrified in the surface. Also a very primitive handle of a lamp; the ornamentation is such as is attempted by men in their earliest efforts. The handle of a vase, with a head, the tragic Muse. A ring-handle, with a fragment of the vessel with which it was connected, very perfect; and then, again, a portion of a handle, with a human head upon it. This is remarkable for having a glazing upon it of vitrified lead. Part of a good handle terminating in a chimæra head, with a frill of leaves behind it. Also the handle of a lamp, with chimæra head. A vine-leaf, forming the handle of a bowl or dish; and lastly, parts of two snakes, probably connected as handles to a vessel; and a harpy's head, which served as a handle.

We have next to notice the handle of a flat dish or tazza, the ornament of which, though rude, is complex, and appears to have a mythological meaning. It has a circular altar or short column in the centre supporting a basket; on each side of which a humped buffalo or Indian bull is couching; over these are two human heads, apparently female, and behind these, fishes: there are others below the fishes, the character of which is not easily determined. The bulls, the fishes, and the female heads have a mythological meaning in harmony with the purpose to which the vessel was appropriated, which was religious. The dish was large, the diameter being nearly 14½ inches, and coated with a red varnish. Also another handle from the same mould, with a small portion of the bowl-part of the dish; this fragment shews the ornamentation was all on the *under* side, and would be unseen when the dish was in use; when out of use, it would be reversed, the concave part would be unseen, and the decorated bottom exposed to view; the very opposite to the construction and use of our dishes. Does not this illustrate a passage in the Bible? 2 Kings, chap. xxi. 13, "I will wipe Jerusalem as a man wipeth a dish, turning it upside down." Next, a small fragment of a red dish, with a part of the handle, having a flower, the syrinx of Pan, and a figure like a running dog. It is on the same plan as the preceding. And in the same category may be placed a very good head of Medusa, in relievo, painted red. It had been applied as an ornament to some vessel, from which it is detached, leaving part of its hair behind. The head of Medusa, it is well known, is sometimes depicted as one of the most beautiful, and at others as one of the most shocking objects in the world; the noble head in the Strozzi collection at Rome is an example of the former. Lastly, a fragment of a beautiful bowl, the outside of which has been ornamented with leaves impressed on it by a punch or die. The handle or lip projected from the rim, and was decorated with scrolls.

In the department of furniture, we find a fragment of a relief, representing a tripod table, with chimæra legs, and some provisions lying upon it; also the side of a chair of state, with a well-formed chimæra in the front. Both these objects appear to have belonged to temples, most probably dedicated to Apollo.

Among the same objects, also, we may notice a ring of glass. It was coated with an enamel made of oxide of silver, and consequently of a yellow or amber colour; but the maker of it did not use silex enough in the composition of the enamel to make it permanent. The article being buried so long in the earth, and thereby exposed to moisture, the enamel has been decomposed, the alkali in it has been carried off, and the oxide of silver, losing its oxygen, has returned to the metallic state, now forming a coat of pure silver upon the glass. The silver being in an imperfect state of crystallisation, causes the spangled appearance. There are several such silver enamels in the British Museum which have not suffered decomposition, having been preserved in dry tombs, &c. As to the purpose for which this ring was used when covered with a smooth coating of enamel, it is more fit to be guessed than described. It was connected with rites which could not stand before the purifying influence of the Christian religion.

In the same collection we find a round disc of pottery, having a hole to hang it by. The panel in front has the character M upon it. It is probably a numeral of the Greeks representing 40. We manufacture similar labels for the purpose of hanging in wine-cellars to distinguish different lots; this was probably used for some like purpose.

Among more miscellaneous objects may be briefly described, an ornamented net containing flowers, and something like our butter-prints; but the subject is in cameo.

TOMB AT ELEUSA, FROM A SKETCH BY MR. LAYARD.

CHAPTER XIII.

MUSICAL INSTRUMENTS.

LYRES—SYRINX.

THERE are several fragments of lyres in the collection, one of them painted red; another with a hand resting upon it, and which formed part of a Muse. These fragments do not throw any light upon the oft-discussed questions as to the original inventor of the lyre and the number of its strings. It is more interesting to us to remember that the Abyssinians have a tradition that this instrument was brought from Egypt into Ethiopia by Thot in the very first ages of the world; and even Greek and Roman authorities will be found to bear out the opinion, that the invention of the primitive lyre with three strings was due to the Egyptian Mercury, Hermes.

Layard found only one musical instrument depicted by the Assyrians, and that was a triangular lyre, the strings of which were *nine* or *ten* in number. The god, says Layard, which Mr. Birch now conjectures to be Baal, is represented at Talmis playing on a triangular lyre.[*]

These last discoveries may well be considered as disposing of the story of Mercury's first affixing thongs to a tortoise-shell; of Choræbus, the son of Atys, adding a fifth string; Hyagnis, a sixth; Terpander, a seventh; and according to some, Pythagoras, or according to others, Lychaon of Samos, an eighth string, by which the octave, which consisted of two disjoint tetrachords, was produced; and which discoveries are seriously discussed by Mr. Spence, Dr. Burney, and others, and which may be now fairly consigned to the same fabulous repositories as Mercury's peace-offering to Apollo, Apollo's vindictive jealousy of Marsyas, the rage of the Theban women against Orpheus, and the building of the seven gates of Thebes to the seven strings of Amphion's lyre.

In this department of the collection may be classed the upper

[*] Rossellini, M.C., Teste, tom. iii. p. 19, tav. ann. Layard, vol. ii. p. 412.

portion of a youth playing the syrinx or Pandean organ, the fabled origin of which, from the conversion of a beautiful naiad pursued by Pan into a tuft of musical reeds, is so well known. The instrument appears to be suspended by a band to his neck, and he regulates it with his right hand, while the left seems to have been free. The pipes are more numerous, and those in the bass part of the instrument much longer than is usually represented. The player seems quite satisfied with his performance.

There is also another fragment giving the middle portion of another figure playing upon a red instrument of a more perfect form. There seems to be little doubt that our modern complicated organs are to be traced to Pan's pipes as their origin. In Hawkins' *History of Music* is an engraving of an ancient monument at Rome, in which is the representation of a primitive organ. It is a small chest placed on a table; in the front is a female playing on keys, and on the other side is a man

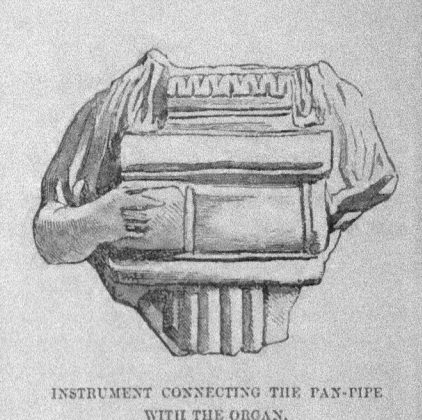

NO. 69.—YOUTH PLAYING THE SYRINX.

INSTRUMENT CONNECTING THE PAN-PIPE WITH THE ORGAN.

blowing into the box with a pair of bellows. This, I believe, is the only known link connecting the organ with the Pandean syrinx. But does not this fragment supply another link in the chain of improvement, and take its place between the simple reeds of Pan and the rude organ just described? It may be unique, and of value in its bearing on the history of music.

Let us look at it again. The instrument consists of a vertical row of pipes, the length unknown, as the lower portion is wanting; they are inserted into a small air-chest, which appears inflated in the middle part. The right hand is operating upon it with a kind of cushion or compress, by which he forces the air into the pipes, and which he seems to apply to different parts at will. There appears to have been a prolongation of the central part of the instrument across the left arm : the loss of this is much to be lamented, as that would have shewn us more of its construction, and also how the left hand was employed in playing it. It is firmly fixed to the body; but the upper ends of the reeds are too low for the performer to blow into them with his mouth. The openings in the tops of the reeds are all perfect, nothing is deficient at that end. This may be looked upon as the very first application of a pneumatic chest to the Pandean organ, which still retains its place on the breast of the player, though he no longer operates upon it with his mouth. It is most desirable to restore this figure ; we should then see whether the left hand or the foot was employed to blow the air into the machine.

In the same collection we have also the representation of a syrinx detached from some figure: there is a fracture on the front, marking the place from which the hand that held it was broken off. The reeds are bound together by a broad ornamented band. Part of the top of the instrument is perfect, and likewise the lower ends of the five treble pipes, but the bass is broken.

CHAPTER XIV.

COMPARATIVE GEOGRAPHY.

ARSUS (RHOSUS)—MYRIANDRUS—ISKANDRUN OR ALEXANDRETTA (ALEXANDRIA AD ISSON)—GODFREY DE BOUILLON'S FORT—BAYLAN (PICTANUS, ERANA ?)—PRIMITIVE CHRISTIAN CHURCH—CASTLES OF IBN DAUD AND OF BAYLAN BUSTANDAH—ALTARS OF ALEXANDER—CASTLE OF MARKATZ—RIVER KERSUS—GATES OF CILICIA AND SYRIA—BAYAS (BALE)—ISSUS—NICOPOLIS—KARA KAYA (CASTABALA)—EPIPHANEA—MATAKH—TAMIR KAPU (IRON GATES, AMANIAN GATES)—AYAS (AGEÆ)—AMMODES—KARA TASH (MALLUS AND MEGARSUS) ALEIAN PLAIN—PYRAMUS—MOPSUESTIA—CASTLES ON THE PLAIN—SARI CAPITA—RHEGMA OF THE CYDNUS—YANIFA KISHLA—MAZARLIK—CASTLE OF KALAK BUGHAZ—KARA SIS—ANABAD AND DUNKALAH.

THIS chapter has reference to the sites of ancient towns or cities in Cilicia, which ought not to be passed over in silence in a general account of the antiquities of the country.

Commencing at the south-easterly extremity of the province, the olden episcopacy of Rhosus or Rhosopolis, now Arsus, we have seen still presents some interesting remains of olden time. There are remains of a Christian church with Corinthian columns, and of an extensive aqueduct, besides other fragments of art. The existing Greek church also presents many features of archæological interest.

According to the distances given by Xenophon of five parasangs from the gates of Cilicia and Syria, the site of Myriandrus (which still remains to be discovered) ought to be on the way from Markatz to Arsus, unless, as is not improbably the case, it was situated at the foot of the Baylan pass, or within the pass itself.

At Alexandretta are the ruins of the Levantine factory, and a little to the southward is a polygonal fort of massive masonry, the construction of which is traditionally attributed to the crusaders under Godfrey de Bouillon; beyond this, again, are fragmentary ruins at a spring called Jacob's Spring by some, but Joseph's Well by Pococke, and which has been supposed by Rennell and others to be the site of Myriandrus.

Baylan is a remarkable town on the crest of the gorge forming the Syrian gates, and it corresponds to the Pictanus of the Jerusalem Itinerary, which was nine miles from Alexandria and eight from Pangrios (Pagræ). It appears also to represent the Pinara of Pliny and Ptolemy, placed by both in the neighbourhood of Pagræ or Pagras, as also, by corruption, the Erana of Cicero, which is described as being in the mountain above the region in which the altars of Alexander are situated.

The mosque of Baylan was built, according to the Mecca Itinerary, by Sultan Selim, and the Khan by Sultan Sulaiman the Magnificent. There are also remains of a causeway, of an aqueduct, and of a bridge, appertaining to the time of the Romans.

Higher up in the mountains, and a few miles northwards of Baylan, are the remains of a well-constructed Christian church of the earliest form after the Basilica; being an oblong area, with colonnades at the sides, supporting an arched or vaulted roof; and at the end opposite the entrance, a semicircular space surmounted by a half cupola. Dr. Pococke, it is also to be observed, met with several Christian sites in the district between Mount Rhosus and Coryphæus.

On the Syrian side of the Baylan pass, we have, to the south, the ruins of a Saracenic castle called that of Ibn Abi Dáúd, at the site of the ancient Pagras or Pangrios; to the east, the ruins of Khan Karamut; and to the north, within the hills, is the castle called Baylan Bustandah, one of the apartments of which is used as a sepulchral chamber, and within which are preserved many arrows—reminiscences of medieval warfare.

To return to Alexandretta: the colossal marble fragment known as Jonas's Pillars is familiar to all travellers. There is much reason to believe, as we have before pointed out, that these are the remains of the altars erected by Alexander to commemorate his victory over the Persians. It was in vain that the traces of such were sought for on the Pinarus. Quintus Curtius may have been in error when he stated that this commemorative monument was erected on the banks of that river. Pliny says that the "Bomitæ," or altars, were between Amanus and Rhosus; and the monument or gateway in question belongs apparently to the Macedonian era. Beyond Jonas's Pillars (Sakal Tutan of the Mecca Itinerary), and to the right on the acclivity of the hills, is a Saracenic castle, called Markatz Kalahsi. Beyond this, again, the

Markatz Su, the Kersus of Xenophon and Andricus of Pliny, close by Mount Crocodile. The way in which the Kersus of Xenophon came to be called Andricus by Pliny is curious, and exemplifies the great difficulty which the comparative geographer sometimes experiences in arriving at a correct identification. There would seem to be at first no sort of relation between Kersus and Andricus. But the Markatz Su, called by Pliny the Andricus, was called by Ptolemy Χερσιας. Pliny has also a Mons Crocodilus on the Andricus, evidently the precipitous rock that rises up above the villages of Markatz, and the site of the Syrian and Cilician gates. The word Kersus, derived from a Coptic and Syriac idiom, refers to the ancient crocodile worship, and is met with in the Axio-Kersus of the Samo-Thracian mysteries. It is explained by Zoega and Münter as the great principle of fecundation; and hence it was explained by Pliny by the word Andricus, which term becomes identified with Kersus. It is to be observed that the crocodile worshipped by the Syrians was also called succoth; but the able commentators of Pancoucke's Pliny suggest an identity between the Syriac Kersus and the Egyptian Kamses, the name of a ferocious crocodile which has been ascertained to be of a different species from the sucko or succoth. It has been seen before that we have the crocodile preserved in the terracottas of Tarsus.

The ruins of a wall can be traced north of the southerly branch of the Markatz Su, from the precipitous rocks to the sea-side, where it terminates in a tower; and to the north of this are also ruins of a tower on the shore, marking the extremities of the other wall, which were three stadia apart. These are the remains of the gates of Cilicia and Syria, to gain which both Cyrus and Alexander despatched a fleet of boats in advance of their respective armies. It is not improbable that it was because the Macedonian hero had gained this point, and attained the heights of the Sakal Tutan, which command the whole Issic Gulf, before he returned to give battle to Darius, that he afterwards erected his altar of thanksgiving at that point.

Bayas has been described in a note to the text; so also with regard to the supposed site of Issus. We have only the authority of Stephanus of Byzantium, that Issus was called Nicopolis after the great victory won there by the Macedonians; but what city in Cilicia is there so worthy of the name? The fact, however, of Strabo and Ptolemy noticing Nicopolis as distinct from Issus renders the identification very doubtful.

The remarkable and extensive ruins of Epiphanea have also been described; and by the distances given of twenty-six Roman miles from

Ægæ, and sixteen miles from Bais (Baiæ), there can be little doubt but that the castle and ruins of Kara Kaya, "the Black Rock," represent the Catabolon of the Antonine Itinerary and the Castabala of writers, as also the castle near Epiphanea, to which Cicero repaired.

There are remains of a Roman causeway and of arches leading from Epiphanea across the Burnuz Su to the mounds and ruins at Matakh, and the Amanian gates, near to the Cyclopean arch, called the Tamir Kapu or iron gates. At Kurt-Kulak there is a fine but ruinous old khan. The castle of Ayas, ancient Ægeæ, is a dilapidated structure of various ages, the walls and towers at the angles alone remaining. To the westward is a round tower with an Arabic inscription; and Admiral Sir Francis Beaufort's party copied a Greek inscription at the same place, which will always possess a melancholy interest as the spot where the much-esteemed hydrographer received a severe wound, and a young midshipman of the *Frederikssteen* was killed. This is the site also of a plaintive story related by Gibbon, of Maria, the Christian maiden of Carthage.

The Ammodes, or sandy cape, noticed by Mela Pomponius as being between the Pyramus and the Cydnus, and now so celebrated for its numerous turtle, leads the way to Kara Tash, a promontory of rock with a port for boats, a village and caravanserai, a ruinous castle like that of Ayas, of various ages, and other fragments of ruins around. A variety of curious considerations, which it is needless to enter upon now, led me at one time to identify Mallus with that portion of Mopsuestia which was on the east or further side of the Pyramus; but a further study of all the details of the question has induced me to return to the views entertained by Admiral Sir Francis Beaufort and by Colonel Leake, and to identify the site of the city of Amphilochus and of the fane of Minerva (Megarsus), as well as of the tombs built out of sight the one of the other, with the ruins at Kara Tash, which are minutely described in Admiral Sir Francis Beaufort's work.

North of Kara Tash is the great Aleian plain, now called Tchukur Uvah; and up the existing bed of the river Pyramus (Jaihun Su) are the ruins of Mopsuestia;* to the east, terminating the rocky ridge called the Jibal al Nur or "Mountain of Light," and overlooking the vast expanse of plain beyond, is the ruinous castle designated as Shah Maran Kalahsi (Jihan Numa, p. 603), or the Castle of the King of the Serpents. Beyond this again, on rocky knolls rising out of the plain, are Tum Kalahsi and Saliyath Kalahsi, which we did not explore; and beyond that again, at the junction of a tributary flowing from the Kuzan Tagh

* See page 110.

with the Pyramus, are the ruins of Anazarba, before noticed, and crowned by a similar rock isolated castle.

Admiral Sir Francis Beaufort has so ably discussed the positions along the coast of the Sari Capita of Pliny, of the second promontory called Zephyrium by Strabo, and of the twice historically united and twice separated waters of the Sarus and the Pyramus, that it is unnecessary to allude to these here. His work contains also a detailed description, with a neatly engraved plan, of the ruins of Soli and Pompeiopolis, which, with the description given of the ruins at Karaduvar (Anchiale?) are more perfect than any that we yet possess of other Cilician cities.

From the extensive ruins at Parshandy to Korghos, ancient Corycus, and thence to Ayash (Sebaste and Eleusa), and for several miles eastward of the latter, the same authority describes the shore as presenting "a continued scene of ruins, all of which being white, and relieved by the dark-wooded hills behind them, give to the country an appearance of splendour and populousness, that serves only, on a nearer approach, to heighten the contrast with its real poverty and degradation."

To return inland, or into what the olden geographers called Mediterranean Cilicia: on our way from Tarsus to the renowned Cilician gates (Kulak Bughaz) are traces of a Roman causeway, with an arch; a ruinous castle called Yanifa Kishla; and a ravine, with sepulchral grottoes and an inscription, now called Masarlik or "the Place of Graves." A castellated building also crowns the crest of the rugged rocks at the narrowest portion of the pass, where the work of the chisel to widen the road is very manifest. We are indebted to Mr. Barker for the first notice of a castle in the same neighbourhood, called after Nimrod, a name which would give evidence of great antiquity, and to which he supposes Syennesis to have retreated.

The country of perpetual rebels, of the lawless Tibareni, of the Cliteans, of the predatory Armenians, and of the unconquered Aushir and Kusan Ughlu tribes, contains, in the present day, the old castles of Kara Sis, and of Andal Kalah, which may correspond to the Cadra and Davara of the Cliteans; and the pass of the Pyramus through Taurus into Cilicia, the bridle-way to Marash, so minutely described by Strabo, is also characterised by its defensive structures, among which the castles of Anabad and Dun Kalah are the most remarkable.

CHAPTER XV.

ANTIOCH AND SELEUCIA.

THE BAY OF ANTIOCH—VILLAGE OF SUWAIDIYAH—GROTTO OF NYMPHÆUS—
ISLAND OF MELIBŒA—RUINS OF SELEUCIA PIERIA—PROJECTED RE-OPENING
OF THE PORT OF SELEUCIA—MOUNT ST. SIMON—MOUNT CASIUS—TEMPLE
OF HAM.

THE bay of Antioch extends from Ras al Khanzir, or Cape Boar, on the north, to Ras Pussit (Ancient Posideum), on the south, a distance of about thirty miles. Hemmed in by Mount Casius—Jibal Akrab, or bald mountain (so called from its summit being covered with snow the greater part of the year), and Anti-Casius to the south; it is bounded to the north by Mount Moses (Jibal Musa), above which again rise the loftier peaks of Jibal Akma, in ancient Rhosus, which attain an elevation of 5,550 feet; and these two ranges are united by low, wood-clad hills in the back-ground, to Mount Saint Simon, a hill that stands in advance of Mount Casius, from which it is separated by a narrow and precipitous but wooded and picturesque ravine, through whose shady depths the river Orontes (Al Asi, " the rebel") forces its way, flowing onwards by the ruins of a monastery, church, and khan—all that remains of the old port of St. Simon—and then by a hamlet or two, constituting the modern port, into the sea.

The modern village of Suwaidiyah, or Suedia, as Seleucia is orientalised, or as it is more commonly called Zaitunli, "the place of olives," embosomed in luxuriant groves of mulberry, olive, grape-vine, pomegranate, and apricot trees, occupies the range of the lower hills; and there are also several large villages in the mountains to the north and south, and on the south bank of the Orontes. Close by the latter is a small grotto, with a spring of clear water; connected with which are many large hewn stones and other fragments of antiquity. The site appears, from a variety of circumstances, to correspond to that of *nymphæum cum specu* of Strabo, situated between the mouth of the Orontes and Mount Casius.

If ever Melibœa, of poetical celebrity, was an island at the mouth of the Orontes, it must be now joined to the mainland, which is not at all an improbable circumstance. We have the explicit authority of Oppianus* in favour of the first fact; and the fabled lover of Orontes, and the nymph of Melibœa, would bear out the latter, as well as the physical features of the soil, the alluvium slowly but steadily adding to the extent of the coast.

On the other hand, we have the combined testimonies of Virgil,

> " Victori chlamydem auratam, quam plurima circum
> Purpura Mæandro duplici Melibœa cucurrit."—ÆNEID, v. 251.

and of Lucretius,

> " Jam tibi barbaricæ vestes, Melibœaque fulgens
> Purpura Thessalico concharum tincta colore."—Lib. i. v. 499.

that Melibœa was a Thessalian island; but this would only shew, what is frequently the case, that there were two of the same name.†

The line of coast from the Orontes northwards is low and sandy on the shore, but pastoral or marshy in the interior to the foot of the hills. Nearly half way to the ruins of Seleucia Pieria is the neatly whitewashed tomb of a holy Mohammedan, which being a ziyarat, or place of pilgrimage, has some ruinous buildings attached to it. Close by is a well of fresh water.

The ruins of the city and port of the Seleucidæ are beyond this at the foot of the rocky range of Jibal Musa, formerly called Πιερια, or Pierius, when Seleucia of Antioch was distinguished from other cities bearing the same name, by the epithet Seleucia Pieria. Strabo calls Mount Pierius a continuation of Amanus; but it is rather an outlying range of Rhosus, or Rhossus. The bare cliffs of Mount Pierius rise at this point abruptly from the low level plain below, and advance in rude promontories into the sea on the other, and the ruins of the once strong, populous, and well-frequented port are still indicated by the now filled-up basin or

---

* Cyneget. vers. 115 to 120.

† There is at the mouth of the Orontes a piece of ground of about a hundred acres, which the Orontes forms (by winding round it) into a peninsula, and which the people of the country call " Geziré," the island, because it is evident that the neck of land has also been traversed by the river at no very distant period. This piece of land belongs to Mr. Barker's garden at Suedia, it being customary there to have a piece of land for each garden, in order that the people who rear the silkworms may have a place on which to cultivate the wheat and barley they require for their immediate use. Without such land it is difficult, almost impossible, to get any one to take charge of a garden. The most delicious melons grow on this peninsula, and the crops are very fertile in consequence of the propinquity of the water in that warm climate. The two vessels which afterwards navigated the river Euphrates were landed at this point, which was called by Colonel Chesney, in his despatches, Amelia Depôt.

dock, the crumbling gates and ramparts, tumbled-down buildings and houses, numerous sarcophagi, and still more interesting sepulchral grottoes, and the remarkable extensive hollow way or excavation cut through the mountain, and attesting in so singular a manner to every successive visitor the industry and perseverance, as well as the skill and ingenuity, of the older inhabitants of this free port.

The walls of the city appear to have been quadrangular, and they had a double line of defence; the northern extremity abutting on the hill, whose summit was crowned by the acropolis. There were also walls of a suburb, triangularly disposed, and reaching down to the mole, traces of which are still extant. A gate led from the suburb towards the sea, and on the opposite side another opened towards Antioch, which was adorned with pilasters, and defended by handsome towers. The space occupied within the walls had a circumference of about four miles, and is filled with the ruins of houses.

The basin is 2000 feet long by 1200 feet wide, occupying an area of 47 acres, and was in fact as large as the export and import basins of the East and West India Docks together. The inner port is entirely excavated, and its canal is 1000 feet long; the area of the outer port is about 18,000 feet square, and it affords good shelter, but is obstructed by sand. There are two moles, 240 paces apart, constructed of enormous stones, and a pier called that of St. Paulæ, which runs west 80 paces, and then turns N.W.

Colonel Chesney proposed some years back to open this port[*] to modern commerce. Since that time, Captain William Allen, R.N., who so distinguished himself in exploring the river Niger, has surveyed and carefully mapped this interesting basin; and his calculations of the expense of clearing the port of mud, and opening it to navigation, chiefly by the natural means formerly used by the inhabitants of letting down the winter floods by the ravine, which is their natural channel, instead of turning them off into the excavated and artificial channel, corresponds almost precisely to that made by Colonel Chesney (30,000*l.*).

Dr. Holt Yates, who has erected a handsome house in the neighbourhood, near the Orontes, has also entered warmly into a project which promises to be of so much benefit to commerce and to the immediate neighbourhood, and has read a paper on the subject to the Syro-Egyptian Society. The great advantages to be gained by opening this port are, that it is nearer at hand than that of Iskandrun or Alexandretta; that it avoids the difficult navigation of the Gulf of Issus;

[*] Description of Seleucia Pieria, in Journal of Royal Geographical Society, vol. viii. p. 228.

that, whereas Alexandretta is infamous as one of the most unhealthy spots on the coast of Syria, and hence few can be induced to reside there, Seleucia is a comparatively healthy spot, and would, if opened to commerce, soon become in all probability a flourishing town; that the road from Seleucia to Antioch, Aleppo, and the Euphrates, is comparatively open, while that from Alexandretta has to cross the formidable Syrian gates—the mountain pass of Baylan (ancient Erana), between Amanus and Rhosus; and lastly, that while Cilicia is constantly disturbed by local dissensions and the rebellion of races, the neighbourhood of Seleucia, chiefly tenanted by peaceful Christians, is remarkable for its tranquillity and security; and lastly, Seleucia would constitute the safest harbour (especially for steamers), on the whole coast of Syria, and would, from that circumstance, and from its greater proximity to Antioch and Aleppo, entirely supersede the ports of Bayrut or Beïrut, of Tripoli, and Latakiyah. The same circumstances that have existed from the period of Mr. John Barker's settling here, and which induced Colonel Chesney to adopt it as the site for landing the steam-boats and equipments of the Euphrates expedition, still exist; and at a very moderate outlay, Seleucia might be again rendered what it once was, the most capable, the most flourishing, the most fertile, the most populous, the most wealthy, the most beautiful, and the most healthy port of Syria. As to the effect which the opening of such a port would have upon the commerce of the interior, the promises it holds out as the key to North Syria, the Euphrates, Mesopotamia, the Tigris, Kurdistan, and Persia, and the line of communication that could be opened, as originally proposed by Colonel Chesney, by this route to India, such subjects are of too great a magnitude to be entered upon here; but once the port opened, they would force themselves upon the Turkish authorities, the Anglo-Indian government, and all concerned or interested in the amelioration of the countries in question, in the progress of commerce, and the general advance in civilisation.

On the side of the city opposite to the harbour are the ruins of two temples, and of an amphitheatre partly cut out of the rock, as is so frequently the case; and here also commence the numerous sepulchral excavations, which extend nearly two miles along the face and up the ravines of the mountain, and in front of which many hundreds of sarcophagi, some of which Mr. W. B. Barker opened, are scattered. One portion of the excavations, called the Tomb of the Kings, has a façade entrance, and suites of apartments, with columns and staircases leading to a set of chambers above. In some of the grottoes were traces of paintings, with remarkably bright colours; in general, however, they were ordinary excavations, devoid of architectural ornaments, and many appear to have been used subsequently as broglodyte dwellings. They are now, however, only tenanted by foxes, jackals, and porcupines.

But the most remarkable feature in the ruins of Seleucia is the great cut or hollow way before noticed, and by which the inhabited and tomb-dotted portion of the mountain is separated from the heights above. This extraordinary work takes its origin from an open valley in Pieria, which is prolonged in a north-easterly direction to beyond the city, upon which it opens to the south-west, above the inner extremity of the harbour. This opening being artificially dammed up, the cutting led the waters away through the mountain to the sea, or to the mouth of the harbour to the north of the city. It is altogether 3074 feet in length, and attains in places an elevation of 120 feet, averaging a width of 22 feet, and it terminates abruptly over the sea. This great excavation is divided into portions, the greater part being an open, hollow way; interrupted, however, by two tunnelled portions or covered ways, the one 102, and the other 293 feet long. The cut is also crossed in its eastern part by an aqueduct supported by a single arch, and its western extremity by another arch, bearing a mutilated inscription of the time of the Cæsars. A recess, with sepulchral grottoes, occurs in another portion.

Water was carried along this hollow way, in addition to what may have flowed along its base, by a little channel hewn in the face of the rock, 18 inches in width; and in one part a narrow staircase leads down to within about 14 feet of the base, and which Colonel Chesney thinks was the ordinary level of the waters. The waters of the valley before mentioned, although no longer artificially dammed up from their natural course, appear still to flow at times along the bed of the hollow way, which they seem to have deepened, for the line of demarcation between the hewn portion and that which has been since excavated by the waters is very distinct, and these waters have forced a passage for themselves through the south-western sides of the excavation leading down to the mouth of the harbour; and hence, according to some, used to keep that mouth open. But the excavation can be traced beyond this opening towards the sea, although the traces of running waters are no longer discernible in that direction.

Appian relates in his *Syriacs* (p. 202), that Seleucia was founded in obedience to an intimation to that effect, obtained from the thunder. Hence it was dedicated to the thunder-god, as may be seen on a coin recorded by Spanheimus, "Jupiter fulminans Seleucensium," and this thunder-god was identified by the Romans with Jupiter Casius.

GEOGRAPHY OF CILICIA.

Seleucia was embellished and strengthened by Seleucus Nicator, who gave the place his own name. It was so strongly fortified, that Strabo designates it an impregnable city; and it was made a free port after the conquest of Syria by the Romans under Pompey, as is recorded on coins belonging to the times of Caius Cæsar, Trajan, and Caracalla. It was one of the four most distinguished cities of the Macedonian dynasty of the Seleucidæ, and which, including Antioch, Apamea (Kalah Mudik), and Laodicea (Latakiyah), were called sisters, on account of the concord which existed between them.

Mount St. Simon, so called from the tomb of that well-known Syrian ascetic, but also denominated Bin Kilisa, or "the thousand churches," from its extensive remains of ecclesiastical structures belonging to an early Christianity, has been described by Mr. Barker, and it need only be added here, that the memory of this fanatic, whose feats of penance have been misrepresented by Lucian, and justly derided, and that without any indecent allusions, by Gibbon, is as much venerated by the Muhammedans as by the Christians of the country; and the Mecca Itinerary contains especial injunctions to pilgrims, on their arrival at Antioch, to pay their respects to the tomb of Hazrat Simun—the holy, or beloved Simon. This will not appear at all extraordinary to those who are aware how much of the legendary and historical portion of the Kuran is borrowed from what had been long before adopted by Syrian monks and priests, and their followers, the Byzantine chronographers. Indeed this use of Christian-Syrian materials is made evident by a comparison of the narrative of the Prophet of the Islamites with the writings of Ephrem Syrus—the Euphrates of the Church, as he has been called by his admirers; yet who was one of the earliest propounders of those systems of scriptural astronomy and geography, for refuting which Galileo was thrown into a dungeon; as also with the works of Syncellus, and the *Paschal Chronicle.**

Mount Casius attains an elevation of 5318 feet above the sea. This was determined by angles taken from the two extremities of a base, measured on the plain below, and by the simultaneous comparison of two barometers, one at the top of the mountain, the other at its base.

---

* The founder of the sect of the Stylites, the fanatical pillar-saint, Simeon Sisanites, the son of a Syrian herdsman, is said to have passed thirty-seven years in religious contemplation on the summits of five successive pillars, each higher than the preceding. The last pillar was forty ells high. He died in the year 461. For seven hundred years there continued to be men who imitated this manner of life, and were called "Sancti columnares" (pillar-saints). Even in Germany, in the diocese of Treves, it was proposed to erect such aerial cloisters; but the bishops opposed the undertaking. (Mosheim, Institut. Hist. Eccles. 1755, p. 215.)

The foot of the mountain is mainly myrtle-clad, at an elevation of 1500 feet; this is succeeded by oak, and the oaks are again succeeded by gloomy pine-forests, which, at an elevation of 3500 feet, are themselves succeeded by open glades of birch, and occasional wild pear, apple, quince, and medlar trees. Vegetation is both luxuriant and beautiful, and in April the patches of gaudy scarlet peonies alternate, and are relieved by patches of yellow asphodel, not far from the snow-clad summit, where violets and pansies are succeeded by dark-green fennel. The extreme summit is composed of naked limestone rock.

Mount Casius is, with the exception of Mount Lebanon, Mount Sinai, and a few hills in Palestine rendered more familiar from frequent Scriptural references, the most celebrated in Syria.* Sacrifices to the Thunderer were offered on its summit from the most remote antiquity; and they were said to have originated with the descendants of Triptolemus, settled at Seleucia, and whom Seleucus Nicator invited to Antioch. These sacrifices were kept up by the Cæsars, who dedicated them to Jupiter Casius. Julian the Apostate, discomfited at Daphne, cheered himself with a hecatomb on Mount Casius; and Pliny relates that Jupiter, yielding to prayers addressed to him on Mount Casius, sent the birds called Seleucidæ, the roseate thrush (*Turdus roseus*), to destroy the scourge of the country—the locusts.

But the most curious tradition connected with the mountain, which the Emperors Hadrian and Julian went especially to witness, and which is described at length by Aristotle (*Meteor.* i. 16) and by Pliny (v. 18), is, that at the fourth watch, or at the second crow of the cock, as Ammianus relates it, day and night are, by the walk round of a few paces, seen at the same time. The elevation of the mountain we have before observed, is 5318 feet above the sea. Now, the rising of the sun commences about one minute sooner at an elevation of 1000 feet than at the level of the sea. Hence the world below is, in these countries, where there is little twilight, wrapped in darkness for five minutes after it is day on the summit of Mount Casius.

* Bochart (Phaleg, p. 333) derives Casius (as more particularly applied to the Phœnician Casius, which was on the boundaries of Syria and Egypt) from the Hebrew signifying a boundary. Another Hebrew origin might be found in Kas, "straw or stubble," as used in Psalm lxxxiii. 14, and Jer. xiii. 24. Homer (Iliad, v. 499) uses Achne in the same sense; and Pliny says of an island of Rhodes, "Casus olim Achne." A'more likely origin may, however, be found in the Syriac and Chaldean Kas, "shining," in reference to its bald summit, whence its actual Arabic name, Jibal Akrab, "Mount Bald." Tin, and also lead, according to Mela and Pliny, were probably called by the Greeks Kasiteros, from their lustre. Tin (in Numbers xxxi. 22) is read Kastira by Jonathan; and in Arabic, Kasdir. This was the origin also of the British Cassiterides.

T

On the acclivity of the same mountain, to the eastward, are the ruins of a very pretty temple or church, now embosomed among woods. It was constructed in the form of the Basilicum, but not so simply so as some of the early Christian churches. The oblong area within the walls is divided into nave and aisles by a handsome row of columns supporting a vaulted roof, and the semicircular space opposite the entrance is supported by a half cupola. This little remnant of early times, placed in so remarkable a position, has been identified by Colonel Chesney with the site of the Pagan temple described by Sanchoniatho (see Cory's *Ancient Fragments*, p. 11) as having been consecrated to Cronus or Hamon on Mount Casius by the descendants of the Dioscuri. It is also noticed by Strabo (xvi. 750) and by Ammianus Marcellinus (xxii. 14).

We cannot do better than close this chapter with an extract from Strabo,* premising that *tetrapole*, a title given to Antioch, means a city consisting of four parts, each fortified separately, and the four collectively forming one city.

"Seleucus Nicator also gathered together at this place the descendants of Triptolemus, of whom I have spoken before. This is why the inhabitants of Antioch render to Triptolemus heroic honours, and celebrate a feast in honour of him at Mount Casius near Seleucia. It is said that this hero, sent by the Argives in search of Io, who had for some time past disappeared from Tyre, and was wandering in Cilicia, was in that country abandoned by some of the Argives who accompanied him, and they founded the city of Tarsus. The rest continued to follow him along the shores of the sea, but despairing of succeeding in the object of their search, they established themselves with Triptolemus on the plains watered by the Orontes. Gordys, the son of Triptolemus, went and founded a colony in Gordiæus † (Γορδαῖα), with a portion of those who had followed his father, the others remained in the country; and it was the descendants of these people that Seleucus united to the inhabitants of Antioch. Forty stadia further on is Daphne, an inconsiderable suburb. An extended and dense wood is met with there, which is watered by live springs; and in the centre there is a sacred enclosure which serves as an asylum, as also a temple of Apollo and of Diana. The people of Antioch and of the neighbourhood are in the habit of assembling there to celebrate festivals. The circumference of the wood is eighty stadia. The Orontes flows near the city. This river, which has its sources in Cœlo-Syria, passes under ground, then

---

* Vol. v. p. 202. British Museum.

† Gordiæus was the most southerly part of Assyria, or of the present Kurdistan, near Lake Van. The inhabitants of Gordiæus have also borne the name of Cardrichi, whence the modern name Kurd.

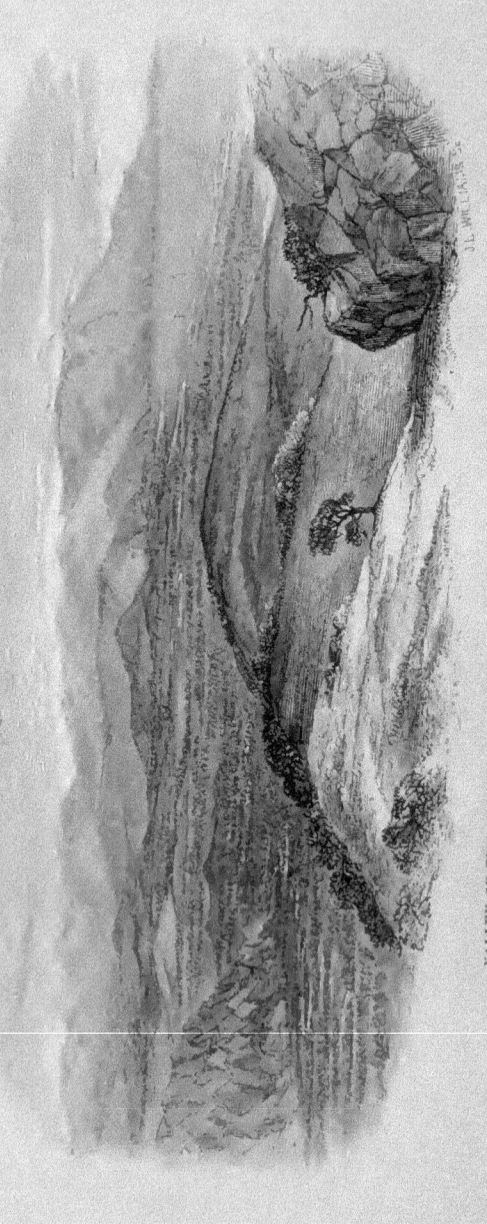

VALLEY OF THE ORONTES, WITH MOUNT CASSIUS IN THE BACKGROUND, BAY OF SUEDIA.

From a Sketch by Mr. C. F. Barker.

shews itself again, to flow through the territory of Apamea and water that of Antioch; and after having passed near the town, it enters the sea near Seleucia. This river, called Orontes, from the name of the person who built a bridge over it, was first called after Typhon; and according to fable, it was in this place that the adventures of Typhon and Arimes (Inarimes) took place. It is said that Typhon, struck by lightning, fled, seeking refuge; this dragon in his flight furrowed the ground so deeply as to cause the source of this river to spring up, and he gave to it his name. The sea is to the west, and is above the territory of Antioch on the side of Seleucia. It is near this latter city, situated forty stadia from the sea and one hundred and twenty stadia from Antioch, that the Orontes flows into the sea. The ascent from the mouth of the river to Antioch can be effected in a day."

RUINS OF AN AQUEDUCT AT ANAZARBA: FROM A SKETCH BY MR. E. B. B. BARKER.

CHAPTER XVI.

NATURAL HISTORY—ZOOLOGY.

THE OUNCE—THE LYNX—BEARS—HYENAS, WOLVES, AND JACKALS—THE FOX—HARES—FALLOW DEER—WHITE GAZELLE (GHAZAL)—GREYHOUNDS—GH'AIK, OR IBEX.

THERE are different species of wild animals in the mountains of Cilicia, among which we may note the *ounce*, the skin of which is much esteemed by the Turks, who use it chiefly to cover their saddles.* I saw a lynx which had been caught in Mount Taurus, but it died after a few months of an inveterate mange, which communicated itself to all the domestic animals in the mansion, and was so virulent that even the fowls died of it. This malady in this incurable state seems to be as indigenous to Tarsus as the fever of the place, which I consider worse than any other: inasmuch as, firstly, it carries off the patient in three days (unless copious bleeding is had recourse to); and secondly, that it is almost impossible to eradicate it out of the system even for years afterwards. The most effective relief I have found to be following up the cold-water system; this seems to possess the best means of alleviating, if not of entirely curing, the evil effects of continued attacks of fever. But with regard to the mange in dogs I will relate one instance that is remarkable.

I had been requested to procure Count Pourtalles two brace of greyhounds, of which the Turkmans possess a very fine breed. One of these greyhounds had had the mange, but was considered cured by a preparation of gunpowder and oil; and as he was quite a champion, and celebrated for his feats, I was tempted to send him among the number; and I have since been informed by the Count, whom I had the honour of visiting when ambassador for Prussia at Constantinople, that

---

* The largest animal of the feline tribe seen by our party in Cilicia was rather a leopard or panther than an ounce. It was called Nimar by the natives, and was probably the same animal that is called Kaplan in Lycia. A smaller species, apparently corresponding to the Felis pardina of Oken and Temminck, was very common. A lynx with black ears (kara kulak) was also met with.—W. F. A.

the malady broke out again and communicated itself to the other dogs, and that they all four died in spite of every exertion to cure them that European knowledge and treatment could afford. From the same malady I have lost the most valuable dogs. At last I discovered that dogs at Tarsus generally died either of this or of the yellow fever, unless they were washed daily with cold water and soap, and confined in a courtyard and kept from all contact even with the ground trodden on by other dogs wherein the seeds of the malady might be left; for I suspect that it is caused by some minute insect that gets into the skin of the animal, and nothing can drive it out that would not be equally pernicious to the life of the dog.

Bears are to be found in Mount Taurus; but as they only prowl about at night, they are not frequently met with. I have had them shot, or rather they shot themselves by a not very ingenious contrivance of the people of the country. As the bears come down into the gardens nearest the mountains to feed upon the vegetables, they walk along the paths and leave marks of their footsteps. The gardener observing this, puts across their road a string which is connected with the trigger of a gun that is set so as to fire on the poor creature as it passes, and the gardener hearing the gun go off, comes up and finishes the work of destruction. The flesh of this animal is remarkably fat, and not unlike beef, but it is not eaten by the people of the country. I have seen one ham which weighed 60 lbs.

The flesh of the porcupine when young is good and tender. The gipsies are constantly in search of them; but it requires some cleverness and patience to get a shot at them; their acute sense of hearing renders them sensible to a person's being in wait, and they cannot easily be compelled to leave their burrows. The native sportsmen even pretend that it is necessary to cover the flint lock of the gun with the left hand when firing, as they discover the flash and dip back into their holes before the shot can reach them! The Turks do not consider them unclean, but few eat them; their flesh is white, and tastes like something between a sucking-pig and a hare.

Hyenas, wolves, and jackals abound, and prowl about at night in search of carrion. I have heard the hyenas howling within a few yards of me, when I have slept on the sands of the sea-shore, where we would light a fire to keep off the innumerable mosquitoes that infest the coast. The people plant the stems of four fir-trees and form a kind of table on the top with branches and leaves; here they climb to the height of twenty to thirty feet, and endeavour to sleep in the air out of the reach of this plague, the most irritating of all insects, and which is believed to have a peculiar relish for a stranger's blood. The jackals frequent the marshes; they are very numerous and noisy, but are so thick-skinned that it is a difficult matter to kill one with a club. I have had to do this with one that had been attacked by my dogs, and I can speak from experience as to their toughness; if a cat has nine lives, the jackal may be said to have nine times nine ! There are two kinds of foxes ; the one large and grey, the other small and brown. These, as well as the jackals, appear to have a fine scent, and they hunt for themselves, destroying a great deal of game, which is, however, very abundant in spite of their depredations. A friend of mine assured me that some years previous to my coming to Tarsus he had been out shooting, and had first counted a hundred francolins, which he put up in the course of an hour and a half, after which he desisted from counting any more. There is but one kind of hare in Cilicia, the large heavy hare. It is of a darker colour than the desert hare, found to the east of Syria. This latter kind is very small, and will often beat the greyhounds in a straight line, without their being able to turn her once. A gentleman of veracity residing at Aleppo related to me an incident having reference to the hare of the desert which I may be allowed to repeat here. He was out coursing on the desert side of the city; and, strange to say, the strength of the hare, dogs, hawk, and horses was so perfectly matched, that after a long chase they all came to a full stop. First the hare came to a stand ; then the dogs, out of breath, a few paces behind ; next the horses of the sportsmen brought to a perfect stand-still ; and lastly, the hawk resting on a stone close by quite exhausted! The gentleman's servant dismounted and took up the hare in his hands.

On the plains of Adana a kind of fallow-deer is met with, called by the natives yumurgia; their skins are dyed and used by the Muhammadans as carpets to say their prayers upon. This animal is very large, but is by no means so swift as the gazelle; the latter are very abundant, and may be seen in flocks of fifty or sixty. They afford the chief sport for coursing, and are seldom taken except by an extraordinary dog, unless they can be driven into a muddy field after heavy rains, which they have the instinct to avoid, by making for the high road as soon as they apprehend pursuit. It requires a great deal of tact and ingenuity to manœuvre so as to get them into the predicament requisite to make them flounder till the dogs can come up to them. I recollect when at Mosul being instrumental in the capture of two, which we took on the plains of Nineveh with dogs that my friend the French consul had in vain taken out on several occasions. The flesh of the red gazelle is barely eatable,—it is always lean and dry; whereas the *rimi*, or white gazelle of the desert, is very fat, and is, perhaps, the most delicious of all venison. The gazelle supplies a tribe of Arabs called Slaih with food, raiment, and tents. These people have a simple method of taking large herds of them for their winter provisions. They build a wall of loose stones about four feet high and about a quarter of a mile long, disposed in a semicircle. In the centre they leave a breach, behind which they dig a deep pit. When they have contrived to drive the gazelles along this cul-de-sac, which is effected by the whole tribe turning out together, the poor animals, seeing no other exit, jump through the breach and fall into the pit, where the men are ready to slaughter them. Their flesh is dried in the sun, and is said to form the only food of the tribe; their skins also serve as covering for the body, and are used as tents to shelter them from the rays of the sun. This Slaih tribe is a remarkable one; with the exception of a very few donkeys, they possess no worldly goods either of camels, sheep, or horses, whereby to tempt the cupidity of their neighbours, with all of whom they are thus enabled to keep at peace.

The dogs used for coursing in Cilicia are very beautiful, having silky hair on their ears and tails; they are bred in the higher regions of Mount Taurus and Anatolia, and are brought down by the Turkmans in the winter, and return to their yaïlas in the summer, as they cannot hold out against the heat of the plains. They are very tame, and, unlike any other dog of the Turks, are much petted, and allowed to lie on their carpets and beds. They are very susceptible of cold, and are always kept covered with cloth-felt. A good dog is much prized, and is often not to be had in exchange for a cow or a horse and a measure of wheat. Such as take hares may be had from half a guinea to a guinea; but one that has taken a gazelle, under the most favourable circumstances, will fetch 2*l.* 10*s.* at least; and then the proprietor will only part with it when constrained to do so by his superior or by his superstitious prejudices; for the Orientals think that if they refuse to part with an animal they have been asked to dispose of, it will be struck with the evil eye and die, or be lost or stolen.[a] They profess, indeed, to despise dogs, and express their contempt of any one refusing to give a dog or horse; and yet the Turkman will never give away either if good for any thing, nor sell either but at an exorbitant price. They have a very fine breed of shepherd-dogs, which they bring up on milk, as they seldom have any bread to spare. (The greater part of their wheat is purchased with the money produced by the sale of their cattle.) This breed is promulgated all over the north of Asia Minor, and I have seen it as perfect on the borders of the Lake of Urumiyah in Persia. It is a large handsome dog, of a light-brown colour, with long woolly hair, and is faithful, courageous, and hardy. Some have been known to possess a good scent, and I have seen them used to find game, and to attack the wild boar, which is very large, and does much mischief to the crops of the villagers, who each pay so much a year to people who make a business of hunting this monster of the marshes. While hunting or hawking I have often come across a sow with seven or eight young ones; but my pointers had no chance with them, and it required larger dogs to overcome them. I recollect encountering one on foot with a lance, and I had to keep the lance in the huge beast to save myself until my companions came up and put a ball into the animal.

There is a kind of antelope in the higher regions of Mount Taurus which the people call Gha-ïk. It is remarkable for the length of its horns, which are sometimes four feet long, and curve over its back in a semicircle without branching off at all. It is as large as the fallow-deer, and its skin is much esteemed by the Muhammadans; it has a strong musk smell, is hard and short in the hair, which is brown, with a darker streak along the back and a dirty yellow white on the stomach.

Some years ago one of these animals being caught before it was three days old, it was brought up by a goat in a village near Kulak Bughaz Castle. If not taken very young, it is impossible to have one alive, and there is much difficulty in getting a shot at them, as they are very alert and live among the highest rocks of Mount Taurus. I offered the sportsmen of Nimrud a handsome present for a live specimen, but in vain.*

* This is evidently the ibex (Capra ibex) which occurs throughout Taurus, and is described by Professor Edward Forbes as inhabiting the mountainous parts of Lycia, where it is known by the same name, spelt by him Caik or Caigi. Professor Forbes says (Travels in Lycia, vol. ii. p. 62) that it is specifically identical with the ibex of Switzerland. The "wild goat" of Crete, whose horns are figured in Mr. Pashley's work, is the same species. A specimen was procured alive and kept tame as a pet on board the *Beacon* (Capt. Graves). In Lycia the ibex frequents the summits of the highest mountains in summer. In the month of October 1841, during Mr. Hoskyn's tour, a herd of them was met with on the summits of the Massicytus, travelling in single file over the steep rocks, at an elevation of 9000 feet. In the winter they are said to descend from the heights. The wild goat of Crete mentioned by Aristotle, and of which he reports that, when wounded, it is said to seek the herb dictamnus, was doubtless this ibex. Its modern name Professor Forbes thinks is only a corruption of the ancient αἴξ.—W. F. A.

CHAPTER XVII.

GAME BIRDS.

GAME BIRDS—MANNER OF TAKING QUAILS—MANNER OF TAKING FRANCOLIN
AND PARTRIDGES—CAPTURE OF WILD DOVES.

QUAILS and woodcocks are very abundant in their respective seasons of passage. The former afford amusement to the peasants, who take them in a very curious manner. A lad walks about till he sees a quail, which he intimidates from rising by holding a jacket extended by two sticks over his head, which the quail mistakes for the wings of a large bird or hawk, and by shaking either of these "wings" he drives the poor little creature in the direction he pleases, till he conducts it into a small net he has fixed some yards further off, and then he takes it with the hand.

I witnessed another plan for entrapping the quail used by the Arabs on the coast of Egypt, which I will here note. The Arab sticks two branches of the date-tree in the earth; and these are joined about a foot high at the top, forming a triangle, of which the ground is the base, and he fastens thereto a small net opposite the side facing the sea; of these he makes several hundred, planting them in regular rows at ten paces from each other; the quails arrive during the night, or rather very early in the morning, and as soon as they begin to feel the heat of the sun, they naturally seek for shade, which is no where to be found in the sandy desert (between Alexandria and Rosetta) except under these artificial bowers, where they are induced to take refuge. About ten o'clock, the Arab knows that all the quails have repaired under his treacherous cover, and he has nothing further to do but to present himself on the side facing the sea, which is open, and the quail, if it attempts to fly at all, must be entangled in the net on the other side. In this way thousands are taken daily and brought in cages to market; but they are never so good as those shot, because they soon fret in captivity and become lean.

Some of the peasants of the plain of Tarsus and Adana employ sparrow-hawks, which they capture a few days before the passage of the quails (which takes place from the 15th of April to the end of May, and again between the 15th of September and 15th of October), and train them to take quails, letting them go again when the season is over. If this useful little hawk is kept two years, it is capable of taking partridges and francolins, to do which it is requisite to practise it at the young birds, which he will continue to take until they are full fledged. But it is the most delicate of all hawks, and it is very seldom that any remain free from accident for so long a period.

Cilicia abounds in francolins and partridges; the latter are of the red-legged species and keep to the mountains, coming down into the hilly part of the plains in the winter, and are at that time to be met with in vast numbers among the bushy mounds of sand on the seashore. The former is a morass bird, and never to be found at any distance from water; the female is exactly like the hen pheasant, but not so the male, which has a little tail; but is quite as variegated in colours and as courageous as any of the gallinaceous breed. The people of the country have a curious way of taking these two kinds of birds, namely, by galloping them down; for when they have flown twice, they generally allow themselves to be taken with the hand, probably from exhaustion. The same method is practised in regard to the cormorant in the shallow waters of some rivers; and Sir John Malcolm, in his Sketches in Persia, mentions the circumstance of the Persians taking the partridge in the same manner in the environs of Bushire (Abu Shahir), when he was on his way from that place towards the capital.

The natives sometimes keep a decoy bird, which they expose in spring-time in its cage, when, by its crowing, it attracts other male birds which come to fight with it, and which are thereupon shot from behind a wall or hedge. It is remarkable that the cock will eat the brains of its fallen enemy, which are generally given to it; and it is curious to see it crow and quite glut itself as if triumphing in its repast. Partridges and francolins are also approached by a man holding in his hand a light framework, on which is fixed a checkered linen cloth, two feet by six, with a small hole to peer through, till he comes within shot, when he sticks it in the ground and fires from behind. Turkman children have also an ingenious way of catching larks or any other small bird. The contrivance is this: they tie at one end of a horse-hair four inches long, a piece of dry sheep or goat's dung, and to the other end an insect or grub of any kind; they throw several of these on the ground and retire to a distance; when they see that a bird has swallowed one of these baits, they run to it, and invariably, on its flying, its wings get entangled in the horse-hair, which is kept hanging down by the weight attached to it, and the bird is thus soon caught.

The natives of Galata, to the west of Mursina, have also a simple yet efficacious method of capturing wild doves; these, like all other birds of passage, on their first arrival, fly in a direct line, never deviating thirty paces to the right or left; the people know this, and in the twilight before sunrise they place across their road a net six feet high by fifty long. On each side of the road, six or eight men stand with crooked branches of trees about three feet long in their hands, and when they see the doves coming, they throw these dark branches up in the air, and the doves imagining them to be hawks coming down upon them fly very low, and consequently come in contact with the nets, and as they go in flights of thirty or more, many are taken in this way.

SCULPTURED ROCKS AT ANAZARBA: FROM A SKETCH BY MR. E. B. B. BARKER.

DIANA STARTING FOR THE CHASE.*

CHAPTER XVIII.

FALCONRY.

THE ancient and aristocratic sport of falconry, formerly much in vogue in Cilicia, has latterly fallen into disuse; even in that province the rich have degenerated to such a point that they cannot conceive any gratification in activity, and the poor are too much occupied in matters more profitable than attending to their hawks, which require constant care and trouble. Still, man is by nature a sportsman, and the Turkmans appreciate the qualities of a good falconer, the term *argi* being still a laudatory one, and many of their chiefs feel flattered by it. When they see a European excel in their own line, they are much pleased, and look upon him as one of themselves. Some of the young chiefs keep hawks; but their dogs are badly trained: when young they are allowed to run wild,

* From the original plaster of Paris sketch modelled by Mr. J. Hancock of Newcastle-on-Tyne.

and are therefore never afterwards under command. They hunt, however, with considerable activity; but it is for themselves, as they generally eat the game they get hold of, if they are not closely watched. Indeed, I once saw a dog swallow a quail—bones, feathers, and all—without giving his master the chance or time to get it out of his mouth.

Of course they cannot be expected to bring the game on which they are fed, to "*induce them to be sharp and look after it!*" as a young Turkman told me; considering it as a matter of course that a dog would not hunt without such incentive. As soon as the dog seizes the bird, the master calls out, "*Husht! husht!*" throwing a stone or any thing he can at him to make him let go the bird, in order to get hold of it himself, and cut its throat before it dies; for if it dies of itself, or is killed by the dog, they look upon it as strangled, and their religion forbids their eating it. But some confirmed sportsmen laugh at this, and cut the bird's throat subsequently, in order to make it appear that this prescribed formality has been gone through in proper time, and thus induce their women to cook the game for them.

The Turkmans have but one kind of sporting dog. It appears to be of a somewhat similar breed to the Scotch terrier, and is well adapted to go through the bushes, as its hair is long, and it is a hardy beast. It is called boji; is small, and has long bristly hair (generally grey, and abounding about the eyes and nose). It is an intelligent animal, and were it brought up by a European, might be rendered subservient and useful for the hawk; and as they are natives of a hot climate, they can stand the heat well, and remain longer without water. Such qualities are valuable; for I have seen my dogs quite knocked up as late in the year as the 25th of November, and chiefly from the heat of the season.

These Turkman bojis have not so acute a scent as some of our best dogs in England, but they are as good as the generality of common breeds, and very persevering. It is really astonishing how these poor creatures hunt at all, for they are nearly starved.

Besides the sparrow-hawk (*accipiter nisus*), *bashek* in Arabic, *atmaja* in Turkish, the Cilicians are acquainted with three species of hawks:

The gos-hawk, *doghan; autour* of Buffon, *aster palumbarius* of Linnæus.

The lanner, *seifee; falco gentilis* or *lanarius* of Linnæus.

The peregrine, *sheheen; falco nobilis* or *peregrinus* of Linnæus.*

---

* The sparrow-hawk is the falco nisus ; the gos-hawk the falco palumbarius ; the falco gentilis is the greater buzzard, falco gallinarius of Temminck. According to the latter author, the falco peregrinus of Linnæus and the falco lanarius of Gmelin are different ages of the true blue-backed falcon.—W. F. A.

The doghan or gos-hawk is a native of Mount Taurus. It is frequently brought up from the nest, as bad sportsmen imagine that by that means a hawk becomes tamer, and not so likely to fly away. But this is an error; and I do not know that there is really any benefit to be derived from an eyas; and I can point out several disadvantages. One is, that unless very carefully and constantly fed when *young*, it gets into the habit of " calling" when it is hungry—a great vice, and one that is catching in birds. No sportsman would keep such among his hawks, as it would spoil the whole lot. Further, the hawk takes to scratching, and will not easily give up the game it seizes, which it often nearly tears to pieces. Besides these disadvantages, the hawk having never caught any thing in the wild state, must be taught; and it requires some time to develop its instinct: whereas haggards, that is, hawks taken by the net *full-fledged*, know what they have to do, having hunted on their own account, and it is merely necessary to tame them in order to render them useful birds. They are also more careful of their wings, the advantages of which they can appreciate better than a bird that has never flown, and they are soon brought into the use of their faculties; whereas the nestling or eyas has to be taught to fly, and practised a long while before it can be brought into *wind*. On the whole, therefore, I lean towards the haggard; and the doghan is so tractable a creature, that in the course of ten days it may be brought to be as tame as can be desired. Generally speaking, a much longer time is taken to train them by timid or inexperienced falconers; but I have myself hunted a doghan and made him take a partridge the eighth day; but then I had dogs accustomed to hunt under the hawk, which is of great consequence, as a dog that does not know what hawks are will do more harm than good.

In England hawks are "*flown at hack* ;" that is, when brought from the nest, they are kept in a shed, where they are regularly fed, and allowed to fly away and return in the evening to their roost.* This is a great advantage, as it enables you to keep your hawk much fatter; and in after times, when hunting, if it is lost or flies away, you know that it will return home. And this is particularly advantageous in case of hawks of the lure, which are most prone to wander. The doghan is so steady a bird that it is extremely difficult to lose it; and he must be a very inexperienced falconer who would allow it to be in that state which would induce it to fly away. Thus, on the whole, the doghan gives the least trouble of any kind of hawk, and requires the least train-

* The falconers in the East cannot do this, as they would be sure to have their hawks stolen.

ing; and we shall see further that it is the bird the best adapted for the present state of the country.

I have lately perused a work of much interest, called *Game Birds and Wild Fowl, their Friends and their Foes*, by A. E. Knox, M.A., F.L.S. The author devotes a chapter to falconry, and gives a graphic account of this exhilarating sport from the experience of his friend, Colonel Bonham, of the 10th Hussars, who, he says, although a good shot and a practised stalker, laid aside the gun and the rifle for the enjoyment of the "noble craft." "Would that others could be tempted to follow his example!" To this I would add, as an inducement, my persuasion, that those who have not felt all the excitement experienced by the falconer cannot be said to have tasted of all the pleasures of life; and surely if there remain to them still one enjoyment which is so refined and innocent, it is worth their while to give it a fair trial, which all can do who have the means of keeping a man, two horses, and a dog, and have the run of an open country.

Knox's description (page 164) of the perfection to which dogs can be brought goes far beyond my experience, as I have not had the advantage of seeing dogs in such good training; and I considered that one dog I had for seven years had reached the acmé of what dogs were capable of; but I find, from what he says, that the intelligence of the Russian setters leads them to distinguish and appreciate the nature of the different characters in which they were alternately required to appear; and when the game was sprung, and the bird fell or flew away, no attempt was made, no inclination was evinced, to break the point; they would "down charge" as instantaneously and perfectly as if the discipline usual in such cases had never been for a moment relaxed in their sport under the hawks. Dogs, in hawking, are expected to run in upon the game directly it rises, and follow the hawk as closely as possible. I had a pointer that would cross the river and hunt alone under the hawk who had pursued the quarry to the other side, and would be on the top of a bush waiting the arrival of his coadjutor to raise the game, which generally takes refuge on the first flight in the closest cover at hand. Doll would first go round the bush to make sure that the partridge had not skulked out, and then entering, would raise it. The bird would then try to fly back to the side of the river from whence it was first started, and would sometimes be struck close to my feet by the hawk. Sometimes the bird fell into the river at the moment of being seized. In this case the hawk would not let go his prey; but both might be seen sailing down the stream, until Doll, swimming back to me, and seeing how matters stood, could go to the rescue, and land hawk and partridge on my side of the river. If the quarry drops in the river before it is caught, the doghan will not lay hold of it, but will return to his master. But it happens that he sometimes overtakes it before it is quite in the water, and yet not sufficiently in the air to enable him to carry it, which he can easily do, to a distance of a couple of hundred yards, when at a sufficient height in the air. Can you imagine any sight more attractive and picturesque than the repose of the party after the excitement of an exploit like the one just mentioned? Often might you see the dog actually hunt alone with the hawk across the river, and return with the hawk, or be in time to rescue it from the stream. My Arab mare appeared, upon these occasions, to understand what was going on, and to take as much interest as the falconer in the sport.* And as the hawk (after having been duly fed) was perched on her back, she would turn round and look approvingly (for horses *can* look approvingly) at the intelligent victor, while the dog, having shaken off the water from its back, would be jumping up to lick her mouth; the sportsman caressing all the three, wondering which he loved best, his gallant hawk, his generous mare, or his faithful dog!

Mr. Knox acknowledges that the movements of the gos-hawk in cover are exceedingly rapid and effective. Its short wings enable it to pass more easily through the interstices of boughs; while with its long and fan-like tail it steers its way and performs marvellously intricate evolutions, as it pursues the pheasant, the black-cock, the hare, or the squirrel, through the tangled labyrinths of coppice and underwood. But he says, "its character is altogether devoid of that energy and perseverance that are so conspicuous in the falcon. If the quarry should gain an advantage at the beginning of the chase, it frequently relinquishes the pursuit altogether, and, settling on the nearest branch, prepares to dart upon the next passer-by."

This is the general complaint made by sportsmen against the gos-

* I am not exaggerating the intelligence of these noble creatures; and I declare that my horse would always distinguish between a hare and any other animal, between the game I sought and any common bird, of which it would take no notice, but always start off in pursuit of the quarry, when put up, if I happened to be looking a different way. It is a known fact, that the Arab horse, when let loose to graze while his master is reposing, will always come up and snort, to apprise him of the approach of an intruder on the privacy of the desert.

In the East the saddles are made to cover the greater part of the back of the horse, and are much more convenient than the English saddle for mounting and dismounting, with the embarrassment of the hawk on the hand, which it is very often requisite to do. The pommel is large enough to form a hold for the left hand; and the hind part of the saddle is raised, so that it is often convenient to perch the hawk upon it. An English rider mounts by the mane of the horse, and not the pommel, in order not to throw too great a strain upon the saddle and saddle-girths.

hawk, but my experience has shewn me that these defects are not inherent in the hawk; but originate generally with the sportsman. If a gos-hawk is *properly* trained, and given something (say the head) of every thing he takes, he will never give up the pursuit until he reaches the bush wherein the quarry has taken refuge; but the dog and the falconer must be alert, and come to his assistance, and never give up the search for that identical bird. If the bird is let go, and the sportsman looks after another, the hawk, whose mind and soul are set upon that *particular* bird, which he will distinguish from among any number that may rise, and will never fail to pursue in preference to the rest, is discouraged from the sport.

Mr. Knox proceeds :—" It was not without reason, therefore, that this species, and some other hawks of similar structure, habits, and character, were styled 'ignoble' by our ancestors, to distinguish them from the long-winged, high-flying, or 'noble' falcons."

I am sorry to differ from an authority of such high standing as the naturalist above quoted; but I would beg to suggest a very different reason for the epithet in question. The gos-hawk, and those of his structure, are birds so much easier to train and keep than the falcons, which require a man for each, that the vulgar herd used them when they could not afford to keep those of a higher flight, which were thus left to the privileged aristocratic and rich falconers. That the gos-hawk is more efficient than the peregrine is clear from the fact that Colonel Bonham, according to Mr. Knox, acknowledges that "*three grouse were sufficient to take from a falcon in one day.*" Colonel Bonham being a great proficient, and having had great practice, must be allowed to be a fair judge; and I am assured that, in general, the peregrine cannot be brought to take so many. One flight, or two at most, daily, is all that is expected of him by the falconers of the present day. Now, the doghan will take as many birds as you can fly him at; and I have repeatedly taken fifteen to twenty francolins in a country where there were no preserves, and where we had to hunt out our game. What would the doghan not do here in England, provided always he had the head of the quarry given him to encourage him? That our forefathers did not look upon the gos-hawk as really ignoble, may be seen from the many elaborate treatises published in the way of treating and hunting this hawk alone; and that they appreciated his good qualities may be inferred from their always keeping one "*to feed their falcons with,*" that is, to secure game for them when the peregrine was not in humour to hunt, a thing of constant occurrence. Indeed, I believe that the uncertainty and caprices of this latter bird have been the chief cause of the noble art of falconry falling into disrepute. People could not afford to keep several of these birds (for each of which, properly speaking, a man is required) in order to secure one flight or two. Sometimes the falconer might, in his zest for the sport, invite a party of friends to witness his exploits, and twenty to one but they were all disappointed, and told that the bird, on being tried out in the field, was not in the humour; was too fat, or too thin, or some other excuse; and you are never sure what your bird will do till you have had the trouble of *going out* to fly him.

Now the gos-hawk, when properly broken in, requires little or no attention; his master need keep no servants or falconer to attend upon him, and carry him day and night on the hand, which is requisite with the peregrine; if in proper trim, he is ready to hunt, and you can count upon him, and you may fly him as often as you please in the course of a day. I do not recollect over seeing my hawks done up from flight after flight, for six hours consecutively; and I have known a gos-hawk belonging to Rizu Kuli Mirza Nayebel Ayaly, a Persian prince residing at Bagdad, take twenty-one francolins consecutively. The prince assured me, and I firmly believe him, that he made sure of the quarry every time he let him fly from his hand. I have myself taken four hares and a dozen francolins, with several minor birds, and some larger birds, in one day; and I invariably found my gos-hawk improve by exercise,—the more I hunted him, the more he was anxious to continue the sport.

If ever falconry is to be revived in England, this bird will be the one to which we must have recourse. The enclosed state of the country has been generally brought forward as a reason for this sport having been discontinued. Such may be the case; and it constitutes the chief impediment in hunting with the peregrine, where life and death are in the scale; for if you do not arrive in time to assist your falcon, he may be killed by the crane or heron. But in following the gos-hawk, you need never go faster than a hand canter; and you will not find more impediments in your way than a fox-hunter is prepared to meet: surely, therefore, this should be no discouragement. Besides, if your dogs know what they are about, they will follow the hawk while you go round by a gate; and when you come up, you will be just in time to see the game raised, and the hawk waiting your arrival on the nearest bush or tree; for the gos-hawk flies in a straight line at his quarry, which he never allows to go beyond a thousand yards from the place it first started from. Indeed, the sport with the gos-hawk is so gentle, and, in a tolerably open country, so easy, that I think it particularly adapted for ladies; and I shall be happy to hear of some of our noble-minded countrywomen setting the example to the sex, and give every encouragement to the sportsman by honouring him with their presence, and cheering him by an interest in his success. With such inducements of so refined a character, I have no doubt that the art of falconry would be revived; and it would be delightful to strive, by patience and attention to our hawks, to gain the approving smile of beauty. Indeed, the presence of the fair sex constituted in former times, no doubt, half the charm of falconry.

Let me not be thought desirous of detracting from the merits of the peregrine or the *lanner*. The latter is one of the most perfect of its race; but both require much attention and an open country, and must be left to those who have attained great perfection in the art of falconry. Generally speaking, the gos-hawk will answer the purposes of most sportsmen.

At the Zoological Gardens there are now five or six gos-hawks imported from Germany; one of these I have trained and sent into the country, consigning it to the care of F. H. Salvin, Esq., Killingbeck Hall, Leeds, who has succeeded in making it take rabbits; and latterly "Juno" has distinguished herself, and taken hares, which is an interesting sight, and one that no person in England has witnessed, except myself and a friend who visited me in Cilicia. I trust this bird, by her feats, may be the cause of once more attracting the attention of the public to an amusement now almost extinct.* I cannot speak too highly of Mr. Salvin's intelligence, patience, and perseverance. He has carried his refinement so far, as to hunt with the otter, and has performed miracles with some cormorants, which he tamed and trained to take fish for him. I am happy that he has turned his attention to the gos-hawk, as, having kept falcons some years back, he will no doubt be better able to do justice to this bird than any one else.

Mr. John Hancock of Newcastle-upon-Tyne, a gentleman well known as one of our first naturalists, has, I believe, carried falconry to perfection. He has kept every kind of hawk, and understands well their habits and mode of life. His collection of stuffed birds and their eggs is quite unique both in its variety and in the way they are got up. No one who has seen them can forget the specimens of taxidermy he exhibited in the transept of the Great Exhibition; and I am happy to hear that he is about to favour the public with lithographic drawings, done by himself, of what I may very properly call "anatomical specimens of stuffed birds," and which stand prominent in the art which he has

* I have since received two trained gos-hawks from Tarsus. They were three months in a cage on their way to England, and came in perfect health. They have just finished moulting in the Zoological Gardens.

carried to such perfection, as to rank, in my opinion, with *the first painters*.

Falconry is, indeed, not quite extinct in England; for I find that the Duke of Leeds takes an interest in this noble sport; and Colonel Thornton, Lord Orford, Sir Thomas Sebright, Colonel Wilson, and the late Duke of St. Alban's (the Grand Falconer of England), have all kept hawks.

So late as 1839, there was a Hawking Society, called the Norfolk Hawking Club; and on its being dissolved, some of the members, such as the Duke of Leeds, the late Honourable C. Wortley, and Mr. E. Cluff Newcome, joined the Loo Club patronised by the present King of Holland.

Mr. Newcome, as well as Captain Verner and some others, still pursue this sport with great success; and I cannot but express the greatest interest in their pursuit, and wish their example may be followed by others.

I am also informed that there are plenty of open districts still in England, upon the chalk formation, suitable to falconry, such as the country between Lincoln and Peterborough, the Berkshire and Wiltshire Downs, seen from the Great Western Railway, and the country about Brighton, Winchester, &c. Those who cannot find time or convenience to go to these places, let them keep the humble, unassuming, useful, and efficient gos-hawk, which I have hunted successfully in a country as bushy as any that nature has produced, and as wild as can be well imagined. The dense thickets that occur between Mount Taurus and the sea-shore, are, indeed, remarkable. The dog can scarcely penetrate them, and sportsmen would generally flinch from flying a hawk there; but living as I did in the vicinity at Mursina, I used to try, day after day, and I soon learned the "dodges" requisite to ensure a good day's sport, even with such difficulties to surmount.

I find that Colonel Thornton and the Earl of Orford were the last sportsmen who took the hare and the kite with the Iceland falcon towards the close of the 17th century (1700). In 1844, Mr. E. C. Newcome, of Hockwold Hall, Brandon, Norfolk, took, with a cast of old "passage-hawks," fifty-seven herons.*

I also hear from my fellow-admirers of this sport, that his Grace the Duke of Leeds, when Marquis of Carmarthen, and living at Dunotar

---

* The herons are not killed; but being taken alive from the hawk, a copper ring, with the name of the captor and date upon it, is fixed to its legs, and it is turned off again; and as the heron is a long-lived bird, I have read of their being recaptured many years after. Indeed, in one instance, a bird was shot at the Cape of Good Hope, bearing on its leg a date so ancient that *I am afraid* to venture upon noting it here.

House, near Stonehaven, in Kincardineshire, Scotland, killed with one peregrine, an old eyas tiercel, "the General," 130 partridges out of 133 flights in one season. *These* instances, and Colonel Bonham's success in Ireland, should, I think, encourage others to enter the field of competition; and I should be happy to afford them every assistance and information in my power, having had great experience for many years, during my residence in the East, in the training of hawks. Indeed, when I visited Persia, Malek Kasem Mirza, the viceroy of Azerbigian, declared to his officers that he had learned a great deal from me in conversation on the subject, when I passed some twenty days in his happy valley near the borders of the lake of Urimiyah; and I confess that I also learned much from him, for the Persians have carried falconry to the greatest perfection possible. As an example of which I will cite one case. Timour Mirza Seif-il-dowly, great grandson of the King of Persia, Feth Ali Shah, now residing with his two elder brothers at Bagdad, when at Aleppo some years ago, was accompanied by my brother in a hawking expedition. He had only a gos-hawk with him, having left his other falcons (of which he has more than a dozen, chiefly lanners) at home. He rode with his slave behind him equally well mounted. On coming to the place where partridges were expected to be found, two rose at the same time. He let off his hawk, which seized one of them immediately in the air at a few paces off. The prince dismounted and took it from the hawk, which he raised in his right hand, concealing the prize with his left. The hawk looked forward, and seeing the other partridge still flying in the open country, proceeded in pursuit of it. The prince remounted, giving the first partridge to his man, and gallopped off after his hawk, coming up just after it had overtaken and seized the partridge that had flown upwards of a quarter of a mile, thus effecting "*un coup double!*" This he did three times successively, taking six partridges one after the other, to the astonishment of my brother, who was aware of the difficulty that is experienced by falconers in extracting the quarry out of the hand of the hawk, so as to enable it to look forward, instead of looking after the missing bird. I must note, however, that the country where this took place was clear of any bush, and that the partridge could scarcely hide itself any where, except under a stone; and that it is not extraordinary that it should be taken in such an open country; the wonder lay in the bird's patient obedience to its master, in allowing him possession of the partridge, and flying immediately after the second. In that open country, I have myself taken forty-two partridges in three days, with a bird I had not had in training ten days, and which Ibrahim Pasha had given me; and I believe that there is no limit to the number of birds a gos-hawk would take when in proper condition—quite as many as he may be flown at, always provided he is not discouraged by being deprived of his right to the head.

Sportsmen have found that it is necessary to keep each falcon to a distinct species of quarry, *i. e.* you cannot properly fly them at fur and feather indiscriminately. But although this rule applies also to the gos-hawk in *some* degree, I have found that it is by no means unexceptionable; for I used to fly my gos-hawk (one I kept seven years) at every thing; and I remember often returning home with every kind of game that I had met with, including hares, ducks, geese, partridges, francolins, curlews, water-birds, small herons, quails, rails, and even crows, and birds of rapine, *three times his size!* Indeed, there was nothing he would not fly at, if I would let him go; and he once actually attacked a vulture, which had carried off one of his companions, a gos-hawk belonging to a sporting friend, who was out with me, and who had neglected his bird in pursuing the game his dogs were hot upon.

Besides the German gos-hawk, there is at the Zoological Gardens, Regent's Park, a precious and beautiful specimen of the Australian gos-hawk; it is perfectly white, and its eyes are the colour of bright rubies. This is a hawk of considerable value for the sportsman; its hands are larger in comparison to the other European and Asiatic gos-hawks, as it is smaller in body. But judging from appearances, I am led to believe that it would be swifter in flight, and, on the whole, a more efficient bird. I have had the pleasure of taming this bird, and could, I think, promise to turn it out a perfect hawk. This is the only specimen in England; but I believe that Mr. Mitchell, the secretary to the society, is daily expecting some more of them from our antipodes. It forms, in my opinion, the beau idea of perfection in a hawk. I consider it worthy of a princely hand, and should be happy to see his Royal Highness Prince Albert patronise the training of this bird to afford amusement to our young Prince of Wales. It is without a defect, and might be brought to perform wonders. There are also peregrines and Iceland falcons to be seen in the same collection. Hitherto, indeed, the natural history of hawks has been much neglected, and we must look forward to more correct and valuable drawings, which we are promised by Mr. Hancock.

The two accompanying illustrations have been kindly furnished me by my friend Mr. John Hancock, to exhibit the different forms of the two tribes of "hawk of the lure" and "hawk of the fist."*

* I cannot avoid making a few remarks here on the wanton destruction of life

In England, hawks are divided into long-winged and short-winged; in the East, they follow the same division, but call them black and yellow-eyed; the peregrine and lanner being of the former, the goshawk and sparrow-hawk of the latter. And it is remarkable how, on almost every point, the sportsmen of the East and West are agreed. Although the communication between them has been interrupted for centuries, the general system of treatment, the many ingenious contrivances, either discovered or handed down from posterity, are in

THE GOS-HAWK.    THE FALCON.

both alike. Each use bells, jesses, leashes, hoods, and gauntlets, that are much alike. They imp the broken feathers in the same way; and both bathe and weather their hawks, give castings, and feed them in the same manner. This alone would prove the ancient origin of falconry, which appears to have had one source, and probably to have been introduced by the Indo-Germanic race from the plains of Hindustan, so favourable to hawking. It appears from all accounts that falconry is more generally attended to there than in any other part of the world; and it was there that Colonel Bonham seems to have acquired his valuable experience, "in spite of Thugs, tigers, and fever," and where his

which the mania for collecting eggs and birds to stuff has generated. At the late sale of the valuable and interesting zoological collection at Knowsley, many a rare animal was bought in order to kill and stuff it; and the exertions made in collecting eggs, an unfair practice and a morbid taste, will soon deprive us of many an interesting bird, unless put a stop to by the execration of public opinion, expressed on all possible occasions.

perseverance has been rewarded by the acquisition of many a sporting trophy.

There is a kind of hawk called by the Easterns *ispir*. I have only seen one of these. They are much esteemed and fetch a great price: I have heard it said that 5*l*., a dog, a horse, a camel, a donkey, a cow, a goat, and a sheep, have been given in exchange for one of these birds. They are very rare in Syria, and always haggards; but I must confess that I have not been able to make a real distinction between them and the doghan, except that, when they have moulted, their eyes remain *yellow*, the pristine colour of the first year, whereas that of the doghan changes into a ruby red. They are certainly more powerful and swifter of flight, flying *up hill* after partridges, and taking them often *comprehensively*, that is, flying at *the covey*, and not singling out any particular bird, by which means the whole lot is brought to a stand-still in a small space, while the hawk is flying about from bush to bush making a whistling noise, which so frightens the partridges that they allow themselves to be taken by the dogs rather than fly again. When the sportsman has thus secured the whole covey, he throws up one to the hawk in waiting, who seizes it in the air, and gives it up, after having been rewarded with the head for his patience and assistance, and is ready to renew the sport until evening, when, of course, he must be well fed on the last taken. Modern sportsmen, in these degenerate days, will perhaps call this proceeding a species of poaching; but when we consider the difficulty and merit of training hawks to be so tractable, we must not, in consideration of the tastes of others, desecrate the noble art of falconry with such an appellation; and we must recollect that, in the East, the chief point looked to is the quantity bagged, which, by the by, is much the same with our present generation, who go out in a preserve to shoot at game as if they were so many barn-door fowls, and glory in the number they bring down without any exertion or trouble. It is related of Charles X. of France, that a shooting day used to cost him thousands of francs in powder alone, as he had a party of keepers sent round to drive up the game (by firing at it in the air without shot), and bring it under the aim of the royal gun!

The yellow-eyed hawks, or hawks of the fist, are never hooded; those of the lure are accustomed to the hood, because, I believe, that, as the latter sit more forward on the hand than the former, they cannot balance themselves so well; and it is necessary to blind them in order to carry them about, as by that means you compel them to have recourse to their "*hands*," instead of constantly opening their "*sails*," to help themselves in their balance. This is the only use I can discover of the hood, and I would never recommend it, except on particular occasions, when necessary to keep the bird quiet. But otherwise I consider the use of the hood should be deprecated.

The *songhur** is a larger species of peregrine. It is sometimes taken in the north of Asia Minor; but I have not seen a specimen of this falcon. It is considered by the Turkmans as the king of birds, and they have assured me that all the feathered tribes " tremble in its presence."

The peregrine of the cliffs of Mount Taurus is smaller than the English peregrine, but more beautifully variegated in plumage. It is known as the " Barbary falcon." It is generally kept in the East by rich men, who can afford to have one man, or even two men, for each bird. The hand of the falconer should be its only perch. Thus treated, its natural wildness is conquered, and it may be brought to take any thing, although it is generally kept to protect the doghan from the attacks of its natural enemies, the eagle and vulture. So we see that the peregrine acts but a secondary, although a loyal part, in the estimation of Eastern falconers.

The lanner, I have said, is the perfection of birds. The older it grows, the more perfect it becomes, it is so gentle and so tractable; but it requires a very experienced sportsman to bring it to hunt at all. If he once succeeds, the bird is without price. It is the hawk most in use in Bagdad, where they are divided into several species, each having a separate name and employment. Some are trained to assist the dogs in taking the gazelles of the neighbouring desert, which it does by fastening itself on the head of the females, which have no horns, until the dogs come up. It is a native of the centre of Asia Minor; and I am *told* that you may see a nest on every tree in front of the habitations of the people of Bur and Nigdy. If naturalists have not called this hawk the " falco *gentilis*," they have given a misnomer to any other species, and deprived it of its rights. Its eyes are of a bluish-black colour; its beak grey, with whitish-grey feet, and black claws. It is not unlike in feathers to the English peregrine in its first year's plumage. I cannot, however, be expected to enter here into a dissertation on the treatment and training of hawks. To do this effectively a separate volume should be devoted to the subject. I have only mentioned cursorily what I thought might be of most interest, and which I trust will attract the attention of the sporting world.

Falconry is a source of healthy and innocent enjoyment; and it is very desirable that some person of distinction should patronise its revival. Being conducted on horseback, *quietly*, it is more adapted to the

---

* The Turkish appellation of this falcon.

generality of sportsmen than fox-hunting or shooting, both of which are too violent exercises for many persons, and subject to many serious accidents, from which falconry is quite free. This "noble craft" combines every advantage, and let us hope will be brought into fashion once again; that we may see, as our ancestors did, those scenes so graphically portrayed by our immortal Walter Scott and other celebrated novelists, when describing this pageant of past glory.

GESRIL HADEED, IN THE PLAINS OF ANTIOCH:
FROM A SKETCH BY MR. C. F. BARKER.

CHAPTER XIX.

MEDICINAL PLANTS.

AMONG the medicinal herbs that have fallen under my notice, I must mention the *Adiantum capillus Veneris*, or maiden-hair, of which the people of the country make a strong decoction to remove dysentery and violent diarrhœa.

There is also a black seed, like a dried black bean, of which I have not learned the name (nor is it, perhaps, used in the materia medica, if known at all). It is remarkably useful in the above maladies; it is a tasteless astringent, and one or two seeds pounded up and taken in coffee bring about the desired effect.

The *Colocynth*, or bitter apple, which grows wild on the sea-coast.

The *Palma Christi*, or castor-oil plant, which the inhabitants cultivate for domestic as well as medicinal purposes.

Mount Taurus produces also the *Scammony* plant, and the gum is collected from the wild plants by persons who come to Tarsus from Latachia expressly for the purpose.

And, lastly, the *Scilla maritima*, which is to be found every where on a sandy ground. The bulb of this plant is dried in an oven and reduced to powder; it forms an excellent gum or glue, used by shoemakers instead of their wax; when required, it is simply rubbed up gradually with a little cold water into a *paste*, and after it is used and has dried, it becomes impervious to moisture, and no insect will touch it. In the state used in Turkey, it is of a brown colour; but I think that, by sifting it of the rind, the remaining pith would be white, and it might be made available in book-binding, saddlery, &c. I brought some of it with me to England, and it has been declared to possess many valuable qualities. In Europe, the squill is a well-known medicinal agent for coughs and consumption; but these maladies are unknown in Cilicia and Syria. So true is this, that the ancient Greek and Roman physicians were in the habit of sending their consumptive patients from Europe to Antioch and Suedia, on account of the beauty and salubrity of the climate: an example which, it is to be hoped, our countrymen will soon learn to follow; for in few places can so fine a climate, such beautiful scenery and vegetation, such resources in learned or philanthropic pursuits, or in field-sports, and such cheap living, be found united together. The country would also benefit infinitely by the occasional residence of our valetudinarians at Suedia, Betias, or the neighbourhood. The reason that these districts have hitherto attracted so little attention is because travellers generally confine themselves to the beaten tract from Beyrut to Palestine. In this respect Mr. Neale's work, lately published, is calculated to do some good.

BETIAS: MR. BARKER'S SUMMER RESIDENCE ON MOUNT RHOSSUS.
FROM A SKETCH BY MR. E. B. B. BARKER.

APPENDIX.

A.

NARRATIVE OF NADIR BEY, WRITTEN FROM HIS OWN DICTATION.*

Depuis l'instant où Dieu tout puissant créa dans le ciel l'étoile qui devait marquer mon existence, et depuis le jour de ma naissance jusqu'à l'âge de onze ans, enfant, je ne savais rien, je n'avais rien vu, si ce n'est les pleurs de ma bien-aimée et très-honorée mère, possédant une âme céleste, qui, au milieu d'un chagrin continuel, n'avait pu m'apprendre autre chose qu'à l'aimer et à partager ses peines. J'appris aussi, avant de l'avoir jamais vu, que mon bien-aimé empereur et père avait été assassiné par son propre frère qui par-là a imprimé sur le front de mon oncle une tache de sang, que rien ne pourra effacer de son vivant, et qui souillera sa mémoire lorsqu'il aura rejoint ses ancêtres dans l'éternité. J'appris encore qu'à l'époque du massacre des innocentes dames de son harem, ce Dieu tout puissant et miséricordieux, qui m'a donné l'être, se servit de la main même d'un des assassins pour sauver les jours de ma tendre mère—barbare assassin, qui montrait des sentimens de générosité et d'humanité supérieurs à ceux d'un oncle souillé de sang—empereur de droit, mais de fait un assassin, qui s'abreuvait du sang de sa propre famille. De cette époque, quoiqu'enfant, mon jeune cœur éprouvait toutes les angoisses d'une pareille tra-

---

* The mistakes left are those in the original, which, though incorrect, is very good for a Turk to dictate to an Italian amanuensis. (For Translation, see p. 310.)

It may be proper to premise here, that the author in no way pretends to guarantee the authenticity of the above extraordinary document. The improbability of the events and the incoherence of the writer are manifest throughout. Little faith can therefore be placed in the princely origin claimed by its author. Still there are such strange things enacted in a country circumstanced as Turkey is, and which receive such frequent illustration in its past history, and there is so much that is romantic in the life of this Oriental adventurer, that there is every excuse for presenting so curious a biography in his own words. If necessary, a further excuse might be found for such a publication, in the fact that the existence of such a personage as Nadir Bey—as a pretender to the throne of the Osmanlis—was very generally known in the countries that border the Mediterranean. Miss Romer, as we shall afterwards see, has already published some account of "the Turkish pretender," as that lady designates him; and frequent allusions have also been made in the Maltese and other newspapers of the day to the same extraordinary personage, whose story has now for some time excited the greatest interest and curiosity in many parts of the world, but has never before been given in the author's own words.

gédie de mon pauvre père, que mes yeux n'avaient pas eu le bonheur de voir, mais que mon cœur avait déviné, et je détestais l'action horrible de mon oncle. Comme enfant, je partageais les chagrins de ma royale mère, l'objet de mon affection la plus dévouée dans mon enfance, et de mon respect, de mon amour, dans l'adolescence, et mon unique consolation dans l'âge viril. Mais hélas! peu de tems après le chagrin qui la consumait termina les jours de cette auguste dame, et elle s'envola, comme je l'espère et le crois fermement, vers les régions du bonheur éternel. Elle me laissa par droit d'héritage les droits de prince impérial, titre que la puissance divine m'accordait, et qu'aucun pouvoir humain ne pouvait me contester, et dont on ne peut sans crime me priver; mais en même tems elle me légua aussi un chagrin profond, et une douleur dont la puissance humaine ne pouvait adoucir l'amertume. Elle me laissa aussi un vêtement superficiel que nul ne pouvait déchirer à l'exception de moi-même; elle me laissa un sentiment de vengéance dont moi seul peut connaître la profondeur; elle me laissa des diamants, preuve de la munificence impériale de son auguste époux le sultan, et son amant; elle me laissa des papiers écris de son auguste main—ajoutez à cela quelle me confia aux soins, à la prudence, et à la protection de Joaniza, homme d'environ soixante-dix ans, qui avait survécu à sa femme et ses enfants, être dévoué et fidèle au service de ma mère, et reconnaissant des bontés et des bienfaits qu'elle avait repandus sur lui pendant sa vie. Elle lui recommanda de me conduire à Constantinople, ayant soin de ne faire connaître ni mon nom ni ma naissance, mais de me faire donner une education ottomane aussi brillante que possible; et lorsque je arriverais à l'âge de majorité, de déclarer mes droits, et de m'engager à les faire valoir. C'est ainsi que la plus cherie des mères expira dans cet espoir. Mais il ne fut pas réalisé; car " l'homme propose, et Dieu dispose." L'honnête vieillard, fidèle exécuteur des ordres de sa bienfaitrice, essaya de me conduire à Constantinople, sans s'inquiéter de ses propres infirmités et de son âge avancé. Peu de tems après la mort de ma mère nous partîmes de Caffa, ville de la Crimée, où ses saintes cendres impériales reposent: nous arrivâmes à Odessa dans l'intention de nous rendre à la capitale où avaient regné mes ancêtres; mais nous fûmes arrêtés dans notre voyage par les lois arbitraires de la Russie, qui ne permettent à aucun sujet de passer la frontière; et quoique le vieux Joaniza fût descendu d'une famille de la Moldavie, et devenu sujet de la Russie par suite d'un séjour de plusieurs années dans cet empire, où la justice est inconnue. Cependant, après avoir été retenu pendant trois ans dans cette ville, le bon vieillard termina sa carrière, et je restai sans protection, isolé, et sans un seul ami, à l'âge de quinze ans. Je connus alors la situation déplorable dans laquelle je me trouvais placé. Je rappellai à ma mémoire les dernières paroles de ma noble mère, que me redisait souvent le bon vieillard, et ce fut alors que la vengeance prit réellement possession de mon cœur ; et ayant arrangé mes projets, j'implorai dans les larmes la protection de Dieu seul, et plaçant toute ma confiance en lui, j'appellai la prudence et le courage à mon aide, et quittai la ville, accompagné d'un Grec nommé Macris, qui allait en Morée, passant par Trieste pour servir son pays, disait-il. Arrivé à Bulta, les Juifs astucieux découvrirent un air de mystère existant entre moi et mon compagnon, attendu que, n'ayant point de passeport, je comptais sur sa prudence ; malgré que j'eusse acheté chèrement l'amitié de ces Juifs, les malheureux n'en suivirent pas moins leurs dispositions à la duplicité, et aussitôt que j'en eus connaissance, je quittai cette ville et mon compagnon, et seul je gagnai Mozilow sur le Dniester. Là je fus assez tranquille, et je fis tout ce que je put pour gagner l'amitié de chacun, et apprendre tout ce que je pouvais. Là j'appris un peu le Polonais ; de-là je me rendis à Lozensk, où, par hasard, je me suis procuré un document d'Elefthery, en Grec, sorte de passeport, qui me mit à même ensuite de voyager en Russie sous ce déguisement, et d'être admis dans la meilleure société de cet empire. Je fus à même d'étudier sa force et sa politique, ses lois, et la faiblesse de ses ressources ; en un mot, je put apprécier son gouvernement avec justesse. Là j'ai vu l'ennemi puissant de mon pays, et par conséquent de mon cœur ; enfin, je quittai la Russie pour me rendre en Pologne, où je trouvai ce peuple guerrier, brave et généreux, et sa brillante armée ; je commençai dès lors à m'attacher à la théorie et aux tactiques de leur armée ; et j'arrivai à dix-huit ans connaissant parfaitement la politique astucieuse de la Russie, et pénétré des souffrances qu'enduraient mon pays natal par suite de la révolte des Grecs. Je fus obligé de quitter la Pologne à cause des soupçons que j'avais inspiré à la police, et je passais en Galicie dans l'intention de me rendre en Moldavie, et de-là dans la capitale de mes ancêtres. Mais à Lembergh on me demanda dans l'hôtel où j'étais descendu, d'où je venais ; mais ne désirant pas les satisfaire sur ce point, ou plutôt craignant le gouvernement russe, je répondis que j'arrivais de la Moldavie, sans penser aux conséquences qui en pouvaient résulter. Lorsqu'on me demanda où j'avais fait quarantaine, je balbutiai, et répondis, "Nulle part." Cette réponse étonna tout le monde, et on me dit que je serais pendu pour m'être soustrait à cette mesure de précaution. Ce que je compris facilement ; mais ne voulant pas être traité comme coupable sans avoir commis un crime, je quittai cette ville, et, sous l'égide de la protection divine, je gagnai, sans être inquiété, la ville de Jassy en Moldavie, faisant partie de l'empire que gouvernait mon oncle. Là, réfléchissant sur ma situation, j'accusai souvent le destin. En peu de tems j'appris la langue moldavienne, seul avantage que je retirais de mon séjour. Je me mis en route pour Constantinople, poussé par la vengeance, et formant des projets imaginaires, batailles, et victoires; la tête pleine de ces rêves je cheminais, et de cette manière je me trouvai lancé au milieu d'une nation étrangère, quoique ce fut ma patrie; des mœurs et des manières toutes nouvelles pour moi ; et lorsque j'étais à etudier ce nouveau pays, la guerre éclata avec la Russie dans les anneés 1828 et 1829. Je n'y comprenais rien, croyant qu'il était de mon devoir de prendre parti contre les agresseurs de mon pays. Je vis alors l'armée des Turcs, lions de courage, honnête par nature, mais commandés par des généraux aussi ignorans que des agneaux, sans en posséder la douceur, qui, dans leur vanité, se croyaient nés pour gouverner. Je ne pouvais que les plaindre et pleurer sur mon pays, et sur le malheureux résultat qui eut lieu à Adrianople, et je le considérai comme un châtiment infligé par la providence à mon oncle le Sultan Mahmout. Je me rendis alors au tombeau révéré de mon légitime empereur, mon père bien-aimé, où je versai les pleurs filiales, et ensuite je vis son assassin placé dans des circonstances les plus critiques, et ce tableau horrible rappellant l'affreuse tragédie dans laquelle mon auguste père avait perdu la vie, mes sens s'égarèrent, et je ne rêvai plus que vengeance ; mais bien malheureux est l'homme qui en fait son idole. Néanmoins me trouvant dans mon pays natal, j'aperçus l'activité qu'il mettait à le civiliser et à en réformer les abus; j'approuvai ces principes ; mais malheureusement il ne pouvait communiquer à d'autres ce qu'il ne connaissait pas lui-même, comme la suite l'a démontré ; ses idées étaient nobles et généreuses, mais il ignorait sur quelles bases il fallait les fonder. Je ne saurais exprimer les combats qui s'élévaient en moi : d'un côté brûlant de vengeance, et de l'autre retenu par la prudence et l'amour de mon pays, qui devait être sauvé, mais non pas remué par des révolutions, me firent prendre la résolution de le haïr, mais de ne pas l'arrêter dans la voie de réforme qu'il avait en vue, et plutôt le seconder comme empereur de ma patrie adorée. Pour ce faire, il était nécessaire de connaître mieux notre empire, et je me rendis en Asie pour examiner de quoi est composée cette grande nation ; et après avoir satisfait ma curiosité sur ce point, je revins à la capitale dans l'intention d'être utile à mon pays. Il fallait connaître les élémens du gouvernement ; je fis la connaissance de tous les amis de mon père, de ceux qui correspondaient avec ma mère sublime, pour qui j'avait des lettres d'elle, et qui en conséquence sont devenu mes vrais amis, et qui me sont encore ; en suite je fis la connaissance de Reis Effendi et de l'interprète de la Sublime Porte: ils devinrent mes vrais amis; et me confiant à leur amitié, je découvris à ce dernier la plaie que j'avais dans le cœur, mon nom, ma naissance, et quelles étaient mes projets. Le brave homme, honnête Mussulman, parut frappé de la foudre, et après un moment de réflexion, il s'exprima ainsi, les yeux baignés de larmes : " Prince, ayez confiance en Dieu, mais jamais dans les hommes. Cachez bien votre origine impériale, et suivez vos intentions pacifiqueés; aimez votre pays, et Dieu vous sera en aide. Quant à moi, je vous suis dévoué jusqu'à mon dernier moment ; mais n'oubliez pas que votre vie est en danger, que vous devez la conserver pour votre pays ; ainsi, que la prudence vous guide, et que Dieu vous protége." J'ai suivi ses conseils ; et en peu de tems je fis beaucoup d'amis; et Hosref Pacha, alors généralissime, qui à cette époque ignorait mon origine, me confia le commandement d'un régiment de cavalerie qu'on devait former à Aldana. Arrivé là, je m'occupai de recruter les soldats; et lorsque j'eus le complément, je reçus l'ordre de les discipliner pour l'infanterie, ce que je fis avec le plus grand zèle. Je contractai là un engagement d'amitié fraternelle avec Hagi Ali Bey, gouverneur de la place, et fils du fameux Hassan Pacha d'Adana. H. Ali Bey avait sous ses ordres environ 19,000 hommes de cavalerie, les plus braves, je crois, du monde entier, et entièrement à sa disposition et à la mienne. Ce fut le moment le plus propice pour venger la mort de mon père; mais ayant déjà resolu de servir mon pays en assistant et participant à la réforme dont il avait besoin, je renonçai à inquiéter mon oncle dans ses projets. Quelques tems après, comme j'avais un goût prononçée pour la cavalerie, je demandai la permission de me rendre à Constantinople, afin de faire un échange et de passer de l'infanterie dans la cavalerie; et en ayant reçu l'autorisation, je me rendis à la capitale. Indépendamment de mes appartemens du Seraskier, je pris un logement particulier à Pera, afin de me trouver en rapport avec les Européens, et apprendre le Français. Peu de tems après les étrangers vinrent à moi, m'appellant Moszinski, à ma grande surprise ; et quoique je déclinasse l'honneur que l'on me faisait, mes devices furent inutiles ; et bientôt, en dépit de moi-même, tout Pera m'appella de ce nom, me félicitant de ce que j'étais si bien avec le gouvernement turc, et dont le motif m'a occasionné des persécutions de la Russie (motif imaginaire).

Un jour, en mon absence, la grande incendie de Pera eut lieu; et lorsque, comme tout le monde, je fus pour sauver ce que je possédais, j'arrivai au moment où tout était en cendre. Près de-là j'aperçus une femme grecque, seule et sans assistance. Le feu avait déjà gagné sa maison; son dénuement excita ma compassion; et avec l'assistance de mes gens, je sauvais sa vie et ses objets les plus précieux ; car ses propres domestiques l'avaient abandonnée à périr, pour se livrer au pillage de sa maison. Après avoir mis en sûreté ce qui avait été sauvé dans le maison de Monsieur Black, qui est batie en pierre, je conduisit cette dame, encore toute effrayée, dans une maison éloignée de l'incendie ; là je lui demandai ses clefs pour aller chercher ses bijoux, argent, et papiers, parceque je considérais prudent qu'elle les eût en sa possession, dans la crainte que dans une confusion semblable ils ne fussent perdus. Je m'aperçus qu'effrayée ; elle craignait de se confier à un étranger ; cependant les larmes aux yeux, et avec cette délicatesse feminine, elle me les remis. Je la quittai, et me dirigeai de suite vers la maison de M. Black ; mais heureusement pour elle je rencontrai par hasard en chemin des gens inconnus, qui emportaient ses malles, qu'ils avaient enlévée dans la confusion du moment ; et quoique je n'en fussent pas précisément certain, j'arrêtai les frippons, et ouvrit les malles avec les clefs qu'elle m'avait remises. J'en sortis les bijoux et papiers, et mis le reste en sûreté dans la maison de M. Bersolesy ; je retournai de suite auprès de l'affligée Mariola (elle s'appellait ainsi), et lui remis ses bijoux et papiers, qu'elle avait cru perdus, et que le hasard seul m'avait fait découvrir. Mariola, étonnée d'une semblable chance et de l'honnêteté, comme elle le disait, d'un étranger, me remercia de la manière la plus gracieuse m'exprimant sa reconnaissance, et me disant qu'il n'était pas possible que je fusse un des Chrétiens du pays ; car la probité et la générosité que j'avais montrée étaient bien rare chez eux. Et pourtant, je considérais que je n'avais fait que mon devoir. Je donnai alors l'ordre à mes gens de lui procurer une maison à Arnaut Kivy, comme elle le désirait ; et après avoir fait transporter ce qui avait été sauvé de l'incendie, je l'accompagnai dans la maison qu'on avait préparée pour sa réception ; mais à peine arrivée, ses pleurs commencèrent à couler abondamment. Je lui en demandai la cause ; et elle me répondit, avec cette délicatesse qui n'appartient qu'à une dame de distinction, que désormais elle ne pouvait plus goûter le bonheur, et que sa réputation se trouvait compromise de ce que je l'avais accompagnée, ce qui était contraire à leurs usages. Ces pleurs me causèrent une vive émotion, et quelque chose même de plus tendre ; et étourdie, comme un jeune homme que j'étais, pour la mettre à l'abri de la calomnie d'une société grecque et injuste, j'offris de l'épouser (vu que la loi mussulman permet à l'homme d'épouser une femme de quelle que religion qu'elle soit) ; et Mariola me répondit qu'elle acceptait volontiers une pareille destinée, quoique je ne fusse pas Grec. Mariola était le plus cher objet de mon cœur.

Un jour Hosref Pacha m'apprit que la révolution faisait des progrès rapides en Pologne, et que l'armée russe avait été battue plusieurs fois. Il me demanda si j'avais voyagé en Pologne, et me fit beaucoup de questions sur cette brave nation; et entr'autres, si j'en connaissais la langue; et l'ayant satisfait sur tous ces points, il jugea à propos de m'envoyer personnellement en Pologne. On me permettra de garder le silence sur l'objet de ma mission. D'après ses ordres je me mis en voyage, et arrivai à Belgrade, porteur de dépêches adressées par Hosref Pacha à Hussein Pacha, gouverneur de cette ville, qui écrivit de suite à Vienne pour obtenir que la quarantaine fût réduite, s'il était possible. Cela lui fut accordé; mais malheureusement j'appris que les Russes étaient entrés dans Varsovie, et que le gouvernement polonais n'existait plus; et quoique Turc, je plaignis alors bien sincèrement cette brave et noble nation; mais pour ne pas exciter des soupçons, je me rendis à Vienne avec l'intention de passer par Trieste pour me rendre à Constantinople. Après avoir reçu pendant plusieurs jours les plus grands honneurs de sa majesté et de la noblesse de Vienne, je fus arrêté avec toute ma suite (comme il est mentionné dans le journal, le *Messager des Chambres* du 27 janvier, 1832); et lorsqu'on m'interrogea, je ne crus pas convenable de répondre à leurs questions sur l'objet de ma mission, et je m'apperçus, par leur conduite et leurs questions insidieuses, qu'ils me prenaient pour un noble Polonais, et je fus dès lors obligé de convenir que je l'étais, puisqu'on m'assurait que sans cet aveu rien ne pouvait me faire recouvrir ma liberté; et il ne me fut pas difficile de confirmer cette qualité, puisque je connaissais la langue, et je n'hésitai pas à céder à leur opinion, afin d'éviter leurs soupçons. Ils me créèrent une famille, père, mère, frères, et sœurs, et une parenté considérable; ajoutant à cela des domaines et d'autres richesses, qui, disait-on, m'appartenaient en Pologne. Je regrettais seulement que ce fut idéal; mais tout à coup un estafette, porteur de dépêches qui me concernaient, et arrivant de Constantinople, vint anéantir ma nouvelle famille et mes propriétés. Vers minuit je fus mandé par le Prince de Metternich; et à la fin de cette entrevue il me dit que j'étais libre, et que l'empereur, ainsi que lui même, régrettaient beaucoup l'erreur qui avait été commise à mon égard, m'accablant de complimens, et me disant qui j'étais libre de continuer mon voyage, et que sa majesté l'Empereur d'Autriche se rappellerait toujours de moi avec plaisir. Je leur offris mes remercîmens, malgré qu'ils fussent plutôt dus à l'estafette. Quittant Vienne, je passai par Trieste, et arrivai à Constantinople. Le matin même de mon arrivée, Namyk Pacha, alors Namyk Bey, m'invita à me rendre chez le Séraskier, qui, disait-il, désirait me voir de suite. Je m'y rendis aussitôt; et après des politesses cérémonieuses, je fus conduit en prison, ou plutôt dans un cachot affreux. Je ne pouvais comprendre ni la conduite infame du Séraskier, ni quelle pouvait être la cause de mon emprisonnement; car n'étant pas d'un naturel méchant, je ne pouvais pas soupçonner l'interprète de la Sublime Porte, qui connaissait mon origine, de m'avoir trahi. Mais là j'étais injuste; et croyant que je devais partager le sort infortuné d'un père chéri, je murmurai contre lui qui m'avait créé pour me faire terminer mes jours d'une manière aussi cruelle dans cette horrible prison. Vingt fois par jour on m'annonçait que la mort m'attendait; et avec tout mon courage, j'étais quelques fois abattu et craintif. Je ne pouvais compter sur aucune assistance—un miracle seul pouvait me sauver; et ma conscience ne me reprochant aucun crime, ni action déshonorable, me faisait espérer un meilleur avenir, car j'étais libre, quoique prisonnier ; tant il est vrai qu'une conscience pure franchit les murs épais du plus noir donjon. Un jour accablé de désespoir, les fidèles domestiques de Hosref Pacha, son Selichtar Aga et un Arménien Marderaki, dignes instruments d'un tel maître et de leur nature vils et envieux du bien d'autrui, s'aperçurent que je possédais des diamans, ceux qui avaient appartenus à ma mère bien aimée; ils les convoitèrent, et sans plus de façon me proposèrent de leur donner trois brillans pour prix de ma liberté; et quoiqu'il me fut bien pénible de me défaire de ces reliques de ma tendre mère, j'aurais sacrifié la moitié de mon existence pour sauver l'autre, car je ne pourrais dépeindre les tortures que j'endurais dans cette affreuse prison. Je leur donnai donc les trois brillans et de l'argent, et les deux misérables me dirent que c'était tout pour le Pacha lui-même, et que par conséquent je pouvais compter sur ma liberté. Je voulus bien le croire ; mais c'était en vain que j'espérais d'être libre, car les hypocrites m'avaient trahis, et je continuai à demeurer prisonnier sans espoir. Par leurs ordres ma captivité fut rendue plus mal; et craignant un jour qu'ils vinrent s'emparer des deux brillans qui me restaient, et des papiers écris de la main de mon auguste mère, j'adoptai un moyen pour les sauver. Ce fut de les faire entrer dans une bouteille, que j'enfouis à plus de trois pieds de profondeur dans ma prison ; où ils sont encore, car je ne pouvais pas les reprendre sans créer des soupçons qui eussent amené des resultats facheux.

Un jour un Grec ivre fut amené dans la prison pour une dette de quarante-neuf piastres; et me voyant, se mit à parler Grec, en me demandant ce qu'un gentilhomme comme moi pouvait faire dans un lieu semblable. "Quel crime," dit-il, "avez-vous pu commettre ?" Je lui répondit que le crime imaginaire pour lequel j'étais détenu me coûterait la vie. "Grand Dieu !" s'écria cet homme ivre, "payez ma dette, seigneur, et vous ne périrez pas." Désirant faire une bonne action, je payai la modique somme pour laquelle il était arrêté. Il s'en dormit; et à son reveil, " Allons, monsieur," me dit-il, " moi, et cinquante palicaris, que j'ai à mes ordres, nous vous délivrerons cette nuit." Je n'attachais aucune croyance à ce que me disait cet homme ; mais il me vint à l'idée de le faire servir d'instrument à mon projet. J'écrivis en langue grecque à l'ambassadeur de France, le suppliant de sauver ma vie. Je la rémis à cet homme, qui fort heureusement la délivra fidèlement. Le ministre chargé d'affaires de France, M. le Baron de Varen, fit aussitôt tout ce qui dépendait de lui, et par des moyens que je ne connais pas, il me procura en peu de jours ma liberté. Je dois certainement ma vie à ce noble Français. Pendant mon emprisonnement, les Russes, qui ne négligeaient rien pour me persécuter, les Grecs et les Patriarches avaient réussi à me séparer pour jamais de ma bien-aimée Mariola, sous le prétexte qu'étant né Grecque, elle ne pouvait épouser un homme qui ne professait pas la même religion. Brûlant de rage contre Hosref Pacha, et tous les évènemens dont j'avais été victime, je partit pour l'Egypte, où j'entrai au service de Méhemet Ali, et reçus le grade de général instructeur et inspecteur de toute la cavalerie, et peu après aide-de-camp d'Ibrahim Pasha, ainsi qu'il en est fait mention au No. 1 de la *Revue Britannique* pour le mois de janvier 1834. Cependant je régrettais de servir sous un homme qui faisait la guerre à mon oncle, c'est-à-dire à ma famille et à mes interêts. J'obtins la permission de venir en Europe pour y rétablir ma santé; mais je ne retournai que pour ne pas agir contre les interêts de ma famille et de mon pays. Depuis, pour mon instruction, j'ai parcouru l'Europe et l'Amérique; mais partout j'ai été en but aux persécutions de la Sainte Alliance, dont tous les calculs étaient déroutés parcequ'elle ne pouvait découvrir mon origine ni l'objet de mes voyages. J'ai étudié les langues anglaises et françaises, et j'ai résolu de servir ma patrie sous l'incognito. Plusieurs fois, sous un déguisement, je me rendis à Constantinople, et je finis comme auparavant par entrer au service militaire. Par les ordres de sa majesté mon oncle, et par l'intermédiaire de son Excellence Reschid Pacha, ministre des affaires étrangères, je fut nommé commandant des troupes de Silistrie, composées d'infanterie, cavalerie, et artillerie; et de plus je fus chargé d'établir une colonie dans les fameuses plaines de Dobrige Ovasse. Mais je m'aperçus en Silistrie, aussi bien que dans les provinces que j'avais traversées, qu'il existait la plus grande confusion et les abus les plus crians dans les administrations civiles et militaires, ainsi que dans tout le système gouvernemental, et que la gangrène de ces abus avait miné et détruit le bonheur du peuple et le pouvoir du souverain ; car ceux qui gouvernaient en son nom, enflé d'orgueil, et agissant plutôt comme ennemi du peuple que dans son intêret, était en général des hommes sans éducation et de l'origine la plus basse, pratiquant dans leur ignorance des cruautés inouies, croyant par-là décevoir leur souverain, ou ceux qui venaient le représenter. Lorsque je découvris un système aussi pernicieux, qui devait amener la ruine de l'empire et de ma maison, mon cœur déchiré ne put le voir et le tolérer plus longtems. Je pris la résolution de me rendre à Constantinople, pour exposer à sa majesté mon oncle le mal qui existait, et l'aider de mes conseils pour y apporter un remède ; et quoique je fusse assez heureux pour gagner la faveur du Sultan et des principaux personnages, cependant je ne pus parvenir à leur faire adopter les moyens que je proposais en faveur de ma patrie bien aimée, en tâchant de leur faire abandonner les principes pernicieux sur lesquels ils fondaient la base du gouvernement, et les changer pour un système pacifique, qui fût favorable à la civilisation. Mais tous mes efforts furent vains, de sorte que, désespérant de réussir, et fatigué d'une lutte semblable, je pris le parti enfin de faire connaître mon origine à sa majesté mon oncle, et de reprendre de ses mains les rênes du gouvernement, dont il ne savait pas diriger la marche, et par ce moyen sauver ma patrie et l'honneur de ma race. Dans cette intention je quittai Constantinople, pour me rendre en Europe, d'où je fis connaître à sa majesté et mon origine et mes intentions pour le bonheur de la nation ; mais la mort, qui ne respecte aucun être, nous l'a enlevé ; et j'espère qu'il sera plus heureux dans les régions célestes qu'il ne le fut sur la terre, où sa vie était abreuvée de douleurs ; et je remercie la Providence de m'avoir préservé l'honneur, en me sauvant de la tache d'être la cause de quelque catastrophe, quelque coupable qu'il fut à mes yeux.

TRANSLATION.

From the moment that almighty God created in heaven the star which was to mark my existence, and since the day of my birth till I was eleven years of age, still a child, I knew nothing, I had seen nothing, except the tears of my much-beloved and ever-honoured mother, who, possessing a heavenly soul in the midst of continual grief, had only been able to teach me to love her and to participate in her sorrows. I also learned (without having ever seen him) that my well-beloved emperor and father had been assassinated by his own brother, who thereby imprinted on the forehead of my uncle a stain of blood which nothing can ever wipe off during his life, and which will darken his memory when he shall have joined his ancestors in eternity. I also learned that, at the time of the massacre of the innocent ladies of the harem, that almighty

Providence which had granted me being, had used the instrumentality of the very hand of one of the assassins to save the life of my tender mother; a barbarous assassin, who evinced sentiments of generosity and humanity superior to those of an uncle whose hands were imbrued with blood; an emperor by force, but in truth an assassin, who bathed himself in the blood of his own family. From this time, although a child, my young heart experienced all the anguish suggested by such a tragedy; and referring to my poor father, whom my eyes had never had the happiness of seeing, but whom my heart could imagine, I detested the horrible action of my uncle. As a child I participated in the griefs of my royal mother, who was the object of my most devoted affection in my infancy, of my respect and love in my adolescence, and my only consolation in my manhood. But alas! a little while after this, the grief which consumed her terminated the life of this august lady, and her soul flew, as I believe and hope firmly, to the regions of eternal happiness. She left to me by right of inheritance the rights of an imperial prince,—a title which divine power gave me, and which no human power can contest with me, and of which I cannot be deprived without a crime; but at the same time she bequeathed to me profound grief and pain, the bitterness of which no human power can soften. She left me also a superficial covering whom no one but myself could tear; she left me a feeling of vengeance of which I alone can know the depth; she left me diamonds, proofs of the imperial munificence of her august spouse the sultan and her lover; she left me papers written with her own august hand;—add to this, she confided me to the care, prudence, and protection of Joaniza, a man of about seventy years of age, who had outlived his wife and children; a person devoted and faithful in the service of my mother, and grateful for the kindness and beneficence she had bestowed on him during her life. She recommended him to take me to Constantinople, being careful not to allow either my name or my birth to be known; to give me an Ottoman education as brilliant as possible; and when I had attained my majority, to declare openly my rights, and induce me to assert them. Thus it was that the fondest of mothers died in hopes, which, however, were not realised; for " man proposes, and God disposes." The honest Ottoman, faithful executor of the orders of his benefactress, endeavoured to take me to Constantinople, regardless of his own infirmities or his advanced age. Soon after the death of my mother we left Caffa, a town in the Crimea, where her holy imperial remains now repose. We arrived at Odessa, with the intention of proceeding to the capital where my ancestors had reigned; but we were detained on our voyage by the arbitrary government of Russia, which allows no subject to pass the frontier; and this in spite of the old Joaniza being descended from a family of Moldavia, and having become a subject of Russia in consequence of a residence of several years in that empire, where justice is unknown. After having been detained three years in this city, the good old man terminated his career; and I remained, at the age of fifteen, isolated, without protection and without a single friend. I then first felt the full force of the deplorable situation in which I found myself placed. I recalled to mind the last words of my noble mother, which the good old man often used to repeat to me; and it was then that vengeance really took possession of my heart; and having laid my plans, I implored with tears the protection only of God, and placing all my confidence in him, I called prudence and courage to my aid, a n left the city accompanied by a Greek named Macris, who was proceeding by way of Trieste to the Morea, as he said, to serve his country. Arrived at Bulta, the cunning Jews discovered that the relations existing between me and my companion were somewhat mysterious, for having no passport I counted on his prudence; but although I purchased the goodwill of these Jews at a dear price, the wretches did not the less follow the suggestions of their evil dispositions to duplicity; which coming to my knowledge, I left the city and my companion, and reached Mozilow on the Dniester alone. There I was pretty quiet, and did every thing in my power to gain the friendship of every one, and to learn all I could. There I learned a little Polish; and thence I went to Lozensk, where I obtained by chance a Greek document of Elefthery, a kind of passport, which enabled me, at an after period, to travel in Russia in disguise, and to be admitted into the best society of that empire. I was even enabled to study its strength and its politics, its laws, and the weakness of its resources; in a word, I could correctly understand its government. I saw there the powerful enemy of my country, and consequently of my heart. At last I left Russia for Poland, where I found that warlike people, so brave and so generous, with its brilliant army. From that time I began to attach myself to the theory and the tactics of their army, and reached my eighteenth year knowing perfectly the astute politics of Russia; and penetrated with the sufferings which my native country endured in consequence of the revolt of the Greeks, I was compelled to leave Poland in consequence of suspicions I had caused in the police; and I passed into Gallicia with the intention of proceeding into Moldavia, and thence to the capital of my ancestors; but at Lembergh I was asked in the hotel at which I put up whence I came; and not wishing to satisfy them on this point, or rather fearing the Russian government, I answered, that I came from Moldavia, without thinking of the consequences that might result therefrom. When I was asked where I had performed quarantine, I stammered and replied "No where." This answer astonished every body, and they told me that I should be hung for having evaded this precautionary measure. This I easily understood; but being unwilling to be treated as guilty without having committed any crime, I left the town, and, under the wing of Divine Providence, I reached without impediment the town of Jassay in Moldavia, which forms a part of the empire governed by my uncle. There, reflecting on my situation, I often lamented my fate. In a short time I learnt the Moldavian language, the only advantage I obtained by my stay here. I started for Constantinople, impelled by vengeance, and forming imaginary projects of battles and victories. With my head full of these dreams, I journeyed, and thus I found myself launched in the midst of a nation strange to me, although in the country of my birth. With manners and customs all new to me, and whilst I was studying this new country, the war broke out with Russia in the years 1828 and 1829. I was unconscious of every thing, and thought it my duty to take part against the aggressors of my country.

I then saw the army of the Turks—lions in courage, honest by nature, but commanded by generals as ignorant as lambs, without possessing the softness of the latter, who, in their vanity, thought themselves born to govern. I could but pity them, and weep over my country, and over the unhappy results which took place at Adrianople, and which I considered as a punishment inflicted by Providence on my uncle, the Sultan Mahmood. It was then that I visited the tomb of my revered and legitimate emperor, my well-beloved parent, and shed filial tears ; and seeing his assassin placed in such critical circumstances, this horrible portrait recalling to mind the dreadful tragedy in which my father had lost his life, I lost my senses, and I dreamt of nothing but vengeance. But unhappy is the individual who makes an idol of this passion. Finding myself in my native country, I could not help being witness of the activity that my uncle employed in civilising it, and in reforming existing abuses, and approved of his good intentions; but unfortunately he could not communicate to others that with which he was himself unacquainted — as the sequel shewed: his ideas were noble and generous; but he was ignorant of the basis on which to found them. I cannot express the tumult of my emotions. I burned with vengeance, but was withheld by prudence and the love of my country, which I thought I ought to save, but not disturb by revolution; so I decided that my hatred of the man should not induce me to impede him in the path of reform which he had taken, but that I would rather second him as the emperor of my adored country. To do this, it was necessary to be better acquainted with our empire; and I passed into Asia to examine the materials of which this great nation is composed; and having satisfied my curiosity on this point, I returned to the capital, with the intention of being useful to my country. It was requisite to be acquainted with the elements of the government. I made the acquaintance of all the friends of my father, as also of those who corresponded with my noble mother, to whom I had letters from her, and who became my real friends, and who are still so. Afterwards I made the acquaintance of the Reis Effendi, and the interpreter of the Sublime Porte. They became my real friends; and trusting to their friendship, I confided to the latter my secret, my name, my birth, and what were my projects.

The good man—an honest Mussulman—was struck with astonishment, and after a little reflection, he expressed himself in the following terms, his eyes wet with tears: " Prince, trust in God, but never in men. Conceal your imperial origin, and follow your pacific intentions; love your country, and God will help you. As for me, I shall be devoted to you to my last moment; but do not forget that your life is in danger, and that it is your duty to preserve it for your country; may prudence therefore guide you, and may God protect you." I followed his advice, and made a great many friends in a short time.

Hosref Pasha, who was then general-in-chief, and who was at that time ignorant of my origin, confided to me the command of a regiment of cavalry that was to be formed at Adana. Arrived at this place, I occupied myself in recruiting for soldiers; and when I had the number required, I received the order to train them as infantry, which I did with the greatest zeal. I contracted here a fraternal friendship with Hagi Ali Bey, governor of the place, and son of the famous Hassan Pasha of Adana.

Hagi Bey had under him about 19,000 horsemen, the bravest, I think, in the world, and entirely at his disposal and at mine. This was the most propitious moment for revenging the death of my father; but having already resolved upon serving my country in assisting and participating in the reform that it required, I persisted in my resolution of not disturbing my uncle in his projects. Some time after, as I had a decided taste for the cavalry service, I asked permission to go to Constantinople, in order to make an exchange, and pass from the infantry to the cavalry; and having received the authorisation I had requested, I returned to the capital.

Besides the apartments at the Seraskier's, I took private lodgings at

Pera, in order to find myself in connexion with Europeans, and to learn French. A little while after, people came to me, and to my great surprise, they called me Moszinski; and although I declined the honour done me, all I could say to the contrary was useless; and soon, in spite of myself, all Pera called me by this name, complimenting me on being so well with the Turkish government, and which motive occasioned me persecutions by Russia; but the motive for this was quite imaginary.

One day in my absence, the great fire at Pera took place; and when, like every one else, I went to save my effects, I arrived and found every thing reduced to cinders. Near to the place I perceived a Greek woman alone and unassisted. The fire had already reached her house; her unprotected state excited my compassion; and with the assistance of my servants, I saved her life and her most valuable effects; her own servants had abandoned her to her fate in order to pillage the house. After I had put in safety what we had saved in the house of Mr. Black, which is of stone, I led this lady, still much frightened, to a house at a distance from the conflagration. I there asked her for her keys, in order to go and bring her her jewels, money, and papers, because I thought it prudent she should have them in her possession, for fear that in such confusion they might be lost. I perceived that she was frightened, and feared to trust a stranger. She, however, with tears in her eyes, and a feminine grace, consigned them to me. I left her, and proceeded immediately to the house of Mr. Black; but fortunately for her, I met some strangers who were carrying away her trunks, which they had stolen in the confusion; and although I was not certain of the fact, I stopped the rascals, and opened the trunks with the keys she had given me. I took out from them her jewels and papers, and placed the rest of the things in safety at the house of Mr. Bersolesy. I then returned to the afflicted Mariora (for that was her name), and consigned to her her jewels and papers, which she had thought lost, and which chance alone had made me discover. Mariora, surprised at such an incident, and pleased with the honesty, as she said, of a stranger, thanked me in the most gracious manner, expressing her gratitude, and saying that it was impossible that I could be one of the Christians of the country, for the probity and generosity I had evinced was very rare among them. And yet I thought I had only done my duty. I then ordered my own servants to procure a house in Arnaut Kivy, as she desired; and having caused what was saved from the fire to be taken there, I accompanied her to the house which had been prepared for her reception; but scarce had we reached it when her tears began to flow again. I asked her the cause of her grief; and she answered me with that delicacy which appertains only to a lady of distinction, that henceforth she could no longer taste of happiness, as her reputation had been compromised by my having accompanied her, which was contrary to their usages. Her tears caused me great emotion, and even a more tender feeling; and like a giddy, foolish young man as I was, in order to protect her from the calumnies of the Greeks, I offered to marry her (as the Mussulman law permits a man to marry a woman of whatever religion she may be); Mariora replied that she accepted willingly such a destiny, even though I was not a Greek. Mariora was the dearest object of my heart.

One day Hosref Pasha informed me that the revolution in Poland was making progress, and that the Russian army had been beaten several times. He asked me if I had travelled in Poland, and questioned me particularly regarding this brave nation, and whether I knew the language. Having satisfied him on all points, he thought proper to send me to Poland. I must be allowed to preserve silence upon the object of my mission. According to his orders, I started for Belgrade with letters addressed by Hosref Pasha to Hussein Pasha, governor of that town, who immediately wrote to Vienna to obtain permission to have the quarantine shortened for me if possible. This was granted; but unfortunately I heard that the Russians had entered Warsaw, and that the Polish government existed no more; and although a Turk myself, I pitied sincerely that brave and noble nation; but in order not to excite suspicions, I proceeded to Vienna with the intention of passing on to Trieste, and thence to Constantinople. After having received during several days the greatest marks of favour from his majesty the Emperor of Austria and the nobles of Vienna, I was arrested, with all my suite (as is mentioned in the journal *le Messager des Chambres*, under date of the 27th Jan. 1832); and when I was questioned, I did not think proper to answer their questions on the subject o my mission, and I perceived by their conduct and their insidious queries that they took me for a noble Pole, and I was obliged to grant that I was so, because I was assured that without such an avowal nothing could make me recover my liberty. It was not difficult for me to confirm this disguise, as I knew the language, and did not hesitate to encourage them in their opinion in order to avoid further suspicions. They created for me in their imagination a family—father, mother, brothers, and sisters, and a large circle of relations, and added to this domains and other riches, which they said belonged to me in Poland. I was sorry that all this was only ideal; when all at once an *estafette* arrived with dispatches regarding me from Constantinople, just in time to annihilate my newly acquired family and property. About twelve o'clock at night I was sent for by Prince Metternich; and at the end of my conference with him, he told me that I was free, and that the Emperor, as well as himself, regretted extremely the error that had been committed regarding me; he loaded me with compliments, and said that I was free to prosecute my journey, and that his majesty the Emperor of Austria would always think of me with pleasure. I offered them my thanks, which were due rather to the *estafette*. Leaving Vienna, I passed by way of Trieste to Constantinople. The same morning of my arrival Namick Pasha, then Namick Bey, invited me to go to the Seraskier, who, he said, wished to see me immediately. I went to him at once, and after much ceremonious politeness I was taken to prison, or rather to a horrible dungeon. I could not understand either the infamous conduct of the Seraskier or what could be the cause of my imprisonment; not being of a wicked character myself, I could only suspect that the interpreter of the Sublime Porte (who knew my story) had betrayed me. But here I was unjust. Believing that I was destined to suffer the same fate as my unfortunate father, I murmured against Him who had created me in order to make me terminate my days in such a cruel manner in this horrible prison. Twenty times a day a proximate death was announced to me, and with all my courage, I was at times cast down and fearful. I could reckon on no assistance; a miracle only could save me; and my conscience reproaching me with no crime nor dishonourable action, made me hope for a happier future; for I was free although a prisoner; so true is it that a pure conscience cannot be restrained by the thick walls of the darkest dungeon. One day, overwhelmed with despair, the faithful servants of Hosref Pasha, his Selichtar Aga and an Armenian Marderake, worthy instruments of such a master and of their vile nature, envious of the goods of their neighbour, perceived that I possessed diamonds, the same which had belonged to my beloved mother. As they coveted their possession, they, without further ceremony, proposed to me to give them these brilliants as a price for my liberty; and although it was very painful for me to deprive myself of these relics of my dear mother, I would have sacrificed the half of my existence to save the other half, for I could not describe the tortures I endured in this dreadful prison. I therefore gave them three diamonds and some money, and these two wretches told me that it was all for the pasha himself, and that consequently I could count on my liberty. I believed them; but it was vain for me to hope for liberty, for these hypocrites had deceived me, and I remained a prisoner without hope. By their order my captivity was rendered more insufferable; and fearing one day that they intended to take possession of the two other diamonds that remained with me, and of papers written by my august mother, I adopted a plan for saving these. This was to put them into a bottle, which I buried at a depth of upwards of three feet in my prison, where they have ever since remained; for I could not take them up again without creating suspicions that would have led to disagreeable consequences.

One day a drunken Greek was brought into prison for a debt of forty-nine piastres; and seeing me, he began to speak in his language, asking me what a gentleman like me could have to do in such a place. "What crime," said he, "can you have committed?" I answered him that the imaginary crime for which I was detained would cost me my life. "Heavens!" exclaimed this desperate man; "pay my debt, sir, and you shall not perish." Anxious to do a good action, I paid the small sums for which he had been arrested. After this he fell asleep; and on awaking, he said: "Well, sir, I and fifty palicaris, whom I have at my orders, will come to-night and deliver you." I put no faith in what this man said; but it came into my mind to make him instrumental to my project. I wrote in the Greek language to the French ambassador, beseeching him to save my life; and I then gave him the letter, which he fortunately delivered. The French *chargé d'affaires*, M. le Baron de Varen, immediately did all that depended on him, and by means with which I am unacquainted he obtained in a few days my liberty. I certainly owe my life to this noble Frenchman. During my imprisonment, the Russians, who neglected nothing to persecute me, and the Greeks and the Patriarchs, had succeeded in separating me for ever from my beloved Mariora, under the pretext that, being born a Greek, she could not marry a man who did not profess the same religion. Burning with rage against Hosref Pasha, and against all the events to which I had been a victim, I left for Egypt, and entered into the service of Mahmed Ali; and I received the grade of general instructor and inspector of all the cavalry, and a little while after of aide-de-camp to Ibrahim Pasha, as is mentioned in No. 1 of the *Révue Britannique* for the month of January, 1834. But it grieved me to serve under a man who was making war against my uncle, that is, against my family and my interests; so I obtained permission to come to Europe for my health, and did not return to act against the interests of my family and of my country. Since then I have travelled in Europe and America for my instruction; but every where I have been subjected to the persecutions of the Holy Alliance, whose calculations were foiled because they could not discover my origin, nor the object of my travels. I have studied the English and French languages; and I resolved to serve my country under an *incognito*. I have several times been to Constantinople in disguise, and finished as before by entering into the military service. By order of his majesty my uncle, and by means of his Excellency Reschid Pasha, minister for foreign affairs, I was named commander of the troops in Silistria, composed of infantry, cavalry, and artillery; and further, I was charged with the order to establish a colony in the famous plains of Dobrige Ovass. But I perceived that in Silistria, as well as in the provinces that I had traversed, there existed the greatest confusion and the most striking abuses in the civil and military administrations, as well as in all the system of government, and that the gangrene had undermined and destroyed the happiness of the people and the power of the sovereign; for those who governed in his name, inflated with pride, acted more like the enemies of the people than as their protectors; and were, generally speaking, men without education, and of the lowest classes, practising, in their ignorance, the most unheard-of cruelties, and believing that they would thereby deceive their sovereign, or those who came to represent him. When I discovered such a pernicious system, which must have led to the ruin of the empire and of my family, my heart, torn by such sights, could no longer tolerate them. I resolved to go to Constantinople in order to expose the evil to his majesty my uncle, and to assist him with my advice in remedying such a state of things. But although I was fortunate enough to gain the favour of the Sultan, and of the principal personages of the government, I could not succeed in making them adopt the means that I proposed in favour of my beloved country, by seeking to make them abandon the pernicious principles on which they based the foundation of their government, and to change them for a pacific system, that might be favourable to civilisation. All my efforts were so futile, that despairing of success, and fatigued with the struggle, I decided at last on making known my origin to his majesty my uncle, and to take from his hands the reins of government, which he did not know how to direct, and thus to save my country and the honour of my race. With this intention I left Constantinople. To this effect I passed into Europe, whence I made known to his majesty my origin and my intentions for the happiness of the nation; but death, which spares no one, took him from us; and I trust that he will be happier in the celestial regions than he was on earth, where his life was steeped in sorrow; and I thank Providence for having preserved my honour by saving me from the shame of being the cause of any catastrophe, however culpable he might have been in my eyes.*

* Long after I had written that which relates to the "Turkish pretender," in the

B.

PETITION OF NADIR BEY.

Agli Eccellentissimi Ambasciatori delle illustre Potenze Cristiane della Europa presso la Corte di sua Maestà il Rè delle due Sicilie.

ECCELLENTISSIMI SIGNORI,—Quantunque la penna sia debole a descrivere il mio penoso destino, spero però, che il loro scelto giudizio, dono felice dei sapienti rappresentanti, sapra intenderne la sostanza.

Io l' infelice Principe Imperiale Achmed Nadir, nato nelle amarezze e le stragi del 1808, in cui fu vittima mio augusto e assai compianto padre, sono stato da lungo tempo perseguito e sospetto, parte per aver celato l'origine mio onde sconcertare i progetti dei malvaggi e degli

---

body of the work, and since my return to England, a friend has pointed out to me that this mysterious personage has already been introduced to my countrymen by Miss Isabella Romer, in a paper entitled "Some Account of the Turkish Pretender," published in Colburn's *New Monthly Magazine*, No. 233, for May 1840; and I avail myself of the opportunity thus afforded to give some further details of the impressions received of so strange a character by that clever and accomplished traveller and authoress.

"If 'travellers see strange sights' in the course of their wanderings, it is quite as natural a consequence that they should also meet with very strange people. In my late tour in the East, it happened that I came in contact with more than one personage of that description; and as their names have since come before the public through newspaper renown, I feel that I am not guilty of any breach of good-feeling in making use of them in the present instance.

"Since the death of Sultan Mahmoud, and during the last few months, I have frequently seen allusions made in the newspapers to a personage who had lately appeared at Malta, and had excited great curiosity and a certain degree of interest in the public mind there, from the romantic character under which he had presented himself to the authorities of that place—no less a one than that of rightful heir to the sabre of Othman, and pretender to the Turkish throne! The story upon which he grounds his claims to such high destinies is, that when Sultan Mustapha (the brother and predecessor of the late Sultan Mahmoud) was deposed and murdered after a brief reign of a few months, a general massacre followed of the ladies of the imperial harem, as the natural consequence of such an event; the bowstring and the sack did their dreadful duty, and the waves of the Bosphorus closed over the unresisting victims. One sultana, however, who was *enceinte* at the time, contrived by some wonderful means to escape the fate of her companions, and in due time became the mother of a son, whom she brought up in the strictest privacy. That boy was Nadir Bey, the person in question —so at least runs the story which he is represented to have told at Malta of his birth and parentage; and I have heard that many persons there fully believed in its truth, and that some even have been found sufficiently confiding to advance him large sums of money to assist in the furtherance of his designs.

"It chanced that on my return from Constantinople to Vienna, in 1838, this identical Nadir Achmet Bey (as he then styled himself) was one of my fellow-passengers on board the Austrian steamer in which I crossed the Black Sea; and he just remained long enough with us to create universal astonishment at his acquirements, and to *intriguer* every one on board most completely as to who or what he could be;

interessati, e parte per amor della patria e dei miei ben amati parenti imperiali ; locche spero non essere delitto in me.

Appena credei il momento propizio ai miei interessi, lasciai il servizio militare di mio zio il fu Sultano Mahmud II. ; il quale regnava allora, ed arrivando in Europa, feci noto la mia nascità, ed il mio diritto al trono. Questo passo non mi giovò punto, attesa la repentina morte del Imperatore mio zio. Da quel momento avvisato dai miei amici, che l'attuale Imperatore mio cugino, profittando della mia lontananza, si era impadronito del impero, ed in seguito per mia somma disgrazia, ed al suo poco onore, ha cercato con ogni mezzo di screditarmi in faccia al

for it seemed to be unanimously decided that he must be any thing but that which he represented himself. I, of course, shared in the general curiosity ; and several pages of my journal were consequently devoted to especial mention of his sayings and doings, and the various speculations to which his presence gave rise among the passengers of the Ferdinando Primo. He came on board in the Golden Horn, accompanied by one of the Armenian bankers of the court, at the precise moment I did, and a very few minutes before the paddles were set in motion, and that we dropped down the Bosphorus to take in more passengers at Therapia and Buyukderé. His companion remained with him to the last moment, and then returned in his caique to Seraglio Point ; while Nadir Bey, left to himself, paced the deck alone for a short time, apparently in deep thought.

"He was dressed in the Turkish uniform, which had been adopted by the Sultan and his officials throughout the empire, namely the Fez cap and blue military surtout ; but his countenance and bearing were so unlike an Osmanli, his clothes so much better made, his firm step and military carriage so different from the shuffling lounging gait of every Turk I had ever before seen, that I at once concluded he must be one of the numerous German military instructors then resident at Pera, whom the Sultan had induced to enter his service, in order that they might organise his army according to European tactics. In short, nothing about him *trahissoit le Turc*, except his beard, which was a genuine Oriental one.

"We had scarcely cleared the Golden Horn, and the various passengers scattered in groups about the deck were admiring the gorgeous appearance produced by the innumerable domes and minarets of Stamboul steeped in the golden light of an eastern morn, and rising proudly above the groves of solemn cypresses which are interspersed among the buildings, and form so picturesque a characteristic of all Oriental cities— when Nadir Bey approached the English party of which I formed one, and with the ease and politeness of high breeding, quite divested of forwardness, addressed us in very good English, spoken without hesitation, but with a foreign accent. He expressed great surprise that an English woman should have trusted herself among the barbarous Turks ! And when I eagerly vindicated their national character from the aspersions which I conceived a prejudiced stranger to be unworthily casting upon it, he thanked me for the partial view I had taken of his country-people, and to the great surprise of our little group, announced himself to be an Asiatic Turk, a native of Caramania.

"'But where,' he was asked, 'did you learn English ? From your manner of speaking it, you must have passed some years in England, and have applied yourself to it at a very early age.' 'No,' he answered, 'I studied it in my own country, and not until I was twenty-two years of age' (he appeared then to be scarcely thirty). 'I never was in England before last year, when I passed four months there with our ambassador, Reschid Pacha ; my life has been passed in Turkey, and if my several absences from it were put together, they would not amount in all to a year and a half,'

mondo, impiegando da per tutto spie per sorvegliarmi, e numerosi assassini per trucidarmi, io per evitargli un tal delitto, ho viaggiato incognito sul continente dell' Europa, reputata essere civilizzata, ospitale, ed umana, onde trovarvi asilo e sicurezza. Ho trovato in vece una continua ed incompreensibile persecuzione.

Per involarmi a qualunque ricerche, condiscesi adottarmi nome plebeo, ch' ad ogni ora tradiva il mio sangue ed il mio aspetto; cagionando vieppiù sospetti e per conseguenza rigori maggiori.

Lasciando nelle mani d'Iddio il mio destino, io sperava di trovare pace ed asilo nel regno felice di sua Maestà il Rè delle due Sicilie;

"He spoke with great delight of the short *séjour* he had made in England, discoursed with considerable shrewdness upon the peculiarities he had remarked in the social structure there, and admired the perfection to which education has been brought.

"Nadir Bey was led by easy transitions to speak of public affairs, and his hearers soon found that he had made himself master of the politics of Europe, and had especially given his attention to fathoming the intricacies and double-dealing of Russian diplomacy, of which he spoke in a strain of the bitterest invective.

"But Nadir Bey presently took occasion to tell us that he was only going as far as Varna in the steamer, and that there horses and attendants awaited to take him by land to Silistria, where he had business to transact from the Porte with the pacha of that place.

"Some of the passengers having joined our group who did not understand English, the conversation was then carried on in French and Italian, and we found that Nadir was still more conversant with those languages than with the English, speaking each with the fluency and purity of a native of France or Italy. But his great triumph was reserved for the hour of dinner, and by the time that repast was concluded, nobody knew what to make of him, but every one agreed in declaring that he could not be a Turk.

"In the first place, before he seated himself at table, he took off his Fez cap (no Osmanli ever uncovers his head), and displayed a *chevelure* of luxuriant chestnut-curls, instead of the Moslem shaven crown, and the single tuft of hair, by which Azrael, the angel of death, is to draw up every true believer into Paradise. Then he sat upon his chair like any Christian, ate with a knife and fork instead of his fingers, called for a bottle of champagne, and, in short, did every thing that a Turk does not do.

"There happened to be among the cabin-passengers the natives of so many different nations, that a Babel-like confusion of tongues prevailed during dinner; but Nadir Bey, to the general surprise, appeared to possess a key to all; he conversed with each man in his own language, and by general admission proved himself to be as great a proficient in German, Greek, Russian, Polish, Hungarian, Wallachian, and Sclavaque, as he had already done in English, French, and Italian. Besides these, he assured us that he understood Persian and Arabic perfectly (the learned tongues of the Turks), which, with Turkish, made thirteen languages with which he was conversant. In short, he appeared to be a reduced copy of that Colossus of linguists, Cardinal Mezzofanti. Such acquirements—prodigious in a European *savant*—in a Turk appeared miraculous! Every body was *émerveillé* by them, and his vanity was evidently gratified by the effect he had produced, although he did not suffer himself to be elated by it into any unbecoming excitement of spirits.

"In short, when we rose from table, half the company were raving about him, and the other half tearing him to pieces.

"The Englishmen united in pronouncing him to be a 'wonderful fellow, whoever he might be,' but inclined to fancy him an agent of Russia, sent purposely on board

stato pacifico e neutro negli affari dell'Oriente; proponendomi di vivervi quietamente; ma anche quest' ultimo progetto, pare aver recato offesa alle Potenze Europee, le quali me lo negano in questo momento, probabilmente colla loro influenza.

Emminentissimi Signori, additemi vi prego qual delitto in me tanto v'offende? Di tutta la mia vita qual fatto ha potuto dar ombra o offendere qualunque Potenza Europea? *Nessuna*. Per cui dopo esservi persuasi del mal inteso, vi prego cessare di perseguitarmi, ma anzi stendere l'ospitalità dei vostri sovrani di cui siete gli onorevoli rappresentanti, ad un prence la cui sola colpa sta nell' essere infelice. Pure non

---

the steamer to *jaufiler* himself with the various strangers he met there, and to gather and turn to account the opinions that escaped from them in the flow of conversation, unchecked by the suspicion that ' a chiel was near them taking notes.'

"As for myself, I knew not what to make of him. Certainly he was unlike every Osmanli I had ever before had any communication with, for that race are proverbially slow of speech, and omit their sentences and their ideas at such long intervals from each other, ruminating so long upon the answers they receive to them, that I always fancied they must fear that a *mental indigestion* would be the consequence of attempting to get on faster. Now this man possessed fluency of language, and a flow of ideas which I had no where seen in the East.

"But, after all, of what consequence could it be to any one there *what* the stranger really was? And I checked in myself an approach to that which I have always condemned in others, and which is but too much the way of the world; namely, a desire to cry down whatever baffles our penetration, and to attribute bad motives to that which is withheld from our confidence; and with perfect indifference as to whether Nadir Bey were Moslem or Christian, spy or statesman, renegade or Osmanli, and a full recognition that whichever of these might be his real character, his talents must remain unquestionable, I proceeded to take my coffee upon deck, where he very soon joined our party.

"We spoke of Sultan Mahmoud and of his accomplishments, his talent as a versifier (for the sultan was accounted one of the most eminent poets in the empire), and the grace and eloquence which he lavished upon his hattischeriffs, which were always written by himself. His highness was also said to be a good musician, and had composed several charming ballads. Nadir Bey insisted upon the high moral qualities of the sultan, his justice, moderation, and humanity—his unwillingness to spill human blood.

"Nadir Bey's admiration of the Sultan amounted to enthusiasm; but he admitted that circumstances rendered it difficult for him to be an impartial judge, and that he could see no imperfections in one who had bestowed upon himself so many signal proofs of favour and esteem. He then told us that the Sultan had just presented him with sixty leagues of territory, extending from the banks of the Danube to the foot of the Balkan mountains in Bulgaria, and that he was then on his way to take possession of it. I asked him if any government was attached to this large grant of land, but he answered, none—that he was not a pacha—that his civil rank was that of Bey (or prince)—his military rank that of general of artillery, and that he had formerly been aide-de-camp to the celebrated Hussein Pacha, and as such had served under him in the Syrian campaign of 1832. In that capacity he had been sent by Hussein to Lady Hester Stanhope, to assure her of his protection, and to place a guard at her disposal; he had passed a day and night in the mountain residence of the noble recluse; and on

voglio credere le Potenze Europee capaci direttamente o indirettamente di voler spingermi verso il coltello pronto a troncare la mia testa.

Tutti i sospetti che hanno potuto dar motivo sul conto mio, sono immaginarii ; e le credo essere i seguenti : l'Inghilterra mi crede segretamente alleato alla Russia, la Russia mi crede unito colla Francia, e la Francia coll' Inghilterra ; l'Austria poi può pensare ch' io sia con tutt' e tre. Questa diffidenza mi cagiona l'inimicizia individuale di ogni Potenza, reducendosi poi ad una persecuzione generale.

In mia diffesa ho il piacere di dire, che sono sin' oggi libero di ogni obligazione, non avendo mai avuto impegno politico con qualunque

his return was asked by Hussein, whether he wished to marry her, in which case he (the Pacha) would summon her to bestow her hand upon him, never dreaming that the eccentric and high-minded old lady could offer any objection to such an arrangement.

"Neither Nadir Bey or his auditors appeared to grow weary of each other, and night came on before the *conversazione* broke up.

"The next morning we anchored off Varna, and the accomplished Turk, taking leave of us, went on shore there.

"Nothing particular happened during the first few days of our passage up the Danube; but at Silistria, where we anchored for some hours, we were, to our great surprise, rejoined by Nadir Bey, who had taken what we supposed to be a final leave of us several days before at Varna. He came to the place of embarkation on horseback, surrounded by the Pacha of Silistria's attendants on foot, and followed by a servant of his own, holding on his wrist a splendid tame falcon. The master, the man, and the bird were the only individuals of the party, however, who were to be our fellow-passengers, and the pleasant recollections of the early part of our voyage across the Black Sea led every one on board to give them a most cordial welcome.

"Nadir Bey told us that he should go as far as Rustchuck with us, where the business of taking possession of his territory would require his presence for some days, and that *chemin faisant* he should have an opportunity of shewing us that part of his new acquisition which lay upon the Bulgarian side of the Danube between Silistria and Rustchuck, and where he proposed to build several villages. He was, if possible, more agreeable than he had previously shewn himself, and up to the hour of dinner, nothing could surpass the harmony that reigned throughout the whole party."

Miss Romer concludes:

"Nadir Bey disembarked at Rustchuck, and we saw no more of him. The next time I heard his name alluded to was more than a year afterwards, when, in a letter from Constantinople, it was stated that the public attention there had lately been occupied with the sudden disappearance of that mysterious personage Nadir Bey, who, after contriving to make himself master of all the secrets of Turkish policy, had fled, no one knew whither. By some he was supposed to be a spy of Mehemet Ali's—by others, a Polish renegade, secretly employed in the interests of Russia—that he understood almost every European language; but no one had ever ascertained to what nation he belonged.

"I forgot to mention that, on the preceding day, when every body was complimenting him on his proficiency in English, one of the gentlemen inquired whether he wrote the language as well as he spoke it ? and upon his replying in the affirmative, I requested he would give me his autograph in English and in Turkish, to add to my collection. The gentleman already alluded to furnished him with a pencil and a flyleaf from his note-book, and in five minutes Nadir Bey presented me with his signature,

Potenza Europea; nemmeno ho offerto, nè progettato, nè mai cercato tale alleanza; dichiaro allo stesso tempo che se mi fosse anche stata offerta, non avrei mai osato accettarla; bramando arrivare al mio trono, col solo ajuto di Dio, col voler dei miei popoli e col sacro diritto mio. Nel corso dei miei viaggi in Europa, non mi sono giammai permesso di offendere o criticare i governi, le società e costumi dei Cristiani; non cercando, in quelli che ho fatto nel mio esilio, altro ch' istruirmi. In Africa ero per rivedere i miei amici, onde ottenerne una assistenza pecuniaria per il mio sostegno; non avendo nessuna speranza, ne diritto di ottenerlo dalla generosità dei Regnanti Cristiani.

In fine posso asserir loro colla sincerità di un Turco, che ho sempre rispettato e rispetto le legge e la società di ogni nazione; ne mai ho proferito parole pregiudiziose ad esse come si può rilevare dai fatti che offre la mia vita.

Essendomi spiegato coll' integrità che da me si deve, mi rimetto alla ospitalità e discrezione dei Rè Europee; pregando i loro onorevoli rappresentanti, se la generosità Cristiana può stendersi sin ad un Musulmano, di prendere in considerazione il mio stato pericoloso e intercedere unitamente presso la sua Maestà il Rè delle due Sicilie; onde mi venga accordata quella tolleranza e quel asilo, da me chiesta come sommo favore.*

TRANSLATION.

To the most illustrious Ambassadors of the Christian Powers of Europe at the Court of his Majesty the King of the two Sicilies.

MOST ILLUSTRIOUS GENTLEMEN,—Although my pen may be weak in describing my painful position, I hope that your judicious judgments, the happy gift of wise representatives, will discern the real truth.

I, the unhappy imperial Prince Ahmed Nadir, born in the revolutions of 1808, to which my august and much-lamented father was a victim, have been for a long time persecuted and suspected, partly for having concealed my origin in order to disconcert the projects of wicked

preceded by four lines in English verse, in which not a single fault of grammar, orthography, or metre was to be detected. The oriental metaphors they contained were evidence of their originality, and as they were, *of course*, very complimentary, I shall not here insert them; but I have preserved them as a literary curiosity, and a relic which may hereafter acquire additional interest, should the extraordinary personage who wrote them succeed in establishing the claims to which he now pretends, and become known to the world, not as a clever adventurer, but as the rightful ' Sultan of the Ottoman Sultans, and Master of the Two Lands and the Two Seas.' *Paris, February 1st, 1840.*"

* The above is without date, but was probably written in 1844. The mistakes that occur are such as may be excused in a foreigner.

and designing men, and partly for my love of my country and of my much-respected parents, which I trust is not a crime in me.

As soon as I thought the time propitious to my interests, I left the military service of my uncle, Sultan Mahmud II., who was then reigning, and arriving in Europe, I made known my birth and my right to the throne. This step profited me nothing, in consequence of the sudden death of my uncle the emperor. From this moment I was informed by my friends that the present emperor, my cousin, profiting by my absence, had taken possession of the empire; and subsequently he has, to his disgrace and my misfortune, endeavoured by every way to discredit me in the face of the world, employing every where spies to watch me and assassins to murder me; and in order to save him from such a crime, I have travelled incognito on the continent of Europe, which bears the reputation of being civilised, hospitable, and humane, seeking an asylum and security, instead of which I have met with continued and incomprehensible persecutions.

In order to screen myself from every requisition, I condescended to adopt a plebeian name, which my appearance and my blood belied at every instant, and thus caused suspicions, and consequently greater rigour.

Leaving in the hands of God my future destiny, I had hoped to have found peace and an asylum in the happy kingdom of his Majesty the King of the two Sicilies—a pacific state, and neutral in the affairs of the Levant. I proposed to myself to live quietly; but even this last project appears to have given offence to the European powers, who deny it to me at this moment probably with their influence.

Illustrious Sirs, point out to me, I pray you, what crime in me offends you. In all my life what deed can have given umbrage or offended any European power? *None whatever*. Therefore, after having been convinced of the existence of a misunderstanding, I beg you will cease to persecute me, and, on the contrary, extend the hospitality of the sovereigns whose honourable representatives you are, to a prince whose only fault is that of being unfortunate. I will not believe that the European powers are capable, directly or indirectly, of desiring to push me towards the knife which is ready to cut off my head.

All suspicions that may have originated on my account are imaginary, and I believe them to be the following: England thinks me secretly allied with Russia; Russia believes me united to France, and France with England; Austria may imagine that I side with all three. This mistrust in me causes me the animosity of each of the powers; and hence all unite in one common persecution.

In my own defence I have much pleasure in declaring that I am to this day free from any obligation, never having had any political engagement with any European power, nor have I ever offered, projected, or sought any such alliance; I also declare that, if it had been offered me, I should not have dared to have accepted it, being desirous to reach my throne by the assistance only of God, by the will of my people, and by my sacred right. In the course of my travels in Europe I have never permitted myself to offend or criticise the governments, the social state, or the customs of Christians, having only sought my own instruction during my peregrinations in my exile. I had passed into Africa to visit my friends and obtain pecuniary assistance for my subsistence, having no hope or right to obtain it from the generosity of reigning Christian powers.

In short, I can assure you, with the sincerity of a Turk, that I have ever respected, and do respect, the laws and customs of every nation, nor have I ever expressed a single word prejudicial to them, as may be learned by the facts that are evinced by my whole life.

Having explained myself with the integrity due by me, I remit myself to the discretion and hospitality of the kings of Europe, praying their honourable representatives (if Christian generosity may be extended to a Mussulman) to take into consideration my dangerous position, and conjointly intercede with H.M. the King of the two Sicilies, in order that that toleration and asylum may be accorded to me which I beg as the highest favour.

C.

HISTORICAL DOCUMENTS.

COPY OF A BUYURDI FROM MUHAMMED IZZET PASHA—INSURRECTION OF LATTA-
KIYAH IN 1804—STATE OF NORTH SYRIA IN 1805 AND IN 1814—PETI-
TION FROM THE CHIEF OF THE TRADES TO MR. JOHN BARKER, 1841—
NOTICE OF BADIR KHAN BEY, THE EXTIRMINATOR OF THE NESTORIAN
CHRISTIANS—STORY OF FAHAL, CHIEF OF THE ARABS OF THE ZOR, OR
FOREST DISTRICT ON THE EUPHRATES.

The subjoined documents are given partly as illustrative of the manners and peculiarities of the country, partly of the evils of an administration of provinces at a distance from the central seat of government, and which were formerly in a retrograde, rather than a progressive state of civilisation. They are also introduced with a view to shew the difference that is already manifest between the present comparatively prosperous and promising condition of the Turkish empire, and the anarchy and misrule of bygone times. The first in the list—the translation of a copy of a *buyurdi* published on the occasion of the Turks resuming the government of Syria, after the expulsion of the Egyptians—strikingly attests that the *intentions* of the Porte are most excellent, and might bear still better fruit than they do, were those intentions strictly attended to and carried out.

1841.

Translation of a copy of a buyurdi from Muhammed Izzet Pasha, Commander-in-chief at Bayrut, to the Mutsellim of Lattakiyah, obtained by the Russian consul at Bayrut, accompanied by a letter from him, and presented by the Greek Bishop at Lattakiyah.

Most honourable of Cadis, present judge of Lattakiyah, Effendi! may you be promoted! Most praised of the honourable learned, authorised to give decisions, Mufti Effendi, may your knowledge increase! Shoot of the odoriferous tree, fringe of Hashem's tiara, constant scribe of the nobles! and you, esteemed and praised, chosen in the service of the Sublime Porte, Kapuj Bashi, Mutsellim of Lattakiyah, Haznadar,

Muhammad Aga, may you be ever respected! and you, equally honoured, learned clergy and nobles, and all citizens, may your knowledge and fame increase! and all subjects in Lattakiyah resident, Muhammadans and Christians: know by these presents—

That, through the great zeal of his Highness the Sultan, proceeding from his benevolence to do all in his power to give peace and tranquillity to his subjects, under the shadow and tutelage of his Highness, among whom there are subjects of the Porte of the Greek persuasion, and others of other Christian denominations, who are either residents or sojourners in the Ottoman dominions; that all of these may partake of the charity of the Porte, in all manner of peace, and happiness, and tranquillity, and that all tyranny and oppression may be prevented in every possible way, this is in very deed the demand and desire of the Sultan, whom God preserve and protect:

Therefore, it has devolved upon me, in very truth, to seek and inquire whether they be really in felicity, because they are subjects and slaves of the Sublime Porte,—"For like unto us are they, and like them are we."* Such is the Sultan's pleasure: therefore it behoves all who are under his excellent authority, to defend their women and property the same as our women and property, and to prevent all manner of evil; and therefore we cannot cease asking and sending spies, going and coming, concerning the existence of our Christian rayas,† if they be truly in confidence and real tranquillity or not? But at the same time I have heard from some persons of veracity, going and coming, that some Turks of Lattakiyah ill-treat and annoy some of our Christian rayas, and for this reason these Christian rayas are not enjoying their wished-for tranquillity. We have been very much astonished that this should happen on the part of our Turkish rayas; and we know not in what manner, or in what way, they dare to ill-treat them, which is contrary to the intentions of the Sublime Porte, and contrary to our own; and for this they deserve condign punishment. Therefore was it necessary that we should write this circular to you all, to enjoin—

1st. We command our said Mutsellim, on the receipt of this, to call a general assembly, and to publish openly, that it may be known to all, both the great and the little, this wish of the Sublime Porte, and that

* I have not seen the original, but should rather think this is a translation of a part of the Koran quotation, wherein is said, "so were you before until God had compassion on you, &c."

كذلك كنتم من قبل فمن الله عليكم فتبينوا ان الله كان بماتعملون خبيرا
I quote from memory.

† Raya in Turkey means a subject.

all may be well restrained from falling in the least tittle contrary to this, and refrain from any thing that may be hurtful to any of our Christian rayas; and you, be you ever watchful in this command, with all vigilance, and both in private and public have overseers and spies; and whatever is proved to have been done by any one in the least annoying, or injurious, or hurtful, to another, do you immediately punish the same without pardon. And because, with all our heart, we desire the protection of our Christian rayas, and their tranquillity, and to prevent all manner of evil and abuse, from wherever it be, from henceforth if we hear of any ill-treatment, and you refrain from executing due punishment on the party offending, we shall not listen to your excuses in any way. There is no need of warning and commanding you further.

And we inform all, of every degree, who may be subjects of his Highness the Sultan, whom God protect and prosper, that it is necessary you all hie you to your several occupations, and gain your livelihoods, and refrain from all abuse and ill-usage, because this is contrary to the will of the Sultan and our own. And he who occupies himself with his own affairs will ever find his happiness therein; but woe to him who commits such abuses. He will find his punishment without mercy. And God says, "You have all a shepherd, and of every shepherd the sheep are demanded." Such is the will of his Highness the Sultan. Therefore pay the greatest attention, for we have now warned you, and have commanded you. For God says, "This is just;" and he will conduct you in the right way. And it is with this intent we have now written you this buyurdi, from the divan of the Commander-in-chief, that on its arrival, when you have understood it, you may act in conformity, and not contrary, but execute it to the letter, without the smallest deviation.

23 *Ramadan*, 1256. (5 *November*, 1841.)

1804.

Extract of a letter from J. Barker, Esq., dated Aleppo, 5th Sept. 1804.

" Insurrection in Lattakiyah—Proceedings of Ali Aga Ibn Rustum.

" Insurrections are become so common in the Turkish empire that a relation of such events are twice-told tales to which it is hard to draw attention. So much is said of Paswan Ughlu, Tarsanik Ughlu, Kutchuk Ali Ughlu, in every part of the Grand Signor's dominions, that a more circumstantial account of the rebels of Syria can scarcely fail to be interesting.

"Let us run over cursorily the principal events that have taken place since the death of Jizzar Pasha, of Acre.

"While Jizzar lived, his power, added to that of Ibrahim Pasha, not only maintained order in the principal cities of Syria, Damascus, and Aleppo, but in a great measure controlled petty rebels. Damascus and the country round it was kept in subjection by the same chief; and Aleppo, with its neighbouring towns, while governed by Ibrahim Pasha, was maintained in the most orderly and submissive subordination.

"But on the demise of Jizzar, Ibrahim Pasha not being able to succeed to his authority in Damascus, and in the absence of Ibrahim Pasha from Aleppo, his son Mahmud Pasha could scarcely hold the reins of government, until the Porte had time to hear of the changes taken place, and invest him with regular authority.

"While the father was endeavouring in vain to establish his authority in Damascus, the son was, on the third day after being proclaimed Pasha of Aleppo, driven out of the city by a general insurrection of the people. Ibrahim retired to Saida, near Acre, with 3000 or 4000 troops, which were, in the very improbable event of the Porte's not coming to an accommodation with Ismail Pasha for the government of Acre, to act in concert with the Capitan Pasha against that place, and the son was at a village near *Killis*, with 1000 or 2000 men skirmishing with the *Kurds* of that district, and endeavouring, hitherto in vain, to enter the latter place, which is little better than a village,* and over which his jurisdiction extends as Pasha of Aleppo.

"This general relaxation of all government has naturally annihilated trade, by exciting just alarms for the security of property; and every one is contemplating with anxiety the daily events that pass in rapid succession, to rob him of the feeble hopes of seeing once again return past days of tranquillity and comparative happiness.

"The Europeans established in these parts have hitherto been mere spectators of tyrannical oppression, because, as there is no hope of the authors of it receiving any punishment adequate to the enormity of their crimes, the example of that impunity must operate most perniciously on the minds of the people of Aleppo.

"The occurrence alluded to is as follows:—On the 31st of July last, there arrived at Lattakiyah, from Constantinople, a new governor, appointed for that place, with 200 men in his suite. He had scarcely taken possession of the government, when the old governor invited the Governor of Jisr al Shughul, named Ali Aga Ibn Rustum, to assist him

* Killis is now a goodly town, with bazaars, barracks, and numerous mosques.

in deposing the new one. Ali Aga willingly obeyed the call; took with him about 400 men, chiefly Arnauts; and, on the first day of his entering Lattakiyah, put the new governor in chains, and set up the old one in his room.

"But perceiving soon after that nothing was to be got out of a Turkish Mutsellim, who had only been ten days in the enjoyment of the emoluments of his post, he released the imprisoned governor, and turning the tables on the other, who had invited him to come to his assistance, threw him into prison, and required from him a hundred *purses*.* As far as the 24th August, the most excruciating torments had only extorted from him forty purses. He probably possesses no more.

"Ali Aga then proceeded to levy a contribution on the town, which he was desirous of fixing at 1500 purses; but after every art to mitigate his rapacity had been exhausted, he still persists in demanding 500 purses. This sum, although enormous, relative to the slender means of the inhabitants of Lattakiyah, was, under the dread of greater evils, collected in part, and laid at his feet; but it had no other effect than that of increasing his avidity, and he returned to his original demand of 1500 purses, as the price on which he consented to quit the town, threatening that if his demand was not immediately complied with, he would give up the place to be plundered by his troops.

"It now, of course, became evident that nothing less than the sack of the town could satiate the rapacity of this brutal horde of robbers; and from that moment no one thought of any thing but the means of flying from the scenes of horror that might naturally be expected to ensue; but only a few had been fortunate enough to escape, when Ali Aga's troops drew a cordon round the town, proceeded immediately to pillage the houses of the fugitives, and to throw into prison individually such of the remaining inhabitants as it was supposed, if put to the sufferance of torture, and in dread of losing their lives, would produce money.

"In this general persecution it was, that Ali Aga quartered six men at the house of each of the Europeans in the place, who consist only of Mr. Nicholas Ducci, British and Imperial agent; Mons. Geoffroy, French commissary; and a Sig. Vidal, Dutch vice-consul, which latter found means to run away, but was laid hold of, and, it is said, thrown into prison at a place called Jibali, between Lattakiyah and Tripoli.

"The business of these six ruffians was, to intimidate, by brutal usage, and by repeated threats of murder, the masters of the houses in which

* A purse contains 500p., and the piastre was then worth 15p. to 1*l*.; *ergo* 33*l*.=one purse of those days.

they were lodged, and thereby extort from them, first a contribution of 3000 piastres from M. Geoffroy, and 1500 piastres from Mr. Ducci.

"The dread of the execution of the threats with which these demands were accompanied, and the hope that they would finish there, induced them at length to comply; but, unfortunately, these persecutions were continued, and up to the 24th past, M. Geoffroy had been compelled, at different times, to disburse 11,000 piastres, and Mr. Ducci 2000 piastres.

"The advices of that date state that the outrages committed by the troops went on increasing in atrocity; that they had pillaged all the warehouses, had plundered several Christians' houses, and ravished their women; and that the tortures which those who were in the prisons were suffering were so great as to endanger their lives.

"The history of Ali Aga Ibn Rustum is succinctly thus :—His ancestors have been, for a century past, in possession of the chief consideration in the town of Jisr Shughul, about two days' journey distant from Aleppo, on the road to Lattakiyah, and thereby kept the government of the place and its vicinity in the hands of the head of their own family in spite of the Pashas of Aleppo, at whose pleasure they ought by right to hold it.

"This family had lately, by feuds and other causes, considerably declined in riches and power, and was reduced to three individuals of note—Cassim, Hussain, and Ali, the hero of this narrative, when Ibrahim Pasha, of Aleppo, about five years ago, formed the design of subduing them. He invited Ali Aga, then a mere lad of eighteen, to Aleppo. He debauched him with prostitutes, and encouraged him in the use of spirituous liquors, a vice that never fails to render a Turk the most abandoned of human creatures. He at length obtained for him, on the passage of the grand vizir through Aleppo, in 1802, an Imperial command as Aga of Jisr Shughul, on his bond for paying 200 purses, when he should have dispossessed his two elder cousins of the government. Ali soon succeeded in murdering both his relations; and, on his assuming the government, Ibrahim Pasha, not finding him so submissive as he had hoped to render him, sent first his son, Mahmud Bey (now Pasha), and afterwards his Kehya, with 3000 men, against him, but was both times repulsed with loss and disgrace.

"Ali Aga's means were, however, little adequate to the support of troops necessary for his defence in these contests; and six months ago, on a chief of 200 or 300 Arnauts quitting his service, he was obliged to put his son into the Arnauts' hands as a pawn for arrears of pay due to him. He then picked a quarrel with Jiwallik Bakir Aga, Mutsellim of Antioch, and went against that town, in hopes of being able to redeem his child by the plunder thereof. He, however, failed in that enterprise; but the grand caravan of pilgrims to Mecca happening to pass on their return to Constantinople, while he lay before Antioch, he obtained a considerable booty by *avanizing* them. He then pillaged Seleucia, modern Suedia, and most of the villages lying between Idlib and the coast, some of which he entirely laid waste. But what is particularly worthy of remark, as affording a just idea of the impoverished state of the country, is, that the fruits of all these ravages, and of those which he is now committing at Lattakiyah, are not only insufficient to enable him to raise the sum for which his son is in pawn, but even unequal to the maintenance and pay of the 400 troops now in his service (8th September). Direct advices from Lattakiyah were, a few days ago, received here up to the 30th August, at which time the persecutions suffered by Mons. Geoffroy and Mr. Ducci were carried on to the most horrible excess. The first was tormented to produce 100 purses more, and the other fifty : sums quite beyond their means.

"We had, however, yesterday the happiness to learn that Ali Aga had been defeated by another rebel, called Mukadim Adra,* inhabiting the mountains of Kastravan. This mountain chief was at the head of a numerous armed peasantry, which forced Ali Aga to fly the place; but on his endeavouring to escape, he was taken and carried back in chains to Lattakiyah.

"There is little doubt of the facts; but details are wanting to inform us of the fate of the inhabitants of Lattakiyah during the contest."

1805.

To give an idea of the then unsettled state of the Turkish government, I subjoin an extract of a letter, dated Antioch, 1 September 1805, written by John Barker, Esq.:

"You have herewith a copy of a recent letter, from which you will see the very precarious situation of Europeans in this revolted province of the Grand Seignior's nominal dominions. The existence of this empire is really a phenomenon in politics, which produces novel circumstances and new matter for reflection that confound the observer who is accustomed to compare living events with the successions of causes and effects in the revolutions recorded in the annals of past times. The Turkish empire, like the fable of Muhammad's coffin, suspended between powers of equal attraction, while sustained by the jealousy of the great

---

* Mukadim Adra was a respectable man, and chief of the Fellah, or Ansayriis, who are very powerful and numerous in those parts.

states of Europe, may be compared to a beautiful captive in the hands of a band of independent Barbary robbers, who every night retires to rest trembling at the thought of an instant assault from some ardent bandit, and every morning awakes in astonishment that another sun has risen to behold her safety. Her fond imagination ascribes the miraculous security to the interposition of Providence; and I have been triumphantly told by a Turk that the truth of the Muhammadan religion obtained an infallible evidence from the supernatural existence of the Ottoman Empire. 'I challenge you, who are a Christian and a consul,' said he, 'to produce me another example, ancient or modern, where a people, long after their power of repelling aggression had ceased, has not only been suffered to continue in the list of independent nations, but whose government is, like ours, assiduously courted, feasted, and flattered, by the ambassadors of all the powerful nations of Europe.'

"There is no part of Syria or Palestine at this time governed by a man in complete subordination to the Porte except the town of Acre, with a very small district round it, which was delivered to Sulaiman Pasha by the troops, who betrayed Ismail Pasha, the successor of Jizzar; but you know that from Acre itself a very trifling revenue can be drawn, and that without the power which Jizzar possessed of rendering the Druzes tributary, a Pasha of that place can find little scope for extortion.

"Abu Marrak Pasha, whom I described in my last letter as occupied in laying waste Palestine, is an Arab of a most atrocious character, who, while the Grand Vizier was in Egypt, was appointed to the government of Jaffa; but having been prevented taking possession by Jizzar, he came to Aleppo in the year 1801, and from thence was sent to govern one and successively another of the cities of Mesopotamia, which were then in arms to resist the entrance of a Pasha who should attempt to establish the authority of the Porte by force. He was, however, admitted, with only a few *chiuhadars* in his suite, and after remaining some time, apparently content with a nominal authority and the daily amusement of playing the gent, he formed and executed the bold design of murdering, with his own hand, while lulled in the security of a festival, almost all the chiefs of the popular faction;*

* This is by no means an unusual occurrence; and we see such constantly reported in the annals of Turkish history: note the destruction of the Janissaries at Aleppo, and of the Mamelukes in Egypt, &c. The facility with which these *coups de main* are executed proceeds from the discord of the chiefs among each other, and from the people being kept down by fear and not by *love* or *interest*. The chiefs are not the head of a *party*, but have seized the government by means of extortion, cruelty, and money.

whereby he struck such terror into the rest of the inhabitants, that they immediately submitted to be reduced literally to sell the ragged carpet which served them for bedding, in order to satisfy, or rather to feed, for nothing could satiate his cruel rapacity. By this glorious exploit he was soon distinguished by the Vizier as an excellent instrument to be employed in cases where the humanity of other pashas had broken through the black cloud of their oppression—who had paused in the direful work of desolation.

"I saw Abu Marrak again last year in his passage from Mesopotamia to Mecca, the ostensible place of his destination; but as that appointment had been forced upon him by the intrigues of his and his patron's enemies as a kind of exile, he proceeded no further than Jaffa, where last winter he played the Porte a notable trick. The Porte had sent him 300 purses by a Kapuji Bashi, who had orders to transmit to him only a few at a time and by degrees, as he might see himself that they had been actually appropriated to the defraying of expenses necessary for the prosecution of his journey to Mecca. With the first and second payments he purchased such articles as satisfied the Kapuji of his intention to proceed to his pashalik; but Abu Marrak quickly discovering his impatience to touch the whole 150,000 piastres, and the officer of the Porte endeavouring to retract, the pasha seized the Khazny at once, and thereby put an end to all further dispute. I saw the Kapuji in his passage through Antioch, on his return to Constantinople with this melancholy story, and he had, of course, a great deal to say on the subject. Since that time Abu Marrak had reared the standard of open rebellion at Jaffa, and the Porte has ordered the other pashas of Syria to send his head to Constantinople.

"These pashas are, Ibrahim Pasha, his son Mahmud Pasha, Abdallah Pasha, Sulaiman Pasha, and Abdin Pasha (of two tails). A few words on each will give you an idea of the present state of Syria.

"Ibrahim Pasha and his son. The first mentioned is a native of Aleppo, who, from the low station of a farrier, has raised himself to the possession of a considerable revenue (while the city was governed by him or his son) of two or three millions of piastres; but these tenures, without their possessing the advantage of their belonging to the Pasha, would probably not yield a tenth part of that sum. Ibrahim Pasha was lately Pasha of Damascus; that is, during two years of his residence there, he has collected the mild, not to say insignificant dues of the *miri*, spent from his private purse a considerable sum of money in conveying the pilgrims (such as they were) to Mecca, and chose to sit out the term of his government a quiet spectator of the prætorian rule of the janissaries over that city, doubtless because he had no personal interest in subduing them equal to the expense of an endeavour to effect it; and you know the Porte, like the superior of the Propaganda Fide in sending out its missionaries, never accompanies its benedictions with any adequate means of their obtaining their ends. 'There,' says the Grand Vizier on the nomination of Abdallah Pasha, successor to Ibrahim Pasha, 'there's a firman for you, with a flaming cipher of his Imperial Majesty the King of Kings, the distributor of all the crowns in the universe; go, and with the magic of this despoil the janissaries of Damascus of the fruits of their long-continued extortions.' And this said to whom? to a man who has scarcely the means of providing a regular supply of rice and butter for the subsistence of half a dozen raggamuffin chinhadars.

"Ibrahim Pasha is now appointed to the government of Diyarbakir; but he, as well as his son Mahmud Pasha, who is named for Tripoli, know much better than to waste their means in the unprofitable and probably unsuccessful enterprise of reducing those towns to subjection; and both are encamped, with one or two thousand men, at a village about ten leagues from Aleppo, where they have too great an interest to abandon easily the hope of being reinstated in its government.

"Meanwhile, however, the janissaries of that ill-fated city are fattening in the clover of supreme dominion, and quaffing its usual sweets, and full gratification of revenge, avarice, pride, lust, and ambition, which are displayed in assassinations, in general monopoly, in contempt of all constituted authorities,—mutsellims, cadis, muftis, custom-officers, and consuls,—in the violation of female and male chastity; in the view of the chiefs towards a more perfect and undivided authority. From this sketch of a picture of Aleppo, your sympathetic mind will readily fill up the dark colours of the present and future miseries of its unhappy inhabitants; *yet sure I am that, great as these sufferings are, the free voice of the people would not be in favour of a change for the government of a pasha!*

"There remains, therefore, only Sulaiman Pasha from whom the Porte can expect the head of Abu Marrak. I understand that he is besieging Jaffa, but I do not know with what prospect of success. The general idea is that Abu Marrak will not be subdued.*

* Abu Marrak, after having been defeated by Sulaiman Pasha, retired to Aleppo, where he had previously married the daughter of Ibrahim Pasha. An order from Constantinople coming for his head, he concealed himself in an *ambar*, a large box for containing provisions of barley. He was seized and strangled by the successor of Ibrahim Pasha, his father-in-law.

"As to Abdin Pasha, you will judge from the following account of his proceedings what good may be expected from him. After the death of Ali Aga Ibn Rustum, about this time last year, the mutsellim of the Porte, who had cut off that rebel, was beheaded in his turn, a few days afterwards, by one Abderrahman Effendi, who had been in usurped possession of the government of Lattakiyah several years previous to the taking of that town by Ibn Rustum. This self-erected governor enjoyed the fruits of that assassination only till May last, about which period a certain Ahmed Pasha, a man of weight, and even of humanity and justice, inhabiting Karamania, was sent to quell a rebellion in Cyprus, where he quickly re-established order and tranquillity, and afterwards sent his brother, Abdin Pasha, with about 1000 men against Lattakiyah. On his approach, all those who had assisted Abderrahman Effendi in oppressing the people immediately fled to the mountains of Kastrawan, and left him to be seized by the oppressed, who joyfully remitted the tyrant into the hands of their deliverer. But I have now to relate what is the usual course of similar events in these parts, that the Lattakiyans soon had reason to exclaim, in agonies of distress, 'Kurban din Abdarrahman Effendi!' 'Kurban Ali Aga!' a strong expression of regret at the disadvantageous change in their situation.

"The foul fame of Abdin Pasha's bad government reached Constantinople almost as soon as the head of the rebel whom he had subdued; and Ibn Chiakal Hussain, an independent man of some consideration and power, of Turkman origin, although now stationary with his tribe, which has converted its black tents into a few small villages in the neighbourhood of Lattakiyah, was named to supersede him in the government of that place, and Abdin Pasha was ordered to proceed to Jidda. But such arrangements not proving agreeable to the latter, a conflict ensued between the Turkman and the Karamanian, which has now lasted three months in bloodless skirmishes. Meanwhile, however, the work of oppression and devastation is going on to the pitch that the place is literally depopulated of men; and consequently none of the necessaries of life, not even bread or grain, is to be had there.

"Many of the fugitives, among whom are all the Franks, with only the clothes on their backs, for they ran away on foot, are come here to claim the compassion and assistance of the people of Antioch; and the crew of a vessel under Ionian colours, of which the rudder had been taken off by the pasha a few days ago, put to sea in their long boat, leaving the ship, with the cargo, to take care of itself.

"M. Ducci, who kept a register of daily occurrences at Lattakiyah subsequent to the pasha's entry, qualifies the 18th May with the emphatic words of 'a bloody day.' He relates that, on the preceding evening, a corps of 300 Arnauts, a remnant of the followers of Ali Aga, who had been driven out of the town on their master's death, seeking an opportunity of revenge, presented themselves to Abdin Pasha, and offered their services; which being declined, an altercation ensued, that ended by their chief firing his pistol at the breast of the pasha, and the instant slaughter of 150 Arnauts, whose heads, says M. Ducci, I counted at the gate of the tower, and whose blood ran in streams down the gutters. The rest retired into a ruined seraglio, where they kept the enemy at bay but a short time, and in flying were so closely pursued that very few could have escaped with their lives.

"I must now close with a description of Abdin Pasha's person and character, many of the extraordinary features of which I shall suppress, because, whatever may be my credit for veracity with you, were I to relate all that has been told me concerning him, or indeed such part as *I* believe, it would form a picture of depravity which, thank God, an Englishman has no opportunity of contemplating, and consequently could not regard in any other light than a caricature.

"Abdin Pasha is a native of Karamania, a short, thick-set, brown man, who seldom shaves his head or changes his dirty clothes, never pares his nails, or uses water in any act of cleanliness. He keeps his breast bare, being afflicted with an asthma, from the paroxysms of which he feels relief by lying on his stomach, and in continual motion; he seldom sits upright, but strikes terror into all who approach him, by transacting business while spitting, scratching, and rubbing his body, and rolling on a dirty carpet, which, as well as his clothes and hands, are generally besmeared with blood. His asthmatic convulsions and perpetual perturbation have established a belief that he is constantly labouring to expel a live pig which is in his stomach. He is his own executioner, and few nights have passed during his stay at Lattakiyah in which his long yatagan has not been imbrued in the bowels of some of his own men, whom he sacrifices on the slightest causes of disgust; yet such an ascendency has he acquired over the minds of his followers, that they patiently see their comrades daily butchered, and obey the orders of their chief with scrupulous exactness. Their numbers are, however, from a thousand reduced by the yatagan of the pasha and by desertion to about four hundred. Night and day his faithful aquavita bottle never quits him, and although he is almost continually taking a small dose, he never loses the use of his faculties, and business goes on with regularity and despatch. He scarcely ever sleeps, and is very often changing place, which he does on horseback, and contrary to the custom of pashas, at great speed. He frequently takes the diversion of the jarid or javelin throwing, and one day amused himself and his troops by forcing the Dutch consul, a very corpulent young man and no jockey, to mount a restive horse, and take his part in the sport, in which he was of course literally the *butt of the company*, to the no small satisfaction of all beholders.

"One good feature in this extraordinary character must not, however, be suppressed by the candid historian : he has ever himself respected, and forces his adherents to entertain an unbounded respect for the asylum of the harem. This fortunate sentiment, from his addiction to the unnatural vice of his country, he must owe to early prejudices of education. The Christian fugitives with whom I have conversed, attribute it to the special bounty of the Virgin Mary, as it afforded them in their distress the resource of flying and leaving the female part of their families, without apprehension, behind them. I have since learned that the families of all his men are in the power of his brother.

"P.S. The crop of corn in the province of Nedjd having, as is reported, this year generally failed, flying parties of Wahabis of 1000 men, more or less, have appeared within a few leagues of Bassora, Bagdad, Aleppo, and Damascus, and again made their enterprises the subject of discourse and apprehension to the people of this country.

"The corps that approached Aleppo a few days ago, probably not more than 600 men, drove the tribe Muwali, which may be considered as the vanguard of that city, to within five miles of its walls, after having carried away the greatest part of the latter's property in corn, cattle, tents, &c. And on the back of this disagreeable information has just reached us the intelligence that Seood or Siwad, chief of the Wahabis, after a long siege, took Medina by famine. The fact is not doubted, but the exact date of that disastrous event is unknown, and the particulars are likewise involved in great obscurity. It is said that the first step Siwad took after entering the Holy City was to demolish all the buildings consecrated to religious uses, not sparing the tomb of the prophet himself; that he prohibited smoking, as a profane practice; and issued a proclamation, which is represented to import as follows :

" ' If you can find better than me do not follow me. If your Sultan should send you armies to war with me, and can vanquish me, while you sustain yourselves in rebellion against my authority, well and good ; but for the present, I have vanquished *you*, and therefore I now appoint a man to rule over you in my name. As for myself I shall go far from you ; but I will send you ullimas (doctors in divinity) to instruct you in Moslemism, because you are ignorant of the true faith.'"

The following bears date 1814, and is also from the pen of Mr. J. Barker, our consul in Aleppo at that time.

Early in 1814 the consular agents received an order from their respective superiors, ordering them in strong terms "not to interfere with the internal affairs of the country, and to refrain particularly from giving protection to the persons belonging to the party which, for some time, had been engaged in a rebellious opposition to the regular government of the provinces."

"Aleppo, Jan. 19th, 1814.

"On the 18th January, at a very early hour, the dragomans of all the European agents were summoned to appear in Mehkamy. They found already assembled in the hall of justice the ayans,* who, as well as the interpreters, had been sent for to take cognisance of the contents of a firman, enjoining the former to aid the pasha in bringing to justice such of the janissaries as had committed crimes with impunity during the rebellion of the Aujak,† and declaring that the Franks must not interfere with any regulations tending to further the grand object of the reformation of that corps, but strictly conform in all things to the tenour of the capitulations.

"After the reading of the firman, a buyurdi was published, addressed to the cadi, enjoining him to summon into his presence all the janissaries in the service of the Europeans, in order that they might be examined, and dismissed or arrested, according to the report that should be made of their conduct for ten years past, founded on the testimony of the ayans of the city.

"On the return of the dragomans from the Mehkamy, I suggested to my colleagues that, without refusing our compliance with the summons, we should endeavour to defer it till the next day; and this with a view to gain the time necessary to soften by presents the ayans, who, being notoriously the bitter enemies of the janissaries, no reasonable hope could be entertained of their testimony proving favourable; but my opinion was overruled: the summons of the cadi was immediately complied with by all the consuls; and six, about half the number of the janissaries that appeared in Mehkamy, who were unable to pass the ordeal, were conveyed thence into the prison of the *Sardar*. Of these

* Primates of the country.
† Quarter of the town occupied by the janissaries.

were the two English janissaries; the others, one French, two Spanish, and one Danish.

"To-day (19th Jan. 1814) we have been obliged to have recourse to the means abovementioned; that is, to endeavour to procure the favourable testimony of the ayans, after they had already caused the arrestation of the janissaries; but as, fortunately, in the corrupted mass of Turkish affairs, men generally sacrifice their personal resentment to their private interests, the ayans left a door open for negociation, by saying only, for those whom they did not befriend, that they had not an adequate knowledge of their conduct to be able to answer for its rectitude. They have now all promised us their good offices for the release of our janissaries, and it is *hoped* that, by using the pretence of having made subsequent inquiries into the characters of the janissaries in arrest, they may still be able to establish their innocence. In the meantime I have thought it proper to-day to present a note to the Pasha on the subject, in order to give my testimony of their good conduct, and to inform him that their long and faithful services naturally impose on me the duty of interceding with his excellency for their pardon and release.

"Their family has, in fact, been for three generations in the British service at Aleppo; and they, men in the middle of life, are burdened with seven or eight children. My intercession in their behalf cannot, therefore, I hope, be construed into an infraction of the duty of a public agent.*

"Although zeal for the good government of Aleppo is the *ostensible* pretext of the Pasha's conduct towards these few insignificant individuals of the Anjak, the principal reason *was, no doubt, a desire of humiliating and degrading the Franks;* a disposition which, I am sorry to say, I have invariably found in every species of Turkish authorities, when they have not been softened by the usual *douceur* of presents. In the present case the Pasha has been indisposed against the Europeans of Aleppo, not only by their total neglect of paying him the customary compliments on his arrival, but likewise by the improper conduct of several of the Jew merchants under French and Austrian protection.†

---

* This phrase shews how strict must have been the *orders* of the ambassadors to force the consuls to the barbarity of giving up to the Turks individuals in their employ, which is without precedent in the East; where the persons employed by the consuls are by custom considered sacred, as much as Europeans themselves; otherwise what chance would there be of finding faithful servants, if they were to be exposed to be traduced by the jealous intrigues of their enemies?

† The Pashas appointed to rule in Aleppo had, since the increase of the power of the janissaries, been held in the greatest contempt. Many came and went without daring to undertake any part of the office allotted them. They were completely at

"On the approach of the Pasha to Aleppo, the janissaries and others had secreted property in most of the Frank warehouses. The simple act of receiving those effects could not reasonably be considered as indicating an improper intercourse with rebels, because the Europeans were in circumstances that would have made a refusal a dangerous experiment; but when the Pasha had seized the principal chiefs, and the whole power of the corps was thereby destroyed, it was clearly the duty of every individual in Aleppo to endeavour to be the first to make a public declaration of all the property belonging to janissaries that was in his possession. Instead of which, there were those, unfortunately, who not only waited till they were called upon, but who discovered so much reluctance to part with their deposits, that the Pasha was forced, in order to obtain them, to find collateral proofs of their existence. It is much to be regretted that the Pasha did not found his complaint against the consuls upon specific facts, as in that case the individuals accused would, of course, have been heard in their own justification; but he foresaw that, by making it a general accusation, each ambassador would flatter himself that the person under his immediate jurisdiction was not the object of the Pasha's displeasure, and be therefore inclined to consent to put into his hands what undoubtedly the Pasha considered as a formal authorisation to seize all the janissaries in our service. It may, indeed, be said that the Pasha, without the letters of the ambassadors, had it, at any time, in his power to order the cadi to summon the janissaries to the Mehkamy, to punish, imprison, or kill them at his pleasure. But as he did not take that step until armed against the consuls, it is unfair to presume it would never have been taken at all, if the letters had not been granted him. There is no law to prevent his seizing, without even the insignificant forms of Turkish justice, a great number of individuals of the Anjak, who have procured protection in the service of the *ayans*, but he has hitherto respected a protection notoriously acquired by money; while the consideration due to Europeans has not been a sufficient safeguard for persons under similar circumstances of proscription, but who had much more legitimate claims on us for protection. Independently of direct infraction of our capitulations, we are therefore naturally inclined to view with a jealous eye every thing that tends to impair that kind of conventional consideration or

the mercy of the janissaries, who made them a certain fixed allowance, or refused to recognise them, just as it suited them; and in one instance a M. Popolani, who had formed the acquaintance of one of the miserable individuals sent as pasha by the Porte, was hailed from the neighbouring house, and entreated to supply him with something to eat; the allotted meal not having been furnished that day by those appointed to feed the great man!

respect, which is, in fact, the only solid basis of the security of our lives and property."

"Aleppo, Jan. 27th, 1814.

"Ahmed Pasha, one of my janissaries, was last night strangled, with Ebn Tubal, the French janissary. The other four are still in prison; but it is supposed their friends will succeed in obtaining their release with money. The distinction that has been made between the punishments of these two men and the others naturally *implies* in them a greater degree of guilt; and although I do not consider myself responsible for the good behaviour of my janissaries, it is necessary to say that I do not believe Ahmed Pasha was guilty of any crime of a nature to warrant the forfeiture of life. During the prosperity of the Aujak, he was perhaps more insolent in his usual deportment towards the ayans than the generality of his comrades; and it is that imprudence, joined to the reputation of possessing forty purses, which has brought him to his untimely end.

"The French janissary was precisely in similar circumstances; all the others are known to possess very little property.

"Ahmed has been in the British service from his childhood, and till six years ago his conduct was as correct as that of Turkish servants usually is. About that time he insinuated himself into the good will of Ahmed Aga, first chief of the janissaries of Aleppo, and insensibly became one of his confidential servants,—a lucrative situation, which placed him in circumstances very ill-suited to the nature of his old employ. The transaction of the complicated and disreputable business of a janissary chief was obviously incompatible with the duty of attending at my door. I therefore made, at different times, every effort in my power to dismiss him, but without effect; for besides what I had to fear from his personal resentment, a request in his behalf from Ahmed Aga, his new master, was to me a peremptory command; so that he continued to be nominally in my service, while the duty was performed by his brother, Abbud Pasha, a foolish, insignificant fellow.

"Upon the approach of Jalal iddeen Pasha (Chiapan Ughlu), he became more officious with me, and sought by degrees to disengage himself from the service of Ahmed Aga.

"The contest between the Aujak and the Pasha remained for some time of a very doubtful issue, when, of course, it would have been still less than ever prudent to discharge a protégé of Ahmed Aga. I was then at Lattakiyah, and had every thing to apprehend from the consequences of his resentment, directed towards Hojiya Nasri Hawa, the person left in charge of my affairs in Aleppo. At length the Pasha got into his power, and in one day executed, all the chiefs of the Aujak, when the whole corps was in an instant dissolved. The large cap and white sash that distinguished them were no longer any where to be seen. The most conspicuous or most guilty fled in disguise; and the rest, more confident in their innocence, or in their resources, threw themselves at the feet of their enemies, the grandees of the town, who, during the reign of the janissaries, had sunk into poverty and contempt. Ahmed was one of those who preferred to run all risks to bearing the certain evils of perpetual banishment. He was soon after thrown into prison by Hadji Effendi, an ayan, for an ancient disputed claim upon him of 2500 piastres. He remained ten days in prison, in butt of his enemies, who, not appearing to accuse him, he flattered himself that he had found means to appease them. When I arrived at Aleppo, I found him duly furnished with a taskary of the Pasha, recognising him as a janissary in the British service; which document he had procured for himself and his brother, when taskaras were given to the other Frank janissaries. Having no special ground of complaint against him, and considering the situation of his pregnant wife and four helpless children, his long services and present misfortune, I thought it would have been an unbecoming and ungenerous act to give him up to the rapacity of the Pasha.

"In public these unfortunate men have not been accused of any specific misdemeanour. After their arrestation in the Mehkamy, they were conveyed to the sardar's house; then removed to the Castle; and thence to execution. In hopes of propitiating the Pasha, I paid him, on the 23d instant, a visit of ceremony. I have endeavoured to procure the intercession and good offices of most of the people of weight in the city; and the consciousness of having strenuously employed every means in my power is the only consolation I can receive in this very disagreeable business.

"On the 28th January, the one Danish, and the two Spanish janissaries were yesterday evening liberated for about 8000 piastres. This morning the Pasha has sent me my janissary Abbud, saying that he made me a present of him!"

"Aleppo, Jan. 30th, 1814.

"On the 20th instant the Pasha made known to the consuls his wish that they should assemble the people under their protection, in order to compel them to make a public declaration of any property they might have belonging to janissaries, dead, living, or absconded. This step was calculated to give considerable uneasiness, because, as most of the Franks had long ago remitted to the Pasha all the effects that had been confided to their custody by the janissaries, it was apprehended that the Pasha meant to follow it up by some more violent measure.

"Myself, the Austrian, Russian, and Danish consuls instantly replied, that we had nothing in our possession belonging to janissaries; but the French consul having a great number of persons under his protection, judged it necessary to convene a general assembly on the occasion. After which, he sent his first dragoman, M. Simion, to the Pasha with a copy of the *procès verbal*. When this paper was put into the pasha's hands, he did not deign to look at it, but said angrily, "What credit would you have me give to your declarations, after having found property in the hands of the Franks, which they had previously denied possessing? This affair must be examined before the cadi, when I shall bring credible witness to prove that there is still property of the rebels in the hands of the Franks, and execute in consequence the orders of the Porte." The dragoman had been charged at the same time to complain that in the preceding days, a French doctor, without having given any provocation, had been beaten with his own cane by a soldier; and that another Frank (also a French subject) had received a box on the ear; to which the Pasha replied, that if the dragoman could point out the persons who had committed these insults, he would order their chastisement. The dragoman said that such a designation was impossible; and then very imprudently suggested that a public crier should be ordered to proclaim in the city that the Franks must not be molested. The Pasha of course refused to comply with so ridiculous a request, when some altercation ensuing, the dragoman says the Pasha insinuated that, if the exigency required it, he would as soon hang him, or any other Frank, as a rajah (Turkish subject).

"Ten days have now elapsed without the Franks having been summoned to appear in Mehkamy,* or the Pasha's having taken any further step in the business of the secreted property of the janissaries; and I am inclined to think, that if the Franks conduct themselves with prudence and temper, the Pasha may yet be induced to act towards them with moderation.

"It is, however, fair to state, that a few days ago the Arnaut who had insulted the doctor was apprehended while sitting in the public bazaar with the gold-headed cane in his hand, without his having received

* It is contrary to all established custom that a European should be compelled to appear at a Turkish tribunal.

any chastisement at all. Besides which circumstance, another French subject has just been insulted in sport, but narrowly escaped a very serious injury. While out riding, he was met by a party of Dalli-Bash playing at the *jarid;* one of them galloped up to him, and when within five yards, threw a jarid with all his force, which pierced the gentleman's hat, and rebounded over a garden-wall.*

"I must also add, that yesterday the Franks were also concerned in a most extraordinary public measure, which touches more or less every man in the city. The Pasha having promulgated a command for the reduction of the currency of coins to the standard of the capital, he fancied that he could likewise regulate and fix the prices of *all* the commodities that are sold in the shops and warehouses. Strange as it may appear, the execution of this project was attempted. Yesterday a great crowd of people assembled in the Mehkamy; and among shoemakers, smiths, Bagdad merchants, petty shopkeepers, manufacturers, &c. &c., there were the house-brokers of the Europeans, who were severally interrogated about the prices at which they vended cochineal, sugar, cloths, red caps, coral, &c., and gravely informed that his excellency the Pasha had ordered that the prices of all their wares should be regulated and fixed! And what is still more ridiculous, it was proposed to limit also the profit of every article as it passed from hand to hand, which was wisely settled by the deputy cadi, the person who presided at this grave assembly, at one para per piastre.†

"On which a facetious shopkeeper disturbed the solemnity of the proceeding, by saying, 'Why, look ye, gentlemen, nothing can be fairer; for my part, I am quite satisfied with the arrangement. I usually sell for five piastres. I shall have earned an ample daily provision for myself and family.'

"After three or four hours sitting without much progress being made in business, the session was prorogued till to-morrow; but it is probable that enough has been already done to prove the impracticability of the undertaking.

"This measure is the more extraordinary, as the Pasha has had sufficient time to see the bad effects of his *maximum* on the necessaries of life; for by fixing their prices three months ago, there is now an alarm-

---

* The instances of insults to Europeans, wherein some were much injured, went on increasing, until Ibrahim Pasha took possession of Syria. To this prince Europeans owe all the little respect accorded them to this day by the people of the country; still, at his time in Damascus, and to this day in Hamma, Christians are not allowed to ride in the streets!

† Forty paras make one piastre.

ing scarcity in the chief articles of meat, butter, bread, and barley, as well as a want of all other provisions.

"If the other price-limiting speculation should be carried into effect, it will be seen that it was conceived with a view to throw obstacles in the way of trade, for the sole purpose of compelling the different branches of industry to unite in a contribution to purchase relief!

"The object, as far as it regards the Franks, will, however, I trust, completely fail, as on this ground we are well armed by the express tenor of our capitulations." *

Translation of a petition in Turkish from the Chiefs of the Trades and the Poor in Antioch, to Mr. John Barker.

O friend of the nation, and zealous in befriending the poor, the honoured Mr. Barker!

We,† the population of this town, the literate and illiterate class, the chiefs of the villages, and the chiefs of the trades, in a body, have previously sent four petitions to the Pasha at Aleppo, borne by persons bare-footed and bare-headed, having been weighed down by the tyranny of Halif Aga (the former mutsellim), praying that he might be removed from power; and his highness listened to our complaints, and placed Shakir Bey, colonel of the sbahis,‡ in his place. From that day we have enjoyed tranquillity. But we have now learnt of a certainty, that Halif Aga has petitioned his highness to the effect that he might send to this town [orders to the Bey], and have fifteen of the chiefs of the trades put in chains and brought to Aleppo, in order that, after having done so, the said Haji Halif Aga may be reinstated in the mutsellimlick.

Since we have a certainty of this, and also that these individuals are not guilty of any crime, but that this proceeds from the enmity of Haji Halif Aga, which is as clear to all as the sun in the heavens, we,

* It was only very lately (1847), that the Pasha of Adana pretended to prohibit the Europeans from selling any thing whatever in *detail;* but on what he founded his pretensions I cannot say. The European shops in Tarsus and Adana had been closed, and complaints sent to Constantinople, with what chance of obtaining success no one can tell; and in Aleppo seventy persons under European protection, some of whom had been for thirty years in the service of various consulates, were seized and put in prison until they paid the Karage, a personal tax on the Christian subjects of the Grand Seigneur, from which all protected have hitherto been exempted. Later, the French ambassador obtained an order of the Porte to the Pasha of Adana to desist from such ridiculous pretensions.

† The persons who presented the petition belong all to the Muhammadan class of the population.

‡ The sbahis are the Sultan's irregular cavalry, of whom a troop is quartered at Antioch.

your servants, the poor, humbly state—firstly, that we will not have Haji Halif Aga return to Antioch [that is, as mutsellim]; and secondly, that these persons should be sent in chains to Aleppo, shall never be with our consent; and in order that there may not be a revolution in the town, we have been in a body to Mr. Michail Adib, the English consular agent in this town, and have laid before him our case. To which he answered, "I have a superior, to whom I will write, and inform of the facts of the case; and please God, Mr. Barker will cause the affair to be properly represented." And we agreed to this advice of Mr. Michail, and we have sent in this petition, that you may take what measures you think fit for our tranquillity. (Signed as above.)

Postscript.—O honoured sir,—
Mr. Michail Adib has written on the subject to the present mutsellim and the council [to ask] why this injustice should be committed? and they answered, "We have no knowledge of it." Upon which Mr. Michail begged that a written document be given to these [fifteen] individuals as a guarantee, which they refused. Mr. Michail then went to them [the mutsellim and council] and procured the paper; but for all this, we, your humble servants, are still in fear, and pray you will strengthen us, because we do not wish to make disturbances, but that justice should be done [to us], and we have [for this purpose] fallen at the feet of the British government, and pray it may protect us from oppression. (Signed as above.)

Dated Rubi Ahir 19, 1257. [June 8th, 1841.]

BADIR KHAN BEY, THE EXTERMINATOR OF THE NESTORIAN CHRISTIANS.

BADIR KHAN BEY belonged to the chief family which has been at the head of the Kurds of Kurdistan Proper for many years, and whose persons are considered by their tribe to be almost sacred. It is problematical whether Badir Khan Bey is the actual head of the family; be this as it may, by his bravery, and the assistance he afforded the Porte, he was about seven years ago raised to the chief command; and he contrived to subdue to his authority, under the sanction of the Porte, a district containing 4000 villages, for which he contributed to the Turkish government a sum of 1000 purses annually; nor has he ever failed in his engagement, so that the Porte had really no cause of complaint; for as to his persecution of the Christians, according to the conscience of most of the great men at Constantinople, Badir Khan Bey cannot be blamed for thus promoting the cause of his religion.

During the time that he governed in Kurdistan, Badir Khan contrived to amass a very large sum of money, great part of which he buried, and caused the persons who had been employed in building up the place where the treasure was concealed to be killed, that the secret of the spot might remain with him alone.

Badir Khan calculated upon rallying 40,000 followers to his standard when he first refused to give up his authority. But when the troops of Osman Pasha approached Jizirah, Iziddin Shir, a lad of seventeen, the son of Mirsirdin,* had been entrusted with one of the passes into Kurdistan, Bughaz Kalaasi, and he broke his trust by openly making protestations to the Pasha of Musul, that he was determined not to fight. On this, three-fourths of the Kurds abandoned Badir Khan, and he found the numbers of his followers reduced first to 12,000, and afterwards to a few hundred men, his immediate dependents. The Turks all admit, that if it had not been for this treachery, the army of the Porte would not have been in sufficient force to conquer the Kurd chief.

When Osman Pasha reached Jizirah, he found that the boats of the bridge over the Tigris had been destroyed, to interrupt communication; and he ordered these to be repaired, and crossed with his whole army, encamping on the other side (where we since pitched our tent). Here he was joined by Iziddin Shir, who had been to Musul, where the Pasha had given him a nishan or honorary decoration, and had treated him with great kindness, naming him governor of Kurdistan, in the place of Badir Khan.

There is a road direct north, at about two hours ride from Jizirah; but as it passes through precipitous hills, the army might have been attacked in those passes at a disadvantage, so Osman Pasha preferred following the course of the stream along a wood, which winds with the river, north-west, for an hour, where they encamped in an open place among some olive-trees. Badir Khan, seeing himself betrayed by his cousin, Iziddin Shir, and fearing that he would lead the Turks through the defile, which was held by his younger brother, Mansur Bey,† he resolved on attacking them, with the hopes of throwing disorder into their ranks before they could enter the gorge. The Turkish army consisted of

* Who had killed his predecessor and brother-in-law, Sayid Bey, and taken the reins of government for a short while previous to the aggrandisement of Badir Khan.

† To shew the spirit of fanaticism still reigning in these parts, I will only state a fact I lately learned at Musul. Mansur Bey and his brother had pressed into their service some horses from Musul to Jizirah to carry their effects; these horses belonged to a Christian, who followed them to bring back the animals; but they were refused to him unless he would consent to turn Turk; on his complaining, Mansur made him open his mouth, and thrust a jarid down his throat. The poor man is now in Musul, and has lost the power of speech.

12,000 regular infantry and cavalry, and 6000 to 8000 irregulars. Badir Khan's troops amounted to only 12,000, the rest being in the mountains, and many siding with Iziddin Shir, others maintaining neutrality. With these Badir Khan surrounded the army at night and kept up a heavy fire till morning, but he killed only twelve men and wounded sixty. The people of Jizirah, who were Kurds, and, at heart, on the side of Badir Khan, pretend that the Pasha caused the bodies of the soldiers to be sown up in sacks and thrown into the river, that the number of the killed should not be known. They also say that one Kurd was so brave, that he actually came up to the cannon to stop it with stones directly after it had been fired off, and that he gave the salam to the soldiers as he did this; on which he was shot by a subordinate officer; but that, collecting his remaining strength, he stabbed the Turk to the heart, on which the colonel of the regiment came forward and cut the Kurd down with his sword. They also say that the Kurds succeeded in carrying off four guns, which they were, however, obliged to abandon in their flight the next morning. As soon as day broke, the Turks, who had returned the fire without moving from their place, charged the Kurds and routed them. The Kurds then retired by the pass near Finik (ancient Phœnicia), where is an old castle, besides several more modern and rudely constructed forts, which have been destroyed since the subjection of Badir Khan, together with several others held by him in the mountains. Iziddin Shir conducted the army through the other pass held by his brother, where there is a castle built by his father, in which there is a little spring of brackish water, and which is *now* garrisoned by twenty Arnauts. This castle is ingeniously situated, commanding a pass through which runs a stream which flows into the Tigris. It is at a sufficient height to render it difficult of access, and still *not* too high to give effect to cannon defending the entrance of the pass. Opposite to it was another fortification, which the Pasha has pulled down. This pass is one hour to the east of the place of engagement, and through it the army made their way to Dar Gul, or the Monastery Lake, two and a half hours further on.*

The army went in four days from Dar Gul to Avrack, and there Badir Khan made his last stand with some two or three hundred men who remained faithful to him. There was some hard fighting at this spot, which was well situated to resist the attacks of the army; but at the end of forty-eight hours, Badir Khan surrendered *on his own terms.*

Now, if it had ever been the intention of the Porte to bring him to condign punishment, there was not the least necessity for their allowing

* An "hour" may be computed to be about 3½ miles at most.

him all he demanded; but the fact is, the Porte had been compelled against its will to make war upon him at the special desire, and in accordance with the reiterated demand, of the British ambassador. At all events, Badir Khan having proceeded to Constantinople, he there pleaded his own cause so effectually, that he has been allowed to retire and live peaceably at Candia.

An account of the horrible atrocities committed by this savage upon the defenceless Nestorians will be found in Layard's *Nineveh and its Remains*, vol. i. p. 173 et seq., and at p. 239 a brief account of the capture of Badir Khan; corroborating, however, the more minute details here given, inasmuch as Layard says, "The Turkish ministers had more than suspected that Osman Pasha had reasons of his own for granting these terms."

The Story of Fahel, Chief of the Arabs of the Zor, or Forest District of the Euphrates; as related by JOHN BARKER, ESQ. Dated, Aleppo, 20th May, 1823.

The Pasha of Aleppo, without having any cause of complaint, but incited merely by the hope of plunder, was induced to make a grand expedition against Fahel, an ancient chief of the tribes of sedentary Arabs who inhabit the Zor, or forest on the banks of the Euphrates. With this view he despatched the mutsellim (governor) of Killis, with four field-pieces, 2000 Turkish soldiers, and half that number of armed peasants, to which force was added 1000 Arabs of the tribe Haddidin, whom he had engaged to act as auxiliaries. This formidable army was calculated to strike terror into the heart of the old patriarch, the fame of whose riches was greater than his power.

Fahel prudently sought to avert the impending danger by an offer of a large sum of money; but that mark of submission and fear served only to stimulate the Pasha's covetousness the more. The latter was already in imagination possessed of the golden hoards of Fahel, when his army was suddenly enveloped, attacked, and dispersed, leaving in the hands of the victors the four cannons and the mutsellim, whose life was spared in the manner related to me by a peasant, who was one of the musketeers.

"It was not," said he, "the affair of a long summer's day—of an hour —of half-an-hour. It was over in a shorter space of time than I have employed to relate it. The first discharge of the artillery killed five of our own men. The cannoneers had hardly time to reload before they were surrounded, having the mutsellim in the midst of them, and were forced to use their swords and pistols. They made an obstinate resistance; but they all fell by the lances of the Fahel, except the mutsellim, whose life was preserved by one of the sons of the chief, who was seen flying in every direction, exclaiming, " No quarter to the Ruam!* but spare the peasant, for he has been brought here against his will."

The auxiliary Arabs abandoned camp and baggage, and saved themselves by flight; but a woman was left behind. On the enemy coming up to the empty tents, she was recognised and accosted by a man, who said to her: " Sister, what are you doing here?" " I am in labour," she replied. " Then thou art the booty that God has assigned me," said the Arab, and respectfully retired to a short distance. There he waited patiently till the woman was delivered. The mother having nothing that could serve to swaddle the infant, he tore off the skirt of his tattered under-garment to cover it.

He then assisted his " sister " to mount his mare, and with the halter in his hand, and words of comfort and urbanity in his conversation, he journeyed on many a weary league in the traces of the fugitive tribe, which he overtook, and restored the woman and the babe to their family. He was introduced to the chief; and the next day, with the view of effecting a reconciliation, he prevailed upon him to accompany him to the tents of the victorious Fahel.

The old man upbraided him gently with having sided with the Osmanlis. He replied, with dignity, " O Fahel! I am a Haddidin. Can you think me capable of uniting in a sincere friendship with those Osmanli dogs? Between you and me there is an honourable warfare. We fight for the goods of this world; but the Ruam are not restrained by the sacred laws of the Arabs. They respect not the chastity of the women. They will slay a brave man whom they have had the chance to unhorse; and, with still greater baseness, stoop to take away his sandals and his water-bottle, and expose him to perish in the desert!"

" Thou art a brave fellow," said Fahel, " and shalt hereafter be esteemed amongst my dearest friends."

The interview between the rival chiefs had scarcely terminated, when the naked and trembling mutsellim was conducted into the tent. *Fahel rose at his entrance.* He was immediately furnished with a proper suit of apparel, and after receiving the assurance of safety, and the ceremonies of the pipe and the coffee being over, he was presented with a cake of unleavened coarse Arab bread. The mutsellim broke it, turned

* Ruam is the plural of Rumi, and is a name the Arabs give to Turkish soldiers without distinction, whether they are from Rumilia (Turkey in Europe) or not.

it over and over in his mouth, and after fruitless efforts to swallow it, declared he could not eat it.

"What!" exclaimed Fahel, sternly; "you cannot eat our bread! Yet this it is which your master envies us the possession of."

When this Lacedæmonian rebuke had made its due impression on the mutsellim, he was regaled with the choicest viands that could be procured, and continued to be treated with respect and even kindness in his captivity.

In the anguish of defeat the Pasha declared his resolution to be revenged. He made some vain demonstrations to raise another army; but was soon after called away to the command of a distant province. Meantime, instead of a prison, the mutsellim had enjoyed in the Zor an asylum against the fury of his master, who sought to wash out his own disgrace in the blood of the unhappy lieutenant.

He was at length dismissed with the honourable gifts of vests and horses, and many other tokens of the hospitality and munificence of the Arabs.

The new Pasha prudently accepted from Fahel the customary tribute for the privilege of selling to the people of Aleppo the surplus of his corn, his sheep, and his butter.

In this little picture of living Arab manners it will be seen that the victorious chief rose from his seat on a distinguished captive being led into his presence; but that mark of civility he shews to the meanest individual, whether Muhammadan, Jew, or Christian. So very distinct are Fahel's manners from those of the Turk in authority, that he never suffers his hand or his vest to be kissed except by women and children. He even always *himself* carries the water-vessel for his ablutions, deeming it impious in a being subject to the wants of nature to exact from a fellow-creature so degrading a service. The sentiment of this religious respect for the dignity of a human being is not peculiar to Fahel. It was displayed by Dr. Johnson, when he himself bought oysters with which he fed his superannuated cat. But the virtue that distinguished a modern British philosopher is so common in Arabia as to attract no attention among a people we please to call barbarians.

D.

BURCKHARDT'S ACCOUNT OF CILICIA.

Mr. Lewis Burckhardt, the celebrated traveller, had a wonderful power of describing even what he saw but casually; witness his description of Palmyra, where he was only permitted to remain a couple of hours, and which he barely traversed on horseback; and yet he gives a plan of the city, and an admirable account of its ruins and edifices. On his first going to the East, he proceeded to reside at Aleppo, in order to prepare himself for being enabled to pass for a Mussulman.

On his way he touched at Tarsus; and his account of this place is so graphic, that we think we cannot do better than insert an extract, together with his relation of his first landing at Suedia, and the difficulties he experienced at Antioch on his first assuming the native costume.

"After we had left Satalia, we sailed for three days along the coast of Caramania, and kept our course constantly ten leagues distant from the shore. The chain of snowy mountains seems to continue in a direction parallel with the shore. At the foot of these mountains I observed every evening thunder-clouds and lightning. During our stay in the port of Satalia we were twice refreshed by heavy showers, though it was now the season when it very seldom rains in other parts of the Levant. I suppose that the vicinity of the snowy mountains, which rapidly condense the copious vapours arising from the heated earth, give rise to these clouds. On the 26th, late at night, we anchored in the roads of Mersin, a collection of villages so called, situated to the west of Tarsus, about fourteen miles distant from it. The next morning some of us went with the Tripoline on shore, where we found a party of about twenty Turkmans encamped under and around a single tent; they were selling grain, with which the buyers loaded several camels. After a short parley, the chief of the party led us to his village, about two miles distant. We remained there the whole day in the chief's house, couched upon carpets, which were spread upon a terrace sheltered from the sun by the shade of two large mulberry-trees. We returned to our ship in the evening, and spent the next four days in the same manner with these hospitable people.

"An aga is at the head of this Turkman tribe; he commands about twenty-five villages, over each of which he appoints a chief to collect the revenue, which is equally divided between the chief and the aga. Many of these chiefs are Greeks, who, by their long residence with the Turkmans, have completely adopted their manners. Their dress is the same, excepting the red cap, which the Greeks do not wear; and but for that mark it would be impossible for a stranger to distinguish them from their masters. The Turkmans are continually moving about on horseback from one village to another; they are tolerably well mounted and well armed, each with a gun, two pistols, a poniard, and a sabre. They never go but armed; but it seems to be chiefly from ostentation, for they live at peace with the inhabitants of the neighbouring villages, have nothing to fear from straggling Arab tribes, and have no opportunity of attacking travellers or caravans, which never pass this way. They occupy the whole plain, which extends in length from Cape Bajarre to beyond Tarsus; its breadth extends from the sea to the lowest ridge of the mountains of Caramania, and varies from four to five or ten miles. This plain, at least as much as I saw of it in my way to Tarsus, is for the greater part sown with barley and wheat; where it is left uncultivated, numerous herds of buffalos and fine cattle feed upon the wild grass. Wild capers grow in great abundance. I found in several rivulets small tortoises; and amongst the ruins of deserted houses we got here and there sight of a zerboa. The Tripoline having made his purchase of grain from the aga, the latter sent on board our ship three fat sheep in earnest of his engagements. In six days the ship was to begin loading. The Tripoline being at leisure during this time, I persuaded him to go with me to Tarsus, in search of a further conveyance for me by sea or land; one of the other Tripolines was likewise desirous of looking out for a passage for Beirout: the excursion was therefore soon agreed upon. We formed a small caravan, and set out on horseback on the morning of the 30th. The road from our anchoring place to Tarsus crosses the above-mentioned plain in an easterly direction: we passed several small rivulets which empty themselves into the sea, and which, to judge from the size of their beds, swell in the rainy season to considerable torrents. We had ridden about an hour, when I saw, at half an hour's distance to the north of our route, the ruins of a large castle, upon a hill of a regular shape in the plain: half an hour further towards Tarsus, at an equal distance from our road, upon a second tumulus, were ruins resembling the former; a third insulated hillock, close to which we passed midway of our route, was overgrown with grass, without any ruins or traces of them. I did not see in the whole plain any other elevations of ground but the three just mentioned. Not far from the first ruins stands in the plain an insulated column. Large groups of trees shew from afar the site of Tarsus. We passed a small river before we entered the town, larger than those we had met on the road. The western outer gate of the town, through which we entered, is of ancient structure; it is a fine arch, the interior vault of which is in perfect preservation: on the outside are some remains of a sculptured frieze. I did not see any inscriptions. To the right and left of this gateway are seen the ancient ruined walls of the city, which extended in this direction further than the town at present does. From the outer gateway,* it is about four hundred paces to the modern entrance of the city; the intermediate ground is filled up by a burying-ground on one side of the road, and several gardens with some miserable huts on the other. We led our horses to the khan of the muleteers, and went ourselves to the khan of the merchants, where we found tolerable accommodation, the brother of the Tripoline being known here. Our room was soon filled with all the foreign merchants who lived in the khan, and the principal town merchants; we sold to them a few silk handkerchiefs and coarse cambric, and were plagued with their company for the whole remaining part of the day. The foreign merchants were a party of Kahines (Kahirines?), several Aleppines, and some Constantinopolitans. In the evening the alley at the gate of the khan was transformed into a dark coffee-room, where every body went to smoke a pipe. As we were strangers, we were greeted at our entrance with the usual politeness of Orientals towards travellers: 'Peace be with you; you are welcome among us; how are you? God send you a happy evening,' &c. &c., were compliments which every one whom we approached addressed to us. We were treated by several merchants with pipes, coffee, ice-water, and bour, which latter drink is water mixed with the juice of liquorice. The ice is brought from the mountains three days' journey distant, at the price of three piastres for about five pounds. A tolerable singer sung some Turkish airs, and accompanied himself upon a sort of mandoline. Many questions were addressed to me about my person and affairs: my neighbour the Tripoline took the trouble of answering them to the satisfaction of the company. 'Allah Kerim!' 'God is great!' was their usual exclamation at hearing that I came from so far. We retired rather late; for my part I had been much entertained with the party. We went to sleep before the door of our room upon a covered terrace built of wood, which runs along the interior circuit of the khan. Before sunrise every body was up; some of the merchants descended into the court-

* It was to the east of this gateway alluded to by Mr. Burckhardt that the terracottas were found.—W. B. B.

yard to perform at the fountain the ablutions which are prescribed to the Mussulman after his night's rest. But in this part of their religious rites, as well as in the performance of their daily prayers, I observed much indifference amongst the plurality of the Turks I saw here, as well as of those with whom I travelled afterwards from Suedieh to Aleppo. Amongst the latter were many who, during eight days, did not pray once; even two Hadjis, who had performed the Mecca pilgrimage, were of that number. Some would pray once, others twice a day, before sunrise and after sunset; only three or four of the caravan were strict in regularly chanting the three daily prayers, to which number the Koran limits the duty of travellers; but I did not find that more respect or deference was paid to them than to the others.

"We remained in the khan that morning, and quitted the town at noon to return to our ship, leaving the Tripoline behind to settle our affairs. The little I saw of Tarsus did not allow me to estimate its extent; the streets through which I passed were all built of wood, and badly; some well-furnished bazaars, and a large and handsome mosque in the vicinity of the khan, make up the whole register of curiosities which I am able to relate of Tarsus. Upon several maps Tarsus is marked as a sea-town: this is incorrect; the sea is above three miles distant from it. On our return home, we started in a S.W. direction, and passed, after two hours and a half's march, Casal (Cazan or Caisanlu), a large village half a mile distant from the sea-shore, called the Port of Tarsus, because vessels freighted for Tarsus usually come to anchor in its neighbourhood. From thence turning towards the west, we arrived at our ship at the end of two hours. The merchants of Tarsus trade principally with the Syrian coast and Cyprus: Imperial ships arrive there from time to time to load grain. The land-trade is of very little consequence, as the caravans from Smyrna arrive very seldom. There is no land-communication at all between Tarsus and Aleppo, which is at ten journeys (caravan travelling) distant from it. The road has been rendered unsafe, especially in later times, by the depredations of Kutshuk Ali, a savage rebel, who has established himself in the mountains to the north of Alexandretta. Tarsus is governed by an aga, who, I have reason to believe, is almost independent. The French have an agent there, who is a rich Greek merchant.

"On the following day the Tripoline rejoined us; he had taken, to my great satisfaction, a passage for me on board a Greek sailing-boat from Tripoli of Syria.* That vessel was at anchor at Casal, and accord-

---

* This Tripoli is distinguished from the city of which my fellow-traveller is a native by the appellation of Tarabolaus fel Shark, or Tripoli of the East.

ing to its master's affirmation was bound for Latikia, which was exactly the place where I wished to land. I left our ship on the second of July; in taking leave of the Tripoline I took off my sash, a sort of red cambric shawl, of Glasgow manufacture, which he had always much admired, thinking it to be Indian stuff, and presented it to him as a keepsake or reward for his good services. He immediately unloosened his turban, and twisted the shawl in its stead round his head, making me many professions of friendship, and assuring me of his hospitality if ever the chance of mercantile pursuits should again engage me to visit the Mediterranean, and perhaps Tripoli in Barbary. The time I hope may come when I shall be enabled to put his assurances to the test. (I think I forgot to mention that the Tripoline was much skilled in languages, which enabled me freely to converse with him; besides his native Arabic tongue, he spoke Turkish, Greek, and Italian.) The vessel on board of which I now embarked was an open boat with three masts, about thirty-five feet long and nine broad, much resembling the representation of the germs of the Nile, which Bruce and other travellers have given. These vessels are very common on the Syrian coast, where they are called Shacktur. I had engaged to pay for my passage twenty-five piastres at my arrival in Latikia; but was no sooner with my baggage on board, than the master informed me that he meant to proceed to Antakia (Antiochia), not to Latikia, and that I was at liberty to return to my own ship if I did not choose to go his way. I thus found myself duped a second time, though I had most distinctly agreed for my passage to Latikia. However, there being no other conveyance to the coast of Syria at hand, I resolved to remain on board. I was afraid of being kept in these parts until after the return of my old ship for Malta, when I should have nobody to recommend me to those in whose company I might continue my way; I knew, moreover, that there was a brisk intercourse between Antakia and Aleppo. There had not been for some time any opportunity from Tarsus to the opposite coast. A crowd of passengers came therefore on board. I counted fifty-six men and women lying upon deck, besides six sailors, and six horses in the ship's hold. We had each just as much space allowed as the body covered, and remained in this state two nights and one day. In general the passage is performed within the twenty-four hours.

"On the morning of the 5th we entered the bay of Suedieh, which is formed on one side by the promontory called Ras Khanzir, on the other by another projecting rocky mountain (Ras Bassit); both are the extremities of chains of barren rocks, which I conceive to be the remotest branches of the Libanus. These mountains come down to the water's edge on both sides of the bay; in the bottom of it, where the Orontes, now called Aasi, empties itself into the sea, begins a level country of four or five miles in width and length. It is to the whole of this tract of level land, which contains several villages, that the name of Suedieh is applied, though that appellation is also given sometimes exclusively to the port.

"The wind being favourable, we entered the river, and anchored, after half an hour's sailing through its sinuosities, at Mina, the port of Antakia, where the ship was laid close to the shore, where the elevated banks of the river form a kind of quay. Mina is a miserable village built close to the river's right bank, consisting of about seven or eight houses, the best of which serves as a place of residence to the aga, whom the aga of Antakia appoints to receive the duties upon exports and imports. Higher up than Mina the Aasi is not navigated; the navigation is rendered impracticable by rocks, though there is plenty of water. Here, at the last stage of its course, it is a fine slow-flowing river, much about the size of the Thames beyond Richmond Bridge; its waters are muddy, and this being the case in the month of June, three or four months after the rainy season, I suppose they can hardly be clear during any other part of the year.

"Arrived at Suedieh, I found myself very uncomfortably situated. I had lost my friend the Tripoline, and though he had warmly recommended me to the master of the Shacktur, yet I found the crew of the vessel to be thievous and treacherous. They spread the rumour amongst the people of Suedieh that I was a Frank; and as the ship was immediately to return to Tarsus, I expected to find myself completely at the mercy of the inhabitants, amongst whom, as well as amongst the crew, there was nobody who understood the Italian, or, as they called it, the Latin tongue. I remained on board the ship that day and the following; and was bargaining for a horse and mules to take me to Antakia, when, to my great satisfaction, a caravan from Aleppo came down to the coast with Indian goods; I soon got acquainted with the muleteers, and made my bargain with one of them for the whole journey from Suedieh to Aleppo. He first asked fifty piastres per kantar (about five hundred pounds English weight). I got him down to thirty, and was afterwards informed at Aleppo that I should not have paid more than twenty-five. It is a great point gained by travellers in these countries if they can make with their mule or camel-drivers the usual bargain of the country. If the muleteer overcharges them, he makes a boast of it wherever he goes; the traveller is immediately known to be a person little conversant with the customs of the country, and he may be sure

MR. BARKER'S VILLA IN THE VALLEY OF SUEDIA, WITH MOUNT ST. SIMON IN THE BACKGROUND

From a Sketch by Mr. C. F. Barker.

to be dealt with accordingly in every respect, wherever the mule-driver accompanies him. I was helping the servants to distribute my baggage into mules' loads, and to tie it round with cords, when the aga sent for me. I found him smoking his pipe in a miserable room, surrounded by his people: entering the room, I pulled off my slippers and sat down on the floor before him. I shall here remark that it is a custom most strictly adhered to never to sit down upon a carpet or even a mat, and in presence of a man of rank, not even upon the bare floor, without pulling off the slippers; and if a person has but one pair on his feet, which is the Moggrebyn and the Greek fashion, he must sit down barefooted.

"After I had drunk a dish of coffee, I asked the aga what his pleasure was; he answered me by making a sign with his thumb and forefinger, like a person counting money. I had several chests for the British consul at Aleppo with me, and had also marked my own baggage with the consul's name, thinking by these means to prevent its being examined. He asked me what the chests contained; I expressed my ignorance about it, telling him only that I thought there was a sort of Frank drink (beer) and some eatables which I had been charged with at Malta for the consul on my way home. He sent one of his people to look over their contents; a bottle of beer had been broken in loading, the man tasted it by putting his finger into the liquor, and found it abominably bitter: such was his report to the aga. As a sample of the eatables, he produced a potato which he had taken out of one of the barrels, and that noble root excited a general laughter in the room: 'It is well worth while,' they said, 'to send such stuff to such a distance.' The aga tasted of the raw potato, and spitting it out again, swore at the Frank's stomach, which could bear such food. The other trunks were now left unexamined; and I was asked fifteen piastres for the permission to depart with them. I gave him ten piastres, and received from him a sort of receipt for that money, because I told him that without it the consul would never believe that I had really paid down the money as duty upon his effects. The aga was very high in his expressions, talking of his grandeur, how little he cared about the sultan, and still less for any consul, &c. He laughed a great deal at my Arabic, which certainly was hardly intelligible; but he did not much trouble himself with questions about my affairs, his mind seeming now solely taken up by the hope of extorting money from the Aleppine merchants; and so I left him; and soon afterwards, about an hour before sunset, departed from Suedieh with part of the caravan, the rest intending to pass the night there. The road from Suedieh to Antakia crosses the plain for about one hour's distance. On the right runs, in a deep bed, a branch of the Aasi, and forms in this place several islands; on your left extends the well-cultivated plain of Suedieh.

"As we approached the mountains which enclose the plain on the western side, we passed several extensive and regularly-planted orchards belonging to the aga of Antakia. The road now lay through lanes thickly overhung on both sides with shrubs, and I was entering a country famous for the beauties of its landscape scenery, when the sun shed its last rays. We continued our way in the dark for about one hour and a half longer, and halted near a rivulet at the entrance of the hills, where men and horses were fed: we remained there till about two hours after midnight.

"From thence the road leads over a mountainous and rocky ground abounding with trees and springs. At the break of day we passed a village and a considerable rivulet flowing towards our right; one hour's march further another rivulet; the country then opens, and the traveller finds himself upon the ridge of a high plain (Carachaiain), encompassed by the two before-mentioned chains of mountains, from which he descends into the valley which the Aasi waters, and where he finds Antakia very picturesquely situated, near the foot of the southern chain of mountains, surrounded with gardens and well-sown fields. It was yet early in the morning when we passed the river and entered the town; a strong-built bridge leads over the river immediately into the town-gate. I was stopped at the gate and asked for one of the two pistols which I wore in my girdle; I had told the people of the caravan that they belonged to the English consul. My muleteer assured me that the pistol would be restored; I therefore gave it up voluntarily, well convinced it would have been forced from me against my will. The aga's man brought it back in the evening; I was asked two piastres for the returning of it; they had taken the flint, and the powder from the pan. Arrived at Antakia, the muleteer led his mules to the khan of the muleteers; I might have gone to the khan of the merchants, but having nobody to accompany me and introduce me there, I preferred staying with the muleteers, whose way of living I also wished to see. The khan is a large courtyard built in a triangular shape: the basis of the triangle is distributed on both sides of the entrance-door into small dark cells, which serve as magazines for the goods and as places to cook in. On another side are the stables; and the whole length of the third side is taken up by a terrace built of stone, about four feet elevated from the ground, and eight feet broad, where the muleteers eat, sleep, and pray, that side of the khan being built in the direction of Mecca. In the midst of the yard is a large water-basin, which affords drink to men and beasts indiscriminately.

"My entrance into the khan excited considerable curiosity, and the little cell I took possession of was soon beset by troublesome inquirers, who unanimously declared that I was a Frank come to the country for evil purposes. I had nobody to take my part except my muleteer, whose remonstrances in my behalf were soon lost in the general cry of djaour (infidel) raised by the other inhabitants of the khan, and by the town's-people who came to visit their friends.

"Whenever I could get any of them to listen to me for half an hour, I found means to appease them; but the town's-people did not even condescend to speak to me, and I evidently saw that their plan was to make religion a pretext for practising an *avanie* upon me. My property fortunately was mixed with that of the consul; a spare shirt and a carpet constituted my whole baggage; besides a pocket-purse, containing the money necessary for my daily expenses, I had about twenty sequins hidden upon me. The aga of Antakia sent his dragoman to get something out of me. This was a wretched Frank, who pretended to be a Frenchman, but whom I should rather suppose to be a Piedmontese. I pretended complete ignorance of the French language; he therefore asked me in Italian minutely about my affairs, and how I could attempt to travel home without any money or goods to defray the expenses of the journey. I answered that I hoped the consul, in remuneration of my having carefully watched his effects, would pay the expense of a camel from Aleppo to Bagdad, and that at the latter place I was sure of finding friends to facilitate my further journey. When the man saw that nothing in my manners betrayed my Frank origin, he made a last trial, and pulling my beard a little with his hand, asked me familiarly 'Why I had let such a thing grow?' I answered him with a blow upon his face, to convince the by-standing Turks how deeply I resented the received insult; and the laugh now turned against the poor dragoman, who did not trouble me any further. I am at a loss to state how far I succeeded in sustaining my assumed character; I thought that the major part of the caravan people were gained over to my side, but the town's-people were constant in their imprecations against me. I had been flattered with an immediate departure for Aleppo, but the caravan was detained four days in the khan. During the whole time of our stay, I spent the daytime in the cell of the goods, amusing myself with cooking our victuals; the town's-people, though often assembled before the door of the room, never entered it; in the evening the gates of the khan were shut, and I then went to sleep with the muleteers upon the terrace.

"I was relieved from this unpleasant situation on the 10th, when it was decided that the caravan should depart. The muleteers began preparing for their departure by dividing the whole court into squares of different sizes, by means of ropes, at the end of which iron wedges are fastened, which are driven into the earth up to their heads; each muleteer takes one of these squares proportionate in size to the number of his beasts, and loads them in it. Though the ropes are little more than one inch above ground, the animals never move out of the square assigned to them, and thus great order prevailed in the khan, though it was dark when we loaded, and the whole court crowded with beasts and bales. At halting-places, when the beasts are fed, the same ropes are extended in front of them to prevent their getting amongst the baggage.

"I cannot say much of Antakia, having seen nothing of it but the streets through which I entered. It looks like a neat town, at least in comparison to Tarsus: living is only half as dear as it is in Aleppo. This circumstance, joined to the beauty of the surrounding country, and the proximity of the sea, would make it a desirable place for Franks to live in, were it not for the fanaticism of its inhabitants, who pride themselves upon being descendants from the Osmanlis the conquerors of Syria. Last year at a tumult raised at Suedieh, these Osmanlis murdered the Greek aga (Barhoom Kehya, grandfather of Jusif Saba) of Suedieh, with his whole family, and a young French physician, who had come to his house to cure his son. The aga of Antakia is appointed by the Grand Signior, and is independent of any pasha.

"We marched the whole night of the 10th over a plain country, and reached early the next morning Hamsie, a village situated at nine hours march from Antakia, on the right bank of the Orontes. We passed the river in a ferry-boat: its banks on both sides are about forty feet high at this place; its breadth is near fifty yards; the depth no where more than five feet. On a little eminence a few hundred paces from the ground on the river's side where we encamped, rises a spring of excellent water; my companions, however, drank of the muddy water of the Orontes in preference to taking the trouble of filling their flasks at the spring. One of the merchants had a tent with him, under the shade of which we passed the whole day. In the evening the village youths kindled a large fire, and amused themselves with music and dancing. The next day we passed a chain of calcareous mountains planted here and there with olives; on the top of one of these mountains lives a custom-house officer, who exacted a toll from each individual, as it was said, in the name of the Grand Signior. The descent on the eastern side is steep, but the mules walked with the greatest firmness. In the valley into which we descended lies the town of Ermenaz, watered by several streams. Though small, it is one of the best towns in this part of Syria; its gardens are cultivated with great care, and its inhabitants are industrious, because they are out of the immediate reach of rapacious pashas and janissaries. They work a glass manufacture which supplies Aleppo. The olives of the country round Aleppo are, next to those of Tripoli, the best in Syria; its grapes are likewise much esteemed. As we rode by, I saw lying on the right-hand side of the road near the town, a broken ancient column of about four feet in diameter; and I was told afterwards in Aleppo that many like remains of antiquity are to be met with in the neighbourhood of Ermenaz. At half an hour's distance from this latter place we again began to mount, and the path became difficult and tiresome for the beasts, from the number of detached rocks with which it is overspread. After nearly eight hours' march (meaning the whole day's work) we descended into the eastern plain of Syria, and encamped at the foot of the mountains, round a large tree in the vicinity of a copious spring. Whenever the beasts were unloaded, it was with much difficulty that I could prevent my luggage from being thrown upon the ground. The caravan people in this country, and I should suppose every where else in the East, are accustomed to loads of bales of goods which do not receive any injury from letting them fall to the ground. The loads on each side of the beast are tied together over its back by a cord. Arrived at the halting-place, the first thing the muleteer does is to go from mule to mule to unloosen that cord; the loads then fall to the ground. This mode of unloading, and the great carelessness of these people, render the transport of many European commodities utterly impracticable, without their being accompanied by a servant sent along with them, for the express purpose of taking off the loads. A Frank merchant of Aleppo received some years ago a load of Venetian looking-glasses which were all dashed to pieces. Provided the chests which contain the merchandise be entire, the muleteer thinks himself free from responsibility. We were joined in the evening by some other travellers, whose curiosity led them to new inquiries about my person and affairs. None of my companions had till now found out any thing which could have directly inculpated myself; they, however, kept a strict watch over all my motions: being obliged at night to go aside, two of the travellers last arrived followed me unseen, and pretended afterwards to have observed some irregularities in the ablutions necessary to be performed on such occasions; in consequence of which, I was told that I was 'Harām,' or in a forbidden unclean state; and notwithstanding every thing I said to defend and excuse myself, I found that from that time I had lost the good opinion of all my companions. We marched the next day six hours, and halted at Mart Mesrin, a village belonging to Ibrahim Pasha, who, in the time of Djezar, was Pasha of Aleppo, afterwards Pasha of Damascus, and who lives now in disgrace and poverty at this place, the whole appearance of which makes it probable that in a few years hence it will be deserted by its inhabitants. The wide-extended plain over which we marched this day consists almost throughout of a fertile soil, but without any trees, and in most places uncultivated, but where a number of ruined and deserted villages indicate that many parts of it must have formerly been cultivated. Having been much plagued during this whole day by my fellow-travellers, and in the evening also by the peasants, who had collected round the caravan, I swore that I would not eat any more with any of them. This declaration being somewhat in the Arab style, they were startled at it; and my muleteer especially much pressed me to rejoin their mess; I assured him that I would rather eat nothing and starve than have any further friendly dealings with men who professed themselves my friends one day, and proved my enemies the next (it should be observed that this was the last stage of our journey; I therefore did not run great risk in making good my words). The tract of country over which we passed on the following day was similar in appearance to that which we had seen on the preceding. The number of deserted and ruined villages increased the nearer we approached Aleppo. We had marched about eight hours when we discerned the castle of Aleppo, at the sight of which the armed horsemen of the caravan set off at a gallop, and repeatedly fired off their guns; the merchants put themselves ahead of the caravan; and after one hour's march further we entered the town. All merchandises coming to Aleppo must be taken to the custom-house khan; they are weighed there to determine the amount of the sum due to the muleteer for freight, and a duty must be paid for them to the Grand Signior, which, together with the taxation-money of the Christians and Jews, is the only branch of revenue which the janissaries, the present masters of the town, still allow the Porte to retain. The English consular house is in that very khan.

"I was now arrived at Aleppo in a shape which entirely left it to my option either to continue in my disguise or to avow my European origin. After a long conversation on that subject with Mr. Barker, I was convinced that it would better answer the purpose of my stay in Aleppo to choose the latter, and my reasons for it were the following: At the time I left England and Malta, I imagined that the intercourse between Cairo and Aleppo was frequent, and that it might easily happen that Cairine merchants might see me here and recognise me afterwards at home, or that travelling Aleppines who knew me here might afterwards see me again in Egypt. The departure of the Syrian pilgrim caravan to Mecca not having taken place for the last three years, has almost annihilated the commercial intercourse overland between the two countries. At the meeting of the Syrian and African caravan near Mecca, Egyptian merchants used formerly to join the former and return with them to Damascus and Aleppo, and *vice versâ*. At present the little commerce carried on between Cairo and Aleppo is entirely in the hands of a few Turkish and Greek houses at Tripoli, Latikia, and Alexandria, and the Egyptian merchants themselves never come to Aleppo. Had I continued in my disguise, and continued to live exclusively amongst the Turks, opportunities would have frequently happened to put the veracity of my story to the test. East Indians come from time to time to Aleppo with the Bagdad caravan, and many of the Bagdad and Bassorah merchants established at Aleppo have been in India. My person would have been infinitely more noticed than it now is, if taking a shop in the bazaar, as I first intended, I should have exposed myself to the curiosity of the whole town; I should have entirely foregone the instruction to be derived from books and masters skilled in the language; and, moreover, I have no doubt that the French consul residing here would have heard of my arrival and have done every thing to put my pursuits in a dubious light. These are the reasons which convinced me that, for the present time, it was more advisable to appear in a shape which would preclude the intrusion of curious inquirers, and afford more facility to my studies. I continue my name of Ibrahim, and pass in my Turkish dress unnoticed in the crowds of the street and the bazaars. The consul receives me at his house as a travelling country merchant of his; and as it frequently happens that people coming into the Levant change their names, nobody wonders at my being called with an oriental name. I had first my doubts whether my fellow caravan travellers might not be over-inquisitive here; but such of them as I have since met greeted me without further questions, and the government of the city is now such, that a man picking a quarrel with me about what I might have told him at Antakia, would only expose himself to be fined for a sum of money by the janissaries, the masters of the town, for their trouble to settle the business with the consul.

"My plans for the present are to remain at Aleppo the whole of the winter and part of next summer. I have been fortunate enough to find a good and willing master of Arabic, and I hope to make progress in the study of the literal as well as vulgar language. As soon as I shall be able to express myself with some precision in the vulgar dialect, and perfectly to understand it, I shall visit the Bedouin Arabs in the Desert, and live with them some months. I can do this in perfect security; and

I have no doubt that you will approve of it, as it will afford me the best opportunity of practising the manners and becoming acquainted with the character of a class of people who are the same, whether they overrun the deserts of Arabia or those of Africa.

"You need not be afraid that the history of my own person, which has taken up so considerable a portion of the preceding pages, will any more be exhibited before you at such a length. I thought it might be of some interest to the Association to see how far I was able to succeed in making good my way to Aleppo in the disguise in which I left London, unaided as I was by a knowledge of Eastern languages, or a familiarity with Eastern manners. This trial has so far been satisfactory to me, that, in the first place, I am persuaded that nothing of my pursuits has transpired at Malta, which will always be of material consequence to me; secondly, in being landed at a remote corner of Syria, I have avoided the general intercourse of a mercantile seaport, such as Acre, Beirout, Tripoli, or Latakia; and finally, it has created within me the confidence that, whenever I may be able to call in support of a similar disguise, a fluent utterance of Arabic, and a habitude of oriental manners, I shall easily find means to triumph over such obstacles as those I met with in the khan at Antakia," in which he succeeded perfectly.

"A few days after my arrival at Aleppo, I was attacked by a strong inflammatory fever, which lasted a fortnight. The want of nights' rest occasioned by the quantity of vermin which had collected upon my person, principally during my stay in the khan of Antakia, was, as I thought, the cause of it. I have enjoyed perfect health since that time, and the climate agrees with me better than I expected.

Aleppo, October 2d, 1809.

Mr. Burckhardt remained two years and a half in Syria, making daily additions to his practical knowledge of the Arabic language, and to his experience of the character of Orientals, and of Mohammadan society and manners. His principal residence was at Aleppo. Having assumed the name of Ibrahim Ibn Abdallah at Malta, he continued to bear it in Syria; but apprehensive of not having yet had sufficient experience thoroughly to act the part of a Mussulman, and finding no necessity for such a disguise at Aleppo, he was not studious to conceal his European origin, and wore only such a Turkish dress as is often assumed in Syria by English travellers, less for the sake of concealment than to avoid occasional insult. Thus he had the benefit of an unmolested intercourse with the Mussulman population of Aleppo, at the same time that he was not prevented from openly accepting the friendship and protection of Mr. Barker, the British consul, nor under the necessity of denying himself the social resources afforded by the houses of the European residents, especially those of Mr. Barker, and of Mr. Masseyk, formerly Dutch consul. Of his obligations to the former of these gentlemen, he omitted no opportunity of bearing testimony.*

I cannot better conclude this long, but I trust not uninteresting extract, than by giving Mr. Salt's account of the last moments of Mr. Lewis Burckhardt; it is to me most heart-rending; and his sensibility and feeling towards his mother, to whom he had been so devoted all his life, are touching in the extreme.

"On the morning of the 15th (1817), conscious of his danger, he proposed and obtained the consent of his physician, that Mr. Salt, his Majesty's consul-general, should be sent for. 'I went over immediately,' says Mr. Salt in a letter to the secretary of the Association; 'and cannot describe how shocked I was to see the change which had taken place in so short a time. On the Tuesday before, he had been walking in my garden with every appearance of health, and conversing with his usual liveliness and vigour; now he could scarcely articulate his words, often made use of one for another, was of a ghastly hue, and had all the appearance of approaching death. Yet he perfectly retained his senses, and was surprisingly firm and collected. He desired that I should take pen and paper and write down what he should dictate. The following is nearly word for word what he said: 'If I should now die, I wish you to draw upon Mr. Hamilton for two hundred and fifty pounds, for money due to me from the Association, and together with what I have in the hands of Mr. Boghoz (two thousand piastres), make the following disposition of it: Pay up my share of the Memnon Head (this he afterwards repeated, as if afraid that I should think he had already contributed enough, as I had once hinted to him). Give two thousand piastres to Osman (an Englishman, whom at Shikh Ibrahim's† particular request I had persuaded the Pasha to release from slavery). Give four hundred piastres to Shaharti my servant. Let my male and female slaves, and whatever I have in the house, which is little, go to Osman. Send one

---

* During his residence at my father's house he was naturally desirous of forming himself as much as possible to the manners and customs of the Mohammedans; and he used to practise in his room the genuflections used by the Turks during their five times of prayer. To do this more at his ease, he would lock himself up in his room. The people of the country, who had some suspicion of his identity, and were desirous of clearing up their minds on the subject, used to peep at him through the keyhole; and as they saw him going through the ceremonies of prayer, they decided that he must be a Mohammedan; and all his assurances to the contrary were ever after useless to change their opinion thus formed of him.

† From the time of his departure from Aleppo, Mr. Burckhardt had continued to pass by this name.

thousand piastres to the poor at Zurich. Let my whole library, with the exception of my European books, go to the University of Cambridge, to the care of Dr. Clarke the librarian; comprising also the manuscripts in the hands of Sir Joseph Banks. My European books (they were only eight in number) I leave to you (Mr. Salt). Of my papers make such a selection as you think fit, and send them to Mr. Hamilton for the African Association; there is nothing on Africa. I was starting in two months' time with the caravan returning from Mecca, and going to Fezzan, thence to Tombuctou; but it is otherwise disposed. For my affairs in Europe, Mr. Rapp has my will.* Give my love to my friends (enumerating several persons with whom he was living upon terms of intimacy at Cairo). Write to Mr. Barker (he then paused, and seemed troubled, and at length with great exertion said)—let Mr. Hamilton acquaint my mother with my death, and say that my last thoughts have been with her. (This subject he had evidently kept back, as not trusting himself with the mention of it until the last.) The Turks,' he added, ' will take my body, I know it; perhaps you had better let them.'— When I tell you that he lived only six hours after this conversation, you will easily conceive what an effort it must have been. The expression of his countenance when he noticed his intended journey, was an evident struggle between disappointed hopes and manly resignation. Less of the weakness of human nature was perhaps never exhibited upon a deathbed. Dr. Richardson and Osman, who has for some time lived with him, were both present at this conversation. He ended by expressing a wish that I should retire, and shook my hand at parting as taking a final leave. So unhappily it proved; he died at a quarter before twelve the same night without a groan. The funeral, as he desired, was Mohammedan, conducted with all proper regard to the respectable rank which he had held in the eyes of the natives. Upon this point I had no difficulty in deciding, after his own expression on the subject. The Arabic manuscripts for the University of Cambridge are in a large chest, and shall be forwarded by the first safe opportunity, together with his papers, which are few, and appear to be chiefly copies of what I believe him to have already transmitted.'

" To those who have perused the preceding extracts from Mr. Burck-

---

* This refers to a will made previous to his departure from England, according to which, in case he had advanced into the interior of Africa, and was not heard of by the 1st of January 1820, he was to be considered as dead. By this will, after shewing his gratitude to a relation to whom he had been indebted while at Leipzig, he appointed his mother residuary legatee for all sums which might accrue to him from his engagements with the African Association.

hardt's correspondence, it will be almost superfluous to add any remarks upon his character. As a traveller he possessed talents and acquirements which were rendered doubly useful by his qualities as a man. To the fortitude and ardour of mind, which had stimulated him to devote his life to the advancement of science in the paths of geographical discovery, he joined a temper and prudence well calculated to ensure his triumph over every difficulty. His liberality and high principles of honour, his admiration of those generous qualities in others, his detestation of injustice and fraud, his disinterestedness and keen sense of gratitude,* were no less remarkable than his warmth of heart and active benevolence, which he often exercised towards persons in distress, to the great prejudice of his limited means. No stronger example can easily be given of sensibility united with greatness of mind, than the feelings which he evinced on his deathbed, when his mother's name, and the failure of the great object of his travels, were the only subjects upon which he could not speak without hesitation. By the African Association his loss is severely felt, nor can they easily hope to supply the place of one whom birth, education, genius, and industry, conspired to render well adapted to whatever great enterprise his fortitude and honourable ambition might have prompted him to undertake. The strongest testimony of their approbation of his zealous services is due from his employers to their late regretted traveller; but it is from the public and from posterity that his memory will receive its due reward of fame; for it cannot be doubted that his name will be held in honourable remembrance as long as any credit is given to those who have fallen in the cause of science."

* His present to the University of Cambridge of the choicest collection of Arabic manuscripts in Europe, was intended as a mark of his gratitude for the literary benefits and the kind attention which he received at Cambridge when preparing himself for his travels. Of his disregard of pecuniary matters, and his generous feeling towards those who were dear to him, a single example will be sufficient. His father having bequeathed at his death about ten thousand pounds to be divided into five equal parts, one to his widow and one to each of his children, Lewis Burckhardt immediately gave up his portion to increase that of his mother. "If," he said, "I perish in my present undertaking, the money will be where it ought to be; if I return to England, my employers will undoubtedly find me some means of subsistence."

APPENDIX

Table I. Commerce of Kaisari[y]

| \multicolumn{4}{c|}{Statistics.} | \multicolumn{3}{c}{Imports from the chief Towns.} |

Name of the towns.	Their population.	Their distance from Kaisariyah in caravan days journey.	How often per annum.	Name of the goods imported.	In what quantity.	Their value.
		Days.	Times.			
Erzerum	75,000	20	5 to 6	Teftic	40,000 okes	6 p. the oke
				Buffalo-skins	600 skins	100 to 130 p. each
				Hare-skins	12,000 ,,	1½ to 2 p. ,,
				Pelisses	8000	100 to 500 p. each
				Merchandise from Persia.	2,000,000 piasters	....
Trebizonde	60,000	16	1 ,, 2	Calicoes	2000	90 to 95 p. ,,
				Buffalo-skins	500	100 to 130 p. cach
Kara-Hisar	30,000	12	3 ,, 5	Goat-skins	20,000	9 to 10 ,,
				Hare-skins	10,000	1½ to 2 ,,
				Trebizond Calicoes	1,000	90 to 95 ,,
				Tragacanth	10,000 okes	10 to 15 p. the oke
Diyar-Bakir	30,000	20	2 ,, 3	Galls	500 cantars	900 ,, 1200 p. the oke
				Alaja	1600 pieces	35 ,, 40 ,,
				Citara	650	50 ,, 55 ,,
Musul	20,000	35	3 ,, 4	Galls	500 cantars	900 ,, 1200 ,,
Damascus	100,000	15	1 ,, 2	Manufactures of the place	3500 pieces	70 ,, 100 ,,
Aleppo	60,000	7	1 ,, 2	Ditto	6000 ,,	40 ,, 50 ,,
				Cotton	6000 ,,	850 p. the cantar
				Soap	5000 sacs, of 100 okes each	900 ,, ,,
Tarsus	6,000	9	30–10	Hinna	150 cantars	800 ,, 900 ,,
				Tobacco	150 ,,	100 ,, 800 ,,

MMERCIAL TABLES.

h the chief Towns of Asia Minor.

	EXPORTS TO THE CHIEF TOWNS.				OBSERVATIONS.
t consumed aisariyah, hat sent out, id where.	Name of the goods exported.	In what quantities.	The value.	Duty.	The cantar weighs 180 okes. The duty paid is, in spite of all regulations and orders, emanated from Constantinople by Sublime Firman.
hole goes myrna chiefly to iman to Smyrna med in country	Cotton of Adana and Tarsus	300 loads	750 to 800 piasters the cantar	2½ pr. cent	Erzerum generally receives what cotton it requires from Rawan, at 15 days' journey off (under the dominion of Russia, and formerly belonging to Persia), but the cold some years kills the plant, and then recourse is had to Adana and Tarsus for the supply needed for the consumption of the place.
Do. s to Syria	Cotton of Tarsus & Adana	200 loads	750 to 800 p. the can.		
fterwards yria consumed country, he other to Smyr. Smyrna.	Cotton of Tarsus & Adana	200 loads	Do.	2¼ pr. cent Do.	Trebizonde receives its English manufactures from Constantinople per steamers, which have much diminished the commerce of Kaisariyah with all towns that can communicate with Constantinople by their means.
e country					
myrna. sumed in ountry, & st goes to na	European manufactures	30,000 lds.	. . . .	. .	The greater part of European manufactures, however, reach this place by way of Aleppo.
he country Do. sumed, ¾ yrna	. . . .	. . . .	. . . .	. .	Do. do. do. The distance between Aleppo and Kaisariyah, by way of Marash, is only 7 days' journey in summer; but in winter the snow impedes the mountain roads, and the caravans go by Adana. The Tarsus and Adana cotton goes also to Kastamuni, Tukat, Amasia, Churum, Zisit, Ladik, &c., without passing thro' the town (to within 6 hours of it).
he country	Amasia silk	50 to 60 lds. of 120 okes each load	110 to 120 p. the oke	. .	
Do. bales for ountry, & est is reirted	Hair sacks	500 lds. of 50 pieces each	16 to 17 p. the piece	2½ pr. cent	
umed in ountry	Yellow leather	1000 pieces	5 to 25 p. each	Do.	
. . . .	Buffalo-skins	400 skins	110 to 130 p. do.	Do.	
. . . .	Ropes	25,000	3½ p. do.	2¼ do.	
	Tukat copper	3000 okes	16 to 21 p. the oke	6 paras the oke	Duty paid in Tukat.
	Constantinople small ware	100,000 p. worth			

Table I. (continued). Commerce of KAISARIYAH

	STATISTICS.			IMPORTS FROM THE CHIEF TOWNS.			
Name of the towns.	Their population.	Their distance from Kaisariyah in caravan days' journey.	How often yearly.	Name of the goods imported into Kaisariyah.	In what quantity.	Their value.	Dut
		Days.	Times.				
Adana	20,000	9	30 to 40	Cotton	12,000 cantars	850 p. the cautar	18 pe cent
Bur and Nigda	10,000	5	52	Ordinary coloured manufactures	10,000 pieces	6 to 8 p. the piece	2¼
	8,000	5	52	Hare-skins	10,000	2 p. the piece	Do
Kastamuni, or Kastambol	35,000	14	15	Ropes	50,000	4 p. each	Do
				Buffalo-skins	800	100 to 120 p. each	Do
				Salip	2 to 3,000 okes	9 p. per oke	Do
				Persian berries	5000 okes	3 to 3½ p. „	D
Tukat	20,000	8	20„30	New copper	60,000 „	16 to 20 p. „	D
Amasia	45,000	8	15	Silk	1000 „	130 to 140 p. the oke	
				Buffalo-skins	500 „	90 „ 100 „	20 p cent Amas only
				Goat-skins	4000 to 5000	9 „ 10 each	
Tossia	10,000	11	10	Rice	60,000 okes	2 p. the oke	2½
Boivat	4,000	9	10	Persian berries of inferior quality	12,000 „	4 to 6 p. „	Do
Timorta	4,000	6	5„6	Do.	10,000 „	14„15 p. „	Do
Iskilub	12,000	8	5„6	Do.	15,000 „	14„16 p. „	Do
Uzgat	8,000	4	15„20	Persian berries	2500 „	20„21 p. „	Do
Angora	50,000	3	8„10	Shawls	3000	100„150 p. „	Do
Karaman	20,000	9	10	Madder-roots	250 cantars	800„1000 „	Do

th the chief Towns of Asia Minor.

	EXPORTS TO THE CHIEF TOWNS.				OBSERVATIONS.
at portion nsumed in iyah, what is ut, & where.	Name of the goods exported.	In what quantity.	Their value.	Duty.	
cantars, rest goes rds Erze-	....	....	....	..	Adana receives the same goods from Kaisariyah as Tarsus, but in treble quantity.
he coun- onsump- ...	European manufactures	250,000 p. worth.	....	..	
Do.	Galls	5 loads...	1200 p. the load ...	2½ pr. cent	
ne coun- to send Adana arsus.	....	....	....	..	The Adana and Tarsus cotton reaches this place direct, passing within eight hours of Kaisariyah.
po rted to n⹁ ..	....	....	....	..	Tukat traffics with Constantinople direct, and receives the cotton of Adana and Tarsus in the same way as Kastambol, without its entering into Kaisariyah. The new copper produced yearly is about 200,000 okes; it is monopolised by the government, and goes to Constantinople. Amasia, for the last thirteen years, traffics with Constantinople by way of Samsun, so that the commerce of Kaisariyah is thus much reduced.
onsumed country, ½ is sent Smyrna	....	....	....	..	
onsumed country, the rest to Smyr.	....	....	....	..	
he country	Soap	10 loads ..	6 p. the oke	..	
whole is umed in ariyah	....	....	....	..	
Do.	European manufactures	20,000 ps. worth ..	....	..	Do. do. do.
Smyrna & antinople	Do.	in small quantities.	....	..	Do. do. do.
Do. do.	....	....	....	..	Do. do. do.
Do. do.	Cotton	70 cantars .	850 p. the cantar ..	..	Do. do. do.
Do. do.	European manufactures	70,000 ps. worth ..	....	..	Here the Pasha of Kaisariyah resides.
the coun- ise .... the con- ption of town ..					

Table I. (continued). Commerce of KAISARIY

	STATISTICS.			IMPORTS FROM THE CHIEF TOWNS.			
Name of the towns.	Their population.	Their distance from Kaisariyah in caravan days' journey.	How often yearly.	Name of the goods imported into Kaisariyah.	In what quantity.	Their value.	
		Days.	Times.				
Karaman cont^d.	20,000	9	10	Currants and raisins	5000 loads	10 paras the oke	2½ ce
Merzehum	15,000	8	10	New copper	5000 to 6000 okes	14 to 15 p. „	
				Teftic and goat-hair.	6000 to 7000 okes	5 „ 6 p. „	2½ c
				Ropes	6000	3 „ 3½ p. „	
Sivas	20,000	5	20	Vegetables, grain, &c.			
				Hare-skins	15,000	20 „ 40 p. „	1
				Buffalo-skins	300 to 400	100 „ 130 p. each	a
Constantinople and Samsun.	60,000	8	15 „ 20	Calicoes, 3 pikes broad	5000 pieces	200 p. each	
				Do. 2½ do.	3000 „	60 p. „	
				Do. 36 yds. do.	13,000 „	70 to 80 p. „	
				Do. 24 yds. do.	8000 „	40 „ 45 p. „	
				Madapolam	5000 „	50 „ 80 p. „	
				2d quality	3000 „	Do.	
				Tangibs	30,000 „	30 p. „	
				Nankin	20,000 „	110 „ 120 p. „	
				2d quality	10,000 „	80. p. „	
				H. Sprigs	3000 „	80 p. „	
				Lappets	10,000 „	28 to 30 p. „	
				Farmaish	24,000 „	30 „ 55 p. „	
				Zebras	15,000 „	25 „ 35 p. „	
Smyrna	135,000	25	27	Striped dimity	4,000 „	80 „ 90 p. „	
				Handkers. of Constantinople imitation	20,000 „	7 „ 12 p. „	
				Chintz	20,000 to 40,000 „	60 „ 100 p. „	
				Coloured dimity	5000 „	70 paras to 3½ p. „	
				White do.	5000 „	Do.	

...h the chief Towns of Asia Minor.

	Exports to the chief Towns.				Observations.
...t portion ...sumed in ...yah, what is ...it, & where.	Name of the goods exported.	In what quantity.	Their value.	Duty.	
...ich 3000 are con-...d in the ...try...	. . . . . .	. . . . . .	. . . . . .	. .	The raisins serve to make a kind of brandy they call raki.
he country	Cotton	30 loads . .	800 p. the cantar . .		
Do.	. . . . . .	. . . . . .	. . . . . .	. .	Of goat-hair they make famous hair-sacks.
xported ...e use of ...untry . .	European manufactures	40,000 ps. worth.			
m yr..a . .	Coffee	10,000 okes.	6 to 7 p. the oke.		
ed in the ...ry . .	Sugar	300 okes . .	4 p. the oke.		
ntity con-...in the coun-...he rest being ...ported.	Boots & shoes	5000 pairs .	20 to 30 p. each . . .	2½p. cent	
pieces . .	Yellow leather .	30,000 . . .	5 „ 25 p. „	. .	For Constantinople.
o 900 „ .	Yellow berries .	400,000 okes	27 to 33 p. the oke.		
„ .	Galls.	200 cantars .	1200 p. the cantar.		
„ .	Wool	50,000 okes	3 p. the oke		
„ .	Scammony . .	500 „	100 to 150 p. the oke.	The duty on goods going to Smyrna and Constantinople is paid in these two places on arrival.	
„ .	Salip	2500 „	10 „ 12 p. „		
00 „ .	Aniseed . . .	10,000 „	3 „ 4 p. „		
„ .	Teftic	20,000 „	15 „ 18 p. „		
00 „ .	Persian berries	300,000 „	28 „ 30 p. „		
„ .	Teftic	5000 „	15 „ 18 p. „		For Smyrna.
„ 6000 „ .	Gum traga- canth . .	20,000 „	9 „ 11 p. „		
00 „ .	Galls	50 cantars .	1200 p. the antar.		*Note.* The steamers that run between Samsun and Constantinople have drawn all the commerce of that quarter to Constantinople. Kaisariyah still communicates with Smyrna by caravan. Tarsus, it has been suggested, might serve Kai-ariyah as a place of deposit, & thus shorten the distance by land to Smyrna, as the roads are very bad, and goods exposed to rain during the journey on mules' backs.
„ .	Wool	30,000 okes	450 p. „		
„ .	Aniseed . . .	20,000 „	3 to 4 p. „		
00 „ .	Hare-skins . .	1000 „	1½ to 2 p. each.		
00 „					
„ 5000 „					

Table I. (concluded). Commerce of KAISARIYAH *with the chief Towns of Asia Minor.*

	IMPORTS FROM THE CHIEF TOWNS.			
Name of the town.	Name of the goods imported.	In what quantity.	Their value.	Quantity consumed in the country; the rest being exported.
Smyrna continued.	Striped dimity	5000 pieces	70 paras to 2½ p. each	4000 ,, 5000 pieces ....
	Handkers.	18,000 ,,	2 to 3 p. ,,	5000 ,,
	Fez	12,000 ,,	8 ,, 30 p. ,,	6000 ,,
	Do. wardi	2000 ,,	80 p. the doz.	500 dozens
	Trieste and French Cloth	150 bales	24 to 52 p. the pike	50 bales
	Sugar	35,000 to 40,000 okes	6 ,, 7 p. the oke	10,000 ,,
	Coffee	200,000 ,,	5 ,, 7 p. ,,	30,000 ,,
	Pepper	20,000 ,,	5 ,, 6 p. ,,	4000 ,,
	Pimento	3,000 ,,	6 p. ,,	1000 ,,
	Cochineal	4,000 ,,	125 ,, 130 p. the oke	1200 ,,
	Indigo	10,000 ,,	90 ,, 135 p. ,,	2000 ,,

COMMERCIAL AND STATISTICAL TABLES. 379

Table II. *Summary of the Commerce of* KAISARIYAH *one year with another.*

PRODUCE OF THE PLACE, OR WHAT IS COLLECTED IN KAISARIYAH ONE YEAR WITH ANOTHER.

Name of the goods.	Quantity.	Value.	Quantity consumed, the rest being exported.	Customs' duty.	Observations.	Statistical Note.
Persian berries[1]	1,000,000 okes	25 to 30 p. the oke	5000 okes		[1] The quantity of this berry produced is increasing every year.	Kaisariyah is under the government of a Mutsellim, who is named by the Pasha of Uygat, who again depends on a superior Pasha at Tivas. The town contains 60,000 inhabitants, and 65,000 in the villages around, equal to 105,000 Muhammadans,—very strict in their religion; 9,500 Greeks, and 10,500 Armenian Catholics. There are no Jews.
Teftic[2]	15,000 to 20,000 do.	7 to 10 p. "	All is exported	If any goods are sent to Smyrna or Constantinople, the duty is paid in *those places*: if to any other part, a duty of 2½ per cent is exacted.	[2] The teftic is cleaned in Kaisariyah.	
Tragacanth gum[3]	15,000 to 20,000 do.	15 to 18 "	Do. do.		[3] One-third yellow, two-thirds white, comes from without.	
Galls[4]	30,000 do.	1000 to 15,000 p. the cantar	3000 okes		[4] Come from Diarbekis and Mossul.	
Wool[5]	75,000 do.	450 to 500 p. the oke	16,000 do		[5] Chiefly white.	
Amasia silk[6]	1000 do.	150 to 180 p. "	For the country		[6] Amasia produces 10,000 to 12,000 okes of silk.	
Salep[7]	10,000 do.	10 to 12 "	100 okes		[7] Comes from Tukat.	
Wax[8]	8000 do.	14 to 16 "	For the country		[8] Is gathered from every where.	
Hare-skins[9]	60,000 skins	2 to 3 p. each	Exported		[9] Come from the environs of Tukat.	
Mahlib[10]	300 cantars	700 to 800 p. the cantar	Do.		[10] Do. do.	Eight Constantinople kilos measure on English quarter as nearly as possible.
Goat-skins[11]	100,000	9 to 10 p. each	{Tanned in the country .. Do. do.		[11] And of this they extract the hair for hair-sacks and for the teftic.	
Cow-hides	15,000 to 20,000	15 to 25 "				
Buffalo-hides[12]	5000	55 to 60 p. every 6 okes	500 skins		[12] A portion comes from Tukat.	
Aniseed	20,000 okes	3 to 4 p. the oke	10,000 okes			
Wheat[13]	1,000,000 kilos of Constantinople	4 to 5 p. the kilo			[13] Grain is cheap, but just sufficient for the consumption of the country.	
Barley	600,000 to 700,000 kilos	2½ to 30 p. "				

Table III. Commercial Table of the Exports of the Pashalik of ADANA and TARSUS.

Name of the goods.	Quantity produced yearly in the Pashalik.	Price current.	Customs.	Quantity exported.	To what places.	OBSERVATIONS.
Cotton[1]	18,000 bales, of 100 okes each	10 to 12 p. the batman of 4 okes	25 paras the oke	16,000 bales	To Kaisariyah and the other towns of Asia Minor	[1] A few hundred bales are sometimes exported to Leghorn as a return for goods from this place sold in Aleppo. But the greatest part goes to the interior. The cotton-seed is sown in the month of May, and the harvest takes place in October; but it is seldom that it can be brought to market before December. The seed is given to oxen to eat, and costs fifteen paras the oke. The quality of the cotton is inferior to that of Egypt or Cyprus.
Wool[2]	600 cantars, of 180 okes each	450 to 510 p. the cantar, ⅓ white, ⅔ black	60 to 92 p. the cantar	600 cantars produced in the country, besides as much from Anatolia	To Marseilles and Leghorn	[2] Wool is brought from Karamân, and hence shipped to Europe and to Smyrna; this being the shortest and least expensive mode of transport. A good deal goes overland to Smyrna, as, being exposed to rain on the road, it increases in weight! Karaman wool is all white; the wool produced in the Pashalik is of a finer texture, but much dirtier: it loses 40 per cent in washing.
Wax[3]	15,000 okes	17 to 18 p. the oke	2 p. the oke	14,500 okes	Marseilles, Cyprus, & Italy	[3] The greatest part goes to Europe, except about 2,000 okes sent to Beyrut.
Wheat[4]	450,000 kilos, weighing 180 okes	50 to 80 p. the kilo	10 p. the kilo	150,000 ,,	Beyrut and Syria	[4] This measure is very nearly an English quarter, and may be calculated the same on a rough valuation. The harvest in grain is generally fine; a few ship-loads go to Malta and Genoa. The quality of the wheat is good, but it looks bad. It is hard, like the Tangaroc wheat. Soft wheat is brought from Karaman—it is very clean, and costs 100 p. the quarter, free on board. When the price of barley rises to 70 piasters the kilo, it is worth while to import it on camels' backs from Karaman. Bread is made of it, for the poor people.
Barley	70,000 kilos do.	30 to 50 p. do.	5 p. the kilo	Consumed in the country	A little to Syria	
Durrah	5000 do.	25 to 40 p. do.	Do. do.	Do. do.	Do.	
Sesam[5]	30,000 kilos, of 125 okes	160 to 220 p. do.	21 p. the kilo	15,000 kilos	Marseilles Malta and Leghorn	[5] In consequence of the great demand, the quantity produced is on the increase. Some has been sent to England, and the expedition proved successful. The harvest takes place in September.
Chickpea[6]	2000 kilos	50 to 60 p. do.	5 p. the kilo	Is consumed in the country		[6] Some is brought from Karaman.
Beans[7]	10,000 ,,	2, 6, 8, & 15 p. each	12½ pr. cent	For the use of the country	to Syria	[7] These are cut off the fir and pine in Mount Taurus.
Boards[8]	150,000 ,,	20 paras to 5 p each	Do. do.	120,000 ,,	to Syria	[8] The mountaineers hew them, and their wives saw them.
Old copper	10,000 okes	8 to 9 p. the oke	45 paras the oke	⅓ to Europe, and ⅔ to Kaisariyah		
Tobacco[9]	1000 cantars	2 p. the oke	10 paras the oke, Miri duty	100 cantars go to ,, 200 ,,	Anatolia Egypt	[9] The quality is ordinary. Tobacco is monopolised by the government, and pays a tenth besides the customs.

COMMERCIAL AND STATISTICAL TABLES. 381

Table IV. *Commercial Table of the Imports of the Pashalik of* ADANA *and* TARSUS.

Name of merchandise.	Prices current.	Quantity imported.	Whence.	Quantity re-exported.	Where sent to.	Customs.	OBSERVATIONS.
Persian berries	15 to 20 p. the oke	2000 okes	Kaisariyah	2000 okes	To Smyrna	2 p. the oke	A duty of 5 p. per load is paid besides at Kuak Bughaz, under the title of bagc (or road-mending duty). A hundred okes of this berry finds its way to Syria.
Linseed	1 p. the oke	300,000	Anatolia	350,000	To England, Marseilles, America, & Trieste	2 paras the oke, and bage 5 p. per load	This is one of the most important articles of commerce. The quality is good; but they have no means of properly sifting the seed.
Madder-roots	1100 p. the cantar	1500 bales of 70 okes each	Karaman	1500 bales	To Smyrna	12½ p. ct, & a bage duty of 5 p. per load	The quality is fine, and much esteemed; and this is a most important article of commerce, any quantity of which can be procured from Karaman.
Copper	26 p. the oke	8500 okes	Tukat	5000 okes	To Syria and Egypt	12½ p. ct, & a bage 5s. per ld.	A duty is also paid at Tukat, and another duty on shipping at Tarsus.
Wool	650 p. the cantar, free on board	500 cantars	Nigde and Bur	1100 cantars	Marseilles	97 p. the cantar and bage	Any quantity of wool may be obtained from Anatolia, by making the usual advances.
Tumbac	10 p. the oke	10,000 okes	From Aleppo & Beyrut	Consumed in the country	..	The duty is paid in Bagdad	
Snuff	10 p. the oke	8000 okes	Roumelia	Do.	..	The duty is paid in Smyrna or Constantinople	This article is monopolised by the government, as well as spits of wine, powder, shot, and alum; and 80,000 p. is paid for the exclusive privilege of trading in these.
Hinny or kina	3 to 12 p. the oke	5000 okes	From Mecca & Egypt	2000 okes	To Anatolia	Comes with teskery bage of 3 p. per load, and 1 oke in kind	
Jaffa soap	850 p. the cantar	6000 sacks of 100 okes each	Jaffa	2000 sacks	Do	Do. Do.	
Tripoli soap	750 ,, ,,	4000 sacks	Tripoli	1500 ,,	Do.	Do.	

APPENDIX.

Table IV. (continued). *Imports of the Pushalik of* ADANA *and* TARSUS.

Name of merchandise.	Price current.	Quantity imported.	Whence.	Quantity re-exported.	Where sent to.	Customs.	Observations.
Dates	300 p. the cantar	5000 cantars	From Egypt	.. ..	Consumed in the country	Comes with a teskery; buge of 3 p. per ld., and 1 oke in kind	The cantar of this country weighs 180 okes.
Rice	400 to 500 p. the ardeb, which weighs 216 okes	400 ardebs ..	Do.	.. ..	Do.	Do.	
Figs	45 paras the oke	500 zembils	Sur	.. ..	Do.	Do.	
Coffee	45 p. to 60 p. the shakié of 9 okes	1000 sacks, weighing 70 okes	Beyrut	.. ..	Do.	Do.	The price of this article is very vacillating, and often rises considerably.
Pepper.. ..	43 to 45 p. the shakié, weighing 9 okes	100 sacks	Do.	.. ..	Do.	It comes with a teskery, the duty being paid in Beyrut ..	
Sugar	5 to 6 of the oke	50 cases, weighing 100 okes each	Do.	.. ..	Do.	Do.	Sometimes the country remains without sugar for many days. In Tarsus there are about 20 tanners, and 50 in Adana.
Indigo	130 to 150 p. the oke .	1000 okes ..	Do.	.. ..	Do.	Do.	
Cochineal ..	90 to 100 p. "	400 okes	Do.	.. ..	Do.	Do.	
Tin and Sal ammoniac .	130 to 135 p.; the 6 okes of one to 3 okes of the other	3000 okes	Do.	.. ..	Do.	Do.	The two are sold together.
		1500 okes.	Do.	.. ..	Do.	Do.	The price of manufactures is always falling, and the sale becoming more and more difficult, as the want of bullion in circulation increases.
Calico of 2½ yards . ..	30 p. the piece . .	3000 pieces .	Do.	.. ..	Do.	Do.	

COMMERCIAL AND STATISTICAL TABLES.

Table IV. (continued). Imports of the Pashalik of ADANA and TARSUS.

Name of merchandise.	Price current.	Quantity imported.	Whence.	Quantity re-exported.	Where sent to.	Customs.	Observations.
Calico of 36 yards	55 p. the piece	1000 pieces	Beyrut	Consumed in the country	Consumed in the country	It comes with a teskery, the duty being paid in Beyrut	1 The value according to the quality. Often the price of manufactures here is cheaper than in Beyrut. The want of money in the country causes a necessity of selling at any price, which ruins all the shopkeepers. The commerce in importations is therefore dangerous, and little useful. 2 Pay a bage of 5 p. per load. 3 Besides the duty of 12 per cent, a bage is paid at Kulak Bughaz of 5 p. per load, plus 65 paras—according to the caprice of the people, who pay to the government 75,000 p. for this monopoly, which is generally in the hands of the Mutsellim of Adana.
Of 52 yards	156 p. „	500 „	Do.	..	Do.	Do.	
Prints[1]	50 to 100 p. „	4000 „	Do.	..	Do.	Do.	
Zebras	19 p. „	3000 „	Do.	..	Do.	Do.	
Fermaish	30 to 40 p. „	1000 „	Do.	..	Do.	Do.	
Muslins	30 to 60 p. „	2000 „	Do.	..	Do.	Do.	
Tanjibs	19 to 23 p. „	800 „	Do.	..	Do.	Do.	
Madapolams	65 p. „	„	Do.	..	Do.	Do.	
Tarbush (caps) Wardi	70 p. the dozen	30 boxes of 80 dozen each	Do.	..	Do.	Do.	
Ropes[2]	3 to 4 p. each	1500 ropes	Kaisariyah	..	Do.	Do.	
Small carpets[3]	22 to 80 p. „	3000 „	Anatolia	3000	To Syria and Egypt	12 p. per cent	
Long carpets	150 to 200 p. „	3000 „	Do.	3000	Do.	Do.	

APPENDIX.

Table V. *Prospectus of the Navigation of* Mursina, *Roadstead of* Tarsus, *1844.*

Name of the nation.	Number of the vessels.	Their tonnage in toto.	Their equipage in toto.	Value of their cargoes imported.	Value of their cargoes exported.	OBSERVATIONS.
Russian	2	410	22	Empty.	400,000	Loaded sesam for the Isles of Archipelago.
French	16	2079	189	..	2,500,000	Loaded sesam wool and wax for Marseilles.
English	2	230	18	..	300,000	Loaded linseed.
Sardinian	7	790	45	..	800,000	Loaded wool, cotton, and wax for Leghorn, and wheat for Genoa.
Austrian	2	265	21	..	250,000	Loaded sesam and linseed for Marseilles.
Tuscan	2	235	20	..	200,000	Loaded wool and cotton for Leghorn.
Jerusalem Flag	9	725	108	600,000 p.	800,000	They bring soap, coffee, and European manufactures from Beyrut, and take to Syria wheat, barley, and cotton.
Arab bombards	63	4275	882	3,000,000 p.	4,000,000	They bring salt and spirits of wine from Cyprus, and take in return sesam and wheat for the Islands of the Archipelago.
Greek	8	225	78	200,000 p.	550,000	
Egyptian frigates	48	..	..	..	8,500,000	Loaded oxen and horses brought from the interior of the country for account of Mehmed Ali Pasha.
Steam-packets	3	..	..	2,400,000	3,500,000	Brought European merchandise from Smyrna, and took back Persian berries, madder-roots, basturma, &c.
Total	162	9,234	1383	6,200,000	21,800,000	

TABLE VI.

Shewing the difference between the Duty paid at CONSTANTINOPLE *per Tariff and the per-centage Duty on Goods from the Interior.*

Name of the articles of commerce.	Value on the spot.	Duty to be paid according to the tariff established between England and the Porte.	Which makes the duty amount to so much per cent, instead of 12 per cent.
			Duty here.
Butter of Turkey	16 p. per 4 okes	3168 aspres per kintal	15 per cent
Raisins	15 p. per ditto	267 ,, the oke..	Do.
Currants	40 p. the Aleppo cantar	ad valorem	Do.
Cotton of Anatolia	2½ p. the oke	3405 aspres the kintal	25 per cent
Buffalo-skins	5 p. the oke	ad valorem	
Morocco of Kaisariyah	10 p. each	ad valorem	
Madder-roots of Cyprus	650 p. the cantar	2592 aspres the kintal	13¼ do.
,, of Anatolia	650 p. ,,		
Grain, wheat	50 p. the kilo of 180 okes	198 aspres the kilo of Constantinople	26½ do.
,, barley	30 p. same measure	90 ditto ditto	27 do.
Indian corn	30 p. ditto	ad valorem	
Wool, ¾ black ,, ¼ white	400 p. the cantar of 180 okes	2952 aspres the kintal	24¾ do.
Honey	2 p. the oke	ad valorem	
Goat and sheep-skins	3 to 4 p. each	64 aspres each	13¾ do.
Lamb-skins	15 paras each	36 ,, ,,	80 do.
Hare-skins	25 paras each	2304 aspres for each 100	31 do.
Cow and buffalo-hides	3 p. the oke	ad valorem	
Leeches*	40 p. do.	288 aspres per oke	6 do.
Old copper	7½ p. do.	192 ,, ,,	13½ do.
Linseed	25 paras the oke	259 ,, every 200 okes	17 do.
Sesam-seed	1½ p. do.	402 ,, ditto	16 do.
Valonea	80 p. the Aleppo cantar	960 ,, per kintal	40 do.
Black raisins	120 p. the cantar of 180 okes	489 ,, ,,	13½ do.
,, currants	1 p. the oke	2160 ,, ,,	40 do.
Persian berries	15 p. do.	403 ,, ,,	22½ do.

* A large sum is paid *besides*, for the sole privilege of fishing for leeches by Europeans who undertake the monopoly. This sum amounts to more than 1000*l.* for the district of Adana and Tarsus. The price of leeches has risen of late years to more than 200 p. the oke.

INDEX.

Abd'ul Hamid I., 71.
Abd'ul Masjid, ascended the throne 1839, 72.
Abdullah Rushdi, 97; falls into disgrace, 103.
Abgar Bar-man, *note*, 172.
Abington, Mr., 151; on the various representations of Perseus, *note*, 197.
Acteon, 189.
Acts xix. 18-20, 159.
Actium, battle of (B.C. 31), 28.
Adana, 111.
Admetus, King, 175.
Adonis as Apollo, with the cloak and brooch, 178.
Æsculapius, 196.
Agrippa, 33.
Ahmed I., 70.
——— II., 71.
——— III., abdicates in favour of his nephew, 71.
——— Izzet Pasha, 97.
——— Minikli Pasha, 112.
Aleium, a plain in Cilicia, 18.
Aleppo, 82.
Alexander the Great marches against Darius, 20; nearly loses his life by bathing, 20; at Issus, 21.
——— Severus, 163.
Alexandretta, small lake of, 114.
——— Jonas pillars, 263.
Alexius succeeded by John Comnenus, 54.
Allen, Captain William, 270.
Al Mamun, expedition into Asia Minor, 46; death of, from eating dates, 46.
Alp-Arslan captures Romanus Diogenes, 50.
Amaxia, iron mines of, 28.
America, central monuments of, 209.
Ammodes, the, or Sandy Cape, 265; celebrated for turtle, 265.
Amorium, siege of, 47.
Amphilochus, city of, 265.
Amurad I., 66.
——— II. besieges Constantinople, 68; marches with a large army into Asia Minor, 68.

Amurad III. strangles five of his brothers 69.
——— IV. enters Cilicia with an immense force, 70; undertakes the conquest of Persia, 70.
Anastasius, 42.
Anatolia, 112.
Anazarba, *note*, 55; ruins of aqueduct at, 56, 275; ruins of, 266; sculptured rocks of, 283.
Anchiale, *note*, 15, 136.
Ancient tomb at Tarsus, 133.
——— bard, 243.
Andronicus, romantic adventures of, 56.
Animals, 249.
Antalcidas, treaty of, 20.
Antelope, 280.
Antioch, 24; tax-gatherers at, *note*, 107; bay of, 268; ruins of, 268.
Antiochus the Great, 23.
——— Epiphanes, 24.
Antipater, a disciple and successor of Diogenes, *note*, 31.
Antiquities in Cilicia, 265.
Apis, 182.
Appian "Syriacs," 129; account of Seleucia, 272.
Apollo Belvidere, 155; winged, 157; as Osiris, 161; head of, radiated, 162; on the Colossus at Rhodes, 162; Belvidere, where found, 184; at Rhodes, various figures of, 195.
Apollodorus, *note*, 13.
Appendix, 301.
Aqueduct, ruins of, at Anazarba, 56, 275.
Arab horse, instinct of, 288.
Aratus, 136.
Arbela, battle of, 21.
Archimedes, 139.
Ariadne and Bacchus, heads of, 216.
Arif Pasha, *note*, 106.
Arimes, adventures of, 275.
Aristotle, 16; relation of circumstance about Mount Casius, 273.
Arrian, 16.
Arsus, 111; description of, *note*, 112.
Art, additional works of, 213.
Artaxerxes, 19.

INDEX.

Artaxerxes Babegan, 37.
Artemisia, Queen of Halicarnassus, 19.
Aski Shaker, 131.
Athenæus, a philosopher of Cilicia, 30.
——————, 134.
Athenodorus the philosopher warns Augustus, 29.
Attalia, 60.
Atys, head of, 227.
Augustus, 29.
Aurelian prepares for his Persian expedition, 38.
Avolio, 201.
Ayass, remarkable for turtles, 111; castle of, 263.
Azof, sea of, 38.

Basil, 226; conjectures on, by Mr. Birch, 259.
Babylon, 234.
Bacchante, 200.
Bacchus, 195; Indian, 226.
Bagdad, khalifs of, 48.
Baldwin, 52.
Barker, Mr. John, British Consul at Aleppo, 83.
——————, Mr. W. Burckhardt, *note*, 161.
Basilica, 263.
Bayas, river of, *note*, 75; fever prevails at, *note*, 81; gulf of, 111.
Bayazid, 66.
—————— II. attacks Kayit Bay, 62; expedition of, into Asia Minor, 68; poisons his father, 69.
Baylan, 263; mosque of, 263; ruins at, 263.
Beard, Rev. Dr., remarks on Tarshish, *note*, 12.
Bears, 277; method of shooting, 277; flesh of, 277.
Beaufort, Admiral Sir Francis, "Karamania," *note*, 24; description of ruins, *note*, 34; views on the antiquities of Cilicia, 265; on the ruins of Soli, &c., 266.
Berenice, widow of Herod, 33.
Berkeley's, Bishop, work, "Siris," 217.
Betias, Mr. Barker's summer residence, 300.
Birch, Mr., on the Apollo Helios, 162.
Birds, 251.
——————, game, of Cilicia, 281.
Bochart, 12; *note*, 13.
—————— (Phaleg, p. 333), derivation of the word Casius, *note*, 273.
Bohemond, death of, 53.
Bomitæ or altars, site of, according to Pliny, 263.
Bonham, Colonel, 289.

Bonomi, "Nineveh and its Palaces," *note*, 199.
Bonzes, 235.
Botta, discoveries of, 213.
Boy and dolphin, 230.
Boys on dolphins, 231.
Brahma, 236.
British Museum, 202; silver enamels in, 257.
Bryant, Mr., "Mythological Dictionary," 148.
Buddist Bonze, 235.
Buffon, 285.
Bulwer's " Rise and Fall of Athens," 173.
Burney, Dr., 259.
Byzantine annals, 48.

Caffa, 62.
Caius Caligula, bust of, with the lorica, 223.
Calchas, 141.
Calisthenes, 21.
Campestris, 135.
Cantacuzene, John, 66.
Cape Boar, 267.
Cappadocia, plains of, 39.
Captive kneeling, from Rosellini's great work, 211.
Caravailas Turkish ships of war, 80.
Carthage, 25.
Cassius, Mount. 268; height of, 273; vegetation, 273; mentioned in Scripture, 273; tradition of, 273.
Casts, making of, 169.
Cato, *note*, 29.
Caucasus, Mount, 28.
Causeway, Roman, traces of, 266.
Cecenius Petus, president of Syria, 33.
Celendris, castle of, 30.
Ceres, head of, 176.
Chaldean astrologers, 235.
Charles X. of France, 240; enormous cost of his hunting expeditions, 296.
Chariots, 253.
Chesney, Colonel, *note*, 269; remarks on the port of Seleucia Pieria, 270.
Chinese, 207.
Christians introduced into the councils of Cilicia, 106.
Christian Church, ruins of, at Rhosus, 262.
Christianity early diffused in Cilicia, 172.
Chronos, 193.
Chorœbus, 259.
Chosroes, 43.
Cicero named proconsul of the province of Cilicia, 26.
Cilicia, early history of, 11; situation,

12; Hypacheans, original inhabitants of, 14; under the Assyrians, 15; death of Xerxes, 19; the gates of, 22; battle of Ipsus, 23; revolt of the citizens of, 24; invasion of Tigranes, 25; Cicero named proconsul, 26; Tarchondemus king of, 28; Tacitus on the trees of, *note*, 30; a Roman province, 33; invaded by Sapor, 37; birthplace of St. George, 40; invasions of the Huns, 41; annexed to the Greek empire, 53; modern history of, 73; extraordinary occurrence at, 93; taxation in, 105; character of tax-gatherers, 107; maladministration of justice, 109; geography of, 110; climate of, 114; forests of, *note*, 122; custom-houses, 126, quarantine laws, 127; Lares and Penates of, 153; potters of, 171; early diffusion of Christianity in. 172; terracottas, 215; situations of towns and cities in, 262; remains of churches and castles in, 263; geography of, 265; antiquities of, 266; Mediterraneum, 266; natural history, 276; coursing and hunting, 278; hawking, 280; birds of, 281; partridges and quails of, 282; falconry and hawking, 285; medicinal plants of, 299.
Cinyras, 13.
Cleanthus, a philosopher of Tarsus, 24; death of, 24.
Cleopatra at Tarsus, 27.
Cliteans, a bold tribe of mountaineers in Cilicia, 32.
Cneius Piso, 30.
Coins, 158.
Colossus of Rhodes, 194.
Comic mask, 177, 178.
Comnenus, John, marches to Antioch and Aleppo, 54; killed in a wild boar hunt, 54.
Conrad III., Emperor of Germany, 55.
Constantius marches against Julian, 39; death of, 40.
Constantinople retaken by the Greeks, A.D. 1261, 59.
Consumption unknown in Cilicia and Syria, 299.
Conybeare and Howson, " Life of St. Paul," 236.
Coracesium, *note*, 26; account of, by Strabo, 129.
Corsica, 63.
Cory's "Ancient Fragments," 274.
Cossnatianus Papito, 33.
Coughs unknown in Cilicia and Syria, 299.
Coursing in Cilicia, 278.

Crates, 142.
Cretins, 239.
Crocodiles, 251; Mount, 264; worship, 264; terra-cottas of, 264; different species, 264.
Crœsus, King of Lydia, 18.
Crusades, 52.
Cupid, head of, 194.
——— and swan, 219.
Curtius Severus, 32.
Cyaxares, 17.
Cybele, 175; mysteries of, 176; head of, 192.
Cydnus River, 17, 20; falls into the Lake Rhegma, 137.
Cyprus, 13; attacked by the Turks, 63; kings of, 130.
Cyrus sends for Syennesis, 19.

D'AGINCOURT, *note*, 202.
Daniel, the prophet, tomb of, 17.
Darius resolves to invade Greece, 18, 198.
David, king, 15.
Deguignes' " Hist. Gen. des Huns, des Turcs, &c.," 207.
D'Herbelot, speculations about the Huns, 207.
Deifying men, 163.
Delian deities, 194.
Delos, island of, 130.
Diana, head and statue of, 156; starting for the chase, 284.
Dioclesian, 39.
Diogenes, *note*, 31.
Dion Cassius, *note*, 29.
Dionysus, 201.
Doghan, one of the hawk species, 286.
Dogs, 249; treatment of, in Cilicia, 276; description of, used for coursing in Cilicia, 279.
Domestic and religious art. 253.
Doria, Philip, a Genoese admiral, 59.
Drinking bowls, 254; vessels generally, 255.
Duc de Luynes, " Essai sur la Numismatique des Satrapes," *note*, 201.
Ducas, Vataces John, 57.
Duda Bey, piratical expeditions of, 84; description of, 84; attack on, 85; betrayed, 86; death of, 86.
Dutch consul, arrest of, 81.
Dwarfs, 239.

EAST India Company, 83.
Egyptian antiquities, 211.
Eleusa, tomb at, 242.
Eleusinian mysteries, 176.

INDEX.

Epiphanea, the birthplace of St. George, 40; extensive ruins of, 264.
Epyaxa, wife of Syennesis, 19.
Eros, winged, 166.
Erotes, 194.
Eudocia, Empress, 50.
Euphrates expedition, *note*, 125.

FAKIRS, 235.
Falconry, 284; gos-hawks and their management, 290; antiquity of, 295.
Fallow-deer seen on the plains of Adana, 278.
Famagosta, capture of, 59.
Figures, fragments of, 245.
Fir-cone, 217.
Forbes, Professor, remarks on the ibex, *note*, 280.
Forster, Rev. Charles, "Historical Geography of Arabia," *note*, 13.
Fortifications at Tarsus, 135.
Francolins, 282.
Frederic I., death of, 57.
Frederickssteen, death on board the, 265.
Furniture, 257.

GALATA, natives of, method of capturing wild doves, 283.
Game-birds of Cilicia, 281.
"Game Birds and Wild Fowl," by A. E. Knox, 287.
Ganymede, 246.
Gates, remains of, in Cilicia and Syria, 264; of Kulak Bughaz, 266.
Gazelles, method of taking them, 279.
Genoese Republic, 58.
George III., 240.
Gerhard, *note*, 193.
Germanicus, 30.
Gesbril-Hadeed in the plains of Antioch, 298.
Gha-ïk, a species of antelope remarkable for its length of horns, 280.
Gibbon, *note*, 48; "Decline and Fall of the Roman Empire," 204.
Gladiator conquered, 244.
Godfrey of Bouillon, 52.
Gordys founds a colony in Gordiæus, 274; situation of, *note*, 274.
Gos-hawk, Australian, the, 294; the training of, 289.
Government, thorough change of, 103.
Granicus, battle of the, 20.
Greece, invasion of, by the Persians, 19.
Greek Church, 262.
Grimaldi, Joe, 239.
Grotefend, Professor, *note*, 16; on the mythology of the Assyrians, *note*, 149, 150.

HADRIAN, 34; emperor, 273.
Haji Ali Bey, capture of, 89.
Hamilton, Mr. William J., "Researches in Asia Minor, &c." *note*, 42.
Handles of vases, lamps, &c. 256; ring, 256; of dishes, 256.
Hardouin, 218.
Hares, 278.
Harpies, 225.
Harpocrates, 181.
Hassan Pasha, 103; anecdote of, *n.*, 103
Hatti Sherif of Gulhanah, 72.
Hawks in England, 286; extraordinary feat of, 293; of the lure, 295; of the fist, 295.
Hawking, description of, in Cilicia, 285; Society, 292.
Hawkins' "History of Music," 260.
Hecate, 198.
Head of a child, 166; of Commodus as Hercules, 167; of a lady with all the attributes of Juno, 167; of a lady, temp. Emperor Claudian, 168; with the attributes of Juno, 177; of a horse, 180; of a lady, 188.
Hellenic divinities, 193.
Hellespont, 39.
Hera of the Assyrians, 217.
Heraclius defeats the Persians, 43.
Hercules, statue of, 46, 167, 169; holding his club, 216.
Hero, 193.
Herodotus, 14, 18.
Herons, *note*, 292.
Hittites, 210.
Homer, 15; mention of Tarsus, *note*, 161; Iliad, v. 499, *note*, 273.
Horses, 250.
Household articles, 257.
Human figures, 243.
Humboldt on the Huns, 203; "Aspects of Nature," 205; "Relation Historique," *note*, 207.
Huns, invasions of, 71; portraits of, 203; their identity with the extinct races of America, 205; speculations about, 207.
Hyenas in Cilicia, 277.
Hypachæans, original inhabitants of Cilicia, 14.

IBEX capra, *note*, 280.
Ibrahim I. fits out an expedition against Candia, 71.
―――― II. besieges Vienna, 71.
―――― Pasha, 90; a hawk, gift of, by, 293.
Idiots, 237; head of, 239; fools and dwarfs, 239.
Imma, battle of, *note*, 38.

INDEX.

Incense-burner, 155.
Io, wanderings of, 274.
Ipsus, battle of, 23.
Irene the Great, 45.
Iris, 177.
Isaurians, a savage horde of Cilicia, 41.
Isis, worship of, 177, 191; priests of, 235.
Isper, a species of eastern hawk, 296.
Issus, the scene of the great battle which decided the fate of the Persian empire, 21; battle at the plains of, 35.

JACKALS abound in Cilicia, 277.
Jam, son of Mohammed II., 62.
Janissaries, 66.
Jeremy, apocryphal book of, 217.
Jerusalem, 2 Kings, ch. xxi. 13, 257.
Jona's Pillars, *note*, 91; a colossal marble fragment, 263.
Jonstonus " Dendographia," 218.
Josephus, *note*, 33; on the depravity of the priests of Isis, 165; "Antiq. Jud." i. c. i, 213.
Jovian, successor to Julian, 41.
Julian, death of, 41.
Juno, 157.
Jupiter, head of, 157.
———— Casius, 273.
Justin I., 42.
Justinian, 43.
Juvenal, 236.

KALAT Kurkass, 129.
Kamses, the Egyptian, the name of a ferocious crocodile, 264.
Kara Kaya, " Black Rock," castle and ruins of, 265.
Karadoghar, ruin at, *note*, 16.
Karadughar, *note*, 105.
Kaisanli, 115.
Kel-Aga, 88.
Khalil Bey, 74; life of, *note*, 74.
Khorsabad, mention of, 224.
Kilitch Arslan, king of Nicæa, defeated by the crusaders, 52.
Kitto, Dr., " Cycl. Bib. Lit." *note*, 12.
Klaproth, speculations of, on Huns, 207.
Knight, Mr. R. P., 152.
Kulak-Bugbaz, 112; lead mines of, 125.
Kurt-Kulak, 100; ruinous khan at, 265.
Kutchuk Ali, 75; extortions of, 76; cruelty of, 77; some account of, 78; imprisons English sailors, 79; unloads and then sinks a French vessel, 80; letter of, to the Dutch consul, 80.
Kuzan Uglu, 102.

LABIENUS marches with a large army into Cilicia, 28; death of, 28.

Labourers, wages of, at Tarsus, 120.
Lamas, aqueduct of, 128.
Lamp, 156, 201.
Languages, peculiarities of, *note*, 205.
Laocoon, 222.
Lares and Penates, 145; explanation of, 146 and *note*; different classes of, 147.
Larnika, 113.
Lascaris, Theodore, 57.
Layard, *note*, 150; discoveries of, 213;
Lajard, M., *note*, 217.
Leake, Colonel, 265.
Leander swimming the Hellespont, 222.
Lebanon, Mount, 273.
Leg of a horse, 175.
Linnæus, 286.
Lion attacking a bull, 187.
Louis VII., 55.
Lucullus, a Roman general, 25.
Lucretius, mention of Melibœa, 269.
Lycophron, v. 18, 227.
Lynx, caught on Mount Taurus, 276.
Lyres, 259.

MACROCEPHALUS, 238.
Magi and monks, 232.
————, bonzes, and fakirs, 235.
Mahmud II., 72.
Malcolm, Sir John, " Sketches in Persia," 282.
Mallos, 21, 141.
Man riding a bear, 226.
Mandarins, 228.
Manuel, Emperor, 55.
Marash, bridle-way to, described by Strabo, 266.
Marc Antony at Tarsus, 27.
Markatz Kalahsi, a Saracen castle, 263.
Marsyas, fable of, 220.
Masseyk, Mr., ill-treatment of, 81.
Matakh, mounds and ruins of, 265.
Mausoleum at Tarsus, ground-plan of, 133.
Maximin, defeat and death of, 39.
Mecca, caravan of, 100.
Medes, the, 17.
———— and Persians, 234.
Medicinal plants of Cilicia, 299.
Mediterranean, pirates of, 25.
Medusa, head of, 267.
Melek Seraf, final conquest of St. Jean d'Acre by, 59.
Melibœa, poetical celebrity of, 269.
Melitus, Bishop of Antioch, 140.
Mercury, 8; origin of, 215.
Mesmerists, modern, 233.
Mesopotamia, 271.
Messalina, head of, 158.
Messiah, the advent of, 29.

INDEX.

Mexico, 207.
Midas, 185.
Minerva as Pallas, 219.
——— and Cupid, 219.
Missis, 110.
Mithridates, king of Pontus, 25.
Mocenigo in communication with Ozun Hassan, 60.
Moguls become masters of all Asia, 67.
——— under Genghiz Khan, 63.
Mohammed adopts and embellishes the cave of the Seven Sleepers, 36.
——— III., cruelties of, 70.
Mohammedan, tomb of, near the ruins of Seleucia Pieria, 269.
Monster, head of, 237.
Monsters and idiots, 237.
Mopsuestia, *note*, 34.
Mopsus, poet and soothsayer, *note*, 25.
———, a celebrated prophet, 111.
Morpheus, 183.
Morocco, Emperor of, 95.
Mosquitoes, 277; method of sleeping out of their reach, 277.
Muhammad I., 68.
——— V., 71.
——— Izzat Pasha, 92.
Muhassil, the, 108.
Musical instruments, 259.
Mustafa I., deposed by Janissaries, 70.
——— II., 71.
——— III., 71.
——— V. proclaimed sultan 1807, 71.
——— Pasha, 86.
——— death of, 102.
Mustuk Bey, 87.
Mutassim besieges Amorium, 47.
Mythological analogies, 174.

NADIR Bey, 93; arrest of, 95; narrative of, by himself, 301; petition, 320.
Naiad, 197.
Napoleon, 240.
Neptune, 183.
Nergat, 251.
Nero, 163.
New Testament, 233.
Nicæa, Turkman dynasty at, 51.
Nicephorus, accession of, 46.
——— Phocas, 48.
Nicopolis, 67.
Nicotia taken by Admiral Catani, 59.
Niger river, 270.
Nimrod, 15.
Nimrud, 115; peculiar broken earthen vase of, 224.
Nineveh, 16; plains of, 278.
Ninias, 15.
Nizam, *note*, 83.

Odenathus, Prince of Palmyra, attacks Sapor, 38.
Olympus, Mount, 135.
Orchan, 65.
Organ, first invention of, 260.
Orinoco, 205.
Orontes, river, 267; course of, 268.
Osiris, 14.
Osman II., 70.
——— III., 71.
Osmanli dynasty, 65.
Othman, 65.
Ottoman Empire, modern history of, 73.
Ounce, the, 275.
Ovid, 146.
Oxen, 249.

PALÆOLOGUS, Michael, 64.
Pallas, 169.
Palma Christi, 299.
Pan, head of, 155, 218.
Pandean organs, 260.
——— syrinx, 260.
Pan-pipes, 260.
Parthia, kingdom of, 37.
Partridges in Cilicia, 282.
Pashalik of Tarsus, revenue of, 125.
Penates of Rome, 149.
Peregrine, the, 297.
Pergamus, library of, 139.
Peruvian carvings, 206.
Perseus, 12; founds Tarsus, 1552 B.C., 14, 197.
Persians, ultimate defeat of, 61.
Pescennius Niger, 35.
Peter the Hermit, 52.
Phallus, 224.
Philemon, a comic poet, 136.
Philip, physician of Alexander the Great, 20.
Philopater, son of Tarchondemus, 29.
Philotas crosses the Aleian plain, 20.
Phocas the Tyrant, 43.
Phree, the Egyptian Sun, 252.
Phrygian head, 197.
Physicians, Greek and Roman, 299.
Pierius, Mount, 269.
——— cliffs of, 269.
Pisa, republic of, 58.
Pliny, "Natural History," *note*, 170; on the site of the Bomitæ or altars, 263.
Plistarchus, 23.
Plutarch's account of Darius, *n.* 21; 147.
Pococke, Dr., 263.
Polemon, king of Cilicia, 33.
Pompeiopolis, ruins of, 130.
Pompey defeats the pirates, 26.
Porcupines in Cilicia, 277; flesh of, 277.
Porphyrogenitus relates the particulars

INDEX. 393

of the execution of the Saracens of Candia, 47.
Pottery-labels, 258.
Priapus. 201.
Priest, with attributes of Apollo, 164.
Priestess, a basso-relievo gem, 199.
Protection, system of, 88.
Ptolemy, Evergetes, invades Syria, 23.
——— Philadelphus, 14.
Publius Servilius, 135.
Pylæ Ciliciæ, 113.
Pyramus river, 18, 19.
Pythagoras, 233.

QUAILS, 281; manner of taking, 281; Arabian method of entrapping, 281.
Quarantine laws, 127.
Quintus Curtius, *note*, 21.

RAMESES III., 210.
Ras Majusi, 227.
Rawlinson, Colonel, 18.
Ray, 218.
Religious art, 253.
Remnius stabs Vonones, 30.
Rhea, the goddess, 253.
Rhegma, 136.
Rhosus, interesting remains of, 262.
Rhossus, Mount, 112.
Rich, Mr., *note*, 13, 146.
Rizu Kuli Mirza, a Persian prince, 290.
Roman ware, 199.
Roman emperors, deification of, 165.
——— causeway, 266.
Romer, Miss, "the Turkish Pretender," *note*, 301.
Rosellini, on Egyptian Antiquities, 210.
———, M. C. " Teste," *note*, 259.
Rotolo, a Turkish weight, *note*, 75.
Russia, wars with, commence, 71.

SADDLES in the East, *note*, 288.
St. George, a native of Cilicia, 40; church of, 136.
St. Jean d'Acre, 59.
St. Paul born at Tarsus, 31; censures elaborately plaited hair, 172; Romans, ch. i. v. 18-32, 224; life of, 236.
Saint Simon, Mount, 268.
Salamis, battle of, 19.
Samosata, city of, 33.
Saracenic castle, Markatz Kalahsi, 263.
Saracens, rise of, 45.
Sarcophagus at Seleucia Picria, 131.
Sapor invades Cilicia, 37.
Sardanapalus, 15.
Saturn, 193.
Schiller, 233.
Schomburgk, Sir Robert, letter to Humboldt, 225.

Scilla, Martima, 299.
Scott, Sir Walter, on the " noble craft" of falconry, 298.
Selene, 201.
Seleucia, 60; Pieria, ruins of the city-walls, 270; gates of, 270; docks, 270; port, 270; the Place of Olives, 268; grotto, 268; ruins of, 269; port and ruins of, 270-272; description of, Journal Royal Geo. Soc., *note*, 270.
Seleucus Nicator, 273.
Selim II. takes the island of Cyprus, 69.
——— III. is put to death, 71.
Senator, image of, with the clavus latus, 186.
Serapis, 14.
Seven Churches, 23.
——— Sleepers, legend of, 86.
Shutz, Colonel, 113.
Sibyl, African, 228.
Silenus, 218.
Silver, oxide of, 257.
Sinai, Mount, 273.
Sinope taken by Mohammed II., 59.
Sis, celebrated monastery at, 111.
Smith's " Dictionary of Antiquities," 186; " Mythology," *note*, 267.
Smyrna, 117.
Soli, Strabo's account of, *note*, 24.
Somnus, 183.
Songhur, the, a large species of peregrine, 297.
Soulouque, emperor of Hayti, 210.
Sparrow-hawks, 281; used for catching quails, 282.
Spartans, war against Artaxerxes, 20.
Spence, Mr., 259.
Stephanus, *note*, 161.
Stephens, " Incidents of Travel," *note*, 203; of Byzantium, 264.
Strabo, account of, *note*, 24; Fables mentioned by, 141.
Sulaiman invades Asia Minor, 50. 66.
——— II. wins the battle of Mohatz, 69.
——— III., 71.
——— pasha, government of, 99; anecdotes of, 101.
Syennesis, 115.
Syrinx, 259.

TACITUS, 13; on the trees of Cilicia, *note*, 30.
———, grandson of the historian, 38; death of, at Tyana, 38.
Tancred, 52.
Tanzimat Khairiyah, 108.
Tarchondemus, king of Cilicia, 28.
Tarshish, *note*, 12.

INDEX.

Tarsus, built by Perseus, 12; Heeren on the situation of, *note*, 12; Scriptural mention of, 13; founded by Perseus, 14; ditto by Sardanapalus according to Grecian historians, 15; tomb of the prophet Daniel, 17; treaty of Antalcidas, 20; visited by Marc Antony and Cleopatra, 27; birthplace of St. Paul, 31; gates of, opened to receive Probus, 39; reduced by famine, 49; 6000 inhabitants in, 113; villages near, 115; merchants of, 115; its advantages and disadvantages in point of commerce, 117; some particulars of, 119; wages of labourers at, 120; cultivation of the soil, 121; Plain of, 122; geology of, 123; great monument at, 133; mountains and fortifications, 135; schools of instruction, 138; illustrious men of, 138; collection of Lares and Penates, 150; discovery of terra cottas, 152; religious system of, 159; Apollo of, 161; mythology of, 227.
Tartars under Genghiz Khan, 63.
Tartarus, representation of, 248.
Tatius, king of the Sabines, 147.
Taurus, Mount, 20.
Taxation in Cilicia, 105.
Terra cottas, discovery of, 152; miscellaneous objects, 201.
Theophilus, 46.
Tibareni, 266.
Tiberius, 165.
Tigranocerta, a city of Armenia, 25.
Tigranes invades Cilicia, 25.
Timur-Lang takes Bagdad, 67; anecdote of, *note*, 67.
Tomb of the Kings, 271.
Tradition connected with Mount Casius, 272.
Trajan, 34; death of, 34.
Trebellius, 32.
Tripod table, 257.
Triptolemus, 274.
Trosobor, chief of the Cliteans, 32.
Troy, 15.
Tugrul Bay, 50.
Tullus Hostilius, 186.
Turkish officials, quarrels of, 97.
Turkmans, 49.

Turkman dynasty at Nicæa, 51.
Turkmans, sporting dogs of the, 285.
Tutulated head, 192.
Typhon, 181; adventures of, 274.

UGLINESS, deification of, 209.
Utensils, 199.
Uzzum Hassan, a powerful Turkman chief, 68.

VALENS, emperor, 140.
Vases, 199.
Venetian fleet, 58.
Venus, head of, 170.
——— at the bath, 193.
Vespasian, 33.
Victory, 189.
Virgil, mention of Celibœa, 269.
Vitellius, governor of Syria, 32.
Voltaire, 24.
Vonones, king of the Parthians, 30.
——— death of, 30.

WARBURTON'S "Crescent and the Cross," 233.
Washington, George, 240.
Wild animals in Cilicia, 276.
Wolff, Rev. Mr., *note*, 13.
Wolves in Cilicia, 277.
Woodcocks, 281.
Works of art, 213.

XENARCHUS, 134.
Xenophon, 19.
Xerxes, expedition of, against Greece, 19; death of, 19.

YATES, Dr. Holt, 270.
Young Atys, 174.
Youth playing the syrinx, 260.

ZAIMS, 89.
Zenicetus the pirate, 135.
Zeno, a philosopher of Tarsus, 24, 42.
Zenobia, wife of Sapor, 38; taken prisoner, 38.
Zeus, 193, 226.
Zimisces, John, 48.
Zoological Gardens, gos-hawks at, 291.
Zoology of Cilicia, 278.

THE END.

LONDON:
PRINTED BY LEVEY, ROBSON, AND FRANKLYN,
Great New Street and Fetter Lane.

Printed in the USA
CPSIA information can be obtained
at www.ICGtesting.com
CBHW031221290524
9246CB00013B/569